Radio Drama in Action

RINEHART RADIO SERIES

▲▲

Erik Barnouw

RADIO DRAMA IN ACTION

Rome and Walter Krulevitch

RADIO DRAMA PRODUCTION, A
HANDBOOK

William B. Levenson

TEACHING THROUGH RADIO

Max Wylie

RADIO WRITING

Radio Drama in Action

TWENTY-FIVE PLAYS
OF A CHANGING WORLD

EDITED BY

Erik Barnouw

Instructor, Radio Writing, Columbia University

Formerly Assistant Manager, Script Division

National Broadcasting Company

RINEHART & COMPANY, INC.
NEW YORK   **TORONTO**

PUBLISHER'S NOTE

Readers in America unanimously approved the size of books produced during the war because they were lighter in weight and more economical in shelf space. We are therefore continuing to issue our books, complete and unabridged, in these popular sizes.

ALL RIGHTS RESERVED

ACKNOWLEDGMENTS

All the plays in this collection have been reprinted with the permission of the following authors, publishers and holders of copyright, to whom especial thanks are due:

Brandt & Brandt, New York, 17, N. Y.: *A Child Is Born* by Stephen Vincent Benét, from WE STAND UNITED AND OTHER RADIO SCRIPTS, Published by Farrar & Rinehart, Inc.

Chevigny, Hector: *Radioman Jack Cooper*

E. I. du Pont de Nemours & Co., Inc., New York 1, N. Y.: *Grandpa and the Statue* by Arthur Miller

Henry Holt and Company, Inc., New York 10, N. Y.: *London by Clipper* by Norman Corwin, from UNTITLED AND OTHER RADIO DRAMAS

Hughes, Langston and Maxim Lieber, New York 17, N. Y.: *Booker T. Washington in Atlanta* by Langston Hughes

Lader, Lawrence: *Pacific Task Force*

Laurents, Arthur: *The Last Day of the War*

Lawrence, Jerome and Lee, Robert E.: *Inside a Kid's Head*

Lloyd, David, New York 16, N. Y.: *Will This Earth Hold?* by Pearl S. Buck. Published by Asia Magazine Inc. in Asia and the Americas, Vo. XLIV, No. 11

Lomax, Alan: *Mister Ledford and the TVA*

Lyon, Peter: *Bretton Woods*

MacDougall, Ranald: *The Boise*

Michael, Sandra: *Against the Storm*

Mulvey, Rev. Timothy J., O.M.J.: *North Atlantic Testament*

National Broadcasting Company, New York 20, N. Y.: *Japanese-Americans* by Harry Kleiner and *Japan's Advance Base: The Bonin Islands* by Arnold Marquis

Oboler, Arch: *The House I Live In*

Ottley, Roi: *The Negro Domestic*

Robson, William N., and the Columbia Broadcasting System, New York 22, N. Y.: *Open Letter on Race Hatred*. Published in Theatre Arts Magazine

Rosten, Norman: *Concerning the Red Army*

Sun Music Co., Inc., New York 19, N. Y.: *The Lonesome Train* by Millard Lampell

The University of Chicago, Chicago, Illinois: *Typhus* by Bernard Victor Dryer

Welles, Orson: *Columbus Day*

Wishengrad, Morton: *The Battle of the Warsaw Ghetto*

WMCA, Incorporated, New York 19, N. Y.: *Halls of Congress* edited by Joseph Gottlieb

FOREWORD

It is now generally agreed that radio, medium of the fireside chat and the Martian panic, Pepsi-Cola Jingles and the NBC University of the Air, can influence human thought and action in powerful ways.

American radio uses the power mainly for merchandising. Drugs, foods and tobaccos, chief financiers of the medium, fill many of the choicest listening periods with gag comedy and escape drama.

But our radio also uses its power—more fitfully—toward pushing back the horizons of public knowledge and understanding. It is with this crucially important function, with "public service" radio, that the present volume is concerned. It assembles for the first time in one volume the contributions of a number of leading radio dramatists to the field of public service radio.

The legal situation surrounding public service radio is not sufficiently understood, either inside or outside radio.

A station is heard at a certain spot on the radio dial. But the station does not *own* the right to broadcast at that spot, that frequency. It holds the privilege on good behavior.

Because the ether wavebands are limited, they have been declared the property of the people. Every spot on the dial is *public property.* The Federal Communications Commission, acting for the public, may grant this or that company a license to broadcast at this or that frequency, and to make a profit on it through the sale of time—provided "the public interest, convenience and necessity" are served.

Those odd words, included in every station's license, have never been exactly defined by law. But the government has increasingly taken the position that the words place important obligations on the station. The Federal Communications Commission now feels that the periodic renewal of a station's license should depend on its genuine contributions to the public interest.

Programs felt to perform such a service, whether through dramatic or other types of programs, include: broadcasts of general edu-

cational or cultural value; programs designed to keep the public informed on world affairs, and on the various aspects of controversial
issues; programs designed to experiment with and develop the radio
medium; programs in support of social services; religious programs;
and programs in support of important government projects, particularly in wartime.

A "public interest" program may of course be sponsored or un-
sponsored. Either way, a newscast, symphony, or historical series can
perform valuable services. If a station owner could persuade all his
sponsors to present programs of genuine social value, his obligation
under his license would certainly be fulfilled.

But a very different set of pressures is at work on the sponsor, and
on his advertising manager. The latter, called on to justify his budgets
in terms of "cost per listener" and "cost per new user," is always likely
to look hungrily for the largest possible audience. And while a skill-
fully informative program, challenging the listener to attention and
thought, never fails to reach a large segment of available listeners, it is
also true that a *larger* audience can generally be found for the program
that invites mental ease instead of thought—that appeals to emotions
more directly than to intelligence, that provides escape into imaginary
wish fulfillment rather than the more demanding attention to actual
problems. The sponsor, facing the choice, again and again chooses the
larger audience. When drama is involved, this means drama with the
old artificial formulas, the pat plots that reinforce childish ways of
thinking, and the stock characters that often strengthen stereotyped
conceptions of whole groups of people.

In the present volume sponsored drama is represented by several
fine plays, which were backed by some of those sponsors who are exceptions to the general rule. But the bulk of the choices inevitably
comes from noncommercial series, produced in unsold time.

Some of these were produced by the broadcasting companies themselves—both networks and stations.

Still others are programs produced, with varying degrees of network or station collaboration, under the auspices of educational institutions, government agencies, or various other kinds of organizations.
"Co-operative" broadcasting of this sort has played an important part
in the story of radio drama, and it is illustrated in this collection by
a number of plays. Among the patrons of drama represented here are:

the Library of Congress, the Treasury Department, the War Department, the American Jewish Committee, Russian War Relief, the University of Chicago, the City-Wide Citizens Committee on Harlem; the Congress of Industrial Organizations, the National Society of Catholic Men.

In notes preceding each of the following plays, some attempt will be made to assess the accomplishments of radio drama "in action," as well as the difficulties under which it labors.

Because the volume is limited in size, it has not been possible to include all writers and series and organizations to which respects should have been paid in a book of this sort.

Also, in order to present as many writers as possible, an arbitrary limit of one script to a writer was decided on. This in turn brought on another injustice: some of the writers could not but be misrepresented by any one script.

The editor is grateful to the many who have helped in preparing the volume. This includes the writers represented and many more not represented. It includes also producers, directors, editors, executives and their secretaries—at networks, stations, and various government and private agencies.

Erik Barnouw

CONTENTS

COLUMBUS DAY

Orson Welles
in collaboration with Robert Meltzer, Norris Houghton

ORSON WELLES has caused successive convulsions in theater, radio, and films. To each he has brought enormous energies, originality, and technical ingenuity.

After Welles, in association with John Houseman, had excited Broadway with productions of *Macbeth, Faustus, Julius Caesar, Shoemaker's Holiday,* and *Heartbreak House,* CBS in 1938 inaugurated the *Mercury Theatre of the Air,* produced and directed by Welles, written in part by him, and with many of its most important roles played by him.

Welles was already an old hand at radio. He had been radio's hero-bogeyman, the Shadow, for some time. He had performed in Archibald MacLeish's famous *Fall of the City.* He had written and performed some *Columbia Workshop* productions. He had acted on the *March of Time.* But when radio gave him free reign he made radio history.

While the public remembers the *Mercury Theatre of the Air* chiefly because of the Martian invasion, the series was far more important in its general impact on radio writing. Most of the broadcasts were in the first person singular. Welles gave a series of brilliant demonstrations of what could be done with the device—and with narrators in general. He did much to loosen up the whole structure of radio drama. In the field of adaptations radio had, before Welles, looked mostly to the stage for material. It was Welles who made clear that the novel was a far richer source, and that many novels could be produced for radio in something closely resembling their original form—with liberal cuts, but retaining the novel's freedom of form, its freedom to zigzag between narration and dialogue, to move quickly from place to place, and also to indulge, when natural to the story, in long stretches of unbroken narration.

In a later series, *Orson Welles' Almanac,* he began to develop into a master of ceremonies full of surprises, who would take the listener from an eight-minute Saki thriller to a reading from the Psalms, to an Americana item like Sherwood Anderson's *I Was a Fool,* all this mixed with birthdays of famous people and cooking recipes. This genial pattern, and the title too, later became part of his syndicated newspaper column.

The following script, one of Welles's few excursions into radio biography, has a lot of the *Almanac* spirit about it. Welles had collaborators assisting him in this script, but the pattern and style and impact were Welles's, and designed by him. In this script Welles is sometimes MC, sometimes dramatic narrator. He can change mood in a moment and have a good time while being deadly serious. He can jump back and forth in the centuries and start on a new tack with almost no warning. He introduces a little girl, blandly fibs to her, quotes Whitman, and reads a message from Henry Wallace. And it all adds up to an arresting program about Christopher Columbus.

This broadcast was originally produced on *Cavalcade of America* on Columbus Day, 1942, under the title *Admiral of the Ocean Sea*. It belongs to a period when hemispheric unity was a crucial matter and many programs were being devoted to the common heritage of the Americas. Many such programs were being translated into Spanish and Portuguese and broadcast to Latin America, to counteract many years of successful Axis propaganda to that area. The Axis, trying to stir Latin America against Anglo-America, had constantly emphasized the differences between the two. It became the job of American radio to emphasize their common experience and essential unity. The series was broadcast to Latin America by the Co-ordinator of Inter-American Affairs.

COLUMBUS DAY

WELLES. Good evening, this is Orson Welles. In an old book in a library in the city of Seville this is written:

VOICE. An age shall come after many years when the ocean will loose the chain of things and a huge land lie revealed.

WELLES. The quotation is from an ancient Roman play by Seneca. "An age shall come after many years when the ocean will loose the chain of things and a huge land lie revealed." In the old book in Seville, these lines are followed by this one:

VOICE. My father fulfilled this prophecy on October 12 in the Year of Our Lord fourteen hundred and ninety-two.

WELLES. Today is October 12. Hello, Americans. This is our birthday.

[Music: Simultaneous with next speech]

This broadcast is part of the celebration. It comes to you in the principal American languages, and you are hearing it in every country of our hemisphere.

Happy birthday, everybody!

Maybe you'd forgotten . . .

LITTLE GIRL. In fourteen hundred and ninety-two
Columbus sailed the ocean blue.

WELLES. That's right. Four and a half centuries ago Columbus found a new world.

PROFESSOR. Mr. Welles, that's a rather dangerous statement.

WELLES. Oh, why's that?

PROFESSOR. It isn't clearly established who first discovered America. I am a full professor of Croviology, Abadabiology, and Cretnics.

WELLES. Glad to know you—but what about Columbus?

PROFESSOR. It is not precisely accurate to say that Columbus discovered America. You see, there is every historical evidence to show that the land masses of the Western Hemisphere were discovered many years—I might even say many centuries—before Columbus. To

4

be exact, in the north and east by the Vikings, under Lief the Lucky and perhaps Eric the Red; in the south and west by natives from the South Seas, traveling in canoes with coconuts for sextants; in the west and north by certain Asiatic peoples bridging the Aleutian Islands; and perhaps even . . .

WELLES. Professor, I agree with you. A lot of men besides Columbus discovered America—probably some before him and many after him—great names like Magellan, Vasco da Gama, Balboa, the Cabots, Hudson—

PROFESSOR. Amerigo Vespucci.

WELLES. That's right, professor.

PROFESSOR. For whom this hemisphere is named.

WELLES. That's right, professor.

[*Music in*]

Now here's my point about America's other discoverers—the great and the anonymous, the conquistadors, the priests, the prospectors, the traders, the trappers, the bandeirantes, and the leatherstockings. Every man of them who moved forward valiantly into any part of the uncharted darkness of our new world is a discoverer of America; every man of these is Columbus—and Columbus is all of them. He's the first man who is going to get to the moon; he's the fellow with the courage of his dreams.

[*Music: Segue*]

FIRST VOICE. I can fly like a bird.

[*Laughter*]

SECOND VOICE. I can sail without a sail.

[*Laughter*]

THIRD VOICE. I can ride my carriage without a horse.

[*Laughter*]

COLUMBUS. I can get to the East by sailing west.

[*Laughter*]

WELLES. The sound you've been hearing was laughter. We bring you now the sound of an airplane . . .

[*Sound*]

a steamboat . . .

[*Sound*]

an automobile.

[*Sound*]

And, by the way, it turns out you can get to the East by going
west because the world is round.

DOUBTING THOMAS. Of course it's round.

WELLES. Then why did you laugh at Columbus?

DOUBTING THOMAS. Who, me?

WELLES. Yes, you. Remember the egg story.

[*Music*]

ANNOUNCER. The Egg Story!

[*Music: Swells, and then down*]

The scene is a castle in Spain. Columbus, who has just discovered America, is the guest of honor at a banquet.

MALE CHORUS [*Heartily finishing the well-known chant*]. And so say
all of us!

[*Applause*]

GUEST [*Sotto voce*]. Why all this fuss about Columbus?

COLUMBUS. You were discussing me, gentlemen?—Yes, I see you were,
and no doubt you were saying that too much is made of my
achievement?

FIRST VOICE. We were only remarking, my Lord Admiral, as the world
goes—sooner or later—somebody else would have done it.

COLUMBUS. There's not much I can say to that; but here you see I
have a hard-boiled egg.

SECOND VOICE. An egg?

THIRD VOICE. Hard-boiled?

DOUBTING THOMAS. Hard-boiled eggs in the fourteen-nineties?

WELLES. Yes. The poached egg hadn't been introduced yet. It was to
be discovered several years later in Mexico by Sister Juana de la
Cruz.

FOURTH VOICE [*Whispering*]. He has an egg.

COLUMBUS. Yes, and I should like to ask you to make this egg stand
on end.

FIFTH VOICE. Stand on end? What a curious request—here, give it
to me.

VOICE. It rolls over!

FIRST VOICE. Of course it rolls over!

ANOTHER VOICE. Here, let me try it!

FIRST VOICE. What's going on?

SECOND VOICE. Wait! Wait! This is obviously quite impossible.

COLUMBUS. Is it impossible?

THIRD VOICE. Impossible.

COLUMBUS. Watch! I crack the shell gently on the bottom and the egg stands.

FOURTH VOICE. Of *course* it stands!

FIFTH VOICE. If you do it *that* way.

COLUMBUS. Yes—but nobody else thought of doing it that way.

[*Music*]

WELLES. I like that yarn because it tells us something about the man himself. He had wit as well as courage, it would seem. Too bad we don't know more about Columbus.

PROFESSOR. Columbus is not necessarily the correct name. It is given severally as Colombo, Colon, Colom, Colomb, and Colonus.

WELLES. Thank you, professor! Anyway, he came from Genoa, which makes him Italian.

PROFESSOR. Evidence has been brought forward that he was Corsican or possibly Majorcan. Another theory would make him a Greek. There are also claims that he was English, Portuguese, German, French, Jewish, Spanish, and Armenian.

WELLES. Probably Italian, though?

PROFESSOR. Indubitably.

WELLES. Thank you, professor! Also everybody seems to agree that his red hair was prematurely gray, that he was freckled.

PROFESSOR. Well, as to the freckles—

WELLES. Never mind about the freckles. What we care about is that four and one-half centuries ago today he arrived on our shores—Christopher Columbus, the admiral of the ocean sea—with three ships in his command. Everybody knows their names: The "Santa Maria," the "Pinto"—

LITTLE GIRL. Excuse me, Mr. Welles.

WELLES. Yes, little girl.

LITTLE GIRL. The name of the ship was the "Pint*a*," not "Pint*o*."

WELLES. The "Pinta," that's right, little girl—and do you know the name of the other boat?

LITTLE GIRL. The other ship was the "Niña."

WELLES. That's what I said.

LITTLE GIRL. Columbus set sail from the coast of Spain on August 3, 1492. It took him thirty-four days to cross the Atlantic, if you count from his last port of call, the Grand Canaries.

[*Music swings in*]

WELLES. The Grand Canaries! There's the glamour of voyaging in that name. His last port of call you said it was—that's the word, all right—call. *Bagdad*—there's a call to that name. Pago-Pago, Timbuktu—and the Grand Canaries. Not that the Grand Canaries can have sounded very special to Columbus. Other words quickened his blood and meant adventure—the Indies, Cipangu, the islands of spice, Cathay, the empire of the Great Khan, Oriental places, the fabled East that he sailed west to find. And there were others—names he'd never heard, singing names for Europeans after him to learn—Cuzsco, Chichen-Itza, Orinoco,

[*Music out*]

Saskatchewan, Mississippi—[*Slight pause*]. Some say that Columbus was only and merely practical. They say all he was after was a short cut to India—just that, a short cut. Maybe. Maybe the unknown can only be explored by men of no imagination; but I think you need imagination to make the try. It can't have been pleasant—that first crossing. Somebody once said that adventure is an attitude taken toward discomfort.

Imagine the first day of that first Atlantic adventure, September eighth, 1492. Here's Columbus ready to upanchor and away—his three caravels dancing in a sharp northeasterly off the Grand Canaries.

[*Music swings in*]

COLUMBUS. My lads, we head away now to the west. There it's still dark—but not quite dark, for, look you, hanging low and so bright—see that westering star. I know that star. I know it well. Our course is set by the Star of the North, lads, but we sail toward that one—the star in the west!

[*Music swells—then down*]

WELLES. Walt Whitman wrote about that voyage. "Passage to India" he called his poem:

Passage to India!
The medieval navigators rise before me,
The world 1492 with its awakened enterprise,
Something swelling in humanity now like the sap of the earth
    in spring.
Passage to India!
Struggles of many a captain, tales of many a sailor dead,
The plans, the voyages again, the expeditions.
Dominating the rest I see the Admiral himself
(History's type of courage, action, faith) . . .
The knowledge gained, the mariner's compass,
Lands found and nations born, thou born America
For purpose vast, man's long probation filled,
Thou rondure of the world at last accomplished.
[*Music out*]
Passage, immediate passage! the blood burns in my veins!
Away, O soul! hoist instantly the anchor!
Cut the hawsers—haul out—shake out every sail!
Have we not stood here like trees in the ground long enough?
Have we not grovel'd here long enough, eating and drinking
    like mere brutes?
Have we not darken'd and dazed ourselves with books long
    enough?
Sail forth—steer for the deep waters only,
For we are bound where mariner has not yet dared to go,
And we will risk the ship, ourselves and all.

O my brave soul!
O farther farther sail!
O farther, farther, farther sail!

[*Music*]

LITTLE GIRL [*Reciting*]. Behind him lay the gray Azores,
    Behind the Gates of Hercules;
Before him not the ghost of shores,
    Before him only shoreless seas.
The good mate said: "Now must we pray,
    For lo! The very stars are gone.

Brave Admiral, speak, what shall I say?"

"Why, say, 'Sail on! Sail on! and on!'"

WELLES. No child grows up in America without hearing again and again the story of that brave first voyage.

LITTLE GIRL. "My men grow mutinous day by day; My men grow ghastly wan and weak."

[*After she says "day by day" the music fades out on her*]

WELLES. Mutiny! None of us got through the fourth grade at school without learning that mutiny was the gravest peril Columbus faced. His men feared to go on, we are told, because they thought their ships would fall off the edge of the world. Perhaps we remember this so vividly because we learned it such a short time after we learned that the world had no edge. The sailors believed in great monsters, sea dragons, fish that could swallow whole fleets. Their dread was real to us then because we'd just been told that dragons don't exist, and we stood with Columbus on these grave questions—on the side of light and logic—by the grace of a mere semester or two.

Frankly, it isn't easy to reconstruct (to re-enact) a fifteenth century mutiny. I don't know how far the mutineers dared to go or got with that clear-eyed gentleman from Genoa. I don't know what they said exactly, but I can guess what it sounded like. Something like this, maybe:

FOURTH VOICE. The Nazi war machine is invincible.

SECOND VOICE. Let's face it—he can't be beaten.

THIRD VOICE. We can't hold out against the Nazis.

WELLES. Of course, Columbus' men weren't talking about the Nazis back then, but it was the same kind of talk.

FIFTH VOICE. He'll be in Moscow in two weeks.

SIXTH VOICE. He'll take Russia by telephone.

SEVENTH VOICE. Hitler is invincible.

WELLES. You've heard that kind of mutiny—remember? Well, there were dragons in 1492, and you could slip off the rim of the earth; but we know now that we can beat Hitler just as sure as the world is round.

[*Music*]

Thirty-two days out, and two days to go—and they nearly turned back. Then on the thirty-third day Columbus made this entry in his log.

[*Music out*]

[*Pause*]

COLUMBUS. Today we saw a bird.

[*Music*]

WELLES. How can we understand a moment in time we never experienced? How can we anticipate something that has already happened? Let's try.—No music, please.

[*Music stops*]

And I'm not going to say anything. We'll all just think about it, try to imagine what it was like on that ship on that night.

[*A big silence—longest silence ever heard on NBC*]

[*The following is very, very hushed*]

COLUMBUS. Hullo, there, mate!

MATE. Aye, Master Admiral?

COLUMBUS. Do you see a light there straight ahead?

MATE. I think I do—yes, there it is!

COLUMBUS. Like a little wax candle it rises and falls!

MATE. It's a light on land, or a little boat.

COLUMBUS. It's gone!

MATE. Wait for a moment. It may return.

COLUMBUS. Aye, there it is!

MATE. I see it too.

COLUMBUS. But no, alas, it's a false alarm. It's my Western star just ready to set, with a wisp of cloud or some low sea mist that gives it that strange warm glow like a lamp—that makes it glimmer and then go out.

[*Pause*]

MATE. Better luck next time, Master Christopher!

[*Music: Simultaneous*]

WELLES. It's four hundred fifty years ago this morning—two o'clock. The three ships speed straight on! Their sails shining white in the moon that now has risen past full in the sky behind. "Pinta" leads. A brave trade wind now blows and the caravels roll and plunge and throw the spray as their bows cut down the last invisible barrier that lies between the Old World and this new one of ours.

[*Music out*]

A moment now—and an era that rose in remotest antiquity will conclude.

[*Another enormous silence*]

VOICE. *Land ho! LAND HO!*

[*Effects, cannons, cheers, then:*]

[*Music to cover. Music's brilliance changes to mood of serenity and optimism*]

COLUMBUS. If this be the Indies, then I've done what I set out to do! But if this should not be, who is there now who is able to say this is not a land far greater still? To that land and the men of that land I say—and to them who follow them through ages to come—to the sons of this land we see here stretching forth—I say:

[*Music out*]

Lock this night in your hearts, for on it a man's dream came true!

WELLES. Passage to more than India!

O secret of the earth and sky!

Of you O waters of the sea! O winding creeks and rivers!

Of you O woods and fields! of you strong mountains. . . .

Of you O prairies! of you gray rocks!

O morning red! O clouds! O rain and snows!

O day and night, passage to you!

O sun and moon and all you stars!

Passage to you!

[*Music: Then down under*]

Columbus died without ever knowing what he had found or how much there was of it. It took a long time to find that out. As a matter of fact we don't know it all yet. There are big sections in our part of the atlas still marked unexplored; but these things we do know: Our island stretches the length of the world. We have great rivers, the Amazon, the Mississippi, the Orinoco, the Columbia, the Yukon, the Paraguay. We have great mountains, the Andes, the Rockies, the Sierra Madres, the Appalachians. We have lakes, Titicaca, the Great Lakes, the Great Salt Lake. We have the brush of the Matto Grosso, the jungles of the Amazon, the swamps of the Everglades, the deserts of Chile and Arizona, the falls of Niagara and Iguassu. We have timber, and quarries, and iron; we can build a world. We have coal, and oil and water; we can run a world. We have wheat, and corn and cattle; we can feed a world.

[*Music out*]

Ours is a tolerant land—summer and winter live in it side by side; and we are so rich that we can change the tide of history with only a small part of our natural wealth. [*Slight pause*] In the crew of Christopher Columbus was a man who is alive today. I will repeat that—a member of Columbus' crew who is alive today. We're happy to have him here with us in the studio. Ladies and gentlemen, I want you to meet José—I'm terribly sorry, I've forgotten your last name.

JOE. I've forgotten the last one myself. Just call me Joe, or José— whatever you like. Yes, sir, man and boy, I've been around for quite some time.

WELLES. How did you happen to sign up with Columbus?

JOE. I just happened to be around. Didn't spend much time here at first. None of us did. Made several crossings. Shipped with a lot of captains on all sorts of craft, the "Mayflower," "Half Moon"— I've forgotten most of the names. Went all over: the Fountain of Youth—never found that; El Dorado—that never turned up; and those Amazon women—*I* never saw any; but that peak in Darien —great view.

WELLES. I suppose you saw a lot of things for the first time, Joe?

JOE. A lot to see—mountains, and lakes and rivers. They were always claiming them in the name of the king. I carried the flag— different flags, of course—different kings—I can't remember their names either: Billy the Bald, Charlie the Flat, Peter the Evil, or whoever they were. Doesn't matter now.

WELLES. What made you finally settle down?

JOE. I don't know. I got used to it—didn't seem any sense going back after a while. Nice people around here—nice country.

WELLES. What did you do?

JOE. A little bit of everything—farmed, prospected, cut down a lot

of trees—sometimes didn't do any work at all; just sat around
and let somebody else do it, for me.

WELLES. Anything else?

JOE. Hunting, fishing [*Thoughtful pause*] —bell ringing.

WELLES. What?

JOE. Bell ringing—there was a time when we were always ringing
bells.

WELLES. What for?

JOE. Celebrating. You see, we claimed all these countries in the name
of the king. But the kings were all too far away to mean much
and after a while they didn't mean anything at all, so we started
doing things in the name of the people. That was a new idea.
That's why we rang the bells.

WELLES. The People—that's something to ring the bell about. And
now there's another new idea—

JOE. Speaking of the People, I'd like you to meet a friend of mine.

WELLES. Oh, how do you do, sir! And your name?

INDIAN JOE. You can call me Joe.

JOE. Indian Joe—he's been around a lot longer than I have. Built
some beautiful cities back in the old days, didn't you, Joe?

INDIAN JOE. Sure.

JOE. He's something to say. Here it is: A lot of good things came
over here from Europe and Africa and Asia; but a lot of good
things were here to begin with. Put 'em all together, and you've
got something new.

INDIAN JOE. Brand new.

WELLES. That's part of what I was starting to say.

JOE. I know what you were starting to say, and it's not such a new
idea either. I heard Bolivar make a speech about it once, and
Henry Clay and a lot of those . . .

WELLES. But right now it's really beginning to come true. Americans
all over the Americas are honestly anxious now to get to know
each other better—to play together, and fight together. Let's put
it this way: America is being discovered again—this time by
Americans. Joe, I think you can start ringing those bells again.
[*Pause*] Any concluding observations?

JOE. Nope, that's it.

[*Music*]

WELLES. Everybody in the American Hemisphere knows that this new idea we've been talking about has no stancher friend than Henry A. Wallace. I went to Washington last week to get his advice on this program, and I also asked him for a few words on this occasion, our American Birthday. He didn't promise he'd prepare us something in a day or two and send it along. He simply picked up a pencil and wrote it out for us there and then. Here it is:

[*Music out*]

"The New World in 450 years has transformed the Latin and Anglo-Saxon cultures into what might be called the New Democracy. The New Democracy looks to the future—not to the past. It looks to the rich soil and bright sunshine of America for strength. It does not exclude the Old World but it will develop its own strength to help the Old World. May October 12 be the symbol of New World strength, of the New Democracy, of abundance for all the peoples of the earth." [*Pause*]

Ladies and gentlemen, that about sums it up. Happy Birthday again and many happy returns of the day.

[*Music*]

WILL THIS EARTH HOLD?

Pearl S. Buck

RADIO has at various times attracted writers who have won fame in other media. One of the most interesting examples is Pearl S. Buck. The first American woman to be awarded the Nobel Prize for literature, winner of almost every major award an author can win, a writer whose works are read throughout the world and who has done much to build "bridges between peoples," she saw early the role that radio was sure to play in the war of ideas.

In the midst of an enormously crowded life of writing, editing, and speaking, she enrolled incognito in a radio writing course at an eastern university. Reading scores of radio plays and writing experimental ones, she explored the new medium throughout one semester, unsuspected by the students who sat beside her. She then became active in radio. For short-wave broadcast to China by the Office of War Information, she wrote a series of six plays entitled *America Speaks to China*. Written in English, they were then translated into Chinese and produced with a cast of Chinese living in America. Pearl Buck subsequently wrote moving pieces for other government agencies and for United China Relief.

Will This Earth Hold? was written for no particular series. It was the result of a conversation with a Chinese friend, just come from China, who told of the men and women who came by the thousands at the call of the government to make airfields for the great B-29s that were to bomb Japan. They had no modern tools to build the airfields—only the short-handled hoe and spade with which they worked on their fields—and they were fearful that these might not be able to make a field strong enough for the great planes. Pearl Buck, from her long years of life in China, knew how to tell this story as no one else could have. And she had already acquired a sure feeling for the radio medium, which she handles with a flexibility rare to writers from other media.

"I feel enormously interested in radio," she writes. "It seems to me that radio is the best dramatic medium that writers can have. . . . I should like best of all to write plays for the radio and eventually radio novels. . . . I see a tremendously important development for radio drama. . . ."

The idea of novels written for radio has often been discussed in radio circles. No network has so far encouraged major novelists to undertake such a venture.

Will This Earth Hold? was published in *Asia and the Americas* in November, 1944. It was first produced over WEVD, a local New York station.

WILL THIS EARTH HOLD?*

[*Music: "America the Beautiful." It is being played by some horns and a drum, and being sung by mixed and garden variety voices, against which three voices are clearer than the rest. These three voices are Mrs. Broder's piercing one, supported by Mr. Broder's bass, which mumbles along in a monotone—and just at the end Mary Broder's clear high soprano, lifting the last line like a banner and flinging it out. There is a confusion of voices as the singing ends, and calls of "Good night," "Glad you're home again, Johnny," and so on. A door shuts and there is silence.*]

MR. BRODER. Take it easy, Johnny. Here, sit in my chair. It's comfortable.

JOHNNY. I'm all right. I don't have to coddle myself.

MRS. BRODER [*Who has been warned through women's magazines against oversympathy for the returning wounded*]. Sure, you're just fine. I can see it. I—I [*Her voice breaks*] I smell the cake burning.

[*Her feet running and a door slams*]

MR. BRODER. Well, now, you mustn't mind mother, Johnny.

JOHNNY. I'm used to—to not walking very well. Plenty of others. You get used to it.

MR. BRODER [*Too heartily*]. Sure you do—sure you do—

MARY [*Abruptly*]. Johnny, you didn't sing!

JOHNNY. Didn't I?

MARY. No, I noticed it. You just stood there on the porch staring out over their heads as though you saw something.

JOHNNY. All of a sudden I remembered something. Funny the way you remember things—not like when you lived 'em day after day. When it's all done you see them in pieces all tossed together anyhow.

* WILL THIS EARTH HOLD? by Pearl S. Buck. Copyright, 1944, by Pearl S. Buck.

MARY. What did you see from the porch?

JOHNNY. Oh—just some people in China.

MARY. You haven't told us anything!

JOHNNY. Oh, I dunno—they weren't anybody, just a family I used to see over there. I dunno why I saw them, sort of, when the folks were singin'.

MARY. How funny, when you were lookin' at our own folks here in Clifton, Pennsylvania.

JOHNNY [*As though a stopper had been removed*]. We was gettin' the big airfield, see? There had to be big airfields, naturally, for the B-29s to take off for Japan. They were goin' to be flown over the Hump and there had to be somewhere for 'em to land. We had our orders to be ready for 'em. Well, over there in China there isn't such a thing as a lot of empty land. It's not like it is over here where you walk a mile and not see anybody. There's people everywhere over there, and villages, they call 'em. When it came to makin' the airfield you just naturally had to smooth off the farms and villages. The farms are little, five acres or so to one. We had to smooth off a lot of farms and villages, see? Well, naturally, it was hard on the people. Like it would be on us here, see?

MR. BRODER. Mary, I don't think you ought to have started this. John, you take it easy.

JOHNNY [*Paying no attention*]. Well, we had our orders. It had to be done. They sent Chinese fellows with us who could speak English so we could explain everything to the people, how we had to take their land for airfields, so we could take off with the bombers against Japan—

[*Music: Simple, not the usual Chinese imitation, fades down under*]

CHINESE [*Speaking a very pure English with a Harvard accent*]. The people do not like to lose their ancestral homes, even though everything has been explained to them, sir. Yet this is not what disturbs them most.

JOHNNY [*His voice in China is very different from what it is in Clifton, Pa. In China it is loud, a little truculent, full of authority*]. Don't they know there's a war on?

CHINESE [*Roughly to the farmers*]. You, farmers, this is war, the foreign soldiers want your land for an airfield.

WONG [*Very deep, quiet voice, without accent but not too cultivated*]. These are the graves of our ancestors. I have told you.

JOHNNY. What does he say?

CHINESE [*Returning to his politeness*]. Sir, he says these are the graves of his ancestors. His own house he gladly gives, but he does not wish to disturb his ancestors.

JOHNNY. Tell him they've dug up plenty of graves in other countries.

CHINESE. Our graves are so old. Our ancestors have been buried so long —for four thousand years.

JOHNNY. Sorry, it's orders.

[*His voice again from the living room of the Broder house, near and close*]. Gosh, I did wish for a bulldozer. If we'd had a coupla bulldozers we could just have gone plowin' over the land and knockin' down the mud houses and it would have been over with quickly. But everything had to be done with people's hands. You can't get bulldozers over the Himalayas. Fifty thousand men and women and children came pourin' in from everywhere to work on that airfield. They had little short-handled hoes and spades and baskets slung on poles. They went pickin' at the graves, kind of gingerly, like they was afraid of ghosts. The Wong family—I got to know them by then—stood there in a little bunch, watchin' their ancestors' graves bein' dug up. Mrs. Wong cried quiet like she was sick. She made me think of mom a little somehow.

[*The door opens . . . Mrs. Broder comes in*]

MRS. BRODER [*Brightly*]. I made you a marble cake, Johnny. Look, I just poured on the icing and you'll have to eat it with a fork.

JOHNNY [*Absently*]. Gosh, that's wonderful, mom—

MR. BRODER [*In a whisper*]. He's talking, mother.

MRS. BRODER [*Half hushed*]. Oh . . .

JOHNNY. Their graves weren't like ours here in the cemetery. They were right out in the middle of a field, maybe, in a circle of low mud wall. After a while I couldn't keep from seein' them the way the Wongs did. At the back was a high old grave that must have belonged to some great-grandfather Wong. Grandfather Wong was still alive. He came out of the house last of all. He was a little old man in a gray robe and a black wool cap over his ears and always a brass tobacco pipe in his hand. When the big grave was opened he tottered forward and bowed to the dust they were takin' out. Mr. Wong rushed up and took the dust himself. Everything was gone and it was only dust. He held out the end of his coat and they poured it in and then he let it fall slowly into a brown jar that Mrs. Wong held. It lay there in the bottom. The next grave was great-grandmother's, I reckon, and so they went, the Wong family bowin' before them all, old men and young men and women and their children. The last grave was the smallest and it had bones in it, the bones of a baby, and the women began to cry out loud and Mrs. Wong held out her arms and took it—the little skeleton.

MRS. BRODER. Oh, Johnny, the poor soul!

JOHNNY. It's funny how I remember that. I saw fellows blown to pieces the days the Japs came over us, and kep' right on eatin' my three square meals a day. When I think of those Wongs I—I can't even eat this cake, mom.

MR. BRODER. Take it easy, son.

JOHNNY. Funny thing, when I was over there I kept seein' home. I thought about grandad and gramma, here in the cemetery, and Aunt Mollie and Little Jim that died before I was old enough even to go to school.

MRS. BRODER [*Weeping a little*]. Oh, Johnny . . .

JOHNNY. Funny, because now I'm home I keep thinkin' about the Wongs. I got to know them so well, see?

MARY. But they couldn't talk to you?

JOHNNY. It was funny, I got so I almost knew what they were sayin'. It was true they minded the graves more than anything, though. We tore down the villages. Fifty thousand people workin' together—well, the Wong village was gone in no time. The bricks turn to dust easy.

MRS. BRODER. Where'd you put the Wongs?

JOHNNY. There wasn't any place to put 'em.

MRS. BRODER [*Her voice outraged*]. You mean to tell me you left those poor innocent people out in the weather without a roof over their heads? And little children, and that good old man?

JOHNNY. Mom, it was war. And we had our orders. We couldn't stop to build a lot of houses. The Wongs put their bedquilts up on some poles.

MARY [*Very quietly*]. Couldn't they have gone somewhere else?

JOHNNY. Well, there didn't seem to be any place for them to go. Anyway, they stayed. It wasn't too bad if it didn't rain. When it rained the earth was mud. They sat on their beds and tables and waited for it to clear off.

MR. BRODER [*Rather solemnly*]. How did Mr. Wong feed the family?

JOHNNY. They worked on the airfield. They all worked. I went out a couple of days after. They were workin' like everybody else, as though it wasn't their own land. Grandpa Wong sat on a coupla of bricks and he had a little stone mallet like all the others and he was poundin' bricks to pieces—poundin' 'em back to dust. Maybe it was his own house. You couldn't tell. They were all there. One of the daughters was nursin' her baby while she pounded the brick to dust, too. They were all poundin', poundin'—

[*As though at a distance the steady, rhythmic pounding of stone mallets upon earth, a dull, dry sound. Against it voices are muted. A child cries*]

MRS. WONG. Hush, my little thing!

MR. WONG. Why does our son cry so much?

MRS. WONG. My breasts are drying. I cannot keep from grief. What will happen to us? We are homeless, living and dead no home!

MR. WONG. What would happen to us if the enemy made us slaves? You must pound the bricks more small. They must be made into dust.

[*The mallets, with no voice, pounding in a rhythmic, click, click, clickety clack . . . Fades out*]

JOHNNY. It was done so quickly. You wouldn't believe it. It made you feel queer to look over the acres and acres of people sitting flat on the ground, the sun beating down on their black heads and on their thousands and thousands of hands rising and falling, rising and falling—

[*The mallets rise to a steady pitch, against which voices speak muted*]

VOICES. Will this land come back to us?
Never if we lose it to the enemy.

We work for victory when we pound this earth of ours, stone
   upon earth.
We offer up our land.
It has become sacred land.
Land where our fathers died.
Land of our children's pride.
Dust under the wheels and the wings of the bombers.
Winged harvest.
   [*The mallets fade to finish*]
JOHNNY. We lived all day with the sound of those beating mallets in
   our ears. Our blood ran to the beat. We talked against it, worked
   against it.
   [*The mallets, steady, so rhythmic it drives you mad . . . Against
   it rough, irritable American voices*]
VOICE. Here you, Joe, get on the job there. Don't let these Chinamen
   see you loafing!
SECOND VOICE. Oh, God, I want to go home—
FIRST VOICE. Shut up!
   [*Sound fades out*]
JOHNNY. The dust was into everything. It got into our clothes and our
   beds, into our food—
   [*The mallets, and angry rough American voices against it*]
VOICES. What's this—ashcake?
   Naw, grits.
   Darned if the sugar hasn't turned to mud.
   Coffee's mud, too.
JOHNNY. At night—the silence—it was so still it made you afraid. They
   stopped at dark, all at the same minute. Your blood had been
   racing along to the beat of the mallets and when they stopped
   your heart seemed to stop too. You were tired to death. You just
   leaned against anything. And you stared over the field where
   the silence was and lights flickered, tiny lantern lights. They were
   eating their rice and a handful of beans apiece. I used to go over
   and see the Wongs.
MR. WONG [*His voice remote as all the Chinese voices are*]. Father,
   you haven't eaten your bowlful.
GRANDPA WONG. I cannot eat.

MR. WONG. You must not work so hard. You will die, and where shall we bury you?

GRANDPA WONG. I will not die until the land is given back to us. That will be my victory.

JOHNNY [*Voice near and clear*]. They sat there with their sticks of furniture under the quilts they had hung on poles for a tent. The jar of ashes was there, too, waiting. As soon as it was dawn the pounding began. It drove some of the fellows crazy. They began to worry about the field. When the B-29s flew in from the Himalayas, could they land or would the field just crumple up under them? Maybe the whole thing would be a flop.

[*Sound of the mallets*]

AMERICAN VOICES. It won't hold up.

It's sheer waste of time.

A couple of steam rollers and we'd have—

You can't haul steam rollers over the Hump.

It ain't gonna do. You can't land them big bombers on a field that Chinks have pounded flat with little toy hammers.

[*Sound fades and out*]

JOHNNY. Somehow or other they got to understand that we thought they weren't any good. Don't ask me how they knew. They got to worryin'. They hadn't even seen a real bomber. They'd ask, with their hands, but we knew what they meant, how long B-29s were. Just for the hell of it, some of the fellows measured off a quarter of a mile or so. Then the whole lot of them would sit around at night and worry.

VOICES [*Remote*]. The Americans think we cannot make the earth hard enough for their bombers.

They don't know us.

They don't know our earth.

We know our earth. It can be rich as river land and hard as stone.

We make our earth into a battlefield for the wheels and the wings of our allies, and they will lift themselves from our earth. We have beaten our earth into the foundation for victory.

JOHNNY [*Half sobbing*]. They'd go back and begin to pound again and pound again and pound again—

MR. BRODER. Take it easy, Johnny.

JOHNNY. The Wongs grew as thin as laths. They'd never been fat, God knows. But they turned the color of the earth under that sun. We didn't have rain for days. The sun beat down on them like fire. Our fellows couldn't hardly stand it and we had sun helmets. The Chinese hadn't anything. A woman maybe would tie a piece of blue cloth over her head. Most of the time they didn't bother. The kids ran around with nothing much on, the little ones, and the big ones worked. The water dried up in the creeks and the wells got low. We began to get scared about water. None of the Chinese washed and we didn't let them see us wash even our hands and faces. They hung around with tin cans and took anything we threw out. I went by the Wongs' one night just to see how they were makin' it. Their faces were parched and their lips were all sores. But they had some incense stuck in a crack in the ground outside their makeshift tent and it was burnin' and the gray smoke curlin' up. I used to talk pretty good with my hands then—

MR. WONG [*His voice remote*]. He wants to know why we are burning the incense.

GRANDPA WONG. I will explain it to him. [*He clears his throat*]

WOMAN. Grandfather, he cannot understand you.

GRANDPA WONG [*Reprovingly*]. These foreigners understand more than you think, if you give them time, and speak slowly, and use your hands. See, I point to heaven—

JOHNNY. I made out they were burnin' incense to heaven to ask their gods to hold off on the rain. The field was nearly done. Another coupla weeks of that poundin' and it would be hard as cement. Then rain wouldn't hurt. But we didn't know if they could hold out.

VOICES [*Against the incessant pounding*]. Water—is there no water in the buckets?

At noon they will give us a cup apiece.

How long is it until noon?

The sun is halfway to the zenith.

[*A child wails*]

MRS. BRODER. Wait a minute, Johnny, I'm goin' to fix a pitcher of lemonade.

JOHNNY. Mom, wait a minute.

MR. BRODER. Take it easy, take it easy.

JOHNNY. We'd had our orders to be done a certain day. Nobody knew if it was the big day or not. We'd talk about it—how it would look to see those big B-29s sailin' in out of the west. Nobody knew if it would be on that day. But the Chinese just took it for granted it would be. They began workin' nights. Then it was night and day. There wasn't a minute's silence. We all got strung up as tight as fiddle strings. Nobody talked. You couldn't. You just went around in a daze. Everything, everybody, doin' what you had to do, just listenin', listenin', not hearin' anything, not thinkin', just movin' and doin' what you had to do.

[*Sound of the mallets and Chinese voices*]

VOICES. How many nights since you have slept, mother of my little son?

Can any of us sleep?

What if we fail? We have never made these floors before. We have only made our threshing floors.

What if the wings cannot rise?

They are foreign machines and we have never seen them.

What if we fail?

JOHNNY. We were all bettin', of course. [*He gives a strange excited laugh*]. The odds were against us.

[*Sound of the mallets and American voices*]

VOICES. Aw, it won't work.

What' ya bet?

You'd oughta see LaGuardia Field at home. It's like a table, hard as stone, smooth as your hand.

Them big bombers—

The earth will crack like paper, I'll betcha.

What' ya bet?

You can't get steam rollers over the Hump.

JOHNNY. Funny thing, I was kind of bettin' on the Wongs. The old man was a shred by now. He made me think of old Mr. Haines. 'Member Mr. Haines, mom? He died when I was a kid.

MRS. BRODER. He was ninety-six when he died. The last five years he couldn't walk. They had to carry him to the sofa while they made his bed up in the mornin'. He didn't weigh more'n ninety pounds.

JOHNNY. Grandpa Wong tottered out every mornin' bright and early and took up his mallet. I could see his old claws of hands trembling. Mr. Wong kept near to kind of watch him.

[*The mallets, quicker now than before and voices against them*]

MR. WONG. Father . . . go and rest, father. We will finish the task.

GRANDPA WONG. Let me finish my work. You young men—you're so —so—

[*Sound dies out*]

JOHNNY. They were pounding straight on the field now. Dust was pounded into stone, hard. They stopped one night and the field was done. Next day was the big day. We couldn't sleep. I guess nobody slept. The lights flickered all night long around the field, like fireflies. The Wongs didn't go to bed. They sat outside their tent, all of them, nobody talkin'. They had incense burnin' again. Everybody had incense burnin'. The air was fragrant with it, like flowers. I never knew how still it could be in the world, at night . . . And then at dawn—

[*Voices remote*]

MR. WONG. They will come in from the western sky.

GRANDPA WONG. Eat, my son.

MR. WONG. I can't eat. What if the earth wrinkles like cloth under their wheels? I will kill myself.

GRANDPA WONG. Trust the earth. I tell you, I know our earth.

MR. WONG. But it has never been put to this great test. The bombers weigh—

GRANDPA WONG. Be quiet—you have said that a hundred times.

MR. WONG. I am going outside. I can't bear this roof. I must see the sky.

GRANDPA WONG [*Chuckling*]. Go on—go on—I want to eat.

JOHNNY [*His voice in the foreground always*]. We did all the last little things all day. We thought they'd be in maybe around the middle of the afternoon. They didn't come. The sky lit up with such a sunset—

MR. WONG. Father, father, look!

GRANDPA WONG. You see the heavens. They light the way. You see the earth how it waits.

GRANDPA WONG. Where?

MR. WONG. There—where I point—

GRANDPA WONG. Eagles!

MR. WONG. No—the bombers—they come—they come—
   [*His words are taken and tossed out by many voices—submerged. Sound of bombers approaching louder, to sudden finish*]
JOHNNY. They came roarin' in out of the west. Nobody said a word when they began to come down. We were all watchin' that field under the wheels. The Wongs were in the front of the crowd, ol' grandpa smilin'. But I saw the sweat pourin' down Mr. Wong's face. When the first bomber hit the ground I was watchin' him. There was a look on his face like the wheels were runnin' over his own body. Then he bust out laughin'—
MR. WONG. This earth holds!
GRANDPA WONG. What did I say?
JOHNNY. Yep, the earth held, like she was cement. The big beauties, they came down as light as feathers and hit and bounced a little and the earth acted like it had always been airfield.
MR. BRODER. Well, by heck—
MRS. BRODER [*Half dazed*]. It's queer how I see it all. I'd like to know those Wongs—
MARY. Johnny, Johnny, don't stop. What happened next?
JOHNNY. Funny thing, nothin' much. Of course we were awfully busy, but the Chinese just seemed to melt away. We thought they'd be trekkin' out that night—they'd all been paid off. But nobody went away. That night the lantern lights around the field were still just like fireflies. Everybody just sat waitin'. They waited that night and the next day and the next night—we began to get a hunch what they were waitin' for. They were waitin' to see the big bombers take off for Japan!
   [*Clatter of voices, Chinese and American, and fragmentary words*]
MR. WONG. We shall all stay to see if the land holds for their going. Who knows? It is more easy to come down than to go up.
GRANDPA WONG. You still do not trust our earth!
JOHNNY. The morning the boys took off—of course it was still nearly dark when we got the propellers spinnin'. I had a queer feeling, I remember when I was workin'. I felt as though a crowd was watchin'. Then the sky split in the east, and light came through, and I saw them. They were all watchin', every one of those men,

women, and children, pressin' around the field, as near as they were allowed to come. I could see the Wongs and I waved to them.

MR. WONG. Now the Americans are in the machines. The wings quiver!

GRANDPA WONG. Be silent!

[*There is an instant of silence, then the sound of the planes, and a loud medley of American and Chinese voices breaks out, the Americans shouting commands, the Chinese as below. This continues for a few seconds and then the confusion resolves itself by a transition that is almost like the precipitation of a chemical, so that out of the confusion a harmony forms. Mr. Wong's voice is the first clear resolution, at the end, then others join.*]

VOICES. Look at the wings—
The wings, the wings!
But we laid the foundations.
They spring from our shoulders, these wings.
Our feet are upon the earth.
Our hands made the foundations.
From which our brothers fly into the heavens.
And over the seas.
All we have and all we are—
Victory!

MR. WONG [*Singing*]. "Arise, ye, who refuse to be bondslaves!"

[*The singing rises to a great chorus, continues for two seconds and recedes, not fading away so much as receding to a finish . . . Out of the silence, Johnny's voice.*]

JOHNNY [*Very matter-of-fact*]. Well, I guess that's all folks. They're usin' the field every day over there. It's a dandy.

THE BATTLE OF THE
WARSAW GHETTO

Morton Wishengrad

M ORTON WISHENGRAD's career is an example of the roundabout ways
in which people have become radio writers. He came into radio
half accidentally, via the labor movement. Once in, he won an
honored place for himself with astonishing speed.

He was the youngest son in a family of seven brothers and two sisters
who were raised on New York's Lower East Side by Russian immigrant
parents. He attended New York University and Brooklyn College. Before
writing radio scripts, or even thinking about it, he ushered one summer
at the New York Paramount Theatre, qualified as an errand boy for a
watch company by having a college degree, then served as an educational
director, editor, researchist, and teacher for the International Ladies'
Garment Workers Union. In 1942 he was named AFL director of a joint
AFL-CIO Labor Shortwave Bureau, through which organized labor addressed trade unionists in England and occupied Europe via the OWI.

Late in 1942 the CIO Textile Workers Union asked him to prepare
a script for the *Labor for Victory* series, which was running on NBC,
telling the stories of various unions. Wishengrad looked through a book
on radio writing and went ahead. The NBC editors, whose chief function
in connection with this series was to watch it nervously, were struck with
the individual quality and sensitive writing of Wishengrad's script, and
asked him to try another for a Red Cross series—then another for the
same series. At that time NBC was looking for a writer for a historical
series of the NBC University of the Air, *Lands of the Free*. The three
scripts Wishengrad had so far written suggested he might be the man.
He was commissioned to write a trial script. His script on *Valley Forge*
immediately won him a contract to write the series. For the next two
seasons he wrote *Lands of the Free*, then went on to the *Eternal Light*,
with occasional scripts for *Cavalcade of America* and several special
broadcasts.

In the summer of 1943 Milton Krents of the American Jewish Committee discussed with Wishengrad a special Yom Kippur program to
propose to NBC. Wishengrad had been deeply moved by the news of the
"Second Battle of Warsaw," and suggested it as a subject. Krents was
immediately enthusiastic and the next day sent Wishengrad a fat folder
of newspaper clippings, diary fragments, and other materials from American Jewish Committee files.

"The more I read," Wishengrad tells, "the more inadequate to the
task I felt. Several times I asked Krents to get another writer. He refused.
I invented all sorts of pretexts. We were moving, my apartment was a

jungle of packing cases, my daughter was sick. But Krents insisted that I do the job.

"So I began. The average script takes me from ten to fifteen hours of steady writing. *Warsaw Ghetto* took nearly ten days. I wrote, rewrote, discarded, began again a dozen times. I hardly knew what I wanted. I neglected to shave, found myself unable to sleep, and littered the floor with paper.

"Then, as I recall, my wife made me sit down, and I talked for nearly three hours about the Warsaw Ghetto. The script opened up after that. I wrote the opening and closing narrations first. I combed *Pirke Aboth*, the Ethics of the Fathers of the Talmud, and in 'It is not for thee to complete the work, but neither art thou free to desist from it,' I felt I had my last scene. The other scenes practically wrote themselves. The scene in which Isaac disrobes Dvora was written in a few minutes. I reread it and threw it away. My wife found it on the floor and made me reinstate it.

"In *The Battle of the Warsaw Ghetto* I wanted to present the tragedy of the people who gave the world its monotheism, its morality, and its concept of the sacredness of human life. I wanted to present Jews as they are, without self-pity, without anger, and with the terrible conviction that, to paraphrase Theodor Herzl, if you cannot march, you must at least remain standing."

The Battle of Warsaw Ghetto was first presented on the eve of the Day of Atonement in 1943 over an NBC network, with Arnold Moss as Isaac Davidson, Frank Papp directing, and a score composed by Morris Mamorsky. Two subsequent performances, directed by Anton M. Leader, featured Raymond Massey. The three performances drew over 12,000 letters. The script was chosen by the Writers' War Board as the War Script of the Month. The War Department sent transcriptions overseas to be played on troop stations in all war theaters. Hundreds of amateur radio groups, Sunday schools, high schools, and colleges have performed it.

This is the first Wishengrad script to be published in any book.

The newspaper *Variety* has awarded the American Jewish Committee a special citation for its contributions to radio broadcasting.

THE BATTLE OF THE
WARSAW GHETTO

[*Cantor: "El Mole Rachamin," unaccompanied—20-30 seconds and fade under following*]

VOICE [*In close softly*]. It is a prayer for the dead . . . "El Mole Rachamin." Hear him with reverence, for it is no ordinary prayer and they are not the ordinary dead. They are the dead of the Warsaw Ghetto—the scapegoats of the centuries. Once the priest robed himself in linen and stood on Sinai in a convocation of Israel; and they brought unto him a live goat, chosen by lot. And he laid his hands on the goat's head and confessed over it the iniquities of the people. And he released the goat, and its name was Azazel, scapegoat; and it fled into the wilderness. But for them in the Ghetto of Warsaw there was no release . . . there was only the abyss. In the Ghetto thirty-five thousand stood their ground against an army of the Third Reich—and twenty-five thousand fell. They sleep in their common graves but they have vindicated their birthright. Therefore, let him sing and hear him with reverence for they have made an offering by fire and an atonement unto the Lord and they have earned their sleep.

[*Cantor: Up and finish*]

[*Music: Establish theme almost as a segue and then fade under following*]

NARRATOR [*Simply*]. My name was Isaac Davidson and I lived in the Polish city of Lublin with my wife, Dvora, and Samuel, our son. When Poland fell, they herded us into a cattle car and transported us to the Ghetto of Warsaw. It was a place in purgatory and around that purgatory they had built a brick wall and around

34

the brick wall another wall of barbed wire and beyond the barbed
wire stood a third wall of soldiers armed with bayonets.

[*Music out*]

[*Fade in shuffling of feet and hold under*]

NAZI 1. All right there, move on. Next, next, next. Lively.

[*Shuffling of feet*]

NAZI 2. Your name?

NARRATOR. Isaac Davidson.

NAZI 2. Who are they?

NARRATOR. Dvora Davidson, Samuel Davidson. My wife, my son.

NAZI 2 [*Stamping three cards in rapid succession*]. Three blue cards.
Get along. Next, next, next, move on. Pick up your feet. There's
no funeral.

[*Shuffling of feet up and take out. . . .*]

[*Music: Fade narrative theme under*]

NARRATOR. Three blue cards stamped with the letter J. Bread cards.
Each card . . . a pound of bread a week. As precious as life.
Dvora held the cards in her hand and we went to the tenement
in the Twarda District . . .

[*Music out*]

to the place where we were to live.

[*Footsteps going up*]

We went up the stairs of the tenement, and Samuel and I
waited in the hall, while Dvora spoke to the woman who lived
there.

DVORA. They said you would know where we are supposed to stay.

WOMAN. Come in, this is where you stay—in this room.

DVORA. But you live here.

WOMAN. In this corner. The other corner is yours.

DVORA. But I thought . . .

WOMAN. You don't know how lucky you are. This room has a
window.

DVORA. Perhaps we shouldn't trouble you. Maybe . . . some other place.

WOMAN [*Laughing bitterly*]. You'll find out. Before they walled the
Ghetto, fifty thousand people lived in these slums . . .

DVORA. Yes, but . . .

WOMAN. Do you know how many are here now? Five hundred thousand! A half million! I know a man who sleeps in a vault in the cemetery. Don't be a fool, come in. It's still better than the cemetery.

[*Music: Theme and under*]

NARRATOR. That was our room. And because Dvora lived in it, it was also our home. There was no soap; but she cleaned it. There were no needles, but she made a cloth for the table. There was no lamp in it, yet she filled it with light. And then when she found a box, our son Samuel scrabbled up some earth and a few pathetic blades of grass . . .

[*Music out*]

and Dvora put the box on the sill of the window.

[*Thump of box coming to rest*]

DVORA. There. Now our house has a garden.

NARRATOR. Yes, Dvora. Our house has a garden.

DVORA. You say it as though it is not true. Look, Isaac . . . look at the sun. There is no land where the sun doesn't shine. Now let it shine here on something green in the Ghetto.

[*Music in under*]

NARRATOR. Green grass in the Warsaw Ghetto . . . a few pathetic blades of green in the scrabbled earth. But a sign of living spirit and a proof that where the spirit lives there can be no degradation. There in this place of death, shut off, walled in, foredoomed, there were things of the spirit done by men and women like Dvora.

[*Music out*]

In the Ghetto of Warsaw there was beauty, and comradeship, and learning.

TEACHER I [*Rabbinical—Fade in*]. And now, we'll see if you have learned your lesson . . . There are seven marks of an uncultured man and seven marks of a wise man. Do you know what they are, Samuel?

BOY. The wise man does not speak before him who is greater in wisdom; and does not break in on the speech of his fellow; he is not hasty to answer; he questions according to the subject matter, and answers to the point; he speaks upon the first things first; and upon the last, last; regarding that which he has not understood, he says, I do not understand it, and he acknowledges the truth.

TEACHER. And the mark of an uncultured man?

BOY. The reverse of all these things.

TEACHER. [*Fading*]. Very good, Samuel. You are a good boy.

[*Cross-fade with classroom voices ad lib*]

GIRL [*She is struggling to make herself heard*]. Weismann's theory of germinal continuity . . . how can I finish the recitation when they talk?

TEACHER 2. Please, all of you. This is a classroom in the Ghetto. It is different from other classrooms. We must be an example.

[*Murmur out*]

Thank you. Go on, Esther. The theory of germinal continuity.

GIRL. The germ contains living material which has come down in unbroken continuity ever since the origin of life and which is destined to persist in some form as long as life itself. [*Fading*] While Weismann's name is chiefly associated with this theory, other . . .

[*Cross-fade with laughter*]

INSTRUCTOR. I thought this was a class in sculpture. Apparently, I'm wrong. What's this supposed to be?

PLUMBER. I don't know. Maybe I'm one of those surrealists.

INSTRUCTOR [*Laughing*]. Well, don't give up, I'll make a sculptor out of you yet.

PLUMBER. It's all right with me. If you're willing, I'm willing. But my father made me a plumber and I guess I'll always be a plumber. Now, if I had my tools and a piece of brass pipe, I'd show you some real sculpture.

[*Both laugh and fade out of laughter into*]

DOCTOR. Say, Ah. Ahhhhh!

BOY [*Almost gagging*]. Aah, aahh.

DOCTOR. Wider . . . a little more . . . There, that will do, boy. Why didn't you bring him earlier?

DVORA. It's my fault. I didn't know there was a clinic.

DOCTOR. His tonsils are badly infected, they'll have to come out.

DVORA. I don't have any money to pay you.

DOCTOR. There's nothing to pay here. Money can't buy what no one will sell to us.

DVORA. No?

DOCTOR. No. We need drugs, instruments, anesthesia.

DVORA. Then—you operate without anesthesia?

BOY. Please, doctor, will it hurt?

DOCTOR. Yes, it will hurt. In the Ghetto, everything hurts. Perhaps tomorrow, it will be different.

[*Music: Short bridge*]

NARRATOR. The Ghetto waited for tomorrow. It tried to do so with dignity and self-respect. Sometimes it was hard. But the Ghetto tried. In the cellars of the tenements the children went to classes, and wherever there was a patch of dirt the older boys studied agriculture; carpenters taught their trade to clerks with thin chests, the watchmakers and the leatherworkers opened trade schools, the artists taught their art. And all of this was free. Whoever wanted to learn was welcome. It was a somber, grim, melancholy place, heavy with a foreboding of death, but we encouraged each other to work and to study and to laugh. Yes, to laugh also—we organized four theaters. But our greatest pride, our finest symbol was our orchestra—the Ghetto Symphony.

[*Fade in tuning of instruments*]

[*Rapping of baton*]

CONDUCTOR. We'll try it again. From the same place. Now watch me. Please! Please, watch the stick. We're going to start together and finish together. All right now. Watch the stick.

[*Orchestra: Air from Smetana's Fatherland Suite—Register and then hold under, dropping out instruments to solo violin*]

NARRATOR. We sat and listened to the Ghetto Symphony, feeding our hunger on the clear, sweet sound. But since the Herrenvolk, the Master Race that erected the walls, since they intended that we should be hungry, they came and confiscated some of the instruments. [*Pause for cue*] First they took only a few, then more. Our orchestra dwindled. It became an ensemble. And then the Herrenvolk came again and stole more instruments. [*Pause for cue*] The ensemble became a quartet. And then [*Pause for cue*] a single solo violin was left. Why did they do it? Perhaps it irritated them—Jews satisfying a hunger.

[*Music out*]

We were left with hunger. And where there is hunger, the plague always follows. The plague came and 17,800 persons died of spotted typhus in Warsaw. And of these 15,758 were Jews. A pestilence imprisoned behind a brick wall, a great achievement of medical science—I say it without irony. Yes, 15,758—and Dvora Davidson, my wife . . . 15,759. [*Gently on cue*]. Samuel, leave her. You cannot help her any more.

BOY. Mamma, mamma!

NARRATOR. Come here. Come here, Samuel. She cannot hear you. You are a big boy. You mustn't cry. Here, let me wash your face. She wouldn't like to see you with a dirty face. Stop crying now.

BOY. I'll try.

NARRATOR. Will you do something for me, Samuel?

BOY. Yes, if I can.

NARRATOR. I want you to go to your corner; I want you to try to go to sleep.

BOY. I couldn't . . . I couldn't sleep, papa.

NARRATOR. Then go to your corner and turn your face away. Mind me. Do as your father says. [*Pause*] That's right, to the wall. You are a good boy, Samuel.

BOY [*Off mike, suggesting face turned away in his following speeches*]. You will not hurt her, papa?

NARRATOR. No one can hurt her. [*Pause*] I am taking off her clothes. Her apron, her dress, Uncle Avrum's shoes—everything. Naked came I out of my mother's womb and naked shall I return thither.

BOY [*Sobbing*]. You are going to carry her into the street.

NARRATOR. Yes, after dark I am going to carry her into the street . . . and I will leave her there . . . cold, naked, nameless. You know why I must do this, Samuel. They must not be able to identify her. They must not know who she is.

BOY [*Sobbing*]. It's because of the bread card, papa.

NARRATOR. Yes, it's because of the bread card. If they identify her as Dvora Davidson, they will take it away. They must not be able to identify her.

BOY. Please, papa, please. Let them take it away. Don't leave her in the street.

NARRATOR. It is her last wish, Samuel. The bread card is for you. Honor her last wish. The blue card with the letter J—a pound of bread a week for her son.

BOY. I won't take it, I can't.

NARRATOR. You must, Samuel. Once you took her milk; now you must take her bread. She leaves you nothing else. You must take it, Samuel—it is your inheritance.

BOY [Sobbing louder and hold under prayer].

NARRATOR. [Very slowly]. Yisgadel ve-yiskadash shmay rabo. Beolmo di-vro chirusay, v'yamlich malchussay, Bechayeichon u'vyo meichon. U'vchayei de-chol-bais yisroal ba-agolo U-vizman Koreev. V'eemeru Omain.

[Music: Fade narrative theme in above and hold under]
[Fade on recitation and sobbing of boy]

NARRATOR. This was our degradation. In the Ghetto of Warsaw we divided dead men's bread. Have you tasted dead men's bread? The taste is bitter, and it is dry in the mouth because the saliva will not flow. This is what we ate and this is how we lived . . . The five hundred thousand of the Warsaw Ghetto. But not five hundred thousand for long. On June 22, 1942, armored cars escorted a convoy of black trucks into the Ghetto. They seized men and women and children and packed them into the trucks and these were the uncoffined dead who never returned. And each day thereafter the black trucks came. And each day when they left there was weeping in the Ghetto. I have seen the faces of the men that did these things—the men who came in armored cars. They were men like other men. Some were old. Some were young, with eyes, with skin and flesh and nails and the requisite number of fingers. I looked into their faces and did not believe. But the trucks continued to come.

[Music out]

And it must be said that if the thing that they did was monstrous, it was a monstrous thing done with order and with method; for they take pride in order.

[Sound of trucks and under voices]

NAZI 1. July 22, 1942.

NAZI 2. Six thousand two hundred and eighty-nine.

NAZI 3. Destination . . . Tremblinka.

NAZI 1. July 23.

NAZI 2. Seven thousand eight hundred and fiifteen.

NAZI 3. Destination . . . Oswiantzem.

NAZI 1. July 24.

NAZI 2. Seven thousand four hundred and forty-four.

NAZI 3. Destination . . . Belzec.

[*Voices and truck sounds hold under Narrator*]

NARRATOR. Done with method, precise, efficient, recorded. To Tremblinka, Oswiantzem, Belzec, Sobibor, Majdany, a lethal gas chamber, an electric furnace, a poison pit, an execution field, a cemetery. And add also ten thousand brave, hopeless, tragic men who seized sticks and stones and knives and bare fists and charged tanks and tried to halt the trucks. Add their bodies to the list for the ten days of June, 1942. Make your total and then add two precise, methodical, documented months in August and September, 1942. Reckon it. Do it carefully. You cannot do it on your fingers. No! Let me give you the sum. Listen, 275,954 fewer bread cards in the Ghetto. Swift, accurate, final. Quicker than typhus, surer than hunger.

[*Music in and under*]

NARRATOR. They sent the black trucks because the hunger and the pestilence were too slow and too merciful. When we were starving, we beseeched the civilized world for food, and when the plague struck us, we appealed for simple things, for soap, medicine, for tools for our physicians. But when the black trucks came we no longer asked for rescue, we no longer asked for mercy—we asked for weapons. Through the Polish underground, which carried our appeals, we asked England, Russia, and the United States for weapons.

[*Music out*]

And there was silence. You did not answer. And then through the Polish underground there came your answer: resolutions of sympathy, phrased with felicity. It was a greater injury than silence. I who know can say to you that the grave does not yield its tenant for such coin, nor will such coin inspire the enemy to lie down and crimson the gutter with his blood. We waited for weapons that did not come. Five hundred thousand waited. [*Pause*] Three hundred thousand waited. [*Pause*] One hundred thousand waited. And finally thirty-five thousand waited who did not know where to look—but the answer came from under their feet—from the sewer under the Warsaw Ghetto.

[*Echo chamber*]

[*Footsteps and ad lib activity*]

POLE. Carry it gently, Pan Meyer. Don't let it fall.

PLUMBER. I'm carrying it as though it were a case of eggs.

POLE. More gently than that, Pan Meyer.

PLUMBER. What could be more fragile than a case of eggs?

POLE. A case of dynamite.

PLUMBER. The Ghetto Council would like to know your name.

POLE. What difference does it make?

PLUMBER. They want to thank you.

POLE. Tell them to thank the Polish underground. [*Pause*] Take good care of those barrels. There are enough grenades in them to blow up every Jew in the Ghetto.

PLUMBER. Then there must be enough grenades in them to blow up every German in Warsaw.

POLE. I'm glad you see it that way.

PLUMBER. What do you think we've been waiting for?

[*Music in and under*]

NARRATOR. April 19, 1943. Thirty-five thousand, men, women, children stood ready. It was the day. Trenches were dug during the night. Every house, every room, every cellar, every roof was prepared. At 4:00 A.M. a detachment of Storm Troopers in light tanks

[*Trucks moving in*]

escorted the black trucks to the walls of the Ghetto. They came as usual on their daily errand. We waited until the vehicles were within range.

TEACHER I. FIRE!

[*Blast of rifle fire and top with battle of machine guns—then distant scream of pain*]

[*Music: Crashing finish*]

NARRATOR. The entire detachment was wiped out. In a few hours they came again. SS troops. Storm Troopers. Our snipers manned the Ghetto wall itself. We were ready.

[*Burst of fire, battle of machine guns under Narrator*]

NARRATOR. They brought up a loudspeaker.

NAZI [*Through loudspeaker*]. Jews, put down your guns. You haven't a chance in the world against us. Put down your guns, Jews. We will give you fifteen minutes to make up your minds and then we will come after you. Jews, put down your guns. It's your last chance.

[*Guns as before*]

NARRATOR. That was the answer. That and the flags of the United Nations which floated over the roofs of the Ghetto.

[*Dynamite explosions one after another rapidly*]

NARRATOR. More answers. [*Explosion*] Eight hundred answers. Eight hundred factories producing material for Germany—blown up by our engineers.

[*Explosion*]

NAZI. [*Loudspeaker*]. Jews, you still have another chance. Put down your guns, Jews. Put them down and come out of the buildings and you will be treated with mercy.

[*Ping of single shot. He gasps and coughs as though he has been hit*]

NARRATOR. That voice was silenced, but they brought up the regular army. The Ghetto had defeated the Storm Troopers and now it was the Ghetto against the German Army. We retreated slowly from our positions as they sent flame throwers, mortars, cannons, tanks and planes against us.

[*Build up volume of sound, planes diving, machine guns, bombs, etc.*]

DOCTOR. April 20 . . . April 25 . . . May 2 . . . May 6 . . . May 10 . . . May 14 . . . May 18 . . . May 20 . . . May 22 . . . May 25 . . .

[*Increase volume of sound*]

NARRATOR. They planted land mines under the tenements

[*Explosions*]

and blew them up one by one. The tenements crumbled but from the rubble of the shattered cellars the snipers kept up a continuous fire. The surviving men and women and children retreated slowly from house to house, erecting barricades in the streets, paying with their lives for every tenement, every room, every step of the way. When their ammunition ran out, they used broken furniture as clubs and hurled stones. On the twentieth day the enemy shut off the water supply and planes dropped incendiary bombs.

[*Tremendous crackle of flames added to sound*]

The entire Ghetto was in flames. Those who were not burned alive were slaughtered by the Nazis.

[*Fade sound to background*]

TEACHER I. [*Gasping*]. Isaac Davidson . . . Isaac . . . here . . . in the trench.

NARRATOR. His right arm had been blown off at the elbow. I spoke to him. . . . Let me tie a tourniquet around your arm.

TEACHER I. Don't waste the bandage on me. Tell me how it is going.

NARRATOR. We're still fighting.

TEACHER I. After thirty-seven days. A few Jews with guns fighting a Nazi army for thirty-seven days.

NARRATOR. The blood ran from the shattered stump and soaked the ground. But he smiled.

TEACHER I. They are really very foolish. They should have known that the Ghetto would explode.

NARRATOR. They know now.

TEACHER I. How many did we kill?

NARRATOR. Some say a thousand, some say twelve hundred. [*Pause*] The smile lingered on his lips even as his eyes began to glaze— and he spoke an epitaph for the Warsaw Ghetto.

TEACHER I. It is not for thee to complete the work, but neither art thou free to desist from it. Tell them to mark that on my grave.

NARRATOR. It is not for thee to complete the work, but neither art thou free to desist from it. Yes, tell them to mark that on our graves.

[*Cantor: Singing unaccompanied solo, "El Mole Rachamin," fade under narration*]

VOICE. Hear him with reverence. For he sings a prayer for the dead— twenty-five thousand dead. It is no ordinary prayer and they are not ordinary dead. For they are the dead of the Warsaw Ghetto—in the year nineteen hundred and forty-three. Tonight they sleep in their last trench, their clothes dispersed in ashes, their holy books sodden in the seventh-month rain, the rubble deep on the thresholds of their houses. They were Jews with guns. Understand that—and hear him with reverence as he chants the prayer. For on the page of their agony they wrote a sentence that shall be an atonement, and it is this: Give me grace and give me dignity and teach me to die; and let my prison be a fortress and my wailing wall a stockade, for I have been to Egypt and I am not departed.

[*Cantor: Up and finish*]

MISTER LEDFORD AND
THE TVA

Alan Lomax

ALAN LOMAX, leading radio exponent of American folklore and folk music, was born in 1915 in Austin, Texas, where his father, John A. Lomax, had been associated most of his life with the University of Texas. Alan Lomax spent his early days around the university campus, except for some time on a West Texas ranch, periods of schooling in the East, and two years collaborating with his father on folk-song collection and in the editing of *American Ballads and Folk Songs* (1937) and *Negro Folk Songs as Sung by Leadbelly* (1939).

In 1936 he arrived in Washington looking for a job. The Library of Congress, for which he had already done folk-song recording in the field, sent him to Haiti to record *Vaudou* and other songs of the Haitian peasantry. His fiancée from Texas joined him at Port-au-Prince; they were married by a Haitian justice of the peace and spent their honeymoon recording songs of the Haitian Mardi Gras. She is Elizabeth Lomax, also a writer.

In 1937 Alan Lomax took charge of the Archive of American Folk Songs in the Library of Congress. For the next few years he was concerned with recording as much as possible of America's still living folk music, as sung and performed by untrained and natural American folk singers and musicians.

In 1939 the Columbia Broadcasting System, largely through the enthusiasm of its Davidson Taylor, put Lomax to work on a folk music series for the American School of the Air—as writer, narrator, and singer. Lomax had never listened to radio, and was somewhat astonished to find himself in a huge studio holding a guitar, gazing at a microphone, and beyond it at the Columbia Symphony Orchestra conducted by Howard Barlow.

School audiences took to the shows. There was an astonishing informality about them that was refreshingly honest, and new in educational radio. Lomax brought to the microphone singers like Leadbelly and the Golden Gate Quartet. Some of his guests were not very familiar with the printed page, so that whole shows had to be planned verbally. An entirely ad lib program from Galax, Virginia, with six mountain musicians, won an award from the Institute for Education by Radio, as the best music education show of the year. In 1941 Lomax's program about the dust bowl, featuring the Okie ballad singer, Woodie Guthrie, won a similar prize. As the series progressed, Lomax began to include dramatic material, using his singers as cast. Thus he gradually evolved into a dramatic writer.

In 1941 he turned to an important type of drama new to American radio, which is represented by the following script. That year the Rocke-feller Foundation gave the Library of Congress a grant for an Experi-mental Radio Project. The group was headed by Philip Cohen, and included Joseph Liss, Charles Harold, Jerome Weisner, and as consultant, Alan Lomax. They took the Library's portable recording equipment into the field to gather material for a series of documentary programs about life in the United States. Programs of this type, using *people,* not actors, had been tried by the British Broadcasting Company, but were almost unknown in America. Archibald MacLeish, Librarian of Congress, whose own fine contributions to radio were later to include a series based on early American "source" documents, saw in such programs an invaluable living record of our own day and a natural extension of a library's function.

The following program is not, in the usual sense, "written." The creator of such a program—in this case Alan Lomax—uses as his material not merely the voices but the minds and emotions and impulses of the people themselves. It was Lomax's job *not* to put words into their mouths, but to draw the people out, to get "on the record" their currents of thought, the feelings they had about their environment. In this case the setting was of particular interest: a valley about to be flooded by the TVA, and from which the people, old pioneer stock, were to be transplanted.

The program was built chiefly around one Paul Ledford, a farmer. Lomax, who is natural and unassuming and puts people at ease, spent many days with him, drawing him out on the story of his county and his people. "For several days I let him do all the talking and make all the decisions about where we were to go and whom we were to talk to. Whenever he said anything that was particularly memorable, which I was unable to record, I tried later on to reproduce the circumstances of the statement, and to record it with the same emotion as it had had originally. By the end of the first morning he was already completely at ease with the microphone and was interviewing his friends and neighbors with more ease than most of us ever accomplish."

Several hours of recorded material were brought back to the Library. Lomax, along with Jerome Weisner, in charge of the Library's Recording Laboratory, spent six weeks in cutting and splicing the material together, giving it a logical arrangement and structure.

The programs were broadcast by some sixty radio stations in 1941, and were very popular in the South. There is unfailing fascination in hearing, in a dramatic broadcast, one's own kind of talk. Paul Ledford and his neighbors, talking about the TVA, could not have been duplicated by any actors in the world. The quality of the dialogue is, of course, similarly difficult to suggest in print.

Wartime developments in recording equipment, which have made possible battle-front recordings of unusual dramatic impact, will undoubtedly stimulate the growth of recorded documentary drama during the coming years.

Lomax wrote and narrated programs for *Transatlantic Call: People to People* throughout most of 1943, then went into the army. He was assigned to the Armed Forces Radio Service, which put him to work, among other things, on a series on American folklore and folk music, for overseas troops.

MISTER LEDFORD AND
THE TVA

SINGERS. It takes a worried man to sing a worried song,
It takes a worried man to sing a worried song,
It takes a worried man to sing a worried song,
I'm worried now, but I won't be worried long.

LOMAX. It takes a worried man to sing a worried song, and that's the
way the folks in Young Harris County, Georgia, felt about things
in the summer of 1941—they were worried.
The Tennessee Valley Administration was building a new dam
to produce more electricity for national defense. The reservoir
lake from this dam was going to flood their valley, and that
meant that many farmers would have to move away from land
that their families had held for generations. The Library of Congress had sent its sound-recording truck into the region to make
recordings of the effect of the TVA program on the mountain
people. The evacuation problem intrigued us, and we decided to
pick one farmer, a good talker—and let him tell the story of
the evacuation. Mr. Paul Ledford was the man we chose—the
sort of fellow who asks questions and starts discussions at county
meetings. This was what we recorded the first afternoon from
Mr. Ledford. . . .

LEDFORD [*Reflectively, looking out across the green farm that has been
his family's for three generations . . . in the background you
can hear the birds and the bees in the honeysuckle along the
fence*]. Been here *all* my life; been here fifty years; *long* time . . .
I know these mountains, and I know these good people in this—
in this country. And we're right here in the foothills of the Blue
Ridge [*Ledford spat and glanced up at the blue kills*] . . . along
this little creek which is a tributary of the Hiawassie River, that
goes into this dam that the TVA is abuildin' . . . I don't like

51

this idee of buildin' a dam on a valley and floodin' a valley like this with water . . . practically *level* country to be in the mountains . . .

[*Music: Mountain fiddle tune, not gay or sad, behind this talk*]

LOMAX. As we sat talking with Mr. Ledford this fine August morning a neighbor came up the road. His name was Barrett and he was a renter, a man without land of his own. Ledford hailed him into the swing under the two great pine trees. . . .

[*Music out*]

LEDFORD. Hello, Mr. Barrett!

BARRETT [*Off*]. How do.

LEDFORD. Come in . . . Set down in the swing under this pine tree here in the shade . . . Pleasant morning—sun shining beautiful, isn't it.

BARRETT [*Nearer*]. Certainly is.

[*Barrett speaks in a soft, almost diffident voice, a complete contrast to Ledford's positive, growling drawl*]

LEDFORD. Well, how you gettin' along?

BARRETT [*In*]. I'm gettin' along pretty well, except my leg—got a big risin' on my leg that's not doin' s' well.

LEDFORD. Well, that's bad—risin's bad. How long you had that risin'?

BARRETT. It's bin acomin' there about three days.

LEDFORD. Well, what do you know about the TVA and buildin' a dam this mornin'?

BARRETT. Well, I don't know much of anything and I just—that's my business out—I thought I'd come out and see when you was agoin' to try to locate your place—thought I'd go with ye.

LEDFORD. Well, I don't know what to tell you about that. You know there's not much use agoin' out to locate a farm until Uncle Sam comes along with the money to pay us off . . . 'Cause we couldn't tie a place down if we's to go without the money, you know. What do you think about it?

BARRETT. Well, I jest think I can't buy a place—I ain't able to buy; and I won't get no money out of it and I—I jest want to rent. . . .

LEDFORD. Well then, the problem you have—you got to get out of here—and you're selling no land and got nothin' to git out on . . . Is that true?

BARRETT. That's true. . . . I ain't *able* to move, as fur as that goes—*anywhere.* . . .

LEDFORD [*Pause*]. Well, have you talked to the TVA anything about gettin' any help?

BARRETT. No . . . I haven't—seen anyone to talk to . . . They never do stop—at my place. [*This last is spoken with a falling inflection of the voice, pathetic and defeated*].

LEDFORD [*After a considerable pause*]. Well, all the good times is past and gone, it looks like—in this country.

BARRETT. They certainly air.

LEDFORD. It's like the song . . . It went on to say: [*He sings*]
"All the good times is past and gone,
Don't cry, little Bonnie, don't cry. . . ."
That's pretty true in this country.

BARRETT. Yeah, it shore is.

[*Music: Banjo sneaks in during following*]

LOMAX. The morning passed in talks about the good old days in the neighborhood . . . Later Mrs. Ledford called us to dinner; and we ate chicken and dumplings, ham with good red gravy, turnip greens, potatoes and a deep apple pie. . . .

SINGER [*With banjo*].
Talk about your old cow meat,
Your mutton and your lamb—
If you want to please these people round yere
Bring on that country ham . . . [*Fade*]

LOMAX. When we finished our coffee, Ledford turned to us and said . . .

LEDFORD. Come on, let's—let's go . . . I want to take you round to see some of m' neighbors. I want you to just see what we've got. I just want you to visit with them—want you to go in their homes—look around their houses—see what they've got to eat—eat with them—I want you to see what they've got to eat, how they're gettin' along . . . They're all out of *debt*—finest people on *earth*—never been none no better—best people I *know* of—best people you've ever been amongst in yore life, I'll bet you

a purty, if you jest—if you jest open yore heart and *say* so . . .
So let's go and see some of 'em.

SINGER [*With banjo*].

Away and away we're bound for the mountain,
Bound for the mountain, bound for the mountain.
Over the mountain, the wild steed's a-boundin',
Away to the chase, away, away. . . .

[*Fades, while banjo continues back of*]

LOMAX. We said, "Ledford, take us to see the man that you consider the most interesting person in the county." . . . And so at
his direction we headed off the main road up Partridge Creek
to a vine-covered cabin set against the foot of the blue mountains . . . There we met Uncle Joe Kirby, the oldest resident of
the county, still lively with all his eighty years. . . . Ledford
did the interviewing. . . .

LEDFORD [*Fade in*], How you gettin' along, Uncle Joe, now?

KIRBY [*A deep, old voice; it rumbles and rattles with age and power
and conviction; each word is weighted and considered*]. Oh, purty
well. I'm gittin' kinda come down to the feeble days, though;
but I'm still purty *healthy* and *hearty*.

LEDFORD. Still able to *work* some?

KIRBY. Yes . . . Made a purty good little *crop* this *yur*. Of course, y'
know, I'm jest a *boy* yit, jist goin' on eighty-one years old.

LEDFORD. Jest a boy yet!

KIRBY. Yes. [*He grins*]

LEDFORD. Well, that's *fine*. . . . What do you think about the old days
and the modern days of today—which do you *like* the best?

KIRBY [*After a pause and thinking it over*]. Well, that's sort of a
hard question with me . . . I don't know whether I can *correctly*
answer it or not. Now, *some* of the old times, I like 'em *pow'ful*
well; but, some of 'em—I like the *modern* times mighty well, much
better. [*He has his teeth into his idea now and he runs along
swiftly*]. I couldn't see how I could *live* if my wife had to go
back and make clothing and make everything with her *fangers*
like my mother *did*—just *couldn't do* it—*never* could have done
it . . .

LEDFORD [*Throwing it in*]. I guess not.

KIRBY. It don't look to me like . . . We raised a good crowd of children and she jest had her *hands* full and she had a good cook stove or a range. . . . When me an' my wife was *married*—I had bought this land *before* we's married, but that's been back about fifty-three or -fo' years ago—'Course money was pretty *hard* and *debts* was hard to pay; and me an' my wife, nary one, had no house stuff scarcely, just enough to sort of *do* with; and I had corn—I didn't *have* no wheat. The year before we was married, I didn't make much; I kinda *baffled about*—and I had enough on hand to pay for the land all except *seventy-five* dollars, but seventy-five dollars were hard to git . . .

LEDFORD. UH-hunh.

KIRBY. . . . and we lived *hard* and paid for our little home and got to whur, atter *bit*, we got to whur we could' buy furniture and 'most anything and we've had a very plenty ever since— [*Rising feeling*] but we jest *starved* there and now for some—the government er somebody to come along and say, "You must jest get *out* of here and give us possession"—it sounds un*just* to me!

LEDFORD [*Pause*]. B'lieve in bein' free!

KIRBY. Yes, I *do*. . . . And I b'lieve in givin' 'em a chance to worship *God* accordin' to the dictates of his own *heart*, jest as our old Con-sti-tu-tion say . . .

LEDFORD. Yeah.

KIRBY. That's what I *b'lieve* in.

LEDFORD [*After pause*]. Well, I believe it's gettin' late, Uncle Joe, and I'm going to have to go on home now . . .

KIRBY [*Changing his tone and swinging into the mountain hospitality formula*]. Why not stay all night with me?—It's been s'long since you bin to see me and we're old friends and—

LEDFORD. I certainly would *enjoy* stayin' all night with yuh, but I can't stay tonight. . . . I'll come back, though, sometime, and I will stay all night and we'll talk more.

KIRBY. All right—I can jest—if I can't fill you on meat and bread, I sho can on hot air!

LEDFORD [*Chuckling*]. All right, that'll be fine.

SINGER [*With banjo*].

Away and away we're bound for the mountain,
Bound for the mountain, bound for the mountain . . .

   [*Fade, continue banjo behind*]

LOMAX. As we drove away from Uncle Joe Kirby's house, Ledford saw two friends putting up their hay in a field near by the road . . . "Let's go down and see what they have to say about the TVA and building the dam," he said. And so we got the turntables rolling and carried our microphone down into the hayfield. . . .

FARMER [*Fade in, talking fast*]. . . . You can hear anything, Paul. And I've gotten so I won't *talk* for hearin' s' doggone many things . . . And then you come along and another fellow will tell you right the other way, and you don't know. . . . The best thing a man can do is to say nothing and listen to what he *hears. . . .*

LEDFORD. Yeah, that's about the best way . . . But then you turn around, on the other hand, I believe they're gonna treat us *right*—in the *end*. We're just drawed up at the idea—we were *scared,* I think, and—

FARMER. Well, I'll tell you, Paul, about the people in this country—they've never been outa here *nowhur*—

LEDFORD. That's hit.

FARMER. —and they don't know they's any other *place*—

LEDFORD. That's hit.

FARMER. That's the way I feel about it . . .

FARMER 2. They jest rushed hit on us s'fast that we—

FARMER. That's hit.

FARMER 2. —we jest got excited [*Chuckles*] and we talked pretty sassy sometimes to 'em.

LEDFORD. They give us too big a "Boo" fer sech a little calf—right on the dash.

FARMER 2 [*Still chuckling*]. Yeah.

LEDFORD. Like the man agoin' along the road and adrivin' a calf—met an *auto*mobile—he's right on the bridge—and he gives his automobile horn a toot and the calf jumps in the river. [*Chuckles*] He got out to apologize about it . . . "Oh," the fellow says, "that's all right. You jest give the calf a little too big a *toot,* that uz all." . . . They give us too big a toot, right on the spur of the moment. . . .

FARMER 2 [*Still laughing*]. Spur of the moment.

FARMER. Well, they say they're gonna try to place us back in as good

a shape as they *found* us, Paul, and, if they *do,* why, of course—
we'll not be at home any more . . . You know, satisfaction is
what *you're* after and what I'm after. We don't keer anything, so
much about prosperity and money—the age I've got on *me, I*
don't—fer I don't feel as if I could *work* much more.

LOMAX. None of these men felt really resentful against the TVA . . .
They were sick at heart and worried . . . They felt their roots
being pulled at. But they knew the job had to be done—more
power for more aluminum for national defense. Nevertheless,
country-style, American-style, they had their fun at the expense
of the TVA engineers. . . .

LEDFORD. Ever oncet in a while I see one of 'em around here with a
load of poles—seems they git lost. [*This is very sarcastic and
there's laughter behind every word*] They don't know whur this
dam *is!*

FARMER. Yeah . . . There was one past my house the other day, had a
John Deere tractor, huntin' the dam. And he was inquirin' of
the Notteley Dam and wanted to know where it was at; and I
said, "Why, the devil, you've done come through Nottelley dam
and gone to another'n!"

FARMER 2. They don't know where they're goin'. They's been s'many
round here you couldn't turn yore team around 'thout steppin' on
'em!

FARMER. There's a while there we couldn't *plow* . . . Our mules just
got scared, you know, and you just couldn't do nothin' with
'em. . . .

  [*The three men go off into gales of high, cackling country
  laughter*]

  [*Music: Mountain fiddle for bridge*]

LOMAX. The day was over and there was Ledford's house behind the
two dark pine trees . . . We'd taken a look at the people of
Young Harris County, Georgia, and we could open our hearts
and agree with Ledford that they were some of the best people
on earth. . . . As for Mr. Ledford, his heart was full of the rich
and quiet peace of the countryside, and he knew now that he
was not going to leave his county. Instead, he'd just move up out
of the reach of the water. . . . With this resolve in every word,

he told us good-bye and invited us to come down and spend a month with him.

LEDFORD. Now, you boys come back 'bout a year from now . . . I tell you the time to come—when I have my vacation off the farm is from the 15th of July till the 15th of August . . . If you'll come back here then, I'll really show you this country—take you into these mountains; I'll show you speckled trout; I'll show you virgin timber, that's been in these woods ever since I s'pose there's been an earth here, s'far as I know—I'll show you cold water runnin' out of the ground that will make your teeth hurt like drinkin' ice water when you drink it. . . . And some of the best people, the best type of people they is in the United States, in here. And they all, their desire and ambition is—is to—they're Americans—their ambition is to defend Ameriky. They'd fight for Ameriky, people in this country would . . . [*He spat*] both old and young. . . . You take these old mountain folks in here would even take up their old hog rifles if they'd git a chance to shoot old Hitler. . . . Genuine Americans—folks in here are. They's not a man in this country but what would fight—to the last drop of blood and the last ditch—to defend Ameriky. . . . That's the kind of people and type of folks we got in here—women and children. . . .

OPEN LETTER ON
RACE HATRED

William N. Robson

*O*pen *Letter on Race Hatred,* by William Northrop Robson, was called by *Time* magazine ". . . one of the most eloquent and outspoken programs in radio history. With no bombast and with a great deal of level, direct statement, CBS told the story of Detroit's recent race riot, and told it with the special impact possible in radio. The fact that a major U.S. network had the courage and took the time to emphasize a crisis in race relations was big radio news."

The history of *Open Letter* is told as follows by Robson: "CBS was approached by the Entertainment Industry Emergency Committee with a request to contribute time in the interests of racial tolerance, after the Detroit race riots of June, 1943. I was brought into the picture by Douglas Coulter,* who knew of my interest in the subject. We were extremely careful in the preparation of the script, since the country at that time was pockmarked with 'tension areas' where it was feared new race riots might break out. Our problem was to throw the light of truth on the Detroit incident, without inciting either whites or Negroes to riot elsewhere. Therefore, it was necessary to show the positive aspects of person helping person, rather than the destructive aspects of the disturbance. This was not an easy task. The entire show was recorded in dress rehearsal on two different occasions, and its broadcast twice canceled before we felt that we had properly balanced the elements. Even then, it was necessary for us to broadcast the entire program over a closed circuit to all CBS stations the day of the show—giving them the opportunity of refusing to carry it, if they so wished. Very few of them turned it down.

"The reactions were as varied and violent as the point of view of the listener. Indiscriminate applause and vile condemnation came from the same localities. . . . The people of Detroit were of two minds about it. I believe that the over-all impression was favorable, and that the broadcast did a certain amount of good."

Wendell Willkie appeared on the program with a brief closing message. Jackson Beck narrated. Robson directed.

Robson is one of radio's leading triple-threat men, equally effective as writer, director, and producer.

He was born in Pittsburgh in 1906, graduated from Yale University and attended its drama school. Immediately afterward he became active in motion pictures, writing for the screen off and on for several years before turning to radio. In 1933, at the bottom of the depression, he was broke

* CBS Vice-President in Charge of Programs.

and out of a job, and glad to accept the $46.50 weekly salary offered him by KHJ, at that time the CBS station in Los Angeles. After several years there as writer and director he came to New York. He attracted wide attention when he succeeded Irving Reis as director of the *Columbia Workshop*.

During recent years he has directed and generally produced (i.e., exercised active supervision over) a number of important series, including *Big Town, Report To the Nation, The Twenty-Second Letter, The Man Behind the Gun,* and *Radio Reader's Digest.* Some comments on his direction will be found in the introduction to *The Boise,* by Ranald MacDougall, in this collection.

Meanwhile he returns to writing now and then with vigorous documentary scripts. Among his best-known writings have been: *No Help Wanted,* a script on depression unemployment which American radio was afraid to touch, but which was broadcast in Great Britain by the British Broadcasting Corporation; *Production Now,* four broadcasts for the War Production Board; and the CBS *Open Letter on Race Hatred.*

OPEN LETTER ON
RACE HATRED*

NARRATOR. Dear fellow Americans. What you are about to hear may anger you. What you are about to hear may sound incredible to you. You may doubt that such things can happen today in this supposedly united nation. But we assure you, everything you are about to hear is true. And so, we ask you to spend thirty minutes with us facing quietly and without passion or prejudice a danger which threatens all of us—a danger so great that if it is not met and conquered now, even though we win this war, we shall be defeated in victory and the peace which follows will for us be a horror of chaos, lawlessness, and bloodshed. This danger is *race hatred!*

Tonight race hatred is breeding and fostering in a score of booming overcrowded war centers. And so tonight we ask you to hear what happened in Detroit, because we believe that no sensible, fully informed American will allow to happen again here at home what he is fighting against all over the world.

[*Orchestra*]

Sunday, June 20, was hot.

[*Orchestra up*]

Detroit, sprawling across the flat Michigan prairie, baked in the nearly vertical sun. In the workers' camps on the fringe of the city, trailers and tents held the heat close and unbreathable. In the crowded flats and overflowing houses along Tireman, and Epworth Boulevard in the Negro district, the heat pressed down like the sweaty hand of John Henry.

[*Orchestra up*]

*OPEN LETTER ON RACE HATRED by William N. Robson. Copyright, 1943, by William N. Robson.

The Poles in Hamtramck felt it. And the two and three families crammed into one family apartments, their tempers grew shorter as the day lengthened from one hot hour to another. Those who could find any way to get there, headed for lovely Belle Isle in the Detroit River, and a breath of fresh air.

[*Orchestra up*]

But when the flat hot sun dropped into the lake on the other side of Michigan, the twilight brought little relief, and still sweating, tempers shortened even more as they started home to another sticky sleepless night. The traffic moved slowly across the bridge from Belle Isle, cars creeping, bumper to bumper, the crowds on foot filling the sidewalk. Something happened there. No one is quite sure what—but something happened that hot Sunday last month—something in itself trivial, something like this—

[*Automobile horns blowing, one in foreground*]

GIRL. Eddie, you're not going to get us home any faster by blowing the horn.

GUY. If that guy ahead'll just move forward, I can get into the other line.

GIRL. Oh, Eddie.

GUY. Shut up—Now I got a break.

[*Car guns in first—Crash of bumpers*]

GIRL [*Squeals*].

GUY. Why, that son of a—he pulled out in front of me—Hey, you stupid jerk!

BLACK GUY [*Off*]. What's the big idea, bud?

GUY. Oh, a Negro. Listen, you, get out that car and I'll show you, you black . . .

BLACK GUY. I'm comin', punk.

[*Car door opens*]

GIRL. Oh, Eddie, please.

GUY. I'll show him.

[*Crowd begins angry ad libs drowning out actual dialogue of two antagonists*]

NARRATOR. You know how crowds are. Nothing like a good fight— You push up as close as you can, and you get pushed, and its usually all in good fun. But this crowd was tired and hot, and full of deep-seated grievances. It promptly took sides, and taking sides, broke up into other fights—and those out on the edge couldn't tell what was going on, and the reports they got were garbled, and they got garbled worse—

[*Crowd fades into music*]

[*Orchestra: Agitato rumor cue backs following*]

NEGRO. What's going on?

SECOND NEGRO. Couple of guys fighting—that black boy's quite a baby with his fists.

[*Orchestra up*]

THIRD NEGRO. A fight about a baby on the Belle Isle Bridge—

[*Orchestra up*]

FOURTH NEGRO [*Woman*]. A baby thrown off the Belle Isle Bridge—

[*Orchestra up*]

FIFTH NEGRO. Yeah, I tell you, Lucius just got back from Belle Isle. He saw it. There was a big fight—and a white fellow threw a colored woman and her baby off the bridge into the river and they was drowned.

[*Orchestra up and out*]

NARRATOR. That's the way the rumor hit the slums of Paradise Valley, the Negro section. And it spread. There was another rumor. The white version.

[*Orchestra: Rumor cue under*]

WHITE. What's the trouble?

SECOND WHITE. I dunno. Tangled bumpers, I guess. That's the white guy's gal sittin' in the car.

[*Orchestra up*]

THIRD WHITE. Fightin' over a white gal on the Belle Isle Bridge.

[*Orchestra up*]

FOURTH WHITE. There's plenty of trouble over on Belle Isle—Negro and a white gal—

[*Orchestra up*]

FIFTH WHITE. Negro attacked a white gal over on Belle Isle—call up the guys—

[*Orchestra up and out*]

NARRATOR. Rumor! More dangerous than dynamite. More deadly than a plague. Rumors tailor-made. One for black ears. One for white ears. The trouble had started.

PUZZLED WOMAN. But just because a couple of men had a fight on Belle Isle Bridge . . .

MR. REASON. Oh, no. It goes much deeper than that. Much further back.

PUZZLED WOMAN. Really?

MR. REASON. Yes, back nearly a quarter of a century. You see, Detroit grew up fast.

MR. DETROIT. I'll say it did, brother. Want some figures on that?

MR. REASON. Why, yes, if you don't mind?

MR. DETROIT. Not at all. Not at all. That's what I'm here for. From 1920 to 1930, while Detroit was putting the world on wheels, our population increased by a half a million. And today we're on our way to . . . er . . . pardon me. Hey, you, mister, how'd you like to work in a de-fense plant in Detroit?

AKRON. Nope, not me. I got a good job at the tire plant right here in Akron.

MR. DETROIT. How about you?

PITTSBURGH. Pittsburgh's good enough for me. We got to make the steel, before you can make the guns.

MR. DETROIT. What do you say, pal?

TOLEDO. Listen, lay off. Toledo's got its own manpower problem.

MR. DETROIT. Okay, okay, no harm in asking. Hey, you down there in South Carolina.

HILLBILLY. Who, me?

MR. DETROIT. Yes, you. How'd you like to come up north and work in a de-fense plant.

HILLBILLY. Well, now, I hadn't thought about it.

MR. DETROIT. Pay the highest wages. Better'n you can make in the cotton mill.

HILLBILLY. Yeah?

MR. DETROIT. You'll be livin' high on the hog in Detroit. Beautiful town. Right on the lake. Bring along the missus and the kids.

HILLBILLY. Well, I'll think about it.

MR. DETROIT. You can clean up quick in Detroit and after the war you can go back down south and retire.

HILLBILLY. I could, huh?

MR. DETROIT. Sure. Report Monday?

HILLBILLY. Yeah, mister. Sure—and thanks.

MR. REASON. Er, pardon me?

MR. DETROIT. Yeah, what?

MR. REASON. Why are you recruiting labor in the South, when you've already got a big pool of labor in Detroit?

MR. DETROIT. What are you talking about?

MR. REASON. The Negroes.

MR. DETROIT. Listen, bud, we're not hirin' any Negroes.

MR. REASON. But the War Manpower Commission has ordered that local labor had to be exhausted before you could—

MR. DETROIT. Maybe they did, but they're not enforcin' the order—and we don't want any black—

STOOGE. Hey, boss.

MR. DETROIT. Yeah?

STOOGE [Whispers].

MR. DETROIT. No? Is that a fact?

STOOGE. Yeah. So you better do something fast.

MR. DETROIT. Okay. Pardon me, pal.

MR. REASON. Go right ahead.

MR. DETROIT. Hey, boy.

NEGRO. Yas, suh?

MR. DETROIT. Want a good job?

NEGRO. Suah do. What I have to do for it?

MR. DETROIT. Nothin'—just come to Detroit.

NEGRO. Detroit?

MR. DETROIT. Sure—work in the war plants makin' tanks and guns.

NEGRO. Suah 'nough?

MR. DETROIT. On the level.

NEGRO. But I'm a field hand; I don't know nothin' about workin' in a factory.

MR. DETROIT. That's all right; we'll teach you.

NEGRO. Well, I don't—

MR. DETROIT. You can make more in a month than you get in a year workin' in the fields.

NEGRO. Is that a fact?

MR. DETROIT. Yeah. Plenty of chance for advancement, too.

NEGRO. Advancement?

MR. DETROIT. Yeah, nothin' to hold you back in Detroit. Why, if you make the grade, we might even promote you to straw boss.

NEGRO. You ain't just joshin' me?

MR. DETROIT. No, sirree—you'll be living in Paradise in Detroit.

NEGRO. Paradise?

MR. DETROIT. Well, Paradise Valley.

NEGRO. Mister, it sounds too good to be true.

MR. DETROIT. I can count on you?

NEGRO. Yes, sir, you sure can. [*Fading*] You sure can.

MR. REASON. But didn't you say a minute ago that you didn't want any Negro labor?

MR. DETROIT. Yeah, but I just got word that the boys back home have changed their minds. They hired all the Negroes in Detroit—and we got to get more. Lots more.

NARRATOR. More. Lots more. In three years Detroit has imported 500,-000 black and white workers from the South.

MR. DETROIT. Yep. As many people as live in New Orleans or the state of Arizona. It's a big operation.

NARRATION. It certainly is. But Detroit doesn't have houses for a half million extra people. Detroit doesn't have enough streetcars and buses to move the state of Arizona back and forth from work. Detroit doesn't have enough parks, or movie houses, or bowling alleys to entertain an additional New Orleans.

[*Pause*]

VOICE. Today it is impossible to rent a decent house within fifty miles of Detroit.

[*Orchestra*]

NARRATOR. No houses. But jobs, plenty of jobs for black and white, for native Americans and Polish-born immigrants, and all the prejudices of Detroit's polyglot population awaited the new army

of war workers. Subversive organizers and native Nazi orators
took to soap boxes outside a dozen war plants—

GEORGIA JERK. I'd rather see Hitler and Hirohito win than work beside
a nigra on the assembly line.

NARRATOR. Detroit was dynamite! The fist fight on the Belle Island
bridge set off the fuse. By the dawn of Monday, June 21, Detroit
blew up.

[*Orchestra up*]

That bloody Monday, Woodward Avenue, the wide boulevard
which divides the city, became a hunting ground upon which no
Negro was safe. Along Hastings Street, in the heart of Paradise
Valley, bands of Negroes, fired by rumors, smashed the windows of white storekeepers, overturned the cars of white motor-
ists, and were shot by the police. On Woodward Avenue a hundred thousand white men armed with lengths of pipe and beer
bottles beat up Negroes until their arms ached.

[*Orchestra under*]

SECOND NARRATOR. And in the great factories of Detroit, which proudly
claims the title of "Arsenal of Democracy," few men worked that
day. From bloody dawn to bloody dawn, in that single day these
insurrectionists wasted one million man-hours.

[*Orchestra up*]

How many of your sons will die for lack of the tanks and planes
and guns which Detroit did not make that day?

NARRATOR. We lost Bataan gallantly. We surrendered Corregidor with
honor. We were defeated at Detroit by ourselves in shame and
humiliation.

[*Orchestra*]

But not all Detroit went blind with blood lust that hot Monday.
There were black people and white people whose conduct proved
them first of all to be human beings. There was a prominent
Negro doctor who was leaving his office on his way to an emergency meeting of city officials, at the Negro Y, when the white
druggist in his building called to him—

DRUGGIST. Dr. Johnson—Dr. Johnson.

JOHNSON. Oh, Mr. Stuart. You shouldn't have opened your store this morning.

DRUGGIST. I didn't know how bad it was. Now I don't know what to do.

JOHNSON. Well, you'd better close up and go home.

DRUGGIST. I'm afraid they'd mob me before I got to Woodward Avenue.

JOHNSON. Yes, they might. I'll tell you, you lock up right now, and I'll drive you through.

DRUGGIST. But you'd be taking a chance, too.

JOHNSON. You're my friend, Mr. Stuart.

[*Orchestra*]

NARRATOR. And the white man was driven through the threatening jeering Negro mob by his colored friend, to safety close to the "no man's land" of Woodward Avenue.

[*Orchestra up*]

And there were white people too who acted with sanity and bravery on that insane day—in a streetcar crawling through the mobs on Woodward Avenue sat a woman and her daughter.

[*Mob outside*]

[*Streetcar, traveling slowly*]

YOUNG WOMAN. Oh, mother, look at them beating up that poor man.

MOTHER. It's disgraceful—outrageous.

YOUNG WOMAN. Oh, look, the mob's coming toward this car.

MOTHER. Now don't get excited, Elsie.

YOUNG WOMAN. And there's a colored man sitting across the aisle. Oh, mother—

MOTHER. Well, they won't get him—psst—you, mister—you—come here—

NEGRO. Yes, ma'am?

MOTHER. Everybody's looking out the windows—quick—get down here under the seat—

YOUNG WOMAN. Mother, what are you—?

MOTHER. Be quiet, Elsie—spread out your skirts so you hide him.

NEGRO. God bless you, ma'am.

MOTHER. Shhh—

[*Banging on car doors*]

[*Car stops—door opens*]

[*Mob up*]

MOBSTER. Any nigras inside? . . . Are there any nigras in there?

MOTHER. There are not!

MOBSTER. Okay ma'am. Just wanted to make sure.

[*Door closes—car starts*]

NEGRO. God bless you, ma'am—God bless you—

MOTHER. Now, you stay right where you are until we get out of this. Those hoodlums—I've lived all my life in Detroit, but today I'm ashamed of it!

[*Orchestra*]

NARRATOR. And there were three sailors that bloody Monday who proved how much courage a mob has.

HOODLUM. There's one!

SECOND HOODLUM. Get the black b—

[*Mob running*]

YOUNG NEGRO. Please, let me go—I ain't done nothin'—I'm just on my way home from work—

HOODLUM. Shut up, you dirty—

[*Smack*]

SECOND HOODLUM. Lemme get a crack at the son of a—

SAILOR. Hey, let that man go.

HOODLUM. Well, well, the U.S. Navy to the rescue—You got friends, eight-ball.

[*Smack*]

YOUNG NEGRO. Don't—please—for the love of God, don't—

SAILOR. Let him go.

SECOND HOODLUM. What's it to you, sailor?

SAILOR. I'll tell you, bum. I'm just payin' off a debt. There was a colored guy on my ship that saved the life of one of my buddies.

HOODLUM. You got me weepin'.

SAILOR. Ace, give this fellow a hand.

SECOND SAILOR. Right.

YOUNG NEGRO. Thank you, sailor, thank you—

HOODLUM. Listen, gob, if you didn't have that uniform on, you wouldn't get away with that.

SAILOR. Okay, I'll be glad to oblige—I'll take it off. Ace, better peel off your jumper too.

SECOND SAILOR. A pleasure.

SAILOR. Would you mind holdin' these for us?

YOUNG NEGRO. Sure thing, sailor.

SAILOR. Okay, you punks, do you want to take us on one at a time or both together?

[Crowd mumbles]

HOODLUM. We ain't pickin' no fights with white men—We're after colored guys.

SAILOR. Yeah, and you're stirrin' up the kind of trouble we went to war to stop. Now you jerks better get off the streets before the army gets into town and starts using you for target practice.

[Orchestra]

NARRATOR. Late that night, the army finally did arrive, and for the first time in twenty-four hours a fitful peace reluctantly fell on the debris-filled streets of Detroit. The score:

VOICE. Eighteen hundred arrested. Eighty-five percent were Negroes.

[Orchestra]

SECOND VOICE. Six hundred injured. The majority Negroes.

[Orchestra]

VOICE. Thirty-five dead.

[Orchestra]

VOICE. Twenty-nine Negroes.

[Orchestra]

VOICE. Seventeen of them shot by the police.

[Orchestra]

NARRATOR. Accomplished?

VOICE. Nothing.

[Orchestra]

NARRATOR. Two nights after the troops arrived, the class of 1943 was graduated at Northeastern High School. Its members included twenty-nine Negro boys and girls. The sincere words of the commencement speaker that night seemed tinged with bitter irony.

SPEAKER [Echo]. See if you can analyze the problems of today. See if you can work out your own destiny through democratic processes. You must if democracy is to survive. The world cannot go on half free and half slave . . . [Fade down, continue under].

NARRATOR. In the park outside the high school, eighty policemen stand on guard. And behind them little groups of hoodlums, toughened by two days of street fighting, gather in the shadows.

SPEAKER [Fade up] . . . Democracy is more than just casting your ballot. It is something that must be lived twenty-four hours each day. It is learning to live collectively . . . [Fade down]

NARRATOR. A lesson their elders had proved they had not learned. A challenge, difficult to accept, when you have for two days watched democracy go up in the smoke of burning automobiles, and trickle away in the bloody gutter. [Pause] It is nearly over, the last moments of their four years together—their last song together—black and white voices blending . . .

[Chorus singing "America," with orchestra]

The hoodlums out in the park hear the song through the open windows.—A mob begins to form. The policemen stiffen, glance nervously about.

[Song up, to end]

And then the song is over, and with congratulations and well-wishes cut short by the ten-o'clock curfew, the Negro and white members of the Northeastern High School class of 1943 step out into the world.

[Cast-angry mumble]

The police line wavers. The girl graduates in their summery dresses cringe. The boys stand there a moment indecisively.

BOY. I'm not going to let them think they can scare me. Come on, who's walking my way?

SECOND BOY. I'll go with you.

THIRD BOY. So will I.

NARRATOR. The three classmates, two Negro, one white, start down the street. Across the way, behind the line of police, the mob paces them.

BOY. Don't walk too fast.

SECOND BOY. Jeez, I'm bein' inducted into the army next week—to fight for them.

THIRD BOY. Doesn't seem worth it.

NARRATOR. At the street corner, the mob breaks through the police line ... sweeps across the street, and then suddenly halts. [*Trucks, motors up to stop*] Four truckloads of soldiers with fixed bayonets roll up to a stop—

OFFICER. All right, boys, on the double—clear the area!

SOLDIERS [*Off*]. Move on there—break it up—get going!

NARRATOR. Slowly, at the point of the bayonet, the rabble of Kluxers, cowards, and crackpots retreat into the shadows whence they came. Northeastern High School Class of '43 has graduated—without bloodshed.

[*Orchestra*]

So an armed peace came to the troubled streets of Detroit, and most of us, knowing little and perhaps caring less why such things occur, forget about it. But not the rest of the world.

GERMAN RADIO [*Filter*]. This is Berlin calling. In the Asiatic Service. The disturbances in Detroit have now also come to an end owing to the intervention of the troops whom Roosevelt dispatched to the scene. There is no doubt about the fact that the problem of labor and capital cannot be solved by the present rulers of the U.S.A.

NARRATOR. And listen to the Voice of Tokyo addressing the billion brown and yellow inhabitants of Asia—

TOKYO RADIO [*Filter*]. The Detroit riots of June the twentieth in which hundreds of Negroes were sacrificed to the altar of American white superiority complex was nothing than the latest of appearings of acts of intolerable cruelty of the people who pay lip service to democracy. How can America hope to bring an order of liberty and equality among the more complicated, vastly more difficult family of races in the world, when it can't manage its own race problem? It simply can't.

NARRATOR. Those words have the ring of logic to millions of people all around the world—millions who look upon us with justified suspicion. And the question those words pose is not rhetoric, but

literal. The answer lies with each one of us. We cannot command
the respect of mankind, with the blood of fellow Americans upon
our hands.

[*Orchestra*]

What happened in Detroit can happen in many another American
city, already has happened to a lesser degree in half a dozen. The
responsibility for these acts of hideous violence lies ultimately at
the doorstep of you, the decent law-abiding citizens to whom this
open letter is addressed. It is you who will pay the final bill for
the race hatred of your fellow Americans. Remember, these street
riots are not new. They have their pattern—a pattern cut in the
streets of Leipzig and Berlin and Munich nearly a generation ago
when gangs of German youth armed with beer bottles and lead
pipe asserted their right to mob rule with the same brawling
methods we have seen at work on our Main Streets. The pattern
is the same, the victim similar. The minority which is most easily
recognized. Adolf Hitler, who invented the technique, predicted
long ago how well it would work here in America.

HITLER. America is permanently on the brink of revolution. It will be
a simple matter for me to produce unrest and revolts in the
United States, so that these gentry will have their hands full with
their own affairs.

NARRATOR. What suckers we are—

[*Orchestra*]

NARRATOR. There are some places in the nation where citizens are
showing common sense, tact, and tolerance. In Houston, Texas,
for instance, last month, rumors were launched that there would
be a race riot on Saturday, June 19, when the Negro population
celebrate the anniversary of the Emancipation Proclamation in
the festival they call Juneteenth. A committee of prominent Negro
and white citizens headed by the mayor stopped the trouble before it started with a full-page advertisement in the Houston
papers.

VOICE OF HOUSTON. Don't Do Hitler's Work. Stop circulating rumors
which create tenseness and interfere with war production, and
attend to your own business. The colored people of this vicinity

are entitled to celebrate their traditional "Juneteenth" holiday Saturday pleasantly and in peace and the fact that they gather for their customary celebrations on that day is no evidence of any intention on their part to create a disturbance. Law-enforcement authorities are prepared to deal with thoughtless hoodlums, white or colored, who provoke trouble. Don't be a rumormonger.

NARRATOR. There was no riot in Houston on June 19 because decent law-abiding citizens saw one coming and did something about it. Each of us can do the same thing in his community. It's not the people who serve on the committee and lead the parades and make the speeches who will stop race hatred. It's each one of us, each anonymous citizen keeping his head on his shoulders, his fists unclenched, and his mouth shut. We've got too tough an enemy to beat overseas to fight each other here at home.

[*Orchestra*]

We hope that this documented account of the irreparable damage race hatred has already done to our prestige, our war effort, and our self-respect will have moved you to make a solemn promise to yourself that, wherever you are and whatever is your color or your creed, you will never allow intolerance or prejudice of any kind to make you forget that you are first of all an American with sacred obligations to every one of your fellow citizens. Sincerely yours,

THE COLUMBIA BROADCASTING SYSTEM.

ANNOUNCER. Ladies and Gentlemen, as a postscript to our open letter to you—we present Mr. Wendell Willkie.

WILLKIE. This is a time for serious thought and sober words. For the situation which flared so tragically in Detroit has its counterpart —actual or potential—in many American cities. Such instances of mob madness cannot be treated as single cases, because they are profound in their effect in this country and lasting in their impression throughout the world.

Two-thirds of the people who are our allies do not have white skins. And they have long, hurtful memories of the white man's superior attitude in his dealings with them. Today the white man is professing friendship and a desire to co-operate and is promising opportunity in the world to come when the war is over. They wonder. When the necessities of war cease to make co-operation valuable to the white man, will his promises mean anything? Race riots in Detroit, Los Angeles, and Beaumont, Texas, do not reassure them.

The situation is grave both at home and, in its effects, abroad. We must therefore seek the basic causes and find the ways for their elimination—practical, direct, positive ways.

One-tenth of the people in this country belong to the Negro race. In the spirit in which our independence was gained and our Republic established, there are certain things these Negro citizens are entitled to—not as a matter of patronage or tolerance, but as a matter of right.

They are entitled to protection under the law. When their safety demands it, to prompt and vigorous enforcement of the law.

It is their right that there shall be no discrimination against them in the administration of the law, in federal, state, or local governments.

They are entitled to the same opportunity to acquire an education—an education of the same quality as that given to other citizens.

They should receive the same per capita expenditure of public moneys for health and hospitalization as is allotted to other citizens.

They have a right—as has every citizen—to the elimination of all arbitrary restrictions on voting, through taxation or otherwise.

Their right to work must equal that of any citizen and their reward should be the same as the reward of any other citizen for the same job.

Their economic opportunity should not be limited by their color.

And last, they should have the rights of every citizen to fight for his country in any branch of her armed services.

These are merely rights that the Negro of our communities shares with other citizens. We must see to it that he gets them.

But in addition to his rights are certain human needs which he also shares with his fellow citizens. And they too must be cared for. The most pressing today, for black and white, is adequate and decent housing. If this cannot be secured through the operation of our private economy, it is an obligation that must be undertaken by government—preferably local but, if necessary, federal.

There is one thing further which seems to me to have a real bearing on the welfare of our Negro citizen. It concerns the Negro's political status.

Our two major political parties have their separate ways of approaching the Negro vote. One has a tendency to ask the Negro for his vote as recompense for an act of simple justice done eighty years ago. The other retains political power by, in effect, depriving the Negro of his right to vote in one part of the country, while seeking his vote in another on the plea of great friendship for his race.

Both attitudes must be changed. One party cannot go on feeling that it has no further obligation to the Negro citizen because Lincoln freed the slave. And the other is not entitled to power if it sanctions and practices one set of principles in Atlanta and another in Harlem.

Our whole purpose today is, with our allies, to defeat fascism. But all the forces of fascism are not with our enemies.

Fascism is an attitude of mind, an attitude which causes men to seek to rule others by economic, military, or political force or through prejudice. Such an attitude within our own borders is as serious a threat to freedom as is the attack without. The desire to deprive some of our citizens of their rights—economic, civic, or political—has the same basic motivation as actuates the fascist mind when it seeks to dominate whole peoples and nations.

It is essential that we eliminate it at home as well as abroad.

BRETTON WOODS

Peter Lyon

A N IMPORTANT phenomenon of recent years has been the increasing
participation of organized labor in radio broadcasting. Regular network broadcasting by organized labor dates from 1942.

Since many years previous, labor has operated its own local radio
stations in a few communities. But it is difficult for a labor-financed station
to compete successfully with network stations featuring the world's most
publicized talent.

During the 1930's, and more particularly in the early 1940's, labor
became increasingly worried over the antilabor slant of some network
commentators. Several of the more rabid of these never seemed to lack
for a sponsor, and were therefore heard at good listening periods over
substantial networks. Noninterference with these commentators was often
defended, by sponsors, networks, and the commentators themselves, in
the name of "freedom of speech." This cogent defense did not solve the
problem: that the other side was not getting the same "freedom of speech."

In 1941 organized labor began to demand regular time on the air.
In 1942 the National Broadcasting Company agreed to set aside a weekly
fifteen-minute period, in which the American Federation of Labor and
the Congress of Industrial Organizations, broadcasting alternate weeks,
might tell of labor's contributions to the war. The series, titled *Labor for
Victory*, was at first supposed to stay away from "controversial issues."
But such issues are hard to define. Just as programs set aside for religion
often seem to deal with matters of political controversy, because such subjects are not easily put into watertight compartments, so it became more
and more difficult to draw a line around what could be treated on *Labor
for Victory*. The CIO, for example, felt that its stand against racial discrimination was an important contribution to the war effort, however
"controversial" it might seem to others. Often programs dealt with proposed legislation, on the ground of its importance to labor and therefore
to war production. NBC gradually shifted to the view that *Labor for
Victory* was labor's platform, on which it might make known its views
on various topics.

Beginning early in 1945, organized labor was heard regularly on the
National Broadcasting Company, the Columbia Broadcasting System, and
the American Broadcasting Company. It was beginning to be heard also
over various regional hookups, and in local broadcasts in Los Angeles,
San Francisco, Washington, Detroit, and other important centers.

Broadcasting time has generally been granted equally to the CIO and
the AFL. It is interesting that the two organizations have approached

programing problems in a very different manner. The AFL has favored talks, interviews, and round tables. It has been more interested in stressing its good relationships than in presenting its grievances. It has tended to avoid controversial issues. The CIO, in the matter of techniques, has leaned toward dramatic presentations. These have occasionally been political operettas, with special scores and lyrics. In tone the CIO programs have often been more aggressive. In subject matter they have ranged widely. They have not hesitated to press their views on such matters as rationing, international relations, racial problems.

The program presented here, broadcast on January 27, 1945, on the American Broadcasting Company series *Labor—USA,* deals with international finance. It is an example of dramatized radio pamphleteering at its most agile. Undoubtedly oversimplifying its subject, and highly effective partly for that reason, it has a quality similar to the lively cartoon-illustrated pamphlets of the CIO's Political Action Committee.

It will be noticed that Henry Morgenthau, Jr., at that time Secretary of the Treasury, appeared for a brief closing statement. Appearances by guests outside the ranks of labor are of course a regular part of labor's strategy on such series. According to an unconfirmed anecdote, which if true is a comment on the vivid cartoon style of the dramatization, Secretary Morgenthau frowned early in the program, then smiled, and at the end of the program said to some friends: "Now at last I understand what Bretton Woods is all about."

Peter Lyon, one of radio's ablest writers of scripts of this type, was born in 1915. He has lived most of his life in New York and New Jersey. He is the son of an executive of the Du Pont Company in New Brunswick, New Jersey, and a grandson—on his mother's side—of S. S. McClure, the publisher. At Williams College, Lyon edited the campus newspaper, and after college naturally gravitated into journalism, working as a minor cog in the machinery of Time, Inc. Later, after a stay in Mexico, he joined the writing staff of the *March of Time* radio series. He has written hundreds of scripts for *March of Time, Cavalcade of America, Radio Reader's Digest,* and for the CIO.

In 1944 he was elected president of the Radio Writers' Guild, one of the component guilds of the Authors League of America, Inc.

BRETTON WOODS

NARRATOR. Very soon now, the Congress will be asked to ratify and make law an agreement of resounding importance to everybody in this country . . . an agreement which carries a long name: "The United Nations Monetary and Financial Conference" . . . what most people call the "Bretton Woods Agreement." Well, now: anything that important, we should talk about, learn more about. That's what we propose to do during the next few minutes. Before we're through, we're going to take you to Washington, to hear from the Secretary of the Treasury, the Honorable Henry Morgenthau, Jr., who wants to tell you about the agreement from his standpoint.

First: Let's explain it, if we can.

It's got two parts. Number One:

A VOICE. The Bank for International Reconstruction and Development.

NARRATOR. And Number Two:

A VOICE. The International Monetary Fund.

NARRATOR. Let's take the Fund first. In order to explain it, we'll need a little cast of actors. There's Joe Worker . . .

JOE. I'll play that part.

NARRATOR. And Mr. Manufacturer . . .

MANUFACTURER. I'll play that part. What do I manufacture?

NARRATOR. Widgets. You manufacture, for the purposes of this little play, widgets. Next we'll need Mr. J. P. Banker . . .

J. P. I'll play that part.

NARRATOR. Good. Finally, and very important, we have Gaston Frenchman.

GASTON [*No accent*]. I'll play Gaston.

NARRATOR. You'll notice that the actor taking the part of Gaston Frenchman is not using a French accent. That's because the way the Bretton Woods Agreement works, every country in the world will be speaking the same language for once. All right? Everybody ready? Music, please . . .

[*Music: A theatrical cue . . . Overture . . . Slightly satirical . . . Sort of "Hearts and Flowers" . . . Register and carry down and out under*]

NARRATOR. First Act: The old way, the way we used to do it before the war. . . .

MANUFACTURER. I, the manufacturer, will make widgets as fast as I can, if there is a market for me to sell them at a reasonable profit.

GASTON. Uh, Mr. Manufacturer, I, Gaston Frenchman, am extremely anxious to buy several thousand gross of your widgets for resale in my country.

MANUFACTURER. Fine, fine. We'll go into production right away.

[*Some industrial effects . . . Register and carry under*]

NARRATOR. A good legitimate business deal. As far as Joe Worker is concerned:

JOE. A steady job, good pay check, coming in every week, security.

NARRATOR. All happy.

[*The industrial effects slow down appreciably*]

NARRATOR. Aha! But soft! The banker approaches . . . Problems?

J. P. It's a question of currency. There seems to be some feeling in this country that the, uh, the government in France . . .

NARRATOR. What's the trouble?

J. P. A certain instability in the currency. As we bankers say, the franc is slipping.

NARRATOR. Oh. The franc is slipping. Which means . . . ?

J. P. It means that instead of the exchange being twenty francs to the dollar, there are now twenty-five francs to the dollar.

GASTON. Hey!

NARRATOR. That you, Gaston? What's the matter?

GASTON. That means widgets are costing me too much! I won't buy!

MANUFACTURER. Won't buy, eh? But if I cut my price per widget?

GASTON. Oh, well, in that case . . .

MANUFACTURER. I'll cut my price per widget, all right. Let's see now. I guess we can shave wages . . . just a leetle . . .

JOE. Hey!

NARRATOR. That's Joe Worker. What happened, Joe?

JOE. The boss is trying to nick five bucks out of my pay check!

NARRATOR. Tsk, tsk, tsk.

JOE. The union will stop him, though.

NARRATOR. That right, Mr. Manufacturer?

MANUFACTURER. Mmmmmm. Maybe. Well, I guess I'll just have to . . .

[*Industrial effects out altogether*]

NARRATOR. What?

MANUFACTURER. Stop exporting altogether. After all, I've got to have a reasonable profit. I guess this means no more widgets.

JOE. Hey!

NARRATOR. What's up now, Joe?

JOE. No job!

[*Music: In for a satirically mournful bridge . . . We can afford to be satirical because*]

NARRATOR. Well, well. That's a sad story. Fortunately, it's an old-time story. Now we will show you how it will work, once Congress has approved the Bretton Woods Agreement. Same cast, same actors, but one new actor:

WORLD BANKER. The representative of the International Monetary Fund.

NARRATOR. That's the official who will work out details of the Bretton Woods Agreement. All right? Are we ready? This is the postwar version of the same story:

MANUFACTURER. I, the manufacturer, will make widgets as fast as I can, at a reasonable profit. Who would like to buy?

GASTON. I, Gaston Frenchman, am delighted to buy some of your widgets.

MANUFACTURER. Fine. Production starts right away.

[*Industrial effects roll merrily along*]

NARRATOR. All happy, including Joe Worker. Enter the Banker again.

J. P. Uh-oh. Same problem again. A little instability in the currency. I'm afraid . . .

[*Industrial effects slow down appreciably*]

NARRATOR. It may be the same problem, but there's a solution. Here comes our new actor.

WORLD BANKER. A little instability in the currency? French franc slipping, is it? Ah, well, these things will sometimes happen, even in the best-regulated . . . Here . . .

NARRATOR. What're you doing?

WORLD BANKER. Lending France enough gold from the International
Monetary Stabilization Fund until she can get her franc stable
again.

[*Industrial effects pick up again*]

NARRATOR. Seems to have done the trick, all right.

WORLD BANKER. Sure.

NARRATOR. Okay, Gaston?

GASTON. Why not? The price of widgets has remained the same.

NARRATOR. Joe?

JOE. Sure. Still got my job. Still got my pay check.

NARRATOR. And Mr. Manufacturer?

MANUFACTURER. All clear here. Still making my reasonable profit.

NARRATOR. Everybody happy?

ALL. [*Ad lib*]. Sure, okay [*etc.*].

[*Music: Up for a gay and triumphant bridge*]

NARRATOR. And that, a little oversimplified, is why the International
Monetary Fund of the Bretton Woods Agreement is a good thing.
We told you there was another part to the Agreement:

VOICE. The Bank for International Reconstruction and Development.

NARRATOR. Yes. For this one we have a different cast of characters.
Music, again, please. Overture . . .

[*Music: Again an overture, satirical in a gentle way*]

This is once more an old-time story. First we'll show you how it
was, then we'll show you how it can be. Once upon a time, there
were three countries.

X [A WOMAN]. Country X . . .

Y. Country Y . . .

Z. And Country Z.

NARRATOR. Country X was a nice little country, but very little indeed.
In order to get along at all, she had to trade with other countries.
But she didn't have much to sell, and she couldn't get much for
what she did sell. What she really needed was equipment for
producing more. Could she borrow the money?

COUNTRY Y [*Villain*]. Don't borrow the money, little Country X. Why
borrow at all? Trade with me, dear little country. Trade with me
and all will be well. What have you to sell to me?

COUNTRY X. I have raw materials, and that is all, alas, for I have no industry to manufacture goods of my own!

COUNTRY Y [*Rubbing his hands*]. What could be better? You have the raw materials—I have the factories. I will pay you well. We will get along together famously. Sign here, please.

COUNTRY Z. Just a moment! Be careful, little Country X! Do not deal with this villainous Country Y! All you will get will be tears and unhappiness! Deal with me, instead!

COUNTRY X. But I need equipment, machinery. Country Y will give me a good price for my raw materials and then I can buy equipment and machinery from her. I think you are nothing but a rich fool, Country Z. Go away and peddle your papers.

COUNTRY Y. Well spoken, my dear. Sign here.

COUNTRY X. There! Now here are my raw materials. Pay me, please.

COUNTRY Y. Uh, pay you. Yes, yes, of course. Excuse me, I have an urgent call I must make . . .

COUNTRY X. Hey! Pay me!

COUNTRY Y. Uh, yes. Just so. Pay you. I'll tell you what. I'll pay you in aspirin tablets and harmonicas. How's that? Fair exchange . . . no robbery . . .

COUNTRY X. I want machinery and equipment or cash on the barrel-head.

COUNTRY Y [*Getting tough*]. Machinery and equipment? I need that for plans of my own. I'll pay you in blocked marks.

COUNTRY X. Blocked marks? What are blocked marks?

COUNTRY Y. They're money, of course . . .

COUNTRY X. Good! What I wanted.

COUNTRY Y. . . . except, of course, that they must stay inside my borders. They'll be put to your credit, of course.

COUNTRY X. Credit! But I don't want credit! I want cash!

COUNTRY Y. You'll take what you get, and like it. Either aspirin tablets and harmonicas, or blocked marks. Remember, you signed the contract. Oh, yes, and by the way, I can't say I like your prime minister. Get rid of him. Kick the rest of the cabinet out too, while you're at it. They've been doing entirely too much talking about nonaggression.

COUNTRY X. Now, just a minute . . . I'll call my friend, Country Z!

COUNTRY Y. Country Z? Oh, yes. Now that I've got your raw materials,

I was thinking about him. I think I'll just go and pick a fight
with him.

[*Music: A bridge . . . down*]

NARRATOR. And so, as we know, they had a fight. Fortunately, Country
Z is winning. Country Y, of course: that's Germany, or it might
be Japan. Yes, that was the way it used to work. Now, when the
Congress approves the Bretton Woods Agreement, it'll go more
like this: Still the same three countries . . .

x. Country X . . .

y. Country Y . . .

z. And Country Z.

NARRATOR. And Country X is still a little country, no industries of her
own. Only now, when she says . . .

COUNTRY X. I must trade with other countries. I haven't enough money
to buy the goods I need. If only I could produce more, I could
buy more. But I have no factories of my own.

NARRATOR. Now, she gets this answer, from the Bank for International
Reconstruction and Development.

WORLD BANKER. We'll give you a loan. Guaranteed.

COUNTRY X. A loan?

WORLD BANKER. So you can build up some industries of your own.
Make your own manufactured goods. Sell 'em to other countries.
Why be poor and dependent?

COUNTRY X. Why, indeed?

WORLD BANKER. No countries dependent, from now on. No countries
entirely independent, either. All countries interdependent. Makes
more sense.

COUNTRY X. But where's the money coming from?

WORLD BANKER. World Bank. Every other country in the United Nations is lending it to you.

COUNTRY X. Aren't they scared that I'll get in competition with them?

WORLD BANKER. The more industry you have, the more well-paid workers you have. The more well-paid workers you have, the better
market your country is for goods from other countries. The more
goods other countries sell you, the more well-paid workers *they*
have. The more well-paid workers *they* have, the better are your
markets for selling what you're going to produce, when you build

the factories and the industries you're going to build with this loan. Okay?

COUNTRY X. Okay!

[*Music: Gay and triumphant . . . down*]

NARRATOR. Not bad, is it? And so they lived happily ever after, all the countries, interdependently. Again, of course, we have oversimplified the picture, but that, after a fashion, is how the other half of the Bretton Woods Agreement will work . . . an agreement that spells security, prosperity, and world peace. And that's why it's an agreement of resounding importance to you, and to everybody else in this country. The man who more than any other is the father of the Bretton Woods Agreement is in his office now, in the United States Treasury Building, waiting at a microphone to speak to you. I have the honor to introduce the Honorable Henry Morgenthau, Secretary of the Treasury. Mr. Morgenthau.

MORGENTHAU. The CIO needs no reminder that the welfare of American labor is tied to the welfare of America as a whole. It demonstrated its knowledge of this fact last fall by taking part actively— and, I may say, fairly effectively—in the political life of the nation. It did so because it understood, as Sidney Hillman put it, that "The activity of such groups in shaping the course of their government is essential to the functioning of our democracy."

The discussion of the Bretton Woods proposals which has taken place on this program indicates that organized labor understands also that it must play a responsible part in the shaping of international affairs. It has a vital stake in the peace no less than in the war.

It is too often assumed that international affairs are beyond the grasp of the ordinary citizen—that they must be left to the diplomats in the political field and to the bankers in the economic field. If they are left entirely in such hands, the chances are that they will be shaped no better than in the past. Your hands must share in the shaping.

There is nothing remote about the Bretton Woods proposals. They involve your bread and butter. They are an essential part of the President's program for the attainment of sixty million jobs here in the United States. We cannot reach such a level of employment at home unless there is a lifting of living standards abroad and a revival of international trade.

The International Monetary Fund is simply a device to make it possible for workers in all parts of the world to exchange the goods they produce on a stable basis and in an orderly way. It would free the flow of commerce from artificial currency barriers. It would substitute economic co-operation for economic warfare among the nations of the earth.

The International Bank, on the other hand, is intended to give economic help to the people of wartorn lands. Only with such help will they be able to buy what we produce. The only good customers are prosperous customers.

And what is even more important is this: The only kind of world in which enduring peace can be assured is a prosperous world—a world in which people everywhere have an opportunity to fulfill their reasonable hopes through honest work and free interchange of the things they grow and make. The agreement reached by the United Nations at Bretton Woods is one of the cornerstones of such a world.

THE LAST DAY OF
THE WAR

Sgt. Arthur Laurents

Aᴄᴛᴇʀ a Cornell degree, Arthur Laurents took a radio course at New York University, and earned back the tuition fee by selling one of his class scripts to the *Columbia Workshop*. During the next year, Laurents tells, "I wrote for practically every half-hour commercial dramatic show on the air. You want the grim names? *Hollywood Playhouse, Dr. Christian, Manhattan at Midnight, Thin Man*—well, you can go on from there. The best part of that was learning to write by writing, and learning that in radio you can sell the same script to as many as four different programs."

In 1941, Laurents went into the army, became a truck driver, a photographer-paratrooper, a message center courier. In spare time, he wrote some scripts for *The Man Behind the Gun*. The result was that in December, 1943, the army assigned him to write *Army Service Forces Presents,* and a year later *Assignment Home.* The purpose of these series was to keep the public informed about life and work in the army. The scripts were so authentic, and so accurately reflected soldier talk and attitudes, that the series were greatly admired by servicemen.

Laurents became particularly effective during the latter part of the war in Europe when the army became concerned about cushioning the readjustment problems of the returning soldier. *Assignment Home* and some of the later programs of *Army Service Forces Presents* had the job of informing civilians about these problems, so that an unenlightened public might not complicate the veteran's reorientation. Sgt. Laurents's powerful scripts, which were official War Department programs, won him a wide wartime reputation.

The Last Day of the War was broadcast twice over the American Broadcasting Company; the first performance was directed by Jerry Devine, the second by the author.

THE LAST DAY OF
THE WAR

[*Music: Curtain raiser*]

VOICE. There was a chunky redheaded kid from Nevada. He got it this way.

[*Machine gun—short, sharp, loud*]
There was a solemn-faced boy from Cape Cod who told jokes with a dead pan. He got it this way.

[*One rifle shot—sniper*]
Then there was this guy—big, lazy shoulders, strong thighs, dirty blond hair. He was from Toledo, Ohio. He got it good.

[*The long shrill scream of a shell. It explodes violently on mike*]

[*Music: A crash and then very short bridge*]

MICKEY [*Groans softly*].

VOICE. That's how it begins . . . with dozens of shell fragments smashing the bone and flesh from Toledo, Ohio. In a few minutes, seconds . . .

[*Battle noise speak in under*]
. . . two company aidmen from the medics belly out over the screaming ground to the bloody, floppy body of—what's his name?

AIDMAN. Hey, it's Ryan! Mickey Ryan!

MEDIC. Washed up?

AIDMAN. Nah. Bleeding like an orange, though.
He'll need a couple of tourniquets.

VOICE. They apply tourniquets to stop the Ohio blood, to save Mickey Ryan from hemorrhages. They give him morphine to stop the fifty million pains. They put sulfa on his wounds and dress them.

AIDMAN. Judas, he's a mess!

MEDIC. Yeah. Nice egg, too.

BOY 1. [*Off . . . groaning*]. Medic . . . medic!

AIDMAN. There's another one.

MEDIC. Okay. We're through here.

AIDMAN. Right. [*Softly*] Hey, Mickey boy, good luck, fellow.

VOICE. They stick his rifle, bayonet down, into the soggy earth as a signal for the litter bearers. Then they crawl farther out to the next poor guy and the poor guy after him and all the poor guys after all of them.

> [*Music: Punctuation . . . Not too dramatic . . . Sneak out under following*]

Mickey Ryan worked in the Toledo freight yards. He's 5 feet 11. He weighs 178 pounds and that ain't hay to the pill rollers who carry him on a litter 650 yards to the battalion aid station behind the lines. He gets blood plasma there, and sulfa and a doctor. And when the litter bearers carry him a mile back to the collecting station, Mickey Ryan doesn't weigh so much. Mickey Ryan's had pieces of shell dug out of him. Mickey Ryan's also had his left leg cut off.

> [*Music: Punctuation . . . Again sneak out under following*]

They go over his wounds at the collecting station, but Mickey Ryan doesn't know this. He doesn't know he almost died. He just wakes up in time to pass out again. But the medics know, the doctors know.

DOCTOR. Swiss cheese.

BOY 2. What, sir?

DOCTOR. Ever see a piece of Swiss cheese?

BOY 2. Yes, sir, but—

DOCTOR. Never mind. Let's get at these dressings. Blood plasma ready?

BOY 2. Yes, sir.

DOCTOR. Good. I think I'll— [*Stops*]

BOY 2. What is it?

DOCTOR. Look at his right leg.

BOY 2. Lousy.

DOCTOR. Yeah . . . Well, we'll try to let him keep that anyway. Let's get going.

> [*Music: As before*]

VOICE. Seven miles behind the lines is the clearing station. Mickey Ryan, who was brought up by an aunt in Toledo, goes there in a jeep. He hurts bad, so they inject morphine again and check his bandages again and give him blood plasma again . . . 53 miles behind the front is the evacuation hospital. Mickey Ryan, who married a girl named Margie one month before he went overseas, goes there in a truck. Yeah . . . They give him more blood plasma. He still doesn't know . . . doesn't know they operate again on that stump of a left leg . . . doesn't know they go over the right leg, the still-whole, still-in-one-piece right leg with sure hands and cool eyes and crying minds. Mickey Ryan doesn't know from nothing till they take him to a big station hospital in a town the war long ago kicked aside like an old sweetheart. Then, one. morning, the fifty million pains take a day off and he comes out of the fog. . . . For a few seconds, Mickey thinks he's in the hotel where he spent his honeymoon with Margie. Then the smell socks him and he opens his eyes to see his right leg hanging in front of him. Nothing registers for a second; he just stares at the leg in a big white cast hanging by ropes from the ceiling.

MICKEY. Holy crow!

VOGEL. Hi.

MICKEY. Oh . . . Hi . . . Some contraption.

VOGEL. The cast?

MICKEY. Yeah. Right out of Rube Goldberg.

VOGEL. I been lying here trying to figure how they rigged it up.

MICKEY. Pretty tricky. Say! Does that piece of steel go right through me?

VOGEL. Looks like it. Does it hurt?

MICKEY. Something hurts. And my other leg's got a cramp in it.

VOGEL. A—cramp?

MICKEY. Yeah. Right down at the toes. You ever get 'em down there?

VOGEL. Yeah. But—hey, look, fellow—

MICKEY. I don't know whether I can reach it with this other— [*Stops abruptly . . . a pause . . . then quietly*] That's a hot one.

VOGEL. Didn't you know?

MICKEY. No . . . Kind of funny to reach down and . . .

VOGEL. Yeah.

MICKEY. Some joke.

VOGEL. Huh?

MICKEY. Me thinking I had a cramp in my—toes.

VOGEL. Oh.

MICKEY. Guess there are nerves in the—stump.

VOGEL. Yeah.

MICKEY. That's a hot one, all right. Me thinking I had a— Hey! I wonder if I got the other one.

VOGEL. Oh, sure. I think the nurse said you had a lot of shrapnel in that one and there were fractures or something.

MICKEY. Oh. That's not so bad.

VOGEL. No. They can fix that.

MICKEY. I'd sure hate to lose 'em both though.

VOGEL. Yeah, but you won't.

MICKEY. What'd you get?

VOGEL. Oh . . . no more one-arm driving for me.

MICKEY. Lose a wing?

VOGEL. Yeah.

MICKEY. Where? At the beach?

VOGEL. Yeah.

MICKEY. Which? Red?

VOGEL. No. Scarlet.

MICKEY. Oh, that was a stinker! Say—when did they chop it off?

VOGEL. Your leg?

MICKEY. Yeah.

VOGEL. I don't know. It was off when they brought you in.

MICKEY. That's a hot one. Me not knowing, I mean. Did you know?

VOGEL. About mine?

MICKEY. Yeah.

VOGEL. Oh, Judas, that arm got clipped smack off before I even hit the beach.

MICKEY. Gee, it's your right one too.

VOGEL. Yeah, but I'm a southpaw, so that's not too bad.

MICKEY. No, that's pretty lucky.

VOGEL. What are you smiling about?

MICKEY. Funny kind of luck.

VOGEL. Yeah.

MICKEY. I wouldn't wish it on my first sergeant.

VOGEL. Me either.

MICKEY. Well . . . I hope this other one gets better. I'd sure hate to lose 'em both.

[*Slight pause*]

VOICE [*Quietly*]. So Mickey Ryan finds out—and takes it. But in the night—he cries.

[*Music: . . . . . .*]

That right leg, that limb which still makes Mickey Ryan 5 feet 11 doesn't come out of the cast. But it does come down from the ceiling halter and Mickey goes back overseas, back to the country he lost a leg for. He goes to a General Hospital there and gets a doctor—Major Crowley, his name is—and a couple of nurses and a tall, tight-faced girl in a blue uniform, Miss Piper. Miss Piper is one of the Blue Angels, one of the physical therapists who work for the Medical Corps. Miss Piper knows her business and doesn't like it. But she does it. Well. She puts Mickey Ryan on a white table and starts to take off the tight, elastic bandage binding the stump that's his left leg.

MICKEY. It's sure gonna be a relief to get that off.

PIPER. It'll go back, right back on when I'm through.

MICKEY. Why?

PIPER. We've got to shrink that stump so it'll fit your artificial leg.

MICKEY. Well, even to have it off for a little while . . .

PIPER. There.

MICKEY. Whew! That feels good. Looks pretty ugly though, doesn't it?

PIPER. I've seen worse.

MICKEY. You're pretty tough.

PIPER. You'd better be.

MICKEY. Why?

PIPER. This is going to hurt.

MICKEY. What are you going to do?

PIPER. Pound that left leg.

MICKEY. That stump, you mean.

PIPER. Okay. That stump.

MICKEY. Why?

PIPER. It's flat now. There are flabby undermuscles and excess fat.

MICKEY. Thanks.

PIPER. I've got to knead it into the shape of a cone so it'll fit your new leg. And we've got to exercise it.

MICKEY. There's not much left to exercise.

PIPER. There's enough. And you've got to keep exercising the muscles even while you're in bed.

MICKEY. What for?

PIPER. So you'll have good control of your new leg.

MICKEY. Okay. Start pounding.

PIPER. It's going to hurt.

MICKEY. You said that.

PIPER. All right.

MICKEY. Hey, Miss Piper . . .

PIPER. Yes?

MICKEY. You've got one of those "this-is-going-to-hurt-me-more-than-it'll-hurt-you" looks.

PIPER. It's not going to hurt me, soldier.

MICKEY. Okay. Let's go.

PIPER. All right.

[*Her manner now changes. She is soft and anxious and we know that this does hurt her*]

MICKEY [*Groans*].

PIPER. Hang on. Hang on tight, Mickey. I know it hurts, but you'll be glad later.

MICKEY [*Tightly*]. Sure.

PIPER. You've got to go through a lot to get the things you really want. Like you've got to go through a war to get a good world and—

MICKEY [*Groans*].

PIPER. Just hang on, Mickey. Don't think about it. Try thinking about something else. Are you married?

MICKEY. Yeah.

PIPER. What's her name?

MICKEY. Margie.

PIPER. What's she like? Is she—

MICKEY [*Groans*].

PIPER. Okay. We'll rest a minute.

MICKEY. Whew!

PIPER [*Back to her old manner*]. I thought you were tough.

MICKEY. I thought you were.

PIPER. Wait till I tell your wife.

MICKEY. You won't have the chance.

PIPER. Oh, no?

MICKEY. You won't see her.

PIPER. The War Department wired her you were here.

MICKEY. I know, but I wrote her not to come.

    [*Slight pause*]

PIPER. So that's the kind of baby you are.

MICKEY. What do you mean?

PIPER. Building up a nice, neat little complex about your leg.

MICKEY. Nuts.

PIPER. You'll be able to get around just as well as you ever did.

MICKEY. Okay.

PIPER. There are lots worse things that can happen, and I'll bet
    your wife knows it.

MICKEY. She's just a kid.

PIPER. So what?

MICKEY. Well . . .

PIPER. Come on. I'm the original Sphinx.

MICKEY. Well . . . you see, Miss Piper, a month after I met Margie,
    we got married. And a month later, I went overseas.

PIPER. Okay. Now you can have the rest of your lives together.

MICKEY. Uh-uh.

PIPER. Why not?

MICKEY. Well . . . the way I figure it . . . just because of two months,
    there's no reason she should be stuck with a—well, me.

PIPER. You *do* have a thing about your leg.

MICKEY. No. I can take it, but—Margie's a kid, Miss Piper. I don't
    want to— Ah, she's better off if she never sees me again.

PIPER. Don't you love her?

MICKEY. Sure. Let's get back to the pounding.

PIPER. I know she loves you.

MICKEY. Ow—it itches!

PIPER. The stump?

MICKEY. No. My right leg.

PIPER. Well, you worry about that and stop worrying about your wife.

MICKEY. Let's get back to the pounding.

PIPER. Mickey . . .

MICKEY. I'm ready. Beat me, daddy.

PIPER. Okay. Hang on.

[*Music*: . . . .]

VOICE. Every day what was Mickey Ryan's left leg is pounded, then strained back into the tight elastic bandage, then exercised in his bed. Every day, the nurses and the doctor, Major Crowley, examine him carefully. Every day, the muscles in the major's long jaw tighten. Then, one day, they go limp. It's all over—and the major knows it.

MAJOR. Miss Piper . . .

PIPER. Yes, major?

MAJOR. How tough are you?

PIPER. What is it?

MAJOR. Ryan's right leg has to come off. Gangrene.

[*Slight pause*]

PIPER. Not that tough.

MAJOR. We've been trying and trying—

PIPER. I'm not that tough. I couldn't tell him.

MAJOR. Somebody has to before the operation. Otherwise, the shock—

PIPER. I couldn't.

MAJOR. It's my job anyway.

[*Pause*]

PIPER. I'll kill them.

MAJOR. What?

PIPER. I'll kill every fascist rat who tries to take away what these kids are fighting for. Does it have to come off?

MAJOR. Yeah.

PIPER. You'd think that we've seen enough of them not to feel anything.

MAJOR. His wife's arriving tomorrow.

PIPER. What?

MAJOR. His wife. She's coming tomorrow.

PIPER. Oh.

MAJOR. Maybe he'll want to see her by then.

PIPER. Maybe. I don't know. When are you going to—?

MAJOR. Operate?

PIPER. Yes.

MAJOR. Today.

PIPER. Well, how tough are you?

MAJOR. I don't know, but I've got to tell him.

[*Music:* . . . .]

MICKEY [*Very flatly*]. Major, you didn't come here just to bull with me. . . . Let's have it.

MAJOR. The leg has to come off, son.

MICKEY. Uh-huh.

MAJOR. Gangrene.

MICKEY. Uh-huh.

MAJOR. We've been trying to save it.

MICKEY. You know what day this is, major?

MAJOR. What?

MICKEY. I'll tell you. It's the last day of the war. Yep. That's what it is.

MAJOR. Mickey . . .

MICKEY. And it's a relief. You know that? It's a relief.

MAJOR. Look. You mustn't—

MICKEY. No, no. Don't get me wrong. I don't care. Cut the leg off. Cut 'em both off. Cut my arms off, cut my head off. You want my heart? Cut that out too. Cut me up to little pieces. I don't care. Go on. Cut.

MAJOR. Mickey . . .

MICKEY. What are you waiting for?

MAJOR. We tried, son.

MICKEY. Okay!

MAJOR. Please . . .

MICKEY. No. I don't want to talk, sir. I don't want to hear. Just— take it. Cut it off. I don't care. [*He cracks*] I don't care one lousy bit.

[*Music: Sting and hold*]

voice. Late that day, they took him to the operating room. Afterwards, Mickey Ryan didn't stand 5 feet 11 any more.

[*Music: ....*]

The sun was warm early the next morning, but in his office the major was cold. Yeah . . . he was there at his desk all night. Business as usual. And he had a customer—a woman, a girl, a kid really. A little blonde kid dressed in woman's clothes, nervously twisting the very thin gold band on her third finger, left hand.

margie. I'm Margie Ryan . . . Mrs. Ryan . . . Mickey Ryan's wife.

major. I'm glad to meet you. Please sit down, Mrs. Ryan.

margie. Thank you, sir.

major. Cigarette?

margie. No, thank you, sir.

major. Do you mind if I do?

margie. Oh, no!

major. He's a fine boy, your Mickey.

margie. Oh, yes. Oh, yes, he is!

major. He told me you were only married a month and then he went overseas.

margie. A month and four days. Sir, how is he?

major. He'll be all right.

margie. Can I—see him, please?

major. He's—sleeping now.

margie. Oh.

major. But you can see him in a little while.

margie. Thank you.

major. You didn't know him very long before you were married, did you?

margie. No, but—

major. It was long enough to know.

margie. Yes, sir. I knew—

major. Yes?

margie. I knew the second time. He was so gentle. Did Mickey lose a leg, sir?

major. Why . . . Yes. How did you know?

margie. Before he was hurt, he wrote almost every day. Then I only got one letter and he told me he— Well, I figured . . .

MAJOR. Go on.

MARGIE. I figured from that something terrible happened to him. Like
losing a leg. Or an arm. Or maybe his face . . . ?

MAJOR. His face is all right.

MARGIE. That's good. He has such a nice face.

MAJOR. You love Mickey very much, don't you?

MARGIE. Yes, sir.

MAJOR. I'm glad.

MARGIE. Oh . . . What's the matter with him?

MAJOR. What?

MARGIE. What else is the matter with him?

MAJOR. His other leg became infected. We tried our best but— Well,
we operated yesterday.

MARGIE. Oh. . . . [*Pause*] Can I see him now, please? ·

MAJOR. Wait.

MARGIE. He must feel terrible.

MAJOR. Mrs. Ryan—

MARGIE. I know Mickey. He must feel terrible. Can't I see him now,
please?

MAJOR. Mrs. Ryan. Sit down . . . please.

MARGIE. Yes, sir.

MAJOR. I want you to see Mickey. I think he needs to see you. But—
he does feel pretty badly. So—you have to be careful what you say.

MARGIE. I'll do whatever you tell me, sir.

MAJOR. Treat him naturally. Don't pretend he has legs. He hasn't.
But don't give him too much sympathy.

MARGIE. No, sir.

MAJOR. And don't treat him as though he's going to be helpless.

MARGIE. Oh, no! Mickey wouldn't like that. He's very independent.

MAJOR. Tell him what you've been doing. Ask him about himself.
Make him talk. Make him relax. Make him want to get better
and get out of here, back to you.

MARGIE. Sir . . .

MAJOR. Yes?

MARGIE. He doesn't want to, does he?

MAJOR. What?

MARGIE. Be married to me any more.

MAJOR. He thinks it's unfair to you.

MARGIE [*Pityingly*]. Oh . . .

MAJOR. You see, what you must do is—

[*Knocking on door*]

MAJOR. Come in.

[*Door opens*]

PIPER [*Coming on*]. Major, did— Oh. Excuse me.

MAJOR. No, come in. Mrs. Ryan, this is the young lady who's been
taking care of your husband. Miss Piper.

MARGIE. I'm pleased to meet you.

PIPER [*The nurse*]. How do you do, Mrs. Ryan.

MAJOR. Is he awake yet?

PIPER. N-o. Could I see you for a moment, major?

MAJOR. Of course. Mrs. Ryan, would you—

MARGIE. Ma'am . . .

PIPER. Yes?

MARGIE. He's awake, isn't he?

PIPER. Mrs. Ryan, I told you—

MARGIE. But he doesn't want to see me.

MAJOR. Now, you mustn't . . .

MARGIE. I know because he wrote me. He doesn't want to see me,
does he?

PIPER. . . . No, Mrs. Ryan. He doesn't. I'm sorry.

MARGIE. Maybe if I just went in anyway—

PIPER. I'm afraid you'd upset him.

MARGIE. We haven't seen each other in so long maybe he—

PIPER. Mrs. Ryan, in your husband's condition—

MAJOR. Miss Piper—please.

PIPER. Yes, sir.

MAJOR. Mrs. Ryan, why don't you come back later?

MARGIE. No. I'll—wait outside. In case he changes his mind. Thank
you very much.

[*Door shuts*]

[*Pause*]

MAJOR. How old do you think she is?

PIPER. The way she loves him, what does it matter?

MAJOR. I wish to God they'd send me overseas.

PIPER. Jenkins over in Ward B says the boys break her heart so much
she has to be tough with the relatives.

MAJOR. Does she?

PIPER. Yes, but she hasn't met Mrs. Ryan. Major—

MAJOR. Yes?

PIPER. Mickey Ryan needs that girl. And if I have to talk for twenty-four hours straight, he's going to see her!

[*Music: . . . .*]

MARGIE. Hello, Mickey.

MICKEY. Hello, Margie. Don't kiss me.

MARGIE. I'm sorry, honey.

MICKEY. Listen. I only said you could come in so I could get rid of Miss Piper. But now that you're here, let's get things straight.

MARGIE. All right, honey.

MICKEY. I wrote you not to come.

MARGIE. I know.

MICKEY. I told you I didn't want to see you.

MARGIE. Why not, honey?

MICKEY. Stop calling me honey! Look, Margie. We had two months. Okay, fine. But this is a lot later. A lot's happened. We're different.

MARGIE. No, we're not, Mickey.

MICKEY. Are you kidding?

MARGIE. We're no different inside.

MICKEY. I am.

MARGIE. No.

MICKEY. Yes. Inside *and* outside. Margie, look. Where I'm pressing the sheet down, look. You see where I end? Well, that's your husband and you don't want a husband like that. You're a kid, a baby. You got your whole life ahead of you. Go out and get yourself a good husband, get a guy who's in one piece.

MARGIE. You're my husband, Mickey.

MICKEY. So you're sticking. You're making the big gesture. Okay. You made it. Now pack up.

MARGIE. Do the legs hurt you much, honey?

MICKEY. Baby, will you listen? Look at me. Don't you know I'm through?

MARGIE. No, honey. All I know is—I love you. Sure, you lost your legs and you feel bad. And I feel bad for you. But—I just love you. So—it doesn't matter. I just love you.

MICKEY. Okay.

MARGIE. The major said you'll get artificial legs and—

MICKEY. Listen!

MARGIE. And—Miss Piper said you ought to be able to walk in about three months.

MICKEY. Margie—

MARGIE. I know how you feel, honey, but—

MICKEY. You don't know how I feel! I hate being like this.

MARGIE. Mickey . . .

MICKEY. I hate having you near me. I hate having you look at me. So go away. Go away! GO AWAY!

[*Music: . . . .*]

VOICE. They put Mickey Ryan to sleep that night, but he wakes up just before dawn in his helpless bed. He thinks of his wife and he shoves his face into the pillow. Then he decides what he's going to do. . . . The tough Miss Piper doesn't find out until later, and then she doesn't say anything until she has him on her table.

PIPER. Remember the first time I had you up here I told you it was going to hurt?

MICKEY. Yeah.

PIPER. Well, I went easy then.

MICKEY. Did you?

PIPER. Yes. And you'll find out how easy I've been.

MICKEY. Okay.

PIPER. Why did you rip off those bandages this morning? [*Pause*] Don't play innocent. Your nurse told me.

MICKEY. I'm not playing innocent.

PIPER. Why did you tear them off?

MICKEY. Are you going to pound today or not?

PIPER. When I'm good and ready. Why did you tear them off? [*Pause*] Okay, I'll tell you. You did it because you don't want to get better. You're afraid to get out of here; afraid to face the world; afraid to face your wife.

MICKEY. Forget my wife!

PIPER. Look, Ryan, we've been riding with you because we were sorry for you. Well, you've gotten soft. You can't take it and you've got to. You've got to get tough, so I'm going to get tough with you.

MICKEY. Go ahead.

PIPER. Not with pounding. That's physical pain; anybody can take that.

MICKEY. Yeah?

PIPER. Yes! You just feel too sorry for yourself. You see your wife and you go to pieces. You get afraid that you won't be able to hold her!

MICKEY. Okay. I'm afraid.

PIPER. Where's the man in you? Don't you want to fight to get better and get out of here and make a home for her?

MICKEY. Are you going to pound or not?

[Pause]

PIPER [Tenderly]. Mickey . . . don't . . . Don't, kid.

MICKEY. I like you better tough, Miss Piper.

PIPER. I met your wife and I can't be. She's a sweet girl. She loves you. She waits here every day just in the hope that—

MICKEY. Be tough, Miss Piper.

PIPER. Look. You love her. She loves you.

MICKEY. Yeah.

PIPER. What are you afraid of? You won't be a burden to her.

MICKEY. Not much.

PIPER. You think you won't get a job? You will. We train you. You think you'll have to hobble around on crutches? You'll have legs! You think everybody'll know? They won't!

MICKEY. If I can really walk—

PIPER. You will!

MICKEY. And really get a job—

PIPER. You will!

MICKEY. And be like before—

PIPER. You will!

MICKEY. Then what are we waiting for? Pound away, Miss Piper, for all you're worth!

PIPER. Okay!

[Music: . . . .]

VOICE. Now Mickey Ryan goes through the paces. It takes time . . .

time to re-establish blood circulation, time to shape the stumps properly, time to heal the raw nerves. Mickey Ryan gets impatient but soon he gets temporary legs which are tightened one day and loosened the next. Finally, the stumps harden and a plaster cast is taken of their shape. Finally, wooden legs that bend at the knee and the ankle and the toes are made and fitted on. Finally, Mickey Ryan learns to walk . . . no one can really know what goes on inside his head as he goes back to his legs and his canes and learns to walk twenty-four years after he first started. But he learns . . . And then one day, the major takes him into a strange room.

MICKEY. What's up, sir?

MAJOR. You see these three steps?

MICKEY. Yes, sir.

MAJOR. You're going to walk up them.

MICKEY. With these?

MAJOR. Yes. With those legs and your two canes.

MICKEY. That's a tough order, sir.

MAJOR. You can do it.

MICKEY. I can try.

MAJOR. You can do it!

MICKEY. Major . . .

MAJOR. Yes?

MICKEY. Nothing.

MAJOR. What's the matter?

MICKEY. Nothing, sir. Let's go.

MAJOR. Do you want to sit down first?

MICKEY. No.

MAJOR. All right. First your right leg.

　　[*Through the following, synchronize with dialogue sound of wooden leg and canes on wooden stairs*]

MICKEY. Feels funny.

MAJOR. Go on . . . That's it. Now the left.

MICKEY. I—

MAJOR. Go on. Don't look at your feet. Let your muscles do it. Lift . . . That's it.

MICKEY. It was easier when I was a kid.

MAJOR. You want to rest?

MICKEY. No, sir.

MAJOR. All right. Right foot again . . . Don't look down. Don't—
That's it. Now the left.

MICKEY. Major—

MAJOR. Don't stop there.

MICKEY. Major, I—

MAJOR. Go on. Lift it—

MICKEY. Major, I'm going to fall!
    [*Clatter on stairs*]

MAJOR [*Through above*]. Ryan! . . . Are you all right?

MICKEY. Yeah. No splinters.

MAJOR. Here. Sit down.

MICKEY. Thanks.

MAJOR. You see, if you—

MICKEY. It's no use, I knew it all along.

MAJOR. What?

MICKEY. It's no use, sir. Who am I kidding? I haven't got any legs.
    I got two pieces of wood and a pair of canes. You say walk.
    So I walk. But like what? Like a guy with no legs on a pair of
    stilts!

MAJOR. Ryan!

MICKEY. You know what I need? A board with wheels on it. Yeah,
    and a tin cup.

MAJOR. Stop it.

MICKEY. Want to buy an apple? How about a pencil? Shoelaces?
    Chewing gum? Yeah—that's what I'm good for!

MAJOR. Ryan, stop it!

MICKEY. I'm a lousy cripple!

MAJOR. Ryan! [*Pause*] Now listen to me. You've walked and you've
    climbed steps. Not well maybe, but that takes time. And in time,
    you'll do it perfectly—and without canes.

MICKEY. What for?

MAJOR. What for? What were you fighting for? To have a house
    for your wife, to have kids maybe, to live like a human being.
    Wasn't that it?

MICKEY. Yeah.

MAJOR. Okay. You lost your legs. Does that mean you lost the war?
    Does that mean you were fighting for nothing? Does that mean
    you're going to lay down and die?

MICKEY. No, but—

MAJOR. There aren't any buts! You're still a man. You can live. You can work. You can fight.

MICKEY. Fight?

MAJOR. Yes! Do you think you must have a gun? There are ways of fighting for everything you want. Do you want your wife?

MICKEY. Yes.

MAJOR. Well, get up and walk to her.

MICKEY. What?

MAJOR. She's waiting outside that door. Go on—walk!

MICKEY. Major—

MAJOR. Walk!

MICKEY. Okay.

[A few footsteps with canes]
The door, sir—

MAJOR *[Off]*. You can open it. Go on.

MICKEY. Yes sir.

[Door opens . . . slow]

MARGIE *[Off]*. Mickey!

MAJOR *[Coming on]*. Don't come down those steps, Mrs. Ryan!

MICKEY. Steps. So that's it.

MAJOR. That's what?

MICKEY. The whole thing, sir. Just a big spiel to get me to walk up three steps.

MAJOR *[Quietly]*. If you think that's all it meant, tell your wife to come down.

[Pause]

MICKEY. Margie . . .

MARGIE *[Off]*. Do you want me to come down, honey?

MICKEY. No. No, stay there. I'm coming up.

[As before, climbing steps, one step here].
That's one.

[Music sneaks in under]
[Same . . . one more step]
That's two.

MARGIE. Mickey . . .

MICKEY. Stay where you are. Because I'm coming up to you.

[Underneath—the last step]

MARGIE. Mickey . . . Oh, Mickey!

[Music: . . . .]

A CHILD IS BORN

Stephen Vincent Benét

I N 1939 Stephen Vincent Benét heard on the *Columbia Workshop* a one-hour radio production of passages from his *John Brown's Body,* arranged and produced by Norman Corwin. It must have been, for Benét, a fascinating demonstration of how the radio medium could be used for the presentation of poetry.

Not long afterwards, Benét began himself to write plays for the air, many of them in verse. *They Burned the Books,* written in 1942, was one of the most influential plays written for radio during the war. Produced twice over the National Broadcasting Company, distributed by the Writers' War Board to hundreds of groups for local broadcasts, used in countless schools over public address systems, and in army camps for "orientation" periods, it drove home its message in a way few other wartime documents have done. This was Benét's eloquence marching to war. There was beautiful anger in it—the anger of a very gentle man who saw the issues.

Benét, putting aside his epic *Western Star,* left unfinished at his untimely death, became during the war years, as Norman Corwin put it, a "one-man task force." For the Council for Democracy he wrote the *Dear Adolf* series and *Listen to the People;* for the Office of War Information he wrote *A Time to Reap;* for the *This Is War* series he wrote *Your Army.* Two of Benét's wartime scripts were written for production on a commercial series, *Cavalcade of America,* which deserves a share of thanks for bringing such plays to a wide midevening audience. One, *The Undefended Border,* dealt with our friendship with Canada; the other was the Christmas play, *A Child Is Born.*

Benét's radio works have been published in one volume under the title *We Stand United and other Radio Scripts.*

In all his radio plays, from the very first, radio seemed to be a natural thing to Benét. It is an interesting fact that poets and novelists have adjusted themselves far more successfully to radio than playwrights of the theater. Benét at once sensed the fluidity of the medium. Its direct appeal to the human mind attracted him. He saw that in this respect the medium was, as he says in the opening narration to *A Child Is Born,* "as old as the human heart."

A Child Is Born had a memorable premier performance on December 21, 1942, with Alfred Lunt and Lynn Fontanne. Homer Fickett directed. The play was repeated a year later, and will be for many a Christmas to come.

A CHILD IS BORN*

NARRATOR. I'm your narrator. It's my task to say
Just where and how things happen in our play,
Set the bare stage with words instead of props
And keep on talking till the curtain drops.
So you shall know, as well as our poor skill
Can show you, whether it is warm or chill,
Indoors or out, a battle or a fair,
In this, our viewless theater of the air.
It's an old task—old as the human heart,
Old as those bygone players and their art
Who, in old days when faith was nearer earth,
Played out the mystery of Jesus' birth
In hall or village green or market square
For all who chose to come and see them there,
And, if they knew that King Herod, in his crown,
Was really Wat, the cobbler of the town,
And Tom, the fool, played Abraham the Wise,
They did not care. They saw with other eyes.
The story was their own—not far away.
As real as if it happened yesterday,
Full of all awe and wonder yet so near,
A marvelous thing that could have happened here
In their own town—a star that could have blazed
On their own shepherds, leaving them amazed.
Frightened and questioning and following still
To the bare stable—and the miracle.

So we, tonight, who are your players too,
Ask but to tell that selfsame tale to you

In our own words, the plain and simple speech
Of human beings, talking each
Troubled with their own cares, not always wise,
And yet, at moments, looking toward the skies.

The time is—time. The place is anywhere.
The voices speak to you across the air
To say that once again a child is born.
A child is born.
"I pray you all, give us your audience
And hear this matter with reverence."

[*Music*]

There is a town where men and women live
Their lives as people do in troubled times,
Times when the world is shaken. There is an inn.
A woman sings there in the early morning.
  [*Music, fading into the voice of a woman—the innkeeper's
  wife—singing as she goes about her household tasks*]
INNKEEPER'S WIFE. In Bethlehem of Judea
There shall be born a child,
A child born of woman
And yet undefiled.

He shall not come to riches,
To riches and might,
But in the bare stable
He shall be Man's light.

He shall not come to conquest,
The conquest of kings,
But in the bare stable
He shall judge all things.

King Herod, King Herod,
Now what will you say
Of the child in the stable
This cold winter day?

I hear the wind blowing
Across the bare thorn,
I fear not King Herod
If this child may be born.
[*Sound of steps coming down a flight of stone stairs. A man's voice, rough and suspicious—the voice of the innkeeper. The innkeeper is middle-aged—his wife somewhat younger*]
INNKEEPER. Singing again! I told you not to sing!
WIFE. I'm sorry. I forgot.
INNKEEPER. Forgot? That's fine!
That's wonderful! That answers everything!
The times are hard enough and bad enough
For anyone who tries to keep an inn,
Get enough bread to stick in his own mouth
And keep things going, somehow, in his town.
The country's occupied. We have no country.
You've heard of that, perhaps?
You've seen their soldiers, haven't you? You know
Just what can happen to our sort of people
Once there's a little trouble? Answer me!
WIFE [*Wearily*]. I've seen. I know.
INNKEEPER. You've seen. You know. And you keep singing songs!
Not ordinary songs—the kind of songs
That might bring in a little bit of trade,
Songs with a kind of pleasant wink in them
That make full men forget the price of the wine,
The kind of songs a handsome girl can sing
After their dinner to good customers
—And thanks to me, the inn still has a few!—
Oh, no! You have to sing rebellious songs
About King Herod!
WIFE. I'm sorry. I forgot.
INNKEEPER. Sorry? Forgot? You're always saying that!
Is it your business what King Herod does?
Is it your place to sing against King Herod?
WIFE. I think that he must be a wicked man.
A very wicked man.
INNKEEPER. Oh, la, la, la!

Sometimes *I* think your ways will drive me mad.
Are you a statesman or a general?
Do you pretend to know the ins and outs
Of politics and why the great folk do
The things they do—and why we have to bear them?
Because it's we—we—we
Who have to bear them, first and last and always,
In every country and in every time.
They grind us like dry wheat between the stones.
Don't you know that?

WIFE. I know that, somehow, kings
Should not be wicked and grind down the people.
I know that kings like Herod should not be.

INNKEEPER. All right—all right. I'm not denying that.
I'm reasonable enough. I know the world.
I'm willing to admit to anyone
At least behind closed doors
[*He drops his voice*]
That Herod isn't quite my sort of king
And that I don't approve of all he does.
Still, there he is. He's king. How will it help
If I go out and write on someone's wall
[*His voice in a whisper*]
"Down with King Herod!"
[*His voice comes up again*]
What's it worth?
The cross for me, the whipping post for you,
The inn burned down, the village fined for treason,
Just because one man didn't like King Herod.
For that's the way things are.

WIFE. Yet there are men—

INNKEEPER. Oh yes, I know—fanatics, rabble, fools,
Outcasts of war, misfits, rebellious souls,
Seekers of some vague kingdom in the stars—
They hide out in the hills and stir up trouble,
Call themselves prophets, too, and prophesy
That something new is coming to the world,
The Lord knows what!

Well, it's a long time coming,
And, meanwhile, we're the wheat between the stones.
WIFE. Something must come.
INNKEEPER. Believe it if you choose,
But, meantime, if we're clever, we can live
And even thrive a little—clever wheat
That slips between the grinding stones and grows
In little green blade-sprinkles on the ground.
At least, if you'll not sing subversive songs
To other people but your poor old husband.
[Changing tone]
Come, wife, I've got some news.
I didn't mean to be so angry with you.
You've some queer fancies in that head of yours
—Lord, don't I know—but you're still the tall girl
With the grave eyes and the brook-running voice
I took without a dower or a price
Out of your father's house because—oh, well—
Because you came. And they've not been so bad,
The years since then. Now have they?
WIFE. No.
INNKEEPER. That's right.
Give us a kiss.
[Pause]
I couldn't help the child.
I know you think of that, this time of year.
He was my son, too, and I think of him.
I couldn't help his dying.
WIFE. No, my husband.
INNKEEPER. He stretched his little arms to me and died.
And yet I had the priest—the high priest, too.
I didn't spare the money.
WIFE, No, my husband.
I am a barren bough. I think and sing
And am a barren bough.
INNKEEPER. Oh, come, come, come!
WIFE. The fault is mine. I had my joyous season,
My season of full ripening and fruit

And then the silence and the aching breast.
I thought I would have children. I was wrong,
But my flesh aches to think I do not have them.
I did not mean to speak of this at all.
I do not speak of it. I will be good.
There is much left—so much.
The kindness and the bond that lasts the years
And all the small and treasurable things
That make up life and living. Do not care
So much. I have forgotten. I'll sing softly,
Not sing at all. It was long past and gone.
Tell me your news. Is it good news?

INNKEEPER [*Eagerly*]. The best!
The prefect comes to dinner here tonight
With all his officers—oh yes, I know,
The enemy—of course, the enemy—
But someone has to feed them.

WIFE. And they'll pay?

INNKEEPER. Cash.

WIFE. On the nail?

INNKEEPER. Yes.

WIFE. Good.

INNKEEPER. I thought you'd say so.
Oh, we'll make no great profit—not tonight—
I've seen the bill of fare they asked of me,
Quails, in midwinter! Well, we'll give them—quails!
And charge them for them, too! You know the trick?

WIFE. Yes.

INNKEEPER. They must be well served. I'll care for that.
The honest innkeeper, the thoughtful man,
Asking, "Your worship, pray another glass
Of our poor wine! Your worship, is the roast
Done to your worship's taste? Oh, nay, nay, nay,
Your worship, all was settled in the bill,
So do not spoil my servants with largesse,
Your worship!"—And he won't. He pinches pennies.
But, once he's come here, he will come again,
And we shall live, not die, and put some coin,

Some solid, enemy and lovely coin
Under the hearthstone, eh?
Spoil the Egyptians, eh?
[*He laughs*]
That's my war and my battle and my faith.
The war of every sane and solid man
And, even if we have no child to follow us,
It shall be won, I tell you!
[*There is a knock at the outer door*]
Hark! What's that?
I'll go—the maids aren't up yet—lazybones!
[*The knock is repeated, imperatively*]

INNKEEPER [*Grumbling*]. A minute—just a minute!
It's early yet—you needn't beat the door down.
This is an honest inn.
[*He shoots the bolts and opens the door, while speaking*]
Good morning.

SOLDIER'S VOICE. Hail Caesar! Are you the keeper of this inn?

INNKEEPER. Yes, sir.

SOLDIER. Orders from the prefect. No other guests shall be entertained
at your inn tonight after sundown. The prefect wishes all the
rooms to be at the disposal of his guests.

INNKEEPER. All the rooms?

SOLDIER. You understand plain Latin, don't you?

INNKEEPER. Yes, sir, but—

SOLDIER, Well?

INNKEEPER. Sir, when the prefect first commanded me,
There was a party of my countrymen
Engaged for a small room—he'd hear no noise—
No noise at all—

SOLDIER. This is the prefect's feast—the Saturnalia—
You've heard your orders.

INNKEEPER. Yes, sir. Yes, indeed, sir.

SOLDIERS. See they are carried out! No other guests! Hail Caesar!

INNKEEPER [*Feebly*]. Hail Caesar!
[*He slams the door*]
Well, that's pleasant.
All rooms at the disposal of the prefect!

No other guests! I'll have to warn Ben Ezra.
But he's a sound man—he will understand.
We'll cook his mutton here and send it to him.
And the wine, too—a bottle of good wine—
The second best and let the prefect pay for it!
That will make up. No other guests. Remember,
No other guests!
WIFE. I will remember.
INNKEEPER. Do so.
   It is an order. Now, about the quail.
   You'll make the sauce. That's the important thing.
   A crow can taste like quail, with a good sauce.
   You have your herbs?
WIFE. Yes.
INNKEEPER. Well then, begin, begin!
   It's morning and we haven't too much time
   And the day's bitter cold. Well, all the better.
   They'll drink the more but—all this work to do
   And the fire barely started! Sarah! Leah!
   Where are those lazy servants? Where's the fish?
   Where's the new bread? Why haven't we begun?
   Leah and Sarah, come and help your mistress!
   I'll rouse the fools! There's work to do today!
      [*He stamps up the stairs. She moves about her business*]
WIFE [*Singing*]. In Bethlehem of Judea
   There was an inn also.
   There was no room within it
   For any but the foe.

   No child might be born there.
   No bud come to bloom
   For there was no chamber
   And there was no room.
      [*Her voice fades off into music which swells up and down*]
NARRATOR. And the day passed and night fell on the town,
   Silent and still and cold. The houses lay
   Huddled and dark beneath the watching stars
   And only the inn windows streamed with light—

[*Fade into offstage noise of a big party going on upstairs*]

FIRST VOICE [*Offstage*]. Ha, ha, ha! And then the Cilician said to the Ethiopian. He said—

SECOND VOICE [*Offstage*]. Well, I remember when we first took over Macedonia. There was a girl there—

THIRD VOICE [*Offstage*]. Quiet, gentlemen, quiet—the prefect wishes to say a few words—

PREFECT [*Off*]. Gentlemen—men of Rome—mindful of Rome's historic destiny—and of our good friend King Herod—who has chosen alliance with Rome rather than a useless struggle—keep them under with a firm hand—

SARAH. What is he saying up there?

LEAH. I don't know.

I don't know the big words. The soldier said—

SARAH. You and your soldier!

LEAH. Oh, he's not so bad.

He brought me a trinket—see!

SARAH. You and your Roman trinkets! I hate serving them.

I'd like to spit in their cups each time I serve them.

LEAH. You wouldn't dare!

SARAH. Wouldn't I, though?

[*There are steps on the stairs as the innkeeper comes down*]

INNKEEPER. Here, here,

What's this, what's this, why are you standing idle?

They're calling for more wine!

SARAH. Let Leah serve them.

She likes their looks!

WIFE. Sarah!

SARAH [*Sighs*]. Yes, mistress.

WIFE. Please, Sarah—we've talked like this so many times.

SARAH. Very well, mistress. But let her go first.

[*To Leah*]

Get up the stairs, you little soldier's comfort!

I hope he pinches you!

LEAH. Mistress, it's not my fault. Does Sarah have to—

WIFE. Oh, go, go—both of you!

[*They mutter and go upstairs*]

INNKEEPER. Well, that's a pretty little tempest for you.

You ought to beat the girl. She's insolent
And shows it.

WIFE. We can't be too hard on her.
Her father's dead, her brother's in the hills,
And yet she used to be a merry child.
I can remember her when she was merry,
A long time since.

INNKEEPER. You always take their side
And yet, you'd think a self-respecting inn
Could have some decent and well-mannered maids!
But no such luck—sullens and sluts, the lot of them!
Give me a stool—I'm tired.
    [*He sits muttering*]
Say thirty dinners
And double for the prefect—and the wine—
Best, second best and common—h'm not bad
But then—
    [*Suddenly*]
Why do you sit there, staring at the fire,
So silent and so waiting and so still?
    [*Unearthly music, very faint at first, begins with the next
    speech and builds through the scene*]

WIFE. I do not know. I'm waiting.

INNKEEPER. Waiting for what?

WIFE. I do not know. For something new and strange,
Something I've dreamt about in some deep sleep,
Truer than any waking,
Heard about, long ago, so long ago,
In sunshine and the summer grass of childhood,
When the sky seems so near.
I do not know its shape, its will, its purpose
And yet all day its will has been upon me,
More real than any voice I ever heard,
More real than yours or mine or our dead child's,
More real than all the voices there upstairs,
Brawling above their cups, more real than light.
And there is light in it and fire and peace,
Newness of heart and strangeness like a sword,

And all my body trembles under it,
And yet I do not know.
INNKEEPER. You're tired, my dear.
Well, we shall sleep soon.
WIFE. No, I am not tired.
I am expectant as a runner is
Before a race, a child before a feast day,
A woman at the gates of life and death,
Expectant for us all, for all of us
Who live and suffer on this little earth
With such small brotherhood. Something begins.
Something is full of change and sparkling stars,
Something is loosed that changes all the world.

[*Music up and down*]

And yet—I cannot read it yet. I wait
And strive—and cannot find it.
[*A knock at the door*]
Hark? What's that?
INNKEEPER. They can't come in. I don't care who they are.
We have no room.
[*Knock is repeated*]
WIFE. Go to the door!
[*He goes and opens the door*]
INNKEEPER. Well?
[*Strain of music*]
JOSEPH [*From outside*]. Is this the inn? Sir, we are travelers,
And it is late and cold. May we enter?
WIFE [*Eagerly*]. Who is it?
INNKEEPER [*To her*]. Just a pair of country people,
A woman and a man. I'm sorry for them
But—
JOSEPH. My wife and I are weary,
May we come in?
INNKEEPER. I'm sorry, my good man.
We have no room tonight. The prefect's orders.
JOSEPH. No room at all?
INNKEEPER. Now, now, it's not my fault.

You look like honest and well-meaning folk
And nobody likes turning trade away
But I'm not my own master. Not tonight.
It may be, in the morning—
    [*He starts to close the door*]
WIFE. Wait!
INNKEEPER [*In a fierce whisper*]. Must you mix in this?
WIFE. Wait!
    [*She goes to the door*]
Good sir, the enemy are in our house
And we—
    [*She sees the Virgin, who does not speak throughout this scene
    but is represented by music*]
Oh.
    [*Music*]
    [*Haltingly*]. I—did not see your wife. I did not know.
JOSEPH [*Simply*]. Her name is Mary. She is near her time.
WIFE. Yes. Yes.
    [*To the innkeeper*]
Go—get a lantern.
Quickly!
INNKEEPER. What?
WIFE. *Quickly!*
    [*To Joseph and Mary*]
I—I once had a child.
We have no room. That's true.
And it would not be right. Not here. Not now.
Not with those men whose voices you can hear,
Voices of death and iron.—King Herod's voices.
Better the friendly beasts. What am I saying?
There is—we have a stable at the inn,
Safe from the cold, at least—and, if you choose,
You shall be very welcome. It is poor
But the poor share the poor their crumbs of bread
Out of God's hand, so gladly,
And that may count for something. Will you share it?
JOSEPH. Gladly and with great joy.
WIFE. The lantern, husband!

JOSEPH. Nay, I will take it. I can see the path.
Come!

[*Music up. Joseph and Mary go. Innkeeper and wife watch them*]

INNKEEPER [*To wife*]. Well, I suppose that you must have your way
And, any other night—They're decent people
Or seem to be—
WIFE. He has his arm about her, smoothing out
The roughness of the path for her.
INNKEEPER.—Although
They are not even people of our town,
As I suppose you know—
WIFE. So rough a path to tread with weary feet!
INNKEEPER. Come in.
[*He shivers*]
Brr, there's a frost upon the air tonight.
I'm cold or—yes, I must be cold. That's it.
That's it, now, to be sure. Come, shut the door.
WIFE. Something begins, begins;
Starlit and sunlit, something walks abroad
In flesh and spirit and fire.
Something is loosed to change the shaken world.

[*Music up and down. A bell strikes the hour*]

NARRATOR. The night deepens. The stars march in the sky.
The prefect's men are gone. The inn is quiet
Save for the sleepy servants and their mistress,
Who clean the last soiled pots.
The innkeeper drowses before the fire.
But, in the street, outside—

[*Music changing into a shepherd's carol*]

FIRST SHEPHERD. As we poor shepherds watched by night,
CHORUS. With a hey, with a ho.
FIRST SHEPHERD. A star shone over us so bright,
We left our flocks to seek its light,

CHORUS. In excelsis Deo,
    Gloria, gloria,
    In excelsis Deo.
FIRST SHEPHERD. We left our silly sheep to stray,
CHORUS. With a hey, with a ho.
FIRST SHEPHERD. They'll think us no good shepherds, they.
    And yet we came a blessed way,
CHORUS. In excelsis Deo,
    Gloria, gloria,
    In excelsis Deo.
FIRST SHEPHERD. Now how may such a matter be?
CHORUS. With a hey, with a ho.
FIRST SHEPHERD. That we of earth, poor shepherds we,
    May look on Jesu's majesty?
    And yet the star says—"It is He!"
SECOND SHEPHERD. It is He!
THIRD SHEPHERD. It is He!
CHORUS. Sing excelsis Deo!
    Gloria, gloria
    In excelsis Deo!
SARAH. Who sings so late? How can they sing so late?
LEAH. I'll go and see.
    Wait—I'll rub the windowpane.
    It's rimed with frost.
    [*She looks out*]
    They're shepherds from the hills.
WIFE. Shepherds?
LEAH. Yes, mistress. They have crooks and staves.
    Their tattered cloaks are ragged on their backs.
    Their hands are blue and stinging with the cold
    And yet they all seem drunken, not with wine
    But with good news. Their faces shine with it.
WIFE. Cold—and so late. Poor creatures—call them in.
    The prefect's men are gone.
LEAH. Aye, but—the master—
WIFE. He's dozing. Do as I tell you.
   LEAH [*Calling out*]. Come in—come in—tarry awhile and rest!

SHEPHERDS [*Joyously*]. We cannot stay. We ollow the bright star.
Gloria, gloria
In excelsis Deo!
WIFE. Where did they go? Would they not stay with us?
Not one?
LEAH. Mistress, they did not even look on me.
They looked ahead. They have gone toward the stable,
The stable of our inn.
LEAH [*Excitedly*]. Aye—gone but—Mistress! Mistress!
Do you hear?
WIFE. Hear what?
LEAH. The tread of steeds on the hard ground,
Iron-hoofed, ringing clear—a company
That comes from out the East. I've never seen
Such things. I am afraid. These are great lords,
Great kings, with strange and memorable beasts,
And crowns upon their heads!
INNKEEPER [*Waking*]. What's that? What's that?
Lords, nobles, kings, here in Bethlehem,
In our poor town? What fortune! O, what fortune!
Stand from the window there, you silly girl,
I'll speak to them!
[*He calls out*]
My gracious noble masters,
Worthy and mighty kings! Our humble inn
Is honored by your high nobility!
Come in—come in—we've fire and beds and wine!
Come in—come in—tarry awhile and rest!
KINGS' VOICES [*Joyfully*]. We cannot stay! We follow the bright star!
Gloria, gloria
In excelsis Deo!
INNKEEPER. I do not understand it. They are gone.
They did not even look at me or pause
Though there's no other inn.
They follow the poor shepherds to the stable.
WIFE. They would not tarry with us—no, not one.
INNKEEPER. And yet—
WIFE. Peace, husband. You know well enough

Why none would tarry with us.
And so do I. I lay awhile in sleep
And a voice said to me, "Gloria, gloria,
Gloria in excelsis Deo.
The child is born, the child, the child is born!"
And yet I did not rise and go to him,
Though I had waited and expected long,
For I was jealous that my child should die
And her child live.
And so—I have my judgment. And it is just.

INNKEEPER. Dreams.

WIFE. Were they dreams, the shepherds and the kings?
Is it a dream, this glory that we feel
Streaming upon us—and yet not for us.

LEAH. Now, mistress, mistress, 'tis my fault not yours.
You told me seek the strangers in the stable
And see they had all care but I—forgot.

SARAH. Kissing your soldier!

LEAH. Sarah!

SARAH. I am sorry, Leah.
My tongue's too sharp. Mistress, the fault was mine.
You told me also and I well remembered
Yet did not go.

WIFE. Sarah.

SARAH. I did not go.
Brooding on mine own wrongs, I did not go.
It was my fault.

INNKEEPER. If there was any fault, wife, it was mine.
I did not wish to turn them from my door
And yet—I know I love the chink of money,
Love it too well, the good, sound, thumping coin,
Love it—oh, God, since I am speaking truth,
Better than wife or fire or chick or child,
Better than country, better than good fame,
Would sell my people for it in the street,
Oh, for a price—but sell them.
And there are many like me. And God pity us.

WIFE. God pity us indeed, for we are human,

And do not always see
The vision when it comes, the shining change,
Or, if we see it, do not follow it,
Because it is too hard, too strange, too new.
Too unbelievable, too difficult,
Warring too much with common, easy ways,
And now I know this, standing in this light,
Who have been half alive these many years,
Brooding on my own sorrow, my own pain,
Saying "I am a barren bough. Expect
Nor fruit nor blossom from a barren bough."
Life is not lost by dying! Life is lost
Minute by minute, day by dragging day,
In all the thousand, small, uncaring ways,
The smooth appeasing compromises of time,
Which are King Herod and King Herod's men,
Always and always. Life can be
Lost without vision but not lost by death,
Lost by not caring, willing, going on
Beyond the ragged edge of fortitude
To something more—something no man has seen.
You who love money, you who love yourself,
You who love bitterness, and I, who loved
And lost and thought I could not love again,
And all the people of this little town,
Rise up! The loves we had were not enough.
Something is loosed to change the shaken world,
And with it we must change!
        [*The voice of Dismas, the thief, breaking in . . . A rather quiz-
        zical, independent voice*]
DISMAS. Now that's well said!
INNKEEPER. Who speaks there? Who are you?
DISMAS. Who? Oh, my name is Dismas. I'm a thief.
        You know the starved, flea-bitten sort of boy
        Who haunts dark alleyways in any town,
        Sleeps on a fruit sack, runs from the police,
        Begs what he can and—borrows what he must.
        That's me!

INNKEEPER. How did you get here?

DISMAS. By the door, innkeeeper,
   The cellar door. The lock upon it's old.
   I could pick locks like that when I was five.

INNKEEPER. What have you taken?

DISMAS. Nothing.
   I tried the stable first—and then your cellar,
   Slipped in, crept up, rolled underneath a bench,
   While all your honest backs were turned—and then—

WIFE. And then?

DISMAS. Well—something happened. I don't know what.
   I didn't see your shepherds or your kings,
   But, in the stable, I did see the child,
   Just through a crack in the boards—one moment's space.
   That's all that I can tell you.
      [*Passionately*]
   Is he for me as well? Is he for me?

WIFE. For you as well.

DISMAS. Is he for all of us?
   There are so many of us, worthy mistress,
   Beggars who show their sores and ask for alms,
   Women who cough their lungs out in the cold,
   Slaves—oh, I've been one!—thieves and runagates
   Who knife each other for a bite of bread,
   Having no other way to get the bread,
   —The vast sea of the wretched and the poor,
   Whose murmur comes so faintly to your ears
   In this fine country.
   Has he come to all of us
   Or just to you?

WIFE. To every man alive.

DISMAS. I wish I could believe.

SARAH [*Scornfully*]. And, if you did,
   No doubt you'd give up thieving!

DISMAS. Gently, lady, gently.
   Thieving's my trade—the only trade I know.
   But, if it were true,
   If he had really come to all of us—

I say, to all of us—
Then, honest man or thief,
I'd hang upon a cross for him!
[*A shocked pause. The others mutter*]
Would *you?*
[*Another pause*]
I see that I've said something you don't like,
Something uncouth and bold and terrifying,
And yet, I'll tell you this:
It won't be till each one of us is willing,
Not you, not me, but every one of us,
To hang upon a cross for every man
Who suffers, starves and dies,
Fight his sore battles as they were our own,
And help him from the darkness and the mire,
That there will be no crosses and no tyrants,
No Herods and no slaves.
[*Another pause*]
Well, it was pleasant, thinking things might be so.
And so I'll say farewell. I've taken nothing.
And he was a fair child to look on.
WIFE. Wait!
DISMAS. Why? What is it you see there, by the window?
WIFE. The dawn, the common day,
The ordinary, poor and mortal day.
The shepherds and the kings have gone away.
The great angelic visitors are gone.
He is alone. He must not be alone.
INNKEEPER. I do not understand you, wife.
DISMAS. Nor I.
WIFE. Do you not see, because I see at last?
Dismas, the thief, is right.
He comes to all of us or comes to none.
Not to my heart in joyous recompense
For what I lost—not to your heart or yours,
But to the ignorant heart of all the world,
So slow to alter, so confused with pain.
Do you not see he must not be alone?

INNKEEPER. I think that I begin to see. And yet—
WIFE. We are the earth his word must sow like wheat
  And, if it finds no earth, it cannot grow.
  We are his earth, the mortal and the dying,
  Led by no star—the sullen and the slut,
  The thief, the selfish man, the barren woman,
  Who have betrayed him once and will betray him,
  Forget his words, be great a moment's space
  Under the strokes of chance,
  And then sink back into our small affairs.
  And yet, unless *we* go, his message fails.
LEAH. Will he bring peace, will he bring brotherhood?
WIFE. He would bring peace, he would bring brotherhood
  And yet he will be mocked at in the street.
SARAH. Will he slay King Herod
  And rule us all?
WIFE. He will not slay King Herod. He will die.
  There will be other Herods, other tyrants,
  Great wars and ceaseless struggles to be free,
  Not always won.
INNKEEPER. These are sad tidings of him.
WIFE. No, no—they are glad tidings of great joy,
  Because he brings man's freedom in his hands,
  Not as a coin that may be spent or lost
  But as a living fire within the heart,
  Never quite quenched—because he brings to all,
  The thought, the wish, the dream of brotherhood,
  Never and never to be wholly lost,
  The water and the bread of the oppressed,
  The stay and succor of the resolute,
  The harness of the valiant and the brave,
  The new word that has changed the shaken world.
  And, though he die, his word shall grow like wheat
  And every time a child is born,
  In pain and love and freedom hardly won,
  Born and gone forth to help and aid mankind,
  There will be women with a right to say

"Gloria, gloria in excelsis Deo!
A child is born!"

SARAH. Gloria!

LEAH. Gloria!

WIFE. Come, let us go. What can we bring to him?
What mortal gifts?

LEAH [*Shyly*]. I have a ribbon. It's my prettiest.
It is not much but—he might play with it.

SARAH. I have a little bell my father gave me.
It used to make me merry. I have kept it.
I—he may have it.

DISMAS. My pocket's empty and my rags are bare.
But I can sing to him. That's what I'll do
And—if he needs a thief to die for him—

INNKEEPER. I would give all my gold.
I will give my heart.

WIFE. And I my faith through all the years and years,
Though I forget, though I am led astray,
Though after this I never see his face,
I will give all my faith.
Come, let us go,
We, the poor earth, but we, the faithful earth,
Not yet the joyful, not yet the triumphant,
But faithful, faithful, through the mortal years!
Come!
      [*Music begins*]

DISMAS [*Sings*]. Come, all ye faithful.

INNKEEPER. Joyful and triumphant.

WOMEN. Come ye, O come ye to Bethlehem!

      [*Their voices rise in chorus in "Come, all ye faithful." The
      chorus and the music swell*]

THE HALLS OF
CONGRESS

Edited by Joseph Gottlieb

E ACH SUNDAY afternoon, on WMCA, New York—a nonnetwork station —*The Halls of Congress* presents reenactments of important legislative debate of the week, taken directly from the Congressional Record. The Congressional Record is reputed to be dull but this series has proved otherwise. Many kinds of drama—from the drama of world events to the drama of personality conflicts—are combined in *The Halls of Congress*. As edited and produced by Joseph Gottlieb, with dramatic skill and an appreciation of his editorial responsibility, *The Halls of Congress* makes exciting listening. Launched late in 1944 as a sustaining "public service" series, it was quickly taken over for sponsorship by the Harman Watch Company. The series is not only helping listeners keep abreast of important issues, and giving them a vivid weekly report on what their senators and representatives are doing, but—even more important—it is giving many people for the first time a picture of how Congress functions.

WHA, Madison, Wisconsin, has for some years broadcast a series along the same lines. Other stations have started similar programs. Audiences throughout the country may in time hear series like *The Halls of Congress*.

It is possible, however, that such a development will meet with opposition; this is indicated by the background of this series.

Nathan Straus, president of WMCA, at first proposed broadcasting actual proceedings from the floor of the House and Senate. When he purchased WMCA in 1943, he at once tried, unsuccessfully, to get permission for such broadcasts. He has announced that WMCA will begin broadcasting sessions of Congress as soon as permission is obtained.

In a letter to Senator Claude Pepper of Florida, urging passage of his joint resolution to open Congressional proceedings to the microphone, Nathan Straus wrote: "I am convinced of the importance of bringing congressional debate to radio listeners. In fact, one of the first things I did on becoming associated with Station WMCA was to make a trip to Washington to explore that possibility. Discussion of the matter at that time with several of the leading members of the House of Representatives gave me little encouragement.

"I was told that it would not be feasible to broadcast congressional debate for two reasons. It was alleged, in the first place, that the installation of microphones in the Chamber would make the private conversations of members audible to radio listeners. I pointed out, in reply, that a switch at each seat would enable the member to disconnect his microphone until he arose to address the house. Therefore, the argument that the installation of radio equipment would violate the privacy of conversation and consultation in the Chamber had no basis in fact.

"Thereupon the second objection was advanced. It was claimed that, as it would be impossible to broadcast all congressional debate, the incompleteness of what the radio audience would hear might convey a false or misleading impression. Again the argument seems to have little validity. If it were sound it would apply with equal force to the printing in the daily papers of quotations of part of speeches of members of Congress. To require that a newspaper print congressional proceedings in their entirety if the paper quoted from the remarks of any senator or member of the House, would obviously be unreasonable. It is equally unreasonable to assert that the value of reporting congressional debate on the air-waves would be dependent on broadcasting the complete proceedings of the day.

"There is, in fact, no valid argument against the resolution which you have introduced. There is no justification for excluding from the radio arguments on which legislators base their decisions. To assert the contrary or to set up hollow objections to the broadcasting of congressional debate is, inevitably, to give enemies of the democratic process the opportunity to say that there is something to conceal, that members of Congress make statements that they would prefer not to have heard by the people. I believe that there is no bad thing that is not helped and no good thing that is not made better by letting in the daylight. Public opinion is a great curative force in a democracy.

"To broadcast the proceedings of Congress would raise the tone of congressional debate and would immeasurably increase public interest in, and understanding of, the processes of government. Radio can perform no greater service than this: To bring the deliberations of those who make our laws and guide our national destiny into every American home."

The ideal way to present a program on the pattern of *The Halls of Congress* is to put it together from recordings of the actual debate. Until Congressional approval makes that possible, *The Halls of Congress* performs one of radio's most valuable current services.

At the 1945 meeting of the Institute for Education by Radio at Columbus, Ohio, Nathan Straus won the Edward L. Bernays Radio Award as the "individual who did most in radio to further democracy in America during the last year."

Joseph Gottlieb was born in Philadelphia and attended the University of Pennsylvania. After some dabbling in playwrighting, a friend suggested radio. Gottlieb's first try was a script entitled *The Broadcast of Opinions,* in which he took a subject in the headlines and dramatized various aspects of it. It was accepted by WCAU, Philadelphia. Gottlieb then went to work for that station, remaining there for eight years, and becoming a director, producer, and finally assistant program director. The desire to do "adult" programs in radio has been with him constantly. Network audiences have heard two of his plays on the *Columbia Workshop*. He feels: "The networks do some magnificent things but nullify their effect by airing them at unsalable hours." His enthusiasm for WMCA, where he feels public service is a matter of first importance to the management, is a heart-warming thing in a field of many frustrations.

This episode of *The Halls of Congress* was broadcast March 18, 1945.

THE HALLS OF

CONGRESS

[*Voices up. Gavel bangs twice. Voices continue in background*]
VOICE 1. Mr. Speaker, I ask unanimous consent . . .
VOICE 2. The gentleman is not in order.
[*Gavel*]
VOICE 1. Mr. Speaker! Mr. Speaker!
[*Gavel*]
Will the gentlemen yield?

[*Music up and out*]

ANNOUNCER. THE HALLS OF CONGRESS!

[*Music: Theme up and down under*]

Each week at this time, WMCA takes its listeners to a front-row
seat in the galleries of the Halls of Congress, as dramatic mo-
ments of the past week of Congressional debate are re-enacted,
thus providing for you a living picture of your Congress in action
. . . This week you will hear . . . a Senate debate on the pro-
posed Missouri Valley Authority!
[*Chord*]
The House debate extension of the Lend-Lease Act.
[*Chord*]
New York Representative Powell's and Representative Rankin's
speeches on the FEPC.
[*Chord*]
And—a report on the new Declaration of Chapultepec. All the
dialogue is taken directly from the Congressional Record for . . .
The Halls of Congress!

[*Music: Theme play-off*]

NARRATOR. On Monday, in the Senate, the proposed Missouri Valley Authority was the subject of a heated debate. The project, based on the Tennessee Valley Authority, had been presented to the last Congress, some months ago. At that time the Senate defeated an amendment to the planned MVA, sponsored by Senator Bailey, Democrat from North Carolina, which would have turned over all power produced at government dams to private utilities. The MVA measure was then sent to the commerce committee, of which Senator Bailey is the chairman. The debate on Monday was introduced by a speech by Senator Murray, Democrat from Montana, in which he endeavored to have the bill transferred to the Senate Agriculture Committee. To do this would require a majority vote of the upper House . . . Senator Murray stated . . .

MURRAY. Ever since the successful inauguration of the TVA in 1933, measures proposing legislation of this character have been uniformly referred to the Committee on Agriculture. If this were the first time such a measure had come before the Senate, and I had the wisdom and the vision to invent this new device for river development, I should have felt impelled to request that the bill be referred to the Committee on Agriculture rather than any other of the several committees of the Senate whose claims for jurisdiction could plausibly be presented.

[*Voices up, fade for narrator*]

NARRATOR. Senator Murray, continuing his speech, declared that he felt that the Chair, namely, Vice-President Truman, had been in error in submitting the Missouri Valley Administration Bill to the commerce committee. He cited the similarity between his bill and the TVA . . . and showed that the Committee on Agriculture had had jurisdiction over the TVA. He concluded . . .

MURRAY. Mr. President. It seems to me that when we have followed a course of procedure for 25 years and legislation of this character has been uniformly referred to the Committee on Agriculture, there is no basis whatsoever, for undertaking to take the bill out of the jurisdiction of that committee. I make that statement especially in view of the fact that it is apparent that the commerce committee has a philosophy with reference to public power which is not in accordance with the philosophy of most of us in the country. We believe that in the development of public power the benefits derived from it should be given to the people and not to the big power corporations of the United States.

[*Voices*]

It seems to me that disagreement with that belief forms the sole basis of the effort to get this bill away from the Committee on Agriculture. Agriculture has demonstrated its sympathy with the national policy which is in force. It has had experience with the subject and I think the bill should be referred to it.

[*Voices up* . . . *Hold through narrator*]

NARRATOR. Senator Bailey, Democrat from North Carolina, chairman of the Committee on Commerce, obtained the floor.

BAILEY. Mr. President, the Senator from Montana rather astonished me by saying that he thought the purpose of having the bill referred to the Committee on Commerce related to some power policy, and had the objective of stating one policy and framing another. That is a rather severe reflection upon the Vice-President of the United States.

[*Voices* . . . *Hold briefly, then fade*]

I shall not discuss the power policy: I do not care to involve it here: but I will say that such policy as we have in this country in respect to the sale of power, such policy as we have with respect to irrigation, to dams and the production of electrical energy has proceeded from the Committee on Commerce, and been approved by the House and the Senate and the President of the United States. So I think that is enough to say in defense of the Committee on Commerce, and, so far as I am concerned, I do not intend to defend it.

[*Voices* . . . *Up and fade*]

I think the Vice-President acted properly in referring the bill. If the title of the bill is to be relied upon, the two most prominent features and purposes of the bill are the promotion of navigation and the development of water control. Of course that means dams and other means, in the interest of the control and prevention of floods. So the bill on its face and by way of its title, which I suppose was written by its author, the junior senator from Montana, declares it to be within the jurisdiction of the commerce committee. Yet the Senator comes before the Senate and protests and makes a special plea on the basis of precedents with respect to the TVA.

MURRAY. Mr. President, will the Senator yield?

[*Voices . . . Hold through narrator*]

BAILEY. Certainly.

NARRATOR. Senator Murray rose to reply to Senator Bailey.

MURRAY. Does not the Senator recognize that the title has a much broader application than the Senator has indicated? The title says to provide for unified water control and resource development on the Missouri River and surrounding region.

BAILEY. Oh, yes. I was just reading the title.

MURRAY. But if the Senator will read the bill itself he will find section after section and page after page which indicate that the main purpose of the bill is the development of the entire region of the Missouri Valley.

BAILEY. I have read the bill, but I am saying to the Senator, and I want him to hear me, that a Senator who introduces a bill in the Senate is supposed to state its purpose in its title.

MURRAY. Yes.

BAILEY. I have read the title. It may be read any way one wishes to, and one may crawl in any direction, but when it is all said and done, here is the declaration in the very title of the bill: "To establish a Missouri Valley Authority." That is there. You may talk about it all you please: but when you get through it is there. "The moving finger . . . having writ" . . . you cannot change a word of it. Does the Senator wish to say anything more?

MURRAY. Yes, if the Senator will yield.

BAILEY. I yield.

MURRAY. The title of the bill is broad enough to cover all the provisions of the bill, because it states that it is "to provide for unified control and resource development on the Missouri River and surrounding region . . . the great purpose and object—"

BAILEY. Mr. President, I did not yield to the Senator for a speech.

[*Voices . . . Mixed laughter*]

AIKIN. Mr. President.

PRESIDING OFFICER. Does the Senator from North Carolina yield to the Senator from Vermont?

BAILEY. Let me answer the Senator from Montana . . . I have read the title of the bill, as written, I presume, by its author: and I stand upon it. Of course I know it takes in more territory. It takes in the general welfare, the national defense, and I suppose the Kingdom of God as well. . . .
[*Slight stir of voices*]
That is not the test. The test is what he wrote by way of interpreting his bill to start with. That is on the threshold of the argument.
[*Voices up . . . Hold through narrator*]
AIKIN. Mr. President, will the Senator yield?
BAILEY. I yield.
NARRATOR. Senator Aikin, Republican from Vermont.
AIKIN. Does not the Tennessee Valley Authority act refer to control of floods and improvement of navigation also?
BAILEY. Yes, I am coming to that.
AIKIN. Those bills have all been referred to the Committee on Agriculture.
BAILEY. I was just coming to that. The TVA began as a scheme to supply the farmers with fertilizer, after having been abandoned as a scheme to create nitrates for munitions. So naturally and reasonably, the TVA and the legislation which followed through the years, was handled by the Committee on Agriculture, largely through the insistence of the late Senator George Norris, a very able man and a man with whom the Senate liked to agree. He was old and he was honest. None of us liked to disappoint him about anything. He insisted, that having begun with the Committee on Agriculture as a fertilizer enterprise, it should remain there. So I consider the TVA as no precedent at all. It is an isolated instance.
MURRAY. Mr. President, will the Senator yield?
BAILEY. I will yield for a question. I do not wish to stand here and hear the Senator read the Congressional Record.
[*Voices . . . Hold through narrator*]
NARRATOR. Senator Murray returned to the debate.
MURRAY. I wish to call the Senator's attention to the fact that the bill which we have before us today is like the bill to which Senator Norris was referring in the debate which took place on the

floor of the Senate on June 3, 1937, when the question of appropriate reference of that bill was under consideration.

BAILEY. I understand the Senator's position. That is an illustration in logic from Montana . . . Because this bill is like the bill which created the Tennessee Valley Authority, it must go the same way. I was just showing how the TVA started. If this bill had started as a fertilizer proposal, the Senator would have some basis for his reasoning.

MURRAY. Let me interrupt the Senator for a moment. This bill does contemplate the development of fertilizer on a large scale.

BAILEY. I want to keep the Senator's mind on the ball.

MURRAY. I have my mind on the ball . . . The senator entirely misconstrues my argument. I do say that when the Committee on Agriculture has for 25 years been handling this sort of legislation, we should not deprive the Senate of the benefit of the experience which the committee has had.

[*Music: Transition, up and fade*]

NARRATOR. The Senate had no opportunity that day to vote on the matter of committee jurisdiction. Debate was interrupted by the presiding officer.

PRESIDING OFFICER. The morning hour having expired, and the consideration of the pending resolution not having been concluded, under the precedents it will be placed on the calendar.

BAILEY. Then we cannot vote on the resolution today?

PRESIDING OFFICER. The resolution goes to the calendar.

[*Music: Play-off up and fade*]

NARRATOR. On Thursday Senator Barkley introduced a resolution to change the reference of the Missouri Valley Authority bill with respect to its submission to committee for study. Approved by the Senate was that three committees should receive it . . . The Committee on Commerce, the Committee on Irrigation and Reclamation, and the Committee on Agriculture.

[*Music: Play-off up and out*]

The Declaration of Chapultepec, a document on stronger ties for nations of the Western Hemisphere, signed in Mexico City on the third of March, received the attention of the House of Representatives on Tuesday of this week. Representative McCormack, Democrat from Massachusetts, addressed the House on the significance of this most important declaration.

MCCORMACK. Mr. Speaker, the Declaration of Chapultepec is a step of the highest significance in the history of inter-American relations. The immediate effect of this declaration is to provide, for the duration of the war, a mechanism whereby the American republics signatory thereto can take effective action against any aggression or threat of aggression against one of the American republics. The declaration provides that, in the event any aggression occurs, or even if good reason exists that such aggression is in preparation, the countries signing this declaration will consult with each other in order to decide what measures they consider advisable to take.

[*Voices up briefly, fade as he resumes*]

On the just grounds that any disruption of the peace among the nations of this hemisphere would constitute a blow to the war interests of the United Nations, to which all the signatory states belong, the Declaration of Chapultepec becomes effective immediately.

[*Voices*]

For the future, the declaration recommends that the American republics enter into a treaty which will formally establish these procedures and continue to be effective after the war. In this declaration we find expressions of the truth that the cause of peace is of equal concern to every nation, large and small. Adoption of this enlightened international agreement emphasizes the leadership which the American republics as a whole have given to the cause of world peace. The United States, as the most powerful of the American republics, has had a special rule and responsibility in the development of the inter-American system. Because of its strength, this country has in the past been feared by some of its smaller and less powerful neighbors. Through our consistent adherence to the good neighbor policy, however, it has been possible for us to convince our friends to the south that the American people are devoted to the same principles of peace and of mutual respect among nations as they are.

[*Voices*]

The enthusiastic formulation of the Declaration of Chapultepec whereby the United States as one of the republics signing that act, is given a necessarily large share of the responsibility for the preservation of the peace in this Hemisphere, by the use of force if necessary, demonstrates that we have been able to win the confidence of our neighbors. . . .

[*Voices*]

MCCORMACK. The American people will welcome the Declaration of Chapultepec as a profound expression of good neighborly confidence and cooperation, and as an indication of the determination of the peoples of the new world to play their part in building a lasting peace on just principles.

[*Music: Play-off up and fade*]

NARRATOR. Thus did Representative McCormack, majority leader in the House, communicate to the lower house an important step in wartime relations among all the nations of the western hemisphere, that is building a foundation for good will in the postwar era.

[*Music: Play-off*]

NARRATOR. The Lend-Lease Act was due to expire on the first of July of this year . . . This week, in the House, representatives voted to extend Lend-Lease for an additional year, making its termination date July 1, 1946. . . . Debate centered around an amendment to the act which was introduced by the chairman of the Foreign Affairs Committee, Representative Bloom, Democrat from New York. . . .

BLOOM. Mr. Speaker, I offer a committee amendment.

[*Murmur of voices . . . Hold through narrator*]

NARRATOR. The clerk read as follows:

CLERK. "Amendment offered by Mr. Bloom: At the end of the bill insert the following new section. That nothing shall be construed to authorize the President to enter into or carry out any contract or agreement with a foreign government for post-war relief, post-war rehabilitation, or post-war reconstruction."

[*Voices briefly . . . Fade as Bloom speaks*]

BLOOM. Mr. Speaker, this amendment was agreed to unanimously by the Committee on Foreign Affairs.

NARRATOR. Representative Rich, Republican from Pennsylvania, obtained the floor.

RICH. Mr. Speaker, I rise in opposition to the amendment. I wish to confine my remarks to an amendment I expect to offer as soon as the pending amendment is disposed of. The amendment would join the Congress of the United States to the President in approving the termination of contracts of Lend-Lease with foreign governments. It seems to me the Lend-Lease was very weak in respect to the termination of the contracts made under it. It is a poor way for America to aid the war. . . . I cannot understand why the Congress of the United States has permitted the chief executive to handle all the affairs of Lend-Lease. Seems to me Congress abdicated.

[*Voices . . . Hold briefly then fade*]

It is true that he has appointed an administrator, but when it comes to the termination of these contracts, more than one or two men should enter into the discussion of how they should be settled . . . If we had a man at the head of our government who loved America as much as Mr. Churchill loves Great Britain . . .

[*No pause*] . . . or as Mr. Stalin loves Russia I would not fear so much the outcome of what happens at the termination of Lend-Lease for America to get her just dues in a final settlement.

[*Voices fade as he resumes*]

But I do not favor altogether the idea that we should permit the power to be lodged in any one man in this country, regardless of who he may be. America might be sold short.

[*Voices . . . Hold through narrator*]

NARRATOR. Representative Miller, Republican from Nebraska, spoke.

MILLER. Mr. Speaker, you know the original purpose of Lend-Lease, as rather loosely stated, was that the United States was to provide the money and material of war and our European friends were to do the fighting and dying and our participation in the war could be avoided . . . Lend-Lease was necessary. But it was not a measure to keep us out of the war. The Prime Minister of England said at one time, "Give us the tools and we will do the job." But what is the picture? We have not only given them the tools, but we are furnishing 75 or 80 per cent of the men on the fighting fronts of Europe. We are having all the casualties of the war, and how many men are we furnishing in the Pacific Theatre? Most of them. England has furnished a few down in India to police that territory. In other words, Lend-Lease did not keep us out of the war.

[*Voices . . . Hold in background*]

MCCORMACK. Mr. Speaker, will the gentleman yield?

WADSWORTH. The gentleman is against the Australians.

SPEAKER. The time of the gentleman from Nebraska has expired.

MCCORMACK. Mr. Speaker, I ask unanimous consent that the gentleman may proceed.

NARRATOR. On the motion made by Representative McCormack, Democrat from Massachusetts, Mr. Miller continued his speech.

MILLER. I am certain that the folks out in my country want the American Congress to stand up and protest most vigorously the wanton waste of our American resources without some promise of a fair return. When I came back from England I made some statements about Lend-Lease and how it was being treated. Of course, some folks in Congress and in England did not like it, and they called me by telephone and wanted me to retract some of my statements. I supported it the last time. With the large amount of money now available for Lend-Lease it is possible it can be used in such a way as to waste the resources of America and destroy our future.

BLOOM. Mr. Speaker, will the gentleman yield?

[*Murmur of voices . . . Hold in background*]

MILLER. I yield to the gentleman from New York.

NARRATOR. Representative Bloom, Democrat from New York.

BLOOM. Do I understand the gentleman to say that when he came back from England he made several statements that the British called him about?

MILLER. Yes: the British Press in New York.

BLOOM. And the gentleman resented it?

MILLER. Yes: I resented it.

BLOOM. That is an unusual thing. I am surprised that the gentleman would make a statement like that.

MILLER. May I tell you one conversation I had with a newspaperman in New York? He said: "Congressman, we were in this war two years before you were. What do you think you owe us for that?"

BLOOM. The gentleman said that a British representative asked him to retract or withdraw his statement: Is that right?

MILLER. Yes, they wanted me to withdraw the statement.

BLOOM. A British representative?

MILLER. A representative of a British newspaper.

BLOOM. That is different.

[*Voices up briefly . . . Then fade*]

MILLER. He represented the thinking of the English.

BLOOM. I would not want it to go out and have the world think that the British Government or any representative called the gentleman up.

[*Voices up . . . Hold through narrator*]

COOLEY. Mr. Speaker, will the gentleman yield?

MILLER. I yield to the gentleman from North Carolina.

NARRATOR. Representative Cooley, Democrat from North Carolina.

COOLEY. The gentleman made the statement that in this Lend-Lease program there has been wanton waste. I am wondering if the gentleman could give the House a bill of particulars and point out where this wanton waste occurred.

MILLER. I do not think that would be very hard. If the gentleman would just look around some of the ports where some of this equipment is piling up. How about the Canol project up in Canada or the Alaskan Highway? Would not the gentleman say that was wanton waste?

COOLEY. No; I do not agree with the gentleman at all.

BULWINKLE. Mr. Chairman, will the gentleman yield?

MILLER. I yield to the gentleman from North Carolina.

[*Voices . . . Hold through narrator*]

NARRATOR. Representative Bulwinkle, Democrat from North Carolina.

BULWINKLE. May I say to the gentleman that he forgets that at the time the Alaskan Highway was built, no one knew what the Japs were going to do in Alaska.

MILLER. I am not yielding for a speech.

BULWINKLE. Not for a speech, but in order to inform the gentleman as to the oil project and the other.

[*Voices . . . Hold through narrator*]

NARRATOR. Representative Flood, Democrat from Pennsylvania.

FLOOD. Mr. Speaker, it is too bad at this late hour in the debate that this question should arise. But I cannot permit any statements to be made such as were made by the gentleman from Pennsylvania, Mr. Rich, a few minutes ago. I say now, and I think I speak for everybody on both sides of the aisle, perhaps with the exception of the gentleman himself, that nobody can question the patriotism of Franklin Delano Roosevelt, the President of the United States.

[*Voices*]

RICH. Mr. Speaker, will the gentleman yield?

FLOOD. I yield to the gentleman for any purpose.

RICH. I was referring to the President of the United States as a spend-thrift, that he did not know the value of the dollar, and he was not protecting the dollars of the American taxpayer. He never has, and he never can, and he never will.

FLOOD. That is probably the best autobiographical statement I have ever heard in the house. But the record of the President stands as an example of great leadership, patriotism, sacrifice, and devotion to his country.

[*Music: Play-off up and fade*]

NARRATOR. At the conclusion of the debate, the Rich amendment was defeated, and the Bloom amendment passed. When the ayes and nays were taken on the extension of the Lend-Lease Act, the vote was "Ayes" 354, "Nays" 28 . . . one Democrat from Idaho, along with 27 Republicans, nearly all of them from the Mid-West, voted against the extension . . . Lend-Lease will operate until July 1st, 1946, as now provided by law.

[*Music: Play-off up and out*]

NARRATOR. The recent passage of the New York State Fair Employ-ment Practices Act provided the Congressional Record of this week with two speeches . . . One, on Tuesday, by Representative Rankin, Democrat from the state of Mississippi, and the other, by Representative Adam Clayton Powell, from New York . . . Mr. Rankin stated . . .

RANKIN. Mr. Speaker, on yesterday Gov. Thomas E. Dewey, using 22 pens, signed the so-called Fair Employment Practice Law, passed by the Legislature of that State, which will go down in history as the greatest betrayal of the white Americans of New York that state has ever known.

[*Voices up . . . Hold briefly then fade*]

The approval of this measure seems to have been the "hand of Esau and the voice of Jacob" . . . The people of New York had reason to expect something better from this Charlie McCarthy who now presides over that great commonwealth, but after his silly performances in the campaign last year, I am sure that many of them were not surprised.

[*Voices*]

As I said on this floor some time ago, the white Gentiles of this country still have some rights left, and should be protected from the persecutions they are now compelled to endure. If this drive continues unabated they will be driven entirely from the business world and from the professions, as well as from public life. Remember that something like 98 per cent of the men who are dying on the high seas and the battle fronts of the world to protect American institutions in this war are white Gentiles. Yet when one speaks up on their behalf on this floor, in the press, on the radio, or elsewhere, we hear the whine of "anti-Semitism," or the cry of "race prejudice."

[*Voices*]

The Communist *Daily Worker,* as well as *PM,* its uptown edition, and Earl Browder, the head of the Communist party, are now gloating over Governor Dewey's capitulation. They are saying in the words of the Holy Writ, "He came to us a stranger, and we took him in." . . . Now the Congress of the United States is asked to support this persecution of American business men throughout the country by the passage of the bill to make permanent the so-called FEPC, which has been set up here in Washington without any legal authority whatsoever, and which is devoting its time to harassing white Americans throughout the country who are trying to carry on their business affairs while their sons are fighting and dying to save this republic. If this is the kind of stuff that is going to be forced on the American people at home, I submit that we had better look into these compacts before we adopt something that might injure, if not destroy, the freedom for which these boys are now offering up their lives.

[*Voices . . . Up, then fade for narrator*]

NARRATOR. On Thursday of this week, Representative Adam Clayton Powell took the floor and addressed the House . . .

POWELL. Mr. Speaker, on the day before yesterday, March 12th, Mr. Thomas E. Dewey, "using 22 pens," signed the Fair Employment Practice Law, passed by the Legislature of the State of New York, which will go down in history as one of the greatest advances in legislation that state has ever seen. The approval of the measure came from every political, religious, social, educational and trade union group in New York State. The members of the Democratic Party voted for it 100 per cent and the vast majority of the Republican Party did likewise.

[*Voices . . . Up and Fade as he continues*]

Protestant, Catholic, and Jewish Church groups supported it whole-heartedly. In truth, it received the greatest support that any legislation has received in the history of the State of New York.

[*Murmur of Voices*]

I rise to speak today because a few un-Americans have distorted the facts concerning this act.

[*Voices up . . . Fade as he resumes*]

It is high time that we start winning the war at home as well as abroad, that we make America safe for democracy, as well as the world. It is my intention, therefore, to refute these distortions. Fortunately, there are only a few such accursed souls left in this nation. Their number is rapidly dwindling. They are the buffoons of American life, but they are still so twisted, so perverted, so vicious, so malicious, so pernicious, and so Fascist . . . that they must be revealed for their un-Americanism . . .

[*Voices up . . . Fade as he resumes*]

Any fair thinking American will respect another's point of view, even though he radically disagrees, but none of us will respect a point of view that is based upon distortions . . . The first distortion was that the New York State Fair Employment Practice Act was a betrayal of the white Americans of New York. The Senate of New York State is composed entirely of whites. And the lower house is 97 per cent white: yet those two houses virtually unanimously passed the state FEPC.

[*Voices*]

The second distortion is the use of Biblical quotations to support race hating, and other forms of anti-religious prejudice. I am a minister of the gospel. From the depths of my religious convictions I state that anyone who is vicious enough to support hatred will be dealt with by a God of vengeance and that God might use the people to execute his own wrath.

[*Voices*]

The third distortion was the statement that the object of the FEPC was to persecute white Americans and drive them from the business world. Recently three hundred employers were chosen at random by the National Urban League, for a survey. They were employers who had never used Negro workers. They now use such workers in all capacities. They were asked if they would retain Negro workers in the post-war world. Two hundred forty-two of them said that they definitely would because Negro workers are just as good as workers of any other race.

[*Voices*]

The fourth distortion stated that the white Gentiles of this country still have some rights left. This is true. Fortunately, the best thinking and, therefore, the majority of the white Gentiles of this country have consistently fought for not the right of whites only but for the rights of all Americans. Only a limited few who are vicious disgraces to the white race and any other race have continued to try to make America a stewing pot instead of a melting pot, but they failed. The fifth distortion is one of the most vicious lies ever conceived. It is stated that 98 per cent of the men who are dying in this war are white Gentiles. Over thirty million of those already killed came from two Oriental countries. The American men whose lives have been placed upon the high altar of patriotism came from every race, color and creed of our national life.

[*Voices*]

The sixth distortion is that the temporary FEPC has harassed white Americans. If it had not been for the work of the temporary FEPC, over 10 per cent of this nation would not be engaged now in turning out the material of warfare. The truth of it is the people are on the march and they are going to crush every fascist, not only in Europe and Japan, but also in America. The people—together united—aren't going to stand much longer for any rabble rousing, demagogic son of a Fascist to continue to besmirch the name of these our United States with outright, downright, filthy distortions.

[*Music: Play-off and segue to theme*]

RADIOMAN JACK COOPER

Hector Chevigny

Rᴀᴅɪᴏᴍᴀɴ Jᴀᴄᴋ Cᴏᴏᴘᴇʀ, one of the most moving programs broadcast by the Treasury Department, is the work of a gifted and versatile writer who has worked successfully in various media: books, films, short stories, radio. He has been totally blind since 1943, but has not allowed it to interfere with his writing career.

Chevigny was born in 1904 in Missoula, Montana, of French-Canadian parents. He went to Gonzaga High School in Spokane, Washington, graduated from Gonzaga University, did some graduate work at the University of Washington, then turned to professional writing. He has written two books on early Alaskan history, *Lost Empire* and *Lord of Alaska,* the latter winning the Commonwealth Award for biography in 1943. He has written stories for many magazines, and motion pictures for Warner Brothers. Most of his work, however, has been in radio.

He began as a staff writer for KOMO, Seattle, in 1928. Staff writing in radio means mass production of scripts of all types, from announcements and continuities to drama.

Chevigny estimates that he has written over five thousand broadcasts during his seventeen years of radio.

In 1936-37 he was director of the CBS Script Division in Hollywood.

Network series for which he has written include *Hollywood Hotel, Woodbury Playhouse* starring Charles Boyer, *Big Town* starring Edward G. Robinson, *Ceiling Unlimited* starring Orson Welles, *Arkansas Traveler* starring Bob Burns.

Late in 1943, suddenly and with very little warning, Chevigny lost his sight. He says: "It was one of those things everyone believes couldn't happen to him." The diagnosis was detachment of both retinas. After three months of hospitalization, and three attempts at surgery, Chevigny was discharged from New York's Eye and Ear Hospital as totally and permanently blind. He immediately undertook the study of Braille and touchtyping, and went to the famous Seeing Eye establishment at Morristown, New Jersey, to be trained in the use of Wizard, the beautiful seventy-five pound male boxer that now accompanies him everywhere and does everything but write scripts for him. He told this story in an article in *Reader's Digest,* "My Eyes Have a Cold Nose."

After a period of experimenting with new methods of work imposed on him, Chevigny took up where he had left off, with the aid of his long-time assistant, Beatrice Dal Negro. He began writing the *Treasury Salute* series for the Treasury Department in September, 1944, and has since contributed seventy-five scripts to the series.

Since the days when war bonds were still "defense bonds," the Treasury has used radio to promote their sale. Many types of programs have been used. Historical programs, often tending to the grandiose, formed a large part of the early productions. Far more effective have been the simple stories of Americans in the services, of which *Radioman Jack Cooper* is an example. These programs have been recorded, and distributed to stations throughout the country for local use. The major network stations, as a matter of principle, either do not broadcast transcriptions so widely distributed or else give them obscure time. These programs are therefore not well known to the radio industry itself. Many network executives are unaware of the fine work done on such series as *Treasury Salute*. The programs are, however, appreciated and welcomed at hundreds of local stations.

At first, the series featured heroes in the news, such as winners of the Congressional Medal. As time went on, it was found that stories about obscure people were often more effective. The Radio Section of the War Finance Division of the Treasury acquired its own research staff to find material, chiefly by talking with men returned from overseas, in such places as Walter Reed Hospital. Interestingly, it was found that only men who were themselves in uniform could successfully get from servicemen the sort of information wanted. Assigned by the armed forces to assist the Treasury in this work were T/Sgt. Norman Agathon, USA, formerly an INS correspondent, and Sgt. Jerry O'Leary, USMC. Sgt. Agathon collected the material for *Radioman Jack Cooper.*

Stories collected have generally been checked by long-distance calls to the families in their home towns, as well as through other sources.

The musical score for *Radioman Jack Cooper* was written and conducted by David Broekman. John Gibson played Jack Cooper. Paul Louis directed.

RADIOMAN JACK COOPER

COOPER. July 15 . . . Drinking sea water now . . . tell Helen I found God.

[*Music: Drum roll and into fanfare*]

ANNOUNCER. THE TREASURY SALUTE! This is a program of the United States Treasury . . . your Treasury . . . and it comes to you thanks to the millions of Americans in uniform who ask you to buy War Bonds. You salute with us a hero of this war: Radioman Jack Cooper.

[*Music: Signature . . . Fade for:*]

NARRATOR. A mother in Elkhart, Indiana, opens a little box. It has just come to her from Washington, sent by the Navy Department. It is a battered box, stained with sea water. Her hands tremble as she opens it and sees the pitiful collection of little objects inside. A compass, a piece of shrapnel, a dime, a bullet, a match case, rusty pliers, a bottle of iodine, a comb, a ring, a mirror, a religious medal. . . . These belonged to her son—they were with him when he was found, his lifeless body floating on a raft in the Central Pacific. There is one more object in the box . . . a wallet of the type that has many little isinglass facings. On these, scratched with a pin, is written a diary . . . the record of Jack Cooper's last days among the living.

[*Music: Hit chord*]

Few things in life could be harder than for a mother to read the day by day, almost hour by hour record of how her son has died. It is infinitely harder when thirst, starvation, and the agony of wounds accompany those last hours. Yet this mother, Mrs. Henry Clevenz, with rare courage said:

MRS. CLEVENZ. My son's diary is something that ordinarily neither Helen nor I would wish the world to see. Only one thing per-

suaded us to let its story be known—people have got to understand what kind of a war is being fought over there . . . what
kind of enemy our boys have to contend with. I hope it will do
its share to keep people from overconfidence.

[*Music: Hit chord*]

NARRATOR. The story begins June 15, 1944.

[*Planes wheeling and zooming, mixed with ack-ack fire*]
An American air squadron bombs a Japanese island base in the
Central Pacific. It's a tough battle—the Japs fight desperately and
it's hard getting in through the ack-ack.

[*Shift to interior of single plane as:*]
These planes left the deck of an unnamed carrier at dawn an
hour ago. One, a torpedo plane, now circles for position over
its target.

STERLING [*Filter*]. Pilot to radio. Take a look at the port wing.

COOPER [*Filter*]. They cut a piece out of it . . . shrapnel's coming up
through the floor—piece just jumped right in my hand.

GITTELSON [*Filter*]. Keep it as a souvenir.

NARRATOR. The crew comprises Ensign Theodore W. Sterling, Jr.,
son of Lt. Commander Theodore W. Sterling of Annapolis,
Maryland, Seymour Gittelson of North Adams, Massachusetts,
and Jack Cooper of Elkhart, Indiana. Cooper is radioman.

[*Plane zooming*]

STERLING [*Filter*]. Hang on—we're going downstairs to let 'em have
it.

[*Heighten plane*]

[*Music: In excitedly*]

NARRATOR. The story doesn't say if their torpedo found its mark. We
know only that the onrushing plane was shot apart in the heavy
Jap fire and that soon—

[*Heavy splash*]

[*Music: Hit chord . . . and out*]

˙Many a navy flier has experienced what followed next: the sinking plane, the hurriedly extracted life raft, finding one's self

afloat on the sea. It's not something to be too much afraid of—
These three lads weren't afraid of it.

[*Waves lapping*]

STERLING. Shucks, they all saw us.

COOPER. Sure, they'll be back to pick us up.

GITTELSON. Don't know why I couldn't have waited till Saturday to
take this bath.

COOPER [*Quickly*]. Hey—careful how you kick that box around.

GITTELSON. For Pete's sake. Cooper grabbed for his hope chest when
we hit the water.

COOPER. Why not? About everything I own's in that box—including
my girl's picture. Didn't want it to get wet.

STERLING. It's liable to—could be there's a storm coming up tonight.

[*Music: in*]

NARRATOR. The long day closes . . . the promise of storm is kept that
night.

[*Fade in storm*]

The boys cling tenaciously as the life raft is lifted by the heavy
swells, then slips sickeningly into the deep troughs. Dawn finds
the heavy sea still running. In the flying scud they see the cruiser
that perhaps has been sent to look for them.

[*Heighten storm*]

THE THREE [*Ad lib, shouting above sound*]. Hey, this way, this way.

NARRATOR. But it is futile . . . When, days later, the storm abates,
they know which way north is, and that is about all.

GITTLESON. Used to wonder what it'd be really like to be—well, like
this.

COOPER. Yeah . . . reading those old stories about Robinson Crusoe
and all that.

STERLING. Only in those days they didn't have planes that could spot
you from the air.

GITTELSON. That doesn't help when all the planes that fly by are Japs.

NARRATOR. They fall silent, staring over the illimitable sea. They
haven't wanted to utter the thought uppermost in their minds.

STERLING. You know, fellows, in spite of all the islands we might drift
to, in spite of the ships and the planes—we can still die out here.

[*Music: Hit chord*]

NARRATOR. Two of the lads are dead two weeks later. How they died may never be known. Exposure, perhaps—perhaps they were strafed from the air by Japanese planes. We know only that on July 6th Jack Cooper is alone, drifting.

[*Music in softly*]

COOPER [*Filter*]. July 6 . . . piece of shrapnel that hit our plane in my box.

NARRATOR. Jack begins a diary—a diary of the days of death. He scratches the letters slowly, painfully, with a sea-rusted pin on the isinglass covers of his wallet. There is nothing else to do . . . nothing else in the whole wide world . . . except to hunger and to thirst . . . and to close the eyes in pain against the searing tropic sun on the sea.

COOPER [*Filter*]. Mom, be sure to check insurance—$10,000, back pay, etc.

NARRATOR. His mother, back in Elkhart. Boyhood there, roaming the Indiana hills . . . high school . . . his two brothers, his sister . . . the job he used to have in the shipping department of the American Coating Mills. Keep your mind on those things, lad . . . that's the way to forget the fever, the pain, the thirst.

COOPER [*Filter*]. Roses to remind me of Helen. I've always loved her. Love and kisses.

NARRATOR. Roses to remind him of Helen. Helen Checchio back in Elkhart. Lovely, dark-eyed, vivacious Helen. The last time he was home on leave he had seen her.

[*Music swells slightly*]

COOPER [*Whispers*]. Gee, Big Eyes, you've made me the happiest man in the world.

HELEN. Oh, Jack—you will come home again soon, won't you?

COOPER. Sure I will—and I'll try to get a really good leave next time. Enough for a honeymoon, too. That is—well, you never can tell when you'll get sent out, of course.

HELEN. Jack . . .

COOPER. Yeah?

HELEN. Know something?

COOPER. What should I know, Big Eyes?

HELEN. Just one thing, darling . . . just one thing I'm, well, afraid of.
I wish you could know . . . God.

COOPER. On that again, huh?

HELEN. It's pretty important to me, Jack.

COOPER. Well . . . I guess right now He doesn't mean much to me.
Maybe I don't get the idea. But you never can tell—I might.

[*Music swells*]

NARRATOR. Two days later the lad scrawls another entry, letter by
letter, in his wallet.

COOPER [*Filter*]. July 8 . . . Feeling weak . . . can't catch fish . . .
no rain . . . I love you, Big Eyes.

NARRATOR. Lying all the time on the rubber floor of the raft now.
Even raising the head to look toward the limitless horizon is a
tremendous effort. The hot sun all day long . . . no rain to fall
inside the raft and be scooped up by the chapped, blackened palms
of the hands. Another long day passes, night falls . . . a little rain.

COOPER [*Filter*]. July 9—Little rain . . . headed west.

NARRATOR. Drifting, drifting. Ocean currents push him a little, the
vagrant winds . . . How near is death? Helen has very definite
ideas about life and death—and God. Head aches too much to
think about those things, though. Best not to think about death—
while there's life there's hope.

COOPER [*Filter*]. July 10—Rain last night—very weak . . . land close
somewhere.

NARRATOR. Land close somewhere . . . but where? Too weak to do
any paddling anyway. Scoop up a little rain water from the
rubber, drink it. It still tastes foul—makes you sick. Suddenly—
[*Airplane overhead*]
An airplane? Raise the head to see . . . strain those burning eyes
to look. No—it's a Jap . . . just another Jap. Got to do something—anything to keep from going nuts. Write a little more
of the diary.

COOPER [*Filter*]. July 11—Jap flew over . . . didn't see me. Left eye
bad shape—still have water—drifting NE.

NARRATOR. Another infinitely long day . . . the little fishline let over
the side . . . when it jerks, hauling it back in takes as much

effort as lifting a tree . . . eating the fish raw . . . can't taste anything any more anyway.

COOPER. July 12—Little cloudy—no land . . . headed north.

[*Planes in*]

NARRATOR. Again that sound . . . planes . . . Japs again . . . this time they see him.

[*Planes zoom down quickly, rattle of machine guns*]

Sweeping down on the raft they machine-gun the prone boy. He quivers under the impact of the bullets. The planes rise again and disappear.

[*Planes fade*]

The boy lies still for a long time, gritting his teeth with the pain —the flail of cruel bullets cut right across his knees. His hand slowly pushes aside the little box—that little box of his own things that he took from the plane—and finds the first-aid kit. Slowly . . . slowly, he sits up and bandages his legs. Hours later he finds the strength to write what happened.

COOPER [*Filter*]. P.M. Jap Nell saw me—strafed—hit me in both legs—bandaged them—drifting east.

NARRATOR. The lad's thoughts are bitter—they saw he couldn't fight back—still they troubled to shoot at him. This could make him die a lot sooner.

COOPER [*Filter*]. July 13. Very weak from loss of blood—land in sight—six ounces of water left.

NARRATOR. Dreams now . . . hallucinations.

HELEN [*Filter*]. Oh, darling, darling—it's so wonderful to have you home.

MOTHER [*Filter*]. No, sir—Jack's getting this extra piece of apple pie—he doesn't come home every day.

HELEN [*Filter*]. Did you find God, Jack—did you try?

[*Music swells slightly*]

COOPER [*Filter*]. Surprise . . . am still alive. Tell Helen I found God. Want my Big Eyes to be happy with someone else. Love and kisses . . . God bless you all . . . no rain . . . drinking sea water.

[*Music swells slightly*]

[*Filter*]. July 16 . . . To Helen—I loved you until the end . . . I love Mom, Dad, and all—wish I could eat some of her cooking.

[*Music: Rise to finish sequence and out*]

COMMANDER. I am the Resurrection and the Life. Whosoever believeth in Me, though he were dead, yet shall he have everlasting life. Whosoever [*Fading*] liveth and believeth in Me shall never die.

NARRATOR. The commander stands at the stern of the small American naval vessel, reading the service of burial at sea. They sighted the life raft this morning—found the body of Jack Cooper on it, found, too, the little box, and the wallet with its tale of slow death. The date is July 21—he had been dead three, perhaps four days. These are full naval honors with which they bury him. The Commander raises his hand in salute as the body slowly slips into the sea.

[*Music in*]

The commander of that vessel wrote to Jack's mother.

COMMANDER [*Writing*]. "I am writing this in hopes that it will in some measure alleviate your sorrow. The story of your son's days on the raft was an inspiration to myself and the officers and men under my command. We are all proud to be able to call ourselves his brothers-in-arms. It is such men who are the cause of our rapid advance in the Pacific. Men like Jack will carry on to bring about the peace we all want. We, my officers and men, salute you and your son."

[*Music: Chord*]

NARRATOR. To Jack's mother went the navy's posthumous awards of the Air Medal and the Purple Heart. If this lad from Elkhart, Indiana, was a hero, it is not hard to tell whence came the heroic quality in him. Said his mother:

MOTHER. They have asked my permission to raise a monument to Jack. I refused it. My son died for his country, yes . . . but so have thousands of others. And the only monument those boys really want is to have this war mean something—and mean it for good, so that their sons won't have to fight another like it.

[*Music: Curtain*]

CONCERNING THE
RED ARMY

Norman Rosten

NORMAN ROSTEN's first volume of poetry, *Return Again, Traveler,* was published in 1940 in the Yale Series of Younger Poets, which was under the editorship of Stephen Vincent Benét. Rosten won a Guggenheim award in 1941-42. In 1943 he published *The Fourth Decade and Other Poems.* He is represented in a number of anthologies. A long narrative poem on the Alcan Highway and the legend of roads is due for early publication.

At the University of Michigan, where he had studied on a playwriting fellowship, Rosten saw his first poetic drama produced. Hearing MacLeish's *Fall of the City* on the *Columbia Workshop,* he realized that radio was "a wonderful carrier for poetry." He wrote his first verse-play for radio at Michigan. Returning to New York—he lives in Brooklyn—he wrote several more, which were produced by NBC. He began to explore commercial radio, and for *Cavalcade of America* he wrote memorable plays on Emily Dickinson, Edgar Allan Poe, and other subjects. But Rosten increasingly felt that radio offered too little freedom of expression, and decided to concentrate on poetry and the drama.

Wartime developments in radio once more stirred his enthusiasm for the medium. The Treasury Department and various war agencies gave him an opportunity to write things he wanted to write. His *Ballad of Bataan* and *Miss Liberty Goes to Town,* both written for the Treasury, caused something of a stir. For the Office of War Information he wrote several programs in the *Uncle Sam* series. For production in war plants by the American Theatre Wing he wrote some *Lunchtime Follies* sketches. For NBC and the War Department he wrote a play on the building of the Alcan by Negro and white troops. Many of these plays were in verse or partly in verse.

Concerning the Red Army was written for Russian War Relief and the Columbia Broadcasting System, on the occasion of the twenty-sixth anniversary of the founding of the Red Army. Broadcast February 22, 1944, it was one of the first dramatic programs about Soviet Russia heard on an American network. Radio drama, like other popular story media in the United States, avoided treatment of the Soviet Union until its successful resistance to Nazi attack. This was true even of educational series dealing · with history. Because of the tension surrounding the subject, a blackout was maintained. Until 1941, the U.S.S.R.'s sole representatives in American radio drama were the occasional bomb-throwing Bolsheviks of comedy and melodrama, who even survived the war in less unfriendly form as "mad Russians." The average listener's picture of the people of the U.S.S.R., at the start of America's wartime alliance with it, was largely conditioned by such figures.

Concerning the Red Army belongs to a period when it began to be possible to write about the Russian war effort, generally in terms of its military aspects only.

Like several network public service plays in this volume, *Concerning the Red Army* was broadcast at 11:30 P.M. to midnight. Commercial sponsors have found little reason to be interested in such periods.

Among enthusiastic comments received were these: "The one regret is that it came so late so many people must have missed it." (Norwalk, Conn.) "The only regret is that it was almost missed but happened to tune in quite casually. . . . Seems a pity that intelligently handled programs of this sort can't be heard more frequently and at a more convenient hour." (Detroit, Mich.) "I only regret that the program was not scheduled for earlier in the evening. Its importance and quality most surely rated it a better spot on your schedule." (Williamsport, Pa.)

The program was directed by Norman Corwin, an ardent Rosten admirer, who had persuaded Rosten to write the script. Martin Gabel was the narrator. The musical score was by Bernard Herrman. Of Corwin's direction the author writes: "Exciting. Particularly the use of sound. His use of the multiple wireless codes toward the end of the script was one of the most dramatic sound improvisations I've ever heard."

The Writers' War Board, in co-operation with the Association for Education by Radio, distributed this script to educational groups throughout the country.

Rosten has hopes and doubts about the future of radio: "The way I see it, the war gave radio a shot in the arm. The war lifted radio out of its bog of mediocrity to a place of distinction. It spoke of man and his world—and radio can speak when it wants to—boldly, honorably. It has become an instrument of social action. It has done some swell shows on the veteran, the problems of peace, world unity, etc. With peace here, however, I wonder if radio drama won't slide right back to its weary formula of love and the creaking door. I hope not."

CONCERNING THE

RED ARMY*

[*Music: Introductory*]

[*Cannon Muffled: One shell hits close*]

GENERAL. Captain?

CAPTAIN. Here, sir.

GENERAL. I can't see you in the dark.

CAPTAIN. I'll relight the candles. Devil knows where the wind comes from. You'd think that in tunnels and caves dug deep under a city the wind would stop blowing. But it blows. [*Striking a match*] There. We'll have some light for a minute. [*Recognizing*] Yes, comrade general!

GENERAL. We are abandoning Sevastopol.

CAPTAIN. So . . . It has come.

GENERAL. The wounded are being withdrawn to Chersonese. They must be covered—until the last man, the last yard, the last breath. [*Pause*] Captain, we have held them off eight months.

CAPTAIN. Yes, I know, sir.

GENERAL. We now ask you to die here. [*Pause*] You may refuse. We don't order you because in these times it is important that a man should order himself.

[*Pause*]

CAPTAIN. I am thinking of my wife.

GENERAL. There is not much time.

CAPTAIN. I should like to send a letter with the last boat.

GENERAL. I shall return and remain with you. But I will see that the letter gets on the boat.

[*Footsteps going off*]

CAPTAIN. My dear Anka, my wife . . . I wanted to refuse, but I could not. I am not a hero and you know it. Death never stood very

* CONCERNING THE RED ARMY by Norman Rosten. Copyright, 1944, by Norman Rosten.

close to me before. Why and for what reason am I doing this? So that others may live. How foolish that we had no children! Life should continue. For its continuation we die the best way we can. I know you love me. I know that when I am dead, for you I will continue to live [*Fading*] and that nobody will edge me away from your careful heart . . .

NARRATOR. All that you have just heard is true. The scene, the setting, and the letter. Who is that man? He is a soldier of the Red Army. He has a name and he is nameless. He is one man and he is five million men whose blood is vanished now into the roots of earth and grass. He sleeps in the frozen snow of the North. He sleeps forever in the warm South. He fell at Kiev, Uman, Zhitomir. ⸙

[*Music: Building under voices*]

VOICES. Rostov
Gomel
Tula
Smolensk
Kalinin
Novgorod
Velikie Luki
Leningrad
Odessa
Orel
Kharkov.

NARRATOR. He lies in the streets of a thousand cities and towns. He lies in the ruined buildings, the open fields, or behind the shattered stone wall. Most often he did not have time for a final letter. Most often he died with a name on his lips. He died without the heroic choice, or he chose a specific act. He is legend and he is a simple man. He is a citizen of the Union of Soviet Socialist Republics as you are a citizen of the United States of America. He lives, or once lived, in a house, on a street, in a certain city. His blood is joined with ours at Salerno and Anzio.

[*Music: Prelude behind*]

Who is the soldier of the Red Army? He is one man dead and five million dead. He is one man living and two hundred million alive. He is one hundred and seventy-five different peoples, speaking one hundred and fifty different languages and dialects. He is Great Russian and Ukrainian, white Russian and Georgian, Usbek, and Kalmyk, Kirghiz and Jew, Turkman and Kazakh. He lives upon one-sixth of the earth's surface. He has climbed from out of the darkness of centuries to take his place among the nations. He is building a new life and is determined that none shall destroy it!

CHILD [Reciting a poem].

"O'er darkened Petrograd there rolled
November's breath of Autumn cold;
And Neva with her boisterous billow [Fading]
Splashed on her shapely bounding wall . . ."

NARRATOR. This little girl is reading a poem of Pushkin in a classroom. Her grandfather could not read.

STUDENT [Giving a mathematical formula].

$S = 1/2 \ a \ h = Vs \ (s\text{-}a)(S\text{-}b) \ (S\text{-}c)$

NARRATOR. This young man is preparing for science. His father never knew of science.

[Tractor motor]

The sound you hear is a tractor working a collective farm. It has replaced the horse-drawn plow forever.

[Riveting]

A new bridge is being built over the Dnieper. There was no bridge here before.

[Blast furnace: roar of metal]

Magnitogorsk—a new city built on an iron mountain, built out of the arid space of Asia. Steel for houses, bridges—steel for tractors and tanks.

[Music: Cadenza of Beethoven violin concerto]

A concert in the Moscow Music Hall. The soloist is sixteen years old. He was chosen to study here. He comes from the Armenian Soviet Republic. His father is a coal miner.

[Effect of great mass of water roaring]

The great Dnieper Dam, bringing light to the valley, bringing power to the basin of the Donets, the promise of a peaceful life, a better life building. What has all this to do with the Red Army? An army is not only men and weapons. It is strength which lives in the people, which the people in turn give to their fighters. It is the belief in the right, and understanding of the right. We know that. We've had our Bataan and El Alamein along with their Stalingrad. The Red Army reaps what it has sown. It has sown strength.

[*Music: Transition*]

At the beginning, there were the doubters. The Red Army? One sentence each, please, for the poll.

VOICE 1. Three weeks and it'll all be over.

VOICE 2. Not a chance.

VOICE 3. Six weeks to three months.

VOICE 4. They're tough people but they can't handle machines.

VOICE 5. I heard a Russian'll drive a truck without oil and when it breaks down he walks the rest of the way.

VOICE 6. The Nazis will go through 'em like a knife through butter.

VOICE 7. Didn't the Russians shoot their generals?

NARRATOR. And the commentators . . .

COMMENTATOR. At this moment the Red Army is in grave danger of being entrapped and cut off. This in itself may not mean a Russian disaster, providing the reserves are brought up in time, which is doubtful due to the questionable transportation—

NARRATOR. Sorry, Mr. Military Commentator. *One* sentence. Any more testimonials?

NAZI. The Russian Army is at this moment being annihilated and smashed never to rise again. Heil Hitler!

[*Music: A Nazi cue*]

[*Coming in swiftly: The swish-swish-swish of the bazooka rocket guns*]

NARRATOR. Hear that? The famous and terrible rocket guns which went into action at Stalingrad. We're a bit ahead of our story, but while the well-meaning or best-paid brains of the world were preparing the last rites, the Red Army was building these rocket guns by the thousand. Just one of the surprises among many. While the military commentators had it all figured out, the Red Army began their great initial retreat. It was the spring being coiled, and it would one day strike.

COMMENTATOR. It seems to us from here that the Red Armies are in great danger of being encircled and wiped out, though of course it depends upon their reserves and the transportation system, which we must remember—

NARRATOR. Excuse me, Mr. Military Commentator. We'd like to get on with the war—if you don't mind.

COMMENTATOR. But you must recognize the danger of their armies being split up. Without transportation, what have you but chaos? It's "Keitel and Kessel" all over again. If Paris fell, how can Moscow stand?

NARRATOR. Our commentator forgot that Moscow was not Paris. The Wehrmacht found no gifts in Russia. No open cities in Russia. Moscow was a closed city, Leningrad was ringed with steel, and the people were ready, whispering . . .

RUSSIAN. Come and take us, you Nazis, come to your graves, there is room for you under the wheat, there is room in our swift rivers. Come, you cannibals, come to your death, you shall not defile us, the air will freeze in your blood, the food turn bitter in your mouth: you shall eat ashes!

[*Plane in dive*]

NARRATOR. A Stormovik on fire, diving towards German fuel tanks. The pilot's name is Nikolai Gastello.

GASTELLO. Hold together, my little bird. Your wings are broken, a moment more, a moment more . . . Their guns have said we must die, but they did not say how. We will give them a taste of thunder, eh? . . . Now, my bird, now, now!

[*Great explosion*]

VOICE A. Today the Red Army engaged the enemy on all fronts.

[*Wireless*]

VOICE B. Today the Red Army engaged the enemy on all fronts.

[*Wireless*]

VOICE C. The Red Army has evacuated Smolensk.

[*Wireless*]

VOICE D. The Red Army has evacuated Rzhev.

[*Wireless*]

VOICE E. Kiev abandoned.

[*Wireless*]

VOICE F. Today the Red Army engaged the enemy on all fronts.

[*Wireless fades*]

NARRATOR. Engaged the enemy on all fronts. We looked at the daily maps in the newspapers, during that first winter in 1941. We saw the lines moving eastward. Kharkov gone. Leningrad caught in the jaw of winter, shelled, starved, laying down a road across the ice of Lake Ladoga. The line on the map moves. The map is unalive. The map does not bleed. We watch the bulge near Bryansk. Four thousand tanks embattled as the ground trembles. Oh, if the map could cry out! If the ink were blood! The loop around Tula . . . Tula, we pray that you hold. The snow is red at Tula, the line bends but does not break.

NAZI. We have Moscow in the sight of our field glasses! Heil Hitler!

NARRATOR. How does it look in your field glasses, von Bock? Reach out, von Bock. Go on, reach out and take Moscow. It is waiting. The road is open. Timoshenko is waiting.

[*Boom of guns: Heavy artillery*]

VOICE. The Red Army engaged the enemy on all fronts.

NARRATOR. To engage the enemy . . . Here are some ways, which the map will never indicate.

[*Fading guns*]

NAZI. Your name, soldier? [*Pause*] Your name. Dog of a Russian, speak! [*Curses in German*] This is your last chance. Tie him to the tanks!

NARRATOR. From the village they herded all to watch. They tied him to the tanks, his arms tied to one, his legs to the other, and the motors of the tanks were idling.

[*Tank motors*]

NAZI. The strength and composition of your unit. Where are the guerrillas hiding? [*Pause*] Pull him a bit!

[*Tanks up and idle*]

NARRATOR. The prisoner is silent. His torn mouth hangs open. His eyes are little stones under a running river. His forehead is a drum where death invisibly beats, and the villagers look silently on and shake their heads . . .

NAZI. Tell us. Tell us and be saved. [*Pause*] Draw him tighter!

[*Tanks up and idle*]

NARRATOR. The bulge at Bryansk . . . Tula holding . . . Rostov holding . . . He turns his head towards the enemy. He tries to spit.

His eyes are burning coals and hatred moves like a flame over them, and he speaks.

PRISONER. Tear me apart! See who is stronger! Tear the Dnieper from the Urals!

NAZI. Pull him apart!

[*Tanks roar up and fade*]

VOICE. Today the Red Army engaged the enemy on all fronts.

[*Music: A thin passage behind*]

NARRATOR. The front is long, it goes through many towns, it touches many people.

ENGINEER. The signal will come from across the river. Be ready with the switch.

WORKER. I'm afraid . . . I won't have the courage.

ENGINEER. Don't worry. We've placed the dynamite well, and deep. It won't fail.

WORKER. Our Dnieperstroy Dam, our blood, our toil, our first dream.

ENGINEER. We'll build it again.

WORKER. Is it true an American engineer helped to build it?

ENGINEER. Yes.

WORKER. Then perhaps he will help us to build again . . . one day.

ENGINEER. There's the signal. Quickly, comrade. What are you waiting for? Here. Take my hand. We'll do it together.

[*Series of explosions*]

VOICE. Today the Red Army engaged the enemy on all fronts.

[*Music: Bridge into*]

[*Freight cars rolling*]

NARRATOR. The sound you are hearing is Kharkov being moved away, far to the east. A thousand freight cars with lathes, tools, dyes, presses, drills. The train will continue eastward for five days and nights. It will come to the middle of a plain, and stop.

[*Train stops*]

FREIGHT MAN 1. We will begin to unload here. As soon as the machines are assembled, hook up the dynamos to the power cars.

FREIGHT MAN 2. On this snow-covered field? Without buildings?

FREIGHT MAN 1. The Red Army fights in the snow-covered fields and we will work in the snow-covered fields.

FREIGHT MAN 2. Impossible, comrade engineer.

FREIGHT MAN 1. Yes. But we will do it.

[*Music under*]

NARRATOR. This is part of the story of the Red Army. It is one of the veins feeding the heart. It is part of the battle. An eighty-five-year-old woman in Leningrad said at a sailor's meeting . . .

OLD WOMAN. For us there is no rear line. The enemy front is everywhere. It goes through our houses, through our hearts, and through our souls.

NARRATOR. A worker named Korshunov spoke and the entire country listened . . .

KORSHUNOV. There is one law for us: If you want victory, over-fulfill the plan of the factory. When it is over-fulfilled, double it, then quadruple it, make it fivefold and tenfold and even then don't stop.

NARRATOR. Journalist Ilya Ehrenburg . . .

EHRENBURG. The time is past for indignation. There is time for one thing only—to slay the assassins!

NARRATOR. The Red Army is the people—and the people testify.

SOLDIER. My motto is: When you see the enemy, kill him!

WORKER. If our fliers need it, we'll make it!

DRIVER. I drove forty-eight hours without a stop across the Lake Ladoga Road. Once a thing has to be done, then it must be done as soon as possible and as well as possible.

PARTISAN. Partisans of N district, we are gathered to report on the German leaflet which says Leningrad is captured. It is decided that detachment N considers Leningrad not taken and states that it can never be taken!

[*Music: Going into piano playing. Chopin waltz*]

NARRATOR. That is Vladimir Sofronitsky, Honored Artist of the Republic, giving a concert in the Pushkin Theater. There is no heat. It is three degrees below zero. The audience is composed of Red Army men, sailors, guerrilla fighters.

PIANIST. I, myself, played in gloves with the finger tips cut out. But frankly I believe I have never played so well. The evening was one of the happiest of my life.

[*Fade piano under*]

NARRATOR. Yes, this is part of the story. American-built trucks are part of the story. Convoys are part of the story. There is laughter and song to the story. Such songs as this one by Konstantin Simonov, Red Army soldier-poet.

SOLO. Wait for me and I'll return
   Dear one, only wait;
   When the leaves of autumn burn
   Round our garden gate;
   Wait, when winter winds blow free;
   Wait, through summer's sun;
   Others may forgotten be
   Ere the fight is won;
But, when days that endless creep
   Bring no word from me;
   Still your lonely vigil keep—
   Dear one, wait for me.

[*Music: Fade theme under*]

NARRATOR. But their battle returns, their song is a moment, their peace is one hour among a million hours. The first year ends. Moscow stands. Leningrad stands. Russia grows stronger. We watch the map in that crucial summer and winter of 1942. Two thousand miles of war put upon a page. The crosses and faded areas . . . territory lost, the first counterattack, arrows (how painless!) indicating new drives . . . the line of battle twisted and curved into pockets, and each is a hell on earth, and each is a place where man is tested and bleeds, where our own life may be decided. The line swings to the east, New England overrun, the Ukraine burning, Boston burning, New York and Pennsylvania, Virginia, Carolina, Tennessee, Ohio, Oklahoma . . . looted and burned, their people murdered, their sons enslaved, daughters taken for brothels . . . Past the Ukraine, the invaders race across the broad valleys of the Don, firing the horizons, towards the Caucasus, the oil, the Volga . . .

COMMENTATOR. It's over, the war's over in Russia! They have fallen back too far and consequently lost the north-south railroads upon which the transportation system of any modern country depends.

NARRATOR. Excuse me, I'd like to go on . . .

COMMENTATOR. No country in the world can sustain such losses of men and material and keep on fighting. Just look at the map! The Red Army *cannot* counterattack without a base of operation and supply! It's against all rules of modern warfare. Look at the map!

NARRATOR. Yes, we *will* look at the map. We conjure up images from the map. We hobble after history with the map. The Crimea bottled up. Sevastopol will fall in a week. Perhaps it's true.

ADMIRAL. Friends, if anyone says to you in my name we must surrender, kill him as a traitor. If I come to you and issue an order for surrender, kill me.

NARRATOR. Admiral Nakhimov spoke these words in Sevastopol a century ago, and those words stand. No surrender. Eight months of ·siege. Three hundred thousand Germans attacking endlessly. The people bled an army here. Eight months, thirty-two weeks, two hundred days and nights of battle. They died at their guns. They died in their bright city of harbors. Honor to them. Honor and silence.

[*Silence. Then kettle drums*]
The buzzards wheel to the east.
The Volga shines with history.
City on the plain, Stalingrad the prize!
Crack the spine of Asia with Stalingrad!
Continents hinge on the gates of Stalingrad!
Reach the Don, across the Don to the Volga;
This time, this summer, they must win,
And "sieg heil" will roll into Asia:
They will sleep with Asia and bear sons!
This time, they see the river ahead,
They are in the city, now, at last . . .
They came on with their heavy tanks
picking ten yards of ground and
grinding through then ten more yards
wave after wave with the planes above
blasting the earth away square by square
with men fighting on the scattered stones
slipping in their own blood

the fascists piling up yard by yard
a thousand deep for every yard
screaming with cotton in their noses
to keep out the stink of their dead
going mad with the sight of victory.
Fighters from the Crimea and Caucasus
the hot Kuban valley and frozen north
from the steppes of Kalumuck to Kirghiz
they came to stand at Stalingrad's river
and the river became a wall.
[*Swish-swish-swish of rocket guns*]
Rocket guns reserved for the master race.
Welcome to the city, the fury of fire!
While at the edge of the River Volga
the famed Guards Division holds out
and will not yield this strip of earth.

GUARD. A guardsman retreats only to another world.

NARRATOR. They threw a continent against Stalingrad,
They threw the disease of the world,
the dregs of Europe, the darkness of time;
the thieves, the treachery, the dung:
all the corruption of history gathered
and flung at this city on the plain,
Bury them, Stalingrad.
Bury the evil of the earth, Stalingrad!

[*Music: Triumphant, rising, then under*]

To the West, the Soviet pincers reach out, larger, until the final
armies—Yeremenko and Rokossovsky—join and lock! The soldiers
run to one another, cheering, swarming across the frozen valleys
of the Don. They kiss, they are not ashamed of tears. They have
trapped a German army! The tide is westward.

VOICES. Voronezh retaken.
The Kuban cleared.
Krasnodar.
Voroshilovgrad.
Rostov.

NARRATOR. The new year of 1943. The Soviet flags returning.

[Wireless code in low register]

VOICE 1. Now it's a stalemate.

VOICE 2. Both armies are going to sit tight.

VOICE 3. Unquestionably, they'll talk peace now.

VOICE 4. It will be a miracle if the Red Army can retake Kharkov this year.

[New code joins in higher register]

NARRATOR. Miracle of Kharkov. Miracle of Belgorod and Orel. Miracle of Taganrog. Honor to the fighters, the airmen, the tankmen. The flags returning. A flag for Mariupol. Flag for Novorossiisk. Flag for Bryansk. Miracle of Smolensk. Miracle of Roslavl.

[Another code, higher. All build]

COMMENTATOR. It is not quite correct to call the German retreat a rout. They obviously have a plan, and they hold the railroads.

NARRATOR. The Cossacks drive towards the Dnieper as they drove towards the Don. A flag for the sight of Kiev! Iron in our hearts for burning Kiev!

COMMENTATOR. We can be sure the German Army has prepared strong defense positions at the Dnieper.

NAZI. We will stand at the Dnieper! Heil Hitler!

[Music: Merge with wireless to climax, and both out]

NARRATOR. Stand at the Dnieper! Stand and die! And they die! and the locusts die, the madmen go down and the Dnieper is flooded with bodies. Zaparozhye. Militopol, the Crimean gate. Perekop. Kiev is ours! The civilian dead uncovered, the hundred thousands, men, women and children. Anger is the air they breathe, is the bread and water, the night's sleeping and the day's waking. Vengeance and justice! Forward beyond Kiev. To the west, to liberation! Westward from Leningrad. Westward from Lake Ilmen and Novgorod. Westward toward Berlin. For the homeless, the tortured, the humiliated, for the bereaved throughout the world— drive them further! The Dnieper Bend—The Dnieper noose— Cherkassy and Nikopol—the little Stalingrads and no request for surrender this time. The hunter is become the hunted. The tide is ever westward, locking the Nazis against the anvil of rivers! Between the Volga and the Don, between the Don and the Donets, between the Dnieper and the Bug—hammer and anvil!

Drive for the Vistula, and the Oder beyond. The victorious soldiers cheer.

[*Special cheering effect*]

The earth thunders to the footsteps of liberating armies. Honor to the Red Army and its commander in chief, Marshal Stalin! Honor to the allies, united and strong! Together our bayonets close around *Festung Europa.*

The justice of man is marching.

The justice of the world is marching.

[*Cheering up*]

[*Music: Closing cue*]

ANNOUNCER. During the period of this broadcast Moscow announced the recapture of thirty populated places in the Ukraine.

[*Pause*]

NARRATOR. The Red Army continues to advance on all fronts.

INSIDE A KID'S
HEAD

*Jerome Lawrence and
Robert E. Lee*

Inside a Kid's Head was first presented as a *Columbia Workshop* play. Before war's demands on radio time pushed this famous series from the CBS network schedule, the noncommercial *Columbia Workshop* gave many a writer a chance to explore fresh fields in radio drama.

Almost every commercial series on the air has a set formula, and rejects many manuscripts on the ground that "it doesn't fit our format." The *Workshop* had no format. Scripts didn't have to fall into three parts, with strong suspense at intermissions to hold an audience through the commercials. Scripts didn't have to have a certain kind of narration, or no narration. Scripts didn't have to have boy and girl leads, written for this and that star. On the *Columbia Workshop* a script could bring its own rules with it. The *Workshop* gave many a new talent an opportunity to develop: Corwin, Robson, Welles, Laurents, to name only a few in this volume, attracted early attention on the *Workshop*. And its editorial policy aroused the interest of distinguished writers from other fields.

To the history of the *Columbia Workshop* belong Irving Reis's early work with filter and echo chamber, Bernard Herrman's demonstrations of what original music could mean to radio drama, Archibald MacLeish's prophetic *Fall of the City,* some of Norman Corwin's early radio adaptations of poetry, and experiments by many writers in radio documentary and fantasy. All these helped develop the flexibility of the medium, and to make radio drama a valuable wartime weapon. Many *Workshop* alumni have played a prominent part in wartime radio.

Jerome Lawrence and Robert E. Lee are both astonishingly young for their many accomplishments. Both have written for dozens of series, and both have published books. Lawrence edited *Off Mike,* a compendium on radio writing; Lee has written a book on *Television.* Both were inducted into the army shortly after the production of *Inside a Kid's Head.* In uniform, they were active in the development of the Armed Forces Radio Service, the network serving overseas troops. At AFRS headquarters in Los Angeles the peacetime collaborators found themselves at adjacent desks, writing programs for men overseas.

The *Columbia Workshop* première of *Inside a Kid's Head* featured Skippy Homeier as Ritchie. Nila Mack directed.

INSIDE A KID'S
HEAD

ANNOUNCER. INSIDE A KID'S HEAD. . . . This personally conducted tour through the brain of a ten-year-old boy was arranged
in script form by Jerome Lawrence and Robert E. Lee. Ladies
and gentlemen, are you ready now? Very good. Right this way,
please. Just follow the guide!

[*Music: "Inside a kid's head" theme . . . establish, then down
and out behind*]

[*Slight echo through this scene*]
[*Group milling about*]

GUIDE. We are now standing inside the brain of—uh—Ritchie Price.
This is not usually included in the fifty-five cent tour, but—
excuse me, sir! Don't stand too close to those nerve centers—
high voltage, you know!

MAN. Oh—sorry.

GUIDE. Right now Ritchie is in his history class in Grade 5B at
Hazeldell Elementary School. We are standing at the medulla
oblongata, looking up into the cerebellum.

WOMAN. Pardon me, guide—but what is all that over there? It looks
like wool.

GUIDE. That *is* wool, madame. This boy has been woolgathering quite
a bit lately. Uh . . . you will notice that the walls here are lined
with gray matter, which absorbs any ideas that may be floating
about.

[*Slide whistle—zoop, zoop!*]

WOMAN. Oh!

MAN. What was that, guide?

GUICE. That was just an idea going in one ear and out the other! And
look!—over there!

183

WOMAN. Where?

GUIDE. Peeking out from behind those brain cells! It's a little date.

MAN. A what?

GUIDE. A date. It's so hazy, I can't quite make out the year . . . !
Oh, yes! It's 1215 A.D.!
  [*Quick ascending "zoop" of slide whistle*]

ALL [*Chuckle*].

GUIDE. Cute little fellow, wasn't he!

MAN. Are all dates as shy as that?

GUIDE. No, I'm afraid this boy doesn't have a very good memory for
dates.

WOMAN. Guide, what did you say this boy's name was?

GUIDE. Ritchie Price, ma'am.
  [*Footsteps*]
Now, if you'll just follow me up this passageway, we'll have a
look at the cerebrum. Oh! careful you don't slip into that crevice!

WOMAN. My, it's deep! What is it, guide?

GUIDE. Lapse of memory—a big one, too!
  [*Hum of automatic, repetitive machinery—such as adding
  machines*]
We're now coming into the cerebrum—the largest section of the
brain. On the right, you see the master control panel for the
automatic functions—such as heartbeats, digestion, breathing, and
so forth.

VOICE 1 [*Filter*]. Inhale!
  [*Gasp of breath intake*]
Exhale!
  [*Gasp of breath exhaled*]
Inhale!
  [*Gasp of breath intake*]
Exhale!
  [*Breath exhaled*]

WOMAN. That must be the breathing mechanism!

GUIDE. That's right, ma'am. And here's the digestion control.

VOICE 2 [*Through a speaking tube*]. Four more licorice drops coming
down the epiglottis.

VOICE 3 [*Filter*]. Okay. Better turn on a little more gastric juice.

VOICE 2 [*Speaking tube*]. Right, chief!

[*Buzz, as of interoffice communication—click!*]

VOICE 3 [*Filter*]. Master control. Go ahead.

VOICE 4 [*Sharp filter*]. Stomach calling. [*Pained*] Look, chief! I'm gonna be upset if this eating between meals isn't cut out! I haven't even digested those peanut-butter sandwiches that came down for lunch! We gotta get some rest down here!

VOICE 3 [*Filter*]. Well, I'll shoot a memo up to the "common-sense" department, and see if we can't get 'em to conserve on the food intake. But we haven't been getting much co-operation from common sense lately . . . [*Fading*] Do the best you can.

VOICE 4 O.K., chief.

[*Click of switch*]

WOMAN. Isn't that wonderful?

GUIDE. Yes, it's quite a complicated apparatus. Now, folks, we've installed an observation booth on the second floor of the cranium. Right up these stairs. [*Footsteps*] From this booth, you can see and hear everything that goes on in this boy's dome. Through these double doors, please . . .

[*Sound of double doors*]

WOMAN. Oh, this is nice . . . !

MAN. Plush chairs, and everything. Can we smoke?

GUIDE. No, Board of Health says no smoking. Might cause a fever. Just a moment . . . I'll turn this loudspeaker on the main thinking channel. . . .

[*Squeals . . . heterodyne . . . then:*]

MISS LUDLOW [*Fading in, but remaining slightly off*]. And, children, don't forget that up to this time King John was the *absolute monarch* of England. Anything he said was *law!*

GUIDE [*Close*]. That's his history teacher talking.

MISS LUDLOW [*Continuing*]. But King John wasn't a good king. He mistreated his subjects, and that's why his barons made him sign the Great Charter. [*Blob of static*] Now, close your history books, children [*More static, squeals*] —and we'll take up the General Science lesson for today.

GUIDE. Reception isn't very good. I'm afraid this boy Ritchie Price isn't paying much attention to his teacher.

[*Music: Bong! Vibraphone, octaves, struck with hard mallets, plus echo*]

[*Fading off*]. Oh-oh! The imagination is coming in on the same wave length! This ought to be interesting . . .

RITCHIE [*Aged ten—fading in*]. Now look here, King John! You've been actin' awful bossy lately! An' we barons are gettin' pretty sick of it!

KING JOHN [*Firmly*]. What dost thou propose, Sir Ritchie? Thou hast no right to challenge the King of England!

RITCHIE. Well, now, your Majesty, we barons have been talkin' this over, jes' between ourselves. An' we come to the conclusion the people oughta have somethin' to say about what's goin' on. How about it, boys?

BARON I. Yes! Sir Ritchie speaks aright!

BARON 2. We are with him!

BARON 3. To the last man!

MARY JANE [*Aged ten*]. Please, father! Why don't you do as Sir Ritchie asks? He's so handsome!

KING JOHN. This is none of thy concern, Princess Mary Jane! My liegemen, this is *treason!*

RITCHIE. Jes' get down off your high horse, King John! All we're askin' yuh do to is put your name on this hunk of paper, so's folks don't have to worry about you not treatin' 'em right. Now, I happen to have a fountain pen right here in my suit of armor. If you'll jes' sign on the dotted line . . .

KING JOHN. I refuse! Thou art traitors! All of you!

RITCHIE [*Very matter-of-fact*]. We mean business, King John! You better sign, or we'll have to get tough!

BARON I. Yes, sign!

BARON 2. Sign, your Majesty!

BARON 3. We demand that thou sign the charter!

KING JOHN [*Riding over the voices*]. Does no man remain loyal to his king?

RITCHIE. We're loyal, King John! But we jes' don't like the idea of you having your own way all the time. We want some say-so, too! That's only fair!

MARY JANE. Sir Ritchie is right! Sign, father!

BARON I. Yes! If you want to keep your throne!

KING JOHN. Very well, Sir Ritchie. Give me the pen.

   [*Scratch of pen*]

KING JOHN [*Pouting like an adolescent*]. There! Take your old paper!
BARONS [*Cheers*].
MARY JANE. Sir Ritchie—you're *so* wonderful!
RITCHIE [*Tossing it off*]. Oh, it was nothing . . . ! [*Over cheers*] Gentlemen! [*As if springing a dramatic piece of information*] Gentlemen! We shall call this—the *Magna Charta!*
BARON I. Three cheers for Sir Ritchie!
ALL. Hurrah for Sir Ritchie! Ritchie! Ritchie!
    [*Simultaneous cross-fade into:*]
MISS LUDLOW [*Fading in, overlapping*]. Ritchie! Ritchie! Ritchie!
RITCHIE. Huh? [*Coming to*] Yes, Miss Ludlow?
MISS LUDLOW. Will you stop daydreaming long enough to answer the question I just asked?
RITCHIE [*Groping*]. Why . . . uh . . . uh . . . [*Timidly*] King John . . . ?
CLASS [*Laughter*].
MISS LUDLOW [*After laughter subsides*]. In fourteen years of teaching, that is the first time a pupil ever told me that King John invented the sewing machine!
CLASS [*Laughter*].
    [*Electric bell rings, scrape of feet*]
MISS LUDLOW. Wait, class! For tomorrow, study Chapter Eight in your General Science book. Class dismissed.
    [*Hurried shuffle of feet. Immediate babbling of released kids*] [*Calling*]. Oh, Ritchie!
RITCHIE [*Gulping*]. Yes, ma'am?
MISS LUDLOW. Ritchie, what do you think we should do with a boy who doesn't pay attention in class?
RITCHIE. I don't know, ma'am . . .
MISS LUDLOW. Do you think we should give him a note to take home to his parents?
RITCHIE [*Meekly*]. Do we have to do anything that—er—severe?
MISS LUDLOW [*As pen scratches*]. I'm afraid so. There you are. [*Envelope folded*] I want you to take this home—have your father sign it, and bring it back to me.
RITCHIE [*Crestfallen*]. Yes, ma'am.
    [*Slow footsteps*]
    [*Suddenly*] Mary Jane! [*Shouting*] Hey! Mary Jane!

[Running footsteps . . . up to walk]

MARY JANE. Go away, silly. I don't want to be seen walking with you.

RITCHIE. Gee whiz, Mary Jane. What's the matter?

MARY JANE. 'Cause you're silly—that's what you are! Why don't you ever study your lessons?

RITCHIE. I do, but— *[Frustrated]* I jes' forget—or something!

MARY JANE. You needn't ask me to walk home with you. Billy Winkler's already asked me.

RITCHIE *[Contemptuously]*. Him? *[Disappointed]* Oh, gee. Gee whiz!

[Music: Fade in "Inside a Kid's Head" theme]

[Slight echo through the following]

WOMAN *[Startled]*. Oh! What's that, guide?

GUIDE. *[Calmly]*. Keep your seats, ladies and gentlemen! There's nothing to worry about. That low gray fog you see rolling in from the cerebellum is nothing but gloom—*pure gloom!*

[Music builds into a bridge—down and out]

MOTHER. Ritchie, just wait until your father sees this note from Miss Ludlow.

RITCHIE. Do we hafta show it to him?

MOTHER *[Reading]*. "Complete lack of classroom spirit," it says. Your father'll be furious.

RITCHIE. Maybe we hadn't oughta bother him, when he's so worried about the election.

MOTHER. When those boys and girls go home and tell their folks the kind of boy you are, do you think they'll vote for Daddy next Tuesday.

RITCHIE *[Hopelessly]*. I don't know.

MOTHER *[Fussy]*. Good heavens, your father'll be home any minute. Be sure to brush your hair and clean your fingernails, Ritchie. Before dinner! Your father's invited the Winklers over.

RITCHIE. Billy, too? Is *he* coming?

MOTHER. Yes. And I want you to be a little gentleman.

RITCHIE. Oh, nuts!

MOTHER. After all, Mr. Winkler is one of the most important men in the county.

RITCHIE *[Almost to himself]*. He's fat—that's what.

MOTHER. And if we want daddy to be elected state assemblyman, we'll have to be very nice to the Winklers. [*Suddenly*] Good heavens! The carpet in here is all scuffed up again! Ritchie, get out the vacuum cleaner and run it over once. [*Fading*] The Winklers are so fussy . . .

RITCHIE [*Tired of it all*]. Okay, mom.

[*Closet door opens—rattle of vacuum cleaner*]
[*Singing to himself, a song of his own composition*]
Billy Winkler. He's a stinkler.
Billy Winkler. He's a stinkler.
[*Vacuum cleaner zooms to start . . . back and forth rhythmically, with vicious tugs . . . on mike, then away from mike, then back on again . . . continue behind the following:*]

RITCHIE [*Muttering to himself*]. Now it's vacuum cleaners. Vacuum cleaners and sewing machines. Who cares about them! Someday I'll invent somethin' BIG—like an airplane! [*Rhythm with the vacuum cleaner*] Zoom! Zoom! Zoom! Zoom!

[*Music: Vibraphone—Bong!—as before . . .*]

[*Cross fade from vacuum cleaner through to crude airplane motor idling . . . coughs . . . onks out*]
[*Sighs*]. Hm. I guess there's dirt in the carburetor. We'll have to take the motor apart.

MAC [*Fading*]. Say, fellows—there's a lady here who wants to meet you. She *says* her name's Miss Ludlow.

RITCHIE. Better watch out, Mac. She might be an enemy spy!

MAC. Naw, I think she's harmless. Miss Ludlow, these are the greatest inventors in the world! I want you to meet—the Wright Brothers! This is the oldest—Ritchie Wright. . . .

RITCHIE. Glad to know you, ma'am.

MAC. And this is his younger brother—Ritchie.

MISS LUDLOW [*Awed*]. How do you do?

RITCHIE [*Gary Cooper modesty*]. We'd like t' give yuh more of our time, ma'am—but my brother an' me are busy inventin' the flyin' machine. Got that carburetor cleaned out, Ritchie?

RITCHIE [*Off, changes his voice only slightly*]. You bet, Ritchie!

RITCHIE [*On mike*]. Okay, Mac! Crank her up!

MAC [*Off*]. Contact?

RITCHIE [*On mike*]. Contact?

[*Old-fashioned propeller wound up—airplane motor catches*]

RITCHIE. Okay! We're going to take off now!

MAC [*Off*]. Good luck, boys!

RITCHIE. Here we go!

[*Motor zooms up*]

MAC [*Shouting*]. Boy, look at that cloud of dust!

[*Plane takes off*]

RITCHIE [*Slightly off*]. Congratulations, Ritchie! It flies!

RITCHIE [*On*] You know what let's call our invention, Ritchie?

RITCHIE [*Slightly off*] What, Ritchie?

RITCHIE [*Triumphantly*] The *airplane!!!!!*

[*Full airplane motor up to dominate scene—hold—then cross-
fade into sound of vacuum cleaner running with bag discon-
nected—lots of fan gust*]

FATHER [*Fading in, coughing*]. What the devil are you doing, Ritchie?
[*Coughs*] Put the bag back on that vacuum cleaner!

MOTHER [*Fading in*]. What's happened? [*Sees*] Ohhhhh! Dust!
All over my nice clean living room! ! ! !

FATHER. For Pete's sake, shut that thing off!

RITCHIE [*Obediently*]. Yes, father.

[*Cut vacuum cleaner*]

FATHER [*Simmering*]. Racing around the room, spraying dust all
over the place!

MOTHER. Look at those piano keys!

FATHER. What will the Winklers think? The one night I wanted to
impress them, and the house looks like a pigsty!

[*Door bell, off*]

FATHER. Good lord! There they are!

[*Music: Bridge, segue into "Inside a Kid's Head" theme*]

[*Slight echo on the following*]

WOMAN. I say there—guide!

GUIDE. Yes, ma'am?

WOMAN. What's happening now?

GUIDE. Well, I think they're at dinner. I can't tell exactly . . .

MAN. Guide, look at the windows of the observation booth! They're
all covered with frost.

GUIDE. Ritchie's father is probably giving him an icy stare. That forms a glacial condition in the brain cells—and probably his thought stream is frozen.

[*Music out*]

[*Dinner effects . . . dishes, etc.*]

RITCHIE [*Meekly*]. May I have another helping of dessert, please?

FATHER [*Icily*]. You may *not!* [*Then warmly*] As I was saying, J.B., we all know how badly the state highway commission has been run. Now, if I'm elected state assemblyman, that graft is going to be stopped.

WINKLER [*An Edward Arnold character—we've met him before as King John*]. A lofty sentiment, Price.

FATHER. Now, I have facts on this highway swindle that'll blow the opposition to bits. It's all typed out, here in this article. [*Taps the newspaper significantly*] But Jeff Green's newspaper won't print it—he's on the other side of the fence, politically.

WINKLER [*Clears this throat*].

FATHER. What's the matter, J.B.?

WINKLER. Well . . . there seems to be a little dust in my coffee.

MOTHER [*Quickly*]. Oh, I'll get you another cup right away, Mr. Winkler! [*Fading*] Gracious!

BILLY [*A nasty kid*]. What are you kickin' about, pop! There was dust all over my mashed potatoes.

WINKLER. Be quiet, Billy.

FATHER [*A little self-conscious laugh*]. Well, as I was saying, here's my idea, J.B. Get an appropriation from the party funds to print up and mail a copy of this exposé to every voter in the county. The election'd be in the bag!

MOTHER. There'll be some more coffee along in a minute. Why don't we all go into the living room and have it there?

[*Shuffling of chairs*]

FATHER. Good idea. [*Pointedly*] Ritchie, you take Billy up to your room and show him your electric train.

BILLY [*Superiorly*]. Oh. Does he still play with electric trains?

WINKLER. Run along, Billy.

BILLY [*Bored*]. Okay.

FATHER [*Fading off*]. Now, it may run into some money, J.B.—but as I see it, it's the only sure way to get the votes we need.

RITCHIE [*Dully*]. Come on.

[*Footsteps, up stairs*]

BILLY. Don't you folks ever clean your house?

RITCHIE. Sure we do!

BILLY. *We* got a maid that comes in every day!

RITCHIE. Aw, who wants an old maid?

[*Door opens*]

RITCHIE. This is my room.

BILLY. Gee, it's small. [*Let's get it over with!*] Let's see your train.

RITCHIE. It's all set up over here. [*Getting enthusiastic*] It's got a variable speed rheostat, automatic signals, an' it'll stop on a dime! Watch!

[*Purr of toy train . . . then stops*]

See? Isn't that keen?

BILLY. Nah. It's punk. That's for kids. What else you got?

RITCHIE [*Grimly*]. I got some boxing gloves. Here. Try 'em on.

BILLY. I don't like boxing gloves.

RITCHIE. C'mon. I'll show yuh somethin'.

BILLY. I don't wanna.

RITCHIE. You said you didn't like kid stuff. Well, this ain't kid stuff. Come on, put up your dukes!

BILLY. Hey, wait a minute! Don't you hurt me!

RITCHIE. It's easy, see? You lead with your right—an' then with your left. Like this . . . one-two—one-two . . . one-two . . .

[*Music: Vibraphone—bong! As before*]

[*Fade in terrific cheers, as at Madison Square Garden . . . Thud of blows landing, heavy breathing of boxers*]

RADIO VOICE. A right to the body and a left to the head! And another! And another! It's the old one-two, one-two! Dempsey's in rare form tonight! It's the fight of his life! [*A big shout from the crowd*] Ooohhhh! The challenger just launched a terrific left to Dempsey's chin! He's reeling—! The champ's against the ropes—!

[*Fight gong*]

And there's the bell that ends the round! The seconds are helping Dempsey back to his corner . . .

[*Fade slightly*]

[*Crowd up and down*]

TRAINER [*Same voice as Mac*]. How are yuh, Ritchie? Are yuh all right, boy?

RITCHIE. It was nothing, Mac! Gimme that towel!

TRAINER. Don't forget—Ritchie Dempsey has never lost a fight!

RITCHIE. Don't worry, Mac—I won't let you down!

TRAINER. It's not just the world's heavyweight championship that's at stake—or that million-dollar purse!—but Mary Jane has promised to walk home from school with the winner of this fight!!!

RITCHIE [*Aglow*]. Did she really say that?

TRAINER. And what's more—she's out there in the audience now, cheering for you!

RITCHIE [*Melodramatically*]. Mary Jane! Here???????

MARY JANE [*Floating over the crowd*]. Hurray for Ritchie Dempsey!
    [*Fight gong*]

RITCHIE [*Gritting, under his breath*]. Let me at that Billy Firpo!
    [*Crowd cheers up*]

RADIO VOICE. They're coming out of their corners . . .
    [*Terrific sock! Crowd goes crazy*]
    Ooooohhhhh! With the first punch of the round, Ritchie Dempsey knocks the challenger *out cold!!!*
    [*Crowd up*]
    Mr. Dempsey! Won't you say something to our radio audience?

RITCHIE [*With magnanimous modesty*]. Gentlemen! I am happy to be the *heavyweight champion of the world!!!!*
    [*Swell crowd up full, then cut abruptly on door slam*]

FATHER. Ritchie! What's happened?

WINKLER. What's Billy doing there on the floor? Wake up, son— wake up!

RITCHIE [*Weakly*]. We was just . . . playin' . . .

FATHER. The boy's out cold! Mother, get some smelling salts!

MOTHER [*Fading*]. Oh, dear . . .

BILLY [*Coming to*]. Huh? What happened?

WINKLER [*Up, to mother*]. Never mind, Mrs. Price. He's coming to.
    [*To Billy*] Are you hurt, son?

BILLY. My chin hurts. [*Tattle tale*] He hit me on the chin!

FATHER. Ritchie!

WINKLER [*Crisply*]. Would you mind getting our coats! I'd better get the boy home.

FATHER [*Panicky*]. But, J.B.! What about the election? What about—
WINKLER. We'll have to forget the whole thing for now. And, Price—
if that was *my* boy, he'd get a good—*talking to!!!!*
[*Door opens*]
Good night.
MOTHER } [*Weakly*]. Good night.
FATHER }
[*Door slams*]
[*There is a menacing pause*]
RITCHIE [*Filling the void*]. I—I guess Mr. Winkler was sorta mad . . .
wasn't he, father?
FATHER. Ritchie.
RITCHIE. Yes, dad?
FATHER [*Not raising his voice, very calmly*]. You wanted me to be
elected state assemblyman next Tuesday, didn't you?
RITCHIE. Sure, dad.
FATHER. There isn't a chance now. Mr. Winkler was the only man
who could get that article of mine published and circulated.
RITCHIE [*Meekly*]. Would you like to take away my allowance for
a week?
FATHER. Ritchie, your mother and I are going to give you just one
more chance. If I hear of your misbehaving just *once* again—
something *drastic* is going to happen.
RITCHIE [*To himself*]. Gee whiz.
FATHER. Is there any aspirin, Ella?
MOTHER. Yes . . . in the medicine chest.
FATHER. I'm going to lie down for a while. [*Fading*] This is one of
the most hectic evenings I've ever spent.
[*Door opens and closes*]
RITCHIE [*With a gulp*]. Mom?
MOTHER. Yes, Ritchie?
RITCHIE. Did you give Dad that note from Miss Ludlow yet?
MOTHER. I gave it to him, but he just stuffed it in his pocket. I don't
think he's read it yet.
RITCHIE. You don't, huh? [*Overly innocent*] Mom . . . was it his
suit coat pocket or his *over*coat pocket?

[*Music: "Inside a Kid's Head" theme . . . down behind*]

[*Echo on the following*]
[*Fire gong, clanging violently*]
WOMAN. Good gracious, guide! What's that?
GUIDE. That's a three-alarm warning from the conscience.
MAN. What's going on?
WOMAN. Is there any danger?
GUIDE. Can't tell exactly, yet. Evidently young Ritchie's up to some-
thing he shouldn't be doing. I haven't heard a racket like that
from his conscience since he cribbed in an arithmetic exam
back in '43.
[*Fire gong becomes fainter and more muffled*]
WOMAN. Say, guide! Isn't it getting fainter?
GUIDE [*With a sigh*]. Yes—I'm afraid he isn't paying much attention
to it.
[*Gong cuts off*]
MAN. Oh-oh! What's happened?
GUIDE. Let's tune in on the visual channel and see what he's up to.
[*Heterodyne squeals, static, etc.*]
[*Shocked whisper*]. Do you see what he's doing? He's sneaking
into his father's closet . . . he's reaching into his father's coat
pocket . . . he's groping around in the dark . . .
WOMAN [*Little fearful gasp*].
GUIDE. He's taking an envelope out of the pocket and slipping it under
his sweater.
[*Sliding chairs, jarring of heavy footsteps*]

[*Music goes into jarring, out-of-beat rhythm*]
MAN ⎫
WOMAN ⎭ [*Gasps, as if being shaken up*].
GUIDE. Hang onto your chairs, ladies and gentlemen! There's nothing
to worry about! Ritchie's just going downstairs *three steps at a
time!!!!*

[*Music swells into bridge . . . down into*]

[*Door open. Fade in hum-clack of linotype machine*]
RITCHIE [*Puffing*]. Hi, Mac!
MAC [*Noncommittal*]. Hi, Ritchie.
[*Treats Ritchie as an adult and an equal. He alone under-
stands Ritchie's problems. He's laconic, slow-speaking*]

[Linotype continues for a while . . . then shuts off]
RITCHIE [*Professionally*]. Puttin' the paper to bed, Mac?
MAC. Yep.
RITCHIE. Got much more to linotype?
MAC. Just the editorials. Then we're all washed up.
RITCHIE. Will yuh let me type some?
MAC. Mebbe. [*Pause*] Well, spill it.
RITCHIE. Huh?
MAC. Spill it. What's on your mind?
RITCHIE. Oh. [*With a heavy sigh*] Gosh, Mac! Nobody understands me—except you! You're the only friend I've got in the world!
MAC. Trouble at home?
RITCHIE [*Wearily*]. Trouble every place! I guess I dinged my dad's chances of bein' state assemblyman . . . I got bawled out at school . . . Mary Jane doesn't like me any more . . . an' everything . . . !
MAC. Mmmmm-hmmmm. Where was yuh runnin' from just now?
RITCHIE. Home. [*Then blurting out the whole story in a burst of words*] I said King John invented the sewing machine, an' Miss Ludlow gave me a note to take home to my dad, an' all kinds of terrible things happened at home, so I took the note out of my dad's pocket so he wouldn't see it . . . and . . . well . . . here I am!
MAC [*Narrowing his eyes*]. Yuh mean yuh went through your pa's pockets?
RITCHIE. I didn't steal anything! I jes' *borrowed* the note for a while . . . so's he wouldn't see it and have more to worry about.
MAC. Lemme see that note.
RITCHIE. Here.
[*Rustle of paper*]
MAC [*Reading*]. Hm. [*Looking up*] Miss Ludlow write this?
RITCHIE. Yeah.
MAC [*Reading*]. "I charge . . . that the state highway commission . . . is rife with graft and corruption . . ."
RITCHIE [*Sunk!*]. Holy Jumpin' Jupiter!!!! I got the wrong paper!!
MAC. I kinda wondered if Miss Ludlow was goin' into politics.
RITCHIE. Oh, Mac—my dad'll skin me! Everything's wrong now!
[*Almost in tears*] Gee whiz, Mac! What'll I do????

MAC. Look. Things'll work out all right. What you gotta do is get your mind offa your troubles. Why don't you go over an' knock out a few lines on the other linotype?

RITCHIE [*Getting out of his sulk*]. Can I? Honest?

MAC. Sure. But watch out you don't get a shock from that Square-D switch on the baseboard.

RITCHIE. Thanks, Mac—gee! Thanks!

[*Hum of linotype starting. Clack of keys*]
Gosh! Now what'll I write?

[*Music: Vibraphone—bong! As before, as Ritchie goes off into another dream*]

[*Calling*]. Oh, Miss Mary Jane!

MARY JANE [*Off*]. Yes, Mr. Franklin?

RITCHIE. Bring your notebook in here. I want to give you some dictation for Poor Ritchie's Almanac.

MARY JANE [*Fading in*]. Yes, Mr. Franklin.

RITCHIE. Take a maxim! "A penny saved is a penny earned." How do you like that, Miss Mary Jane?

MARY JANE. A lofty sentiment, Mr. Franklin.

RITCHIE. You may call me Ritchie, if you like.

MARY JANE. Oh, thank you . . . Ritchie!

RITCHIE. And here's another one that I thought of yesterday afternoon while I was inventing the rocking chair. "A stitch in time saves nine."

MARY JANE. Oh, you're so clever, Ritchie Franklin.

RITCHIE. Take those down to the pressroom—and see that they get in this issue of Poor Ritchie's Almanac.

MARY JANE. Yes, Mr. Franklin.

RITCHIE. Hmmmm. I have a free hour. What do you suppose I ought to invent?

MARY JANE. *You're* the clever one, Mr. Franklin.

RITCHIE [*A sudden idea*]. I know! It's an idea I had while I was in France last year buying Louisiana! Thought I'd call it the harmonica!

MARY JANE [*Fading*]. I'll take these maxims right down to the print shop.

RITCHIE. Very well.

[*Door closes*]

[*Considering*]. Now, let me see . . .

[*Whistles while there is a bit of hammering, scraping of tools*]

[*Door opens*]

MARY JANE [*Fading in*]. Is there anything else, Mr. Franklin?

RITCHIE. Well, it's all finished! Listen!

[*Quick run, up and down the scale, on a harmonica*]

MARY JANE. Oh, it's *wonderful!* You're so *clever*, Ritchie Franklin!

RITCHIE [*Spencer Tracy modesty*]. It's nothing, really . . .

[*Loud hammering on the door*]

[*Calling*]. Come in!

[*Door opens*]

MINUTEMAN [*The voice is his father's*]. Mr. Franklin! I have a scoop for Poor Ritchie's Almanac! [*Very excited*]

RITCHIE. Now, just calm down, young man, and tell me what this is all about.

MINUTEMAN [*Very excitedly*]. Mr. Franklin, I charge that the Continental Congress is rife with graft and corruption! Here—this paper will explain everything!

RITCHIE. Miss Mary Jane, would you please hand me my bifocals? Thank you. Hmmmm. Why, this will blow the opposition to bits!!!

MINUTEMAN. Every voter in the American colonies should see a copy of this exposé! And you're the only man who can publish and circulate it—in Poor Ritchie's Almanac!

RITCHIE. It's very fortunate that yesterday I invented the linotype machine. Otherwise, we could never get this out in time for today's issue. Come with me!

[*Footsteps . . . Door opening and close . . . fade in hum-clack of linotype machine*]

MINUTEMAN. What an amazing machine! Where did you ever get the idea?

RITCHIE. It came to me like a flash while I was signing the Declaration of Independence. Give me that exposé. I'll set it up myself!

[*Linotype machine runs for a while . . . Then sudden clap of thunder, off*]

What was that?

MARY JANE. It's beginning to thunder and lightning out, Mr. Franklin!

RITCHIE. Lightning! That's just what I've been waiting for! Miss Mary
Jane, get me my kite!

MARY JANE. Here it is, Mr. Franklin!

[*Footsteps, door opens, fade in terrific storm—wind, rain, and
thunder*]

MINUTEMAN. I'll help you launch it, Mr. Franklin!

RITCHIE. Thank you, son! There she goes! Now! Hand me that key,
Miss Mary Jane!

MARY JANE. Here you are, sir! [*Aside, hero-worshiping*] Oh, I wonder
what he's going to invent now!

RITCHIE. I think the kite's up high enough! Now, watch carefully,
everyone! I'm going to touch this key to the kite string!

[*Sputter of electric arc. Cheat storm down a little to emphasize
this*]

ALL [*"Ohhhs" and "Ahhhhhs"*]. . .

RITCHIE [*Dramatically*]. Gentlemen! I have decided to call my invention—*electricity!!!!*

[*Sputter of arc up sharply*]

OUCH!!!!

[*Storm cuts out abruptly*]

MAC. Ritchie, I told yuh you'd get a shock if yuh touched that
Square-D switch. After all the times I've let you play with that
linotype, you oughta know better!

RITCHIE. Gosh! I burned my finger!—an' it hurts . . . !

MAC. Here . . . let me see it.

RITCHIE. Ow!

MAC. That's kind of a bad burn. We better go next door, an' I'll
give yuh some first aid. [*Calling*] Joe! Lock up that editorial
page, will you?

[*Music: Bridge . . . segue into "Inside a Kid's Head" theme*]

WOMAN. Guide, what's happening now? I can't see a thing!

GUIDE. Nothing's happening, ma'am. The boy's asleep—and he's not
even dreaming.

MAN. How come?

GUIDE. I think he's blown a fuse in his imagination. Besides, he's had
a pretty tough day. But something ought to be happening soon.
You see, it's morning already.

MOTHER [*Distant and muffled*]. Ritchie! Ritchie! Wake up!

GUIDE [*Fading*]. That's his mother calling him now.

MOTHER [*On mike, clear*]. Wake up, Ritchie!

[*Babble of voices in the background*].

RITCHIE [*Waking up*]. Huh? [*With a start*] Say! What's going on downstairs?

MOTHER. Put on your bathrobe and come down. Just about everybody in town's here! [*Fading*] Your father's so excited he can hardly talk.

RITCHIE [*Half to himself*]. Gee whiz! *Now* what have I done? [*Rustle of bedclothes*] Dawgone! This sleeve's always wrong side out!

[*Footsteps—slippers. Gallop downstairs. Babbling of crowd fades in*]

VOICE [*Fading in*]. Price, that's the cleverest political move that's ever been made in this state. You're as good as in office right now!

FATHER [*Beaming*]. Thank you! Thank you!

SECOND VOICE. That editorial of yours has blasted the state highway commission wide open!

WINKLER. What *I* can't understand, Price, is how you got the opposition paper to print that editorial of yours!

FATHER [*On thin ice*]. Well . . . you're not the only one, J.B.! [*An uncertain little laugh*]

RITCHIE [*Tugging at his mother's skirts*]. Mom, what's happened?

MOTHER. Well, that article of your father's is in the morning paper.

RITCHIE [*Fearing the worst*]. Oh, gee! [*Suddenly*] Hey! What's Mary Jane doing here!?

MOTHER. She came over with her father. [*Distressed*] Oh, dear! I wish I'd put those new curtains up yesterday! Everybody in town's here to congratulate your father!

VOICE [*Fading in*]. A brilliant article, Price—brilliant! Frankly, though, I didn't quite get that reference in the last paragraph to the "Continental Congress."

FATHER [*Self-conscious laugh*]. Well, there are a *number* of people here who didn't understand that!

MOTHER [*Fading in—low, confidential, to Father*]. Ralph, I'm so proud of you. But how *did* that article get printed in the paper?

FATHER [*Low*]. Darned if I know. Somebody must've just taken it out of my pocket, and . . . [*Comes the dawn*] Sa-a-ay! [*Eyes narrowing*] Ritchie!

RITCHIE [*With a wholly futile front of innocence*]. Yes, father?

FATHER [*Slowly*]. You didn't happen to take anything out of my pocket last night, did you?

RITCHIE [*Groping*]. As a matter of fact, I did. . . . [*Then blurting, fast*] But I jes' meant to get the note from Miss Ludlow, 'cause you were so upset! I got your article by mistake, an' I was gonna put it back! Honest I was!

FATHER. But how in blazes did it get in the paper?

RITCHIE [*Very fast*]. Well . . . I went down to see Mac . . . an' he let me play with the linotype machine . . . an' I guess I set up your speech . . . an' I guess Joe put it in the form . . . [*Trailing off, weakly*] an' I guess it got in the paper! [*Pleading*] Please don't be mad!

FATHER. Mad! [*Expansive, full voice*] *Folks! I want you to meet my boy!!!*

RITCHIE [*Nonplussed*]. Gee whiz!

FATHER. If I'm elected on Tuesday . . .

VOICE [*Off confidently*]. You will be, Ralph!

FATHER. Well, then—all the credit goes to Ritchie here! If it weren't for what he did, I wouldn't stand a chance of being state assemblyman!

ALL [*Babble of exclamation*].

MARY JANE [*Fading in*]. Oh, Ritchie! I'm so proud of you! [*Kisses him audibly*]

RITCHIE [*Bubbling*]. Gosh, Mary Jane! You kissed me! Gee whiz! You kissed me on the cheek!!!!

FATHER [*Still expansive*]. You know—I'd like to make a prediction right now! I'll bet dollars to doughnuts my boy Ritchie will be one of the great political leaders of his day!!!!

[*Music: Vibraphone—bong! As before—and Ritchie goes off into another dream*]

RITCHIE [*Solemnly*]. Gentlemen! I shall be very happy to speak at Gettysburg!

[*Music: Big curtain*]

LONDON BY CLIPPER

Norman Corwin

SOON AFTER our part in World War II began, and it became ever more important that Americans understand how our allies were living and fighting, CBS sent Norman Corwin overseas to write of Britain at war as he found her. The OWI had urged that such a series be done, and CBS took on the challenge, asking Corwin to do the series. Hardly any other radio writer could have seized on the possibilities of the assignment as imaginatively as Corwin did; few could have handled it with so sound a feeling for the needs of the moment.

Postwar American radio needs to develop the sort of thing Corwin did in the *American in England* series—of which we include here the first script. In peace even more than in war we need such series. We need constantly increasing knowledge of other lands, and the roving radio playwright can do his part.

Corwin is important to radio not only because of his own outstanding writing and directing, but also because of the influence he has had on others. There used to be among radio writers pro-Corwin and anti-Corwin factions, but the latter has gradually dissolved, and Corwin now holds among fellow writers a kind of esteem no one else in the field possesses.

Corwin, one of the best informed of radio writers, never went to college. He spent those years writing for the Springfield *Republican*—as movie critic, sports reporter, and various other things.

He slid into radio gradually. The *Republican* assigned him to read, over stations WBZ-WBZA, a nightly news commentary which the newspaper had agreed to furnish. He won some regional renown out of it and it got under his skin. Later, when his brother Emil got him a job in New York writing promotional radio scripts for Twentieth Century-Fox Films, he persuaded New York's station WQXR to let him read poems, talk about them, and experiment in ways of presenting them on the air. The program attracted the attention of CBS, which hired him for its staff.

Network audiences began to notice Corwin first when, on Sunday afternoons, he launched his memorable *Words Without Music* series, a further development of his WQXR experiments. The series consisted of radio arrangements of poems, from nursery rhymes to large works like Sandburg's *The People, Yes*. The method varied according to the poem. It made use of any devices that would heighten the effect of a poem: sound effects, music, dramatization, choral speech, and even silence. The choral speech was regarded by some people as "arty," but was so successful with listeners that before long producers of dramatized commercials began to use Corwin's choral speech group for spot announcements to sell soap flakes.

For *Words Without Music* Corwin wrote some original poetry-for-radio, and so did many others. The series drew astonishing mail response, which included contributions from well-known poets. Listening to Corwin's broadcasts, they had felt a desire to contribute to something new and exciting. Radio poetry, which had stirred into life as a result of MacLeish's *Fall of the City,* received enormous impetus from *Words Without Music.*

After this series Corwin was assigned by CBS to produce an Americana variety series, *Pursuit of Happiness.* On this he introduced to radio *Ballad for Americans,* which also started something new—the short radio opera. The story of this form is sketched in the introduction to *The Lonesome Train,* in this collection. Corwin contributed to it with writings of his own, and by making known to large radio audiences the talents of Earl Robinson, Millard Lampell, and others.

During the war Corwin became one of the most effective of war writers. His magnificent *We Hold These Truths,* his scripts for *American in England,* and his V-E Day program *On a Note of Triumph,* each crystallized the meaning of the hour.

On the eve of the crucial election of 1944, Corwin produced for the Democratic National Committee a program in which many of the actors were not actors but people, speaking as themselves, in effective montages arranged by Corwin, and scored with music and choral backgrounds. This dramatico-musical use of actual people and of "remote pickups" from many points was also a feature of the one-hour program produced by Corwin for the opening of the San Francisco Conference on international organization. These programs clinched Corwin's position as the outstanding creator of special-event programs.

Corwin writes in many moods and styles. When using narration, as he generally does in his more ambitious scripts, the style varies with the narrator he is writing for. In several of his earlier documentaries he wrote for House Jameson. Jameson's voice is a magnificently mellow instrument; he is a master of language cadences and has a fine gift for irony. Narrative roles written for him by Corwin tend toward an elaborate style, with an Olympian quality about them. In these Corwin seems to look on the human scene from somewhere else.

In a number of wartime scripts Corwin wrote for Joe Julian as narrator. He has a down-to-earth, GI quality. In narration written for him, Corwin takes a people's-eye view, and writes with eloquence of a simpler kind.

In some recent programs, Corwin has used Martin Gabel. Gabel has a brusque quality and a sort of smoldering anger in his voice. He is Corwin's voice of challenge. Elaborate structures and figures of speech reappear, but with an aggressive quality replacing the polite irony of earlier programs.

American in England, including *London by Clipper,* was written for Joe Julian, who flew with Corwin on his trip.

LONDON BY CLIPPER*

JOE [*Annoyed*]. Hello! . . . hello! . . . What's the matter with this line?

[*Jiggling hook*]

Hello, reservations? I guess we were cut off. I was asking how much baggage I can take on the Clipper tomorrow . . . yes, to England. Huh? [*Incredulous*] *Forty-four pounds!* Is that all? [*Protesting*] Why, my suitcase and a couple of neckties weigh forty-four pounds! . . . Well, can't I take more if I *pay?* . . . [*Amazed*] You mean to say I'd have to get an order from the War Department if I want to carry more baggage? . . . Well, no, not in that case. . . . No. Take too much time. . . . All right. . . . When do I show up at the airport? . . . Four in the *morning?* And you leave at six. . . . Okay. Thank you. . . . G'by.

[*Receiver up*]

[*Music: Passage conveying the excitement of anticipation. Suddenly it segues, retarding into good-natured morning music. Over the concluding phrases:*]

I took exactly forty-four pounds of luggage with me, and I said good-bye to my folks and my girl and my friends, and at 6:30 in the morning I walked down a ramp to board a Clipper bound for England. . . .

OFFICER. Good morning, sir.

JOE. Good morning.

OFFICER. I'm afraid we're a little late getting started, but we're going to fly direct. We ought to be there in good time.

JOE. That's fine. Thank you.

OFFICER. Yes, sir.

JOE [*To audience*]. That was an officer of the crew. Did you hear what he said? *Direct!* Atlantic *nonstop!* . . .

OFFICER. All passengers aboard, please. . . .

JOE. You get on board and take an assigned seat. You look around

* LONDON BY CLIPPER by Norman Corwin. Copyright, 1945, by Norman Corwin.

at your fellow passengers. Nothing odd about them. Pretty much like the average pay load on the eight-o'clock plane to Washington. . . .

BISHOP. Do you mind if I put my bag on your seat for a moment?

JOE. Go right ahead. Perfectly all right. [*To audience*] That was a bishop. You had an idea only generals and diplomats and business executives went on these flights. . . .

GIRL [*Fifteen years old*]. Pardon me, how soon do we take off?

JOE [*Startled*]. What?

GIRL. How soon do we take off?

JOE. Why, any minute now, I should think.

GIRL. Thank you.

JOE [*To audience*]. Where did she come from? A *kid!* Can't be more than fifteen years old, if she's that. What kind of war is this, anyway? Kids flying the oceans nonstop in a Clipper! Trouble with that kind of thing, it puts you in your place. Up to then you were feeling important. [*Low; apprehensively*] Oh-oh . . . looks like we won't get to see the take-off! . . .

STEWARDESS. I'm sorry, but curtains must be pulled down over the windows until we're twenty minutes out. War regulations. . . .

JOE. Stewardess. For a while you thought she might be English, but you find out later she comes from New Jersey. Life can be just a series of disillusionments sometimes. Jersey takes care of the curtains; then she goes down the passageway to shut the door of the ship.

[*Door slams*]

That, you say to yourself, is no ordinary door. That door won't be opened again until you've crossed an ocean. . . .

OFFICER. Tell the captain we're all set back here, Miss Malone.

STEWARDESS. Yes, sir. . . .

JOE. Well, so we're all set. And with our nose pointed in the general direction of war, we take off.

[*Music: A brief passage symbolic of take-off. It cross-fades to the effect of engines in full flight, as heard from inside the cabin. This sustains behind all but the indicated musical interpolations in the following:*]

Twenty minutes out, and the curtains go up. You look below and see your country gliding westward; you see the farms and woods and towns of two of the forty-eight states and the blue Atlantic. It's a calm day—a fine North American summer morning, just a little mist. . . .

PASSENGER. I say, aren't those some warships down there?

JOE. Where? [*Patronizingly; to audience*] Obviously this passenger hasn't traveled much by air. Can't gauge altitudes. [*To passenger*] No, those aren't warships. Just a couple of fishing boats.

PASSENGER. But they're bigger than fishing boats. We're up pretty high. They must be destroyers.

JOE. No, we're only up a couple of thousand feet.

PASSENGER. All the same they're good-sized ships.

JOE [*Genially*]. Okay. [*Pause*] The last of the land is slipping away now. Only islands ahead. The ship flies steady. The air is smooth; cabin's settled down now. Everything's quiet. . . .

PASSENGER. Hey, what's that stuff on the water there?

JOE. What stuff? [*Pause; to audience*] You look out of the window and see something that hits you like a sledge hammer.

[*Music: A sudden and dark presence, forte. It sustains, somberly and sinuously, under the following:*]

Oil, thick oil. Far as the eye can see. Great patches of oil, spread out over mile after square mile of water, covering the ocean with a gray-green scum. That's war, drifting inshore with the tide. These patches are all that's left of American and Allied ships torpedoed recently along the coast. You wonder how many good men lie in those waters—how many thousands of tons of munitions and food for England and Russia are rotting beneath the surface of this oil. Gives you a new slant, looking down on this tremendous oil slick, about people who act careless with the dim-out, as though it were a kind of nuisance, a kind of make-believe. Well, it's not. That oil down there ain't kidding.

[*Music: Crosses with sound*]

[*Motors again*]

You find yourself thinking about the boys who sail those ships.

You wonder whether you would have the guts to sign on to the crew of a tanker. . . .

PASSENGER. Will you have a cigarette?

JOE. [*Coming out of it*]. Oh—yes, thanks.

PASSENGER [*Qualifying his offer*]. It's English—

JOE. That's okay. I like English cigarettes.

PASSENGER. Then that's one problem you won't have to face in England.

JOE. Yeah. [*Chuckles; to himself*] Say, that's right. You *are* going to *England*, aren't you? Almost forgot that in the last-minute rush. You pinch yourself and wake up to the fact that you're very much on your way—that you're actually flying the Atlantic nonstop. Been out of sight of land for some time now.

Sure enough, going to England. You wonder whether you will like the people as much as you like their cigarettes. Are the people a mild, mixed blend, like their tobacco? Nonirritating? It occurs to you that we Americans as a whole know very little about Britishers, although we've been speaking their language all our lives, and half our cities are named after theirs. We know more about English dogs and muffins and tweeds than about English people. According to what we've always imagined, England is made up of three or four distinct types. There's the upper-class old-school-tie Lord Smudgepot type, who's filed away in your mind as a stuffed shirt, and who talks like this:

[*Motors out*]

SMUDGEPOT. Absolutely ripping, old fruit. I remember at Ascot one year early in June. It was really remarkable. Believe it or not, the jolly old horse actually stopped running.

[*Motors in*]

JOE. That's the fellow you blame for the loss of Singapore. And then there's another type you're sure represents most of Great Britain —the cockney. You gather from the movies that all cockneys are natural-born comedians who break into song at the slightest opportunity, like this:

COCKNEY. Talk about a toff—blimey, you ought to see him sitting around Covent Garden in a—

[*Music: Tremendous exaggerated opening to song, which then*

*reduces rapidly to a mere patter of accompaniment. The whole
effect fades under:*]

[*Motors in*]

JOE. And then there's the high-spiriter type who founded the Empire
and has been losing it, cheerfully, ever since. . . .

[*Motors out*]

CHEERFUL. Chin up, cheerio, carry on, old chap—bear up, righto,
wot? . . .

JOE. So altogether, when you try to picture the average Englishman,
he seems to you mainly one of two things: a cold, calm, aloof
highbrow or a funny little guy who sings.

Oh, well . . . you look out of the window at a sky full of
broken clouds and wonder where you got some of those ideas.
Maybe from the movies, or the novels, or the short-wave radio.
BBC news broadcasts, perhaps—very calm, very cultured they are
about the news. They don't go in for the shouting and wheezing
and high-pressure opinionizing that we do at home. No question
about it—they're a cool bunch. Why, if the world were to come
to an end at three tomorrow afternoon, they'd wait until the
regular six o'clock broadcast and go on as usual. . . .

NEWS. This is London calling. Here is the news, and this is John
Snagge reading it. The world came to an end at two minutes
after three this afternoon, during a debate in the House of Com-
mons. A summary of the debate will be given at the end of this
bulletin. Due to the unusual nature of the event and also to the
fact that he was away at the time, Mr. Churchill could not
be reached immediately to comment on the policy that His
Majesty's Government intends to pursue regarding the situation. . . .

JOE. Yes, that's about how it would be. [*Chuckles; then sobers suddenly*] Hey, look—there's a convoy directly beneath you. Ten
freighters. Headed the same way you are. Wonder if there were
more than ten when they started out? Your friend in the seat
opposite also sights the ships. . . .

PASSENGER. Say, isn't that a convoy down there?

JOE. Either that or a reasonable facsimile.

PASSENGER. They seem to be pitching, don't they? Must be a heavy sea. Certainly looks like a millpond from up here.

JOE. Certainly does. [*After pause; to audience*] We're leaving them behind pretty fast now. So long, convoy. You take the low road and we take the high road, and we'll get to London before you. [*Abstractedly humming "Loch Lomond"*] Getting a little stuffy in the cabin now. Let's see, you were figuring how much you know about the British. Hmmmm. [*New thought*] What's the lowdown about them as *fighters?* That's the important thing right now, isn't it? Not how they talk and broadcast news. You wonder how much one can believe of what one hears. Are they really starving, for example? Eating horsemeat and seaweed? Have they lost confidence in themselves after the shellackings they took? Maybe they're just sitting back waiting for America and Russia to win the war for them.

Someone said the island was chock-full of well-trained, fully equipped troops hanging around doing nothing because they lack the courage and the audacity to attack. Were they really hard and tough during the bombings, or was that just propaganda? Well—all these things are what you're going over to find out about. Have to check into those stories about their sympathy for Russia and the rubbing out of old class distinctions. Yes, you'll see—you'll give a good look around when you get there. Oh, dear—yawn coming on. [*Yawns*] Pretty tired now. No sleep for the past two nights.

You yawn two or three more times, and then you decide that, war or no war, you're going to leave the Clipper to its crew and the Atlantic to its weather and England to tomorrow—and get some sleep. You crawl into your berth and do acrobatics to undress, and then you lie in a sort of stupor, drugged by the noise of the motors.

[*Motors behind this*]
After a while you become conscious of a sound from the bridge—radio code. . . .
[*Slow code. A fat spark—dot-dot-dot-dash*]
Isn't that the V symbol? V for victory? What's it doing on that receiver? You're too tired to wonder. . . . And then, for no good reason, you begin to think of *music.* Maybe because of

the rhythms set up by the vibration. You try to recall what little
English music you've heard, and it isn't at all hard to remember.
It very obligingly runs through your head.

[*Music: A mnemonic melange, sneaking in as:*]

[*Motors fade slightly. The effect goes on under:*]
And somehow or other, as you drop away into a spongy sleep,
it all gets mixed up like a radioman's nightmare—code, and
motors, and Gilbert and Sullivan, and static, and "Pomp and
Circumstance" and V for victory—and the night. . . .

[*Music: A disturbed montage as described, with sounds of
motors and code interspersed ad libitum. At length a sustained
quiet passage suggestive of sleep. Then suddenly a flourish of
awakening*]

STEWARDESS [*Announcing*]. An hour and ten minutes to your destination! One hour and ten minutes to your destination! . . .
JOE. That's how the passengers are awakened. By Miss Malone of
New Jersey, the self-winding cuckoo clock with the English
accent. Of course she doesn't say "Your destination"—she names
the place. Naturally we can't do the same on the air for obvious
reasons—censorship. . . .
STEWARDESS. Good morning.
JOE. Good morning, Miss Malone. [*To audience*] Wartime censorship
isn't a gag—it's a protection. [*Yawning*] Heeaaww. That wasn't
much sleep. Flying east as fast as we've flown, the night gets
folded up like an accordion. [*Returning to the thought*] Why is
it nobody loves a censor? He's like a baseball umpire—everybody
wants to kill the bum. Yet he does an important job—a vital
job, in fact. Any man who keeps information away from the swine
is a friend of mine. Well, so the Clipper (which you feel you've
been on all your life by now) makes a beautiful landing at a
place called—
CENSOR. Censored.
JOE. And she tears around in the water like a speed boat for a while,
and then finally she moors; and you disembark; and you go
through the customs in a building overlooking the beautiful—
CENSOR. Censored.

JOE. Then you have breakfast, and you all pile into a —

CENSOR. Censored.

JOE. And you travel for a censored number of miles to a censored place, where you are met by a censored type of camouflaged airship whose windows are censored by white paint. It's a white-out—allows light to come through, but keeps you from seeing anything. And you get into that plane and fly for a censored number of hours, and then—well, then you're *there!*

[*Music: Landing; arrival; a stern passage with suggestion of excitement and premonition of grimness. It sustains for some time under:*]

You are on the soil of England. You're on the island that fought the Nazis alone for a year. You look around. . . .

OFFICER. This way, please. . . .

JOE. And on your way to the customs and censorship you catch a glimpse of the airfield on which your plane landed. It's heavily guarded, heavily camouflaged—warplanes perched here and there —you walk right under the nose of a big Lancaster bomber, and it lifts your heart to see it. It's a strange sensation. You've seen brand-new Flying Fortresses fresh off an American assembly line, and that was a pleasant enough sight—but that was nothing compared to seeing this grizzly old battle-worn giant with bullet holes in his fuselage and one of his wings slightly ruffled. This fellow, you can wager, was over Germany last night. This baby has been carrying the war to where it belongs—right on the front doorstep of the Fascists. . . .

CUSTOMS. Passport, please? . . .

JOE. You're asked some questions by customs officials. . . .

CUSTOMS. Have you credentials? . . .

JOE. You have, and you show them. . . .

CUSTOMS. How long to you plan to stay, please? . . .

JOE. You tell him. . . .

CUSTOMS. Where will you be living in England? . . .

JOE. You tell him. . . .

CUSTOMS. What is the purpose of your visit? Have you documents in your possession? What are your references in England and the United States? . . .

JOE. It's all cordial and routine, and then you move along to the censor. He inspects the contents of your brief case. . . .

CENSOR. Any letters or articles?

JOE. Yes. These. [*Pause*] He reads them. One is a clipping from the New York *Times*—an article damning the British for the loss of Tobruk. Another is a carbon of a letter you wrote to a friend, in which, among other things, you criticize certain British government policies. . . .

CENSOR. Interesting letter, this.

JOE. Thank you.

CENSOR. And this clipping is from the New York *Times?*

JOE. Yes.

CENSOR. These are quite all right. You may go through, sir. I hope I haven't delayed you from catching the special train to London.

JOE. Oh, that's quite all right. [*To audience*] It develops that you *have* lost the train, but in doing so you've gained the comforting knowledge that here, in this small detail, is one of the thousand yardsticks by which one can measure the issues in this war. If anybody in Germany were foolish enough to be found carrying literature critical of the government, he'd either be shot or slapped into a concentration camp.

[*An auto horn blows, about fifty yards away*]
That's the coach that takes you to the London train. It's going to be a long ride to the city, and you're hungry enough to eat a horse. Are horses rationed, by the way? [*To driver*] Driver, I take it there's a dining car on the train to London?

DRIVER. Oh, no, sir. No dining cars on any of the trains. Haven't had them for some time now.

JOE [*Dryly*]. I see. [*To audience*] When you reach the station, you have four minutes in which to get something to eat. You rush into a place marked "Refreshments" and dash up to the counter. . . .

WAITRESS. Yes, sir. What will you have?

JOE. A sandwich, please.

WAITRESS. We have meat pastes, that's all.

JOE. Any milk?

WAITRESS [*Scandalized*]. *Milk?* Of *course* no milk. Coffee!

JOE. All right. Coffee. [*Down*] The train saves you from having to drink the coffee. You feel such coffee is a blow to the Allied cause. And with your forty-four pounds of luggage you board your first English train.

[*Starter's whistle. Then train effect, starting up. It continues in the background all the way under:*]

The train is crowded. It's a warm Sunday, and people are apparently returning to London from outings in the country. Everybody in the compartment looks tired, but none can be as tired as you.

You look at their faces. Good, average, unspectacular, kindly people. No signs of malnutrition in this batch. A little shabby, perhaps—not a new hat or suit or dress in the lot. For a long while you ride in silence. Then you look up, look casually out of the window; and there—right in front of your eyes . . .

[*Music: Shock. It tapers off under:*]

. . . are the first bomb ruins you have ever seen. It's an ordinary suburban house such as you'd find in Chevy Chase, Oak Park, Glendale—any of ten thousand towns in the States. But the roof of this one is burnt away and the insides blasted out . . . and now you're passing a church, a little church like the one in Winthrop, Massachusetts, or Kent, Ohio, or Pleasantville, Mississippi. Only this one is just four hollow walls.

It's different from the pictures in the roto, somehow; different from the newsreels—it's the difference between seeing an actress on the screen and seeing her in person. *This* is the brick and mortar—this is the flesh and blood. It makes you mad—mad enough to forget your fatigue. You catch the eye of the man sitting opposite. [*To the man*] When did they have a crack at this place?

MAN. Fairly recently. About three weeks ago.

JOE. That's the first I've seen.

MAN. Oh. Just come over?

JOE. Well, uh, yes. I'm an American.

MAN. I'm afraid you'll see a good deal more.

JOE. Might be a good idea to ship one of these ruins intact to America and set it up stone by stone in Times Square, so we could see what a bombed house really looks like.

MAN [*Good-naturedly*]. Why do that?

JOE. Because I'm afraid it's hard for some of us to visualize these things at such a distance. To a lot of us the war exists mainly in the newspapers. Here it's blown up your houses and killed your neighbours.

MAN. Yes, I see what you mean.

JOE [*After a pause*]. You have a long conversation with this fellow. He speaks seriously of the war, its aims, the peace after victory. . . .

MAN. You see, I really believe this war is part and parcel of a great revolution which began long before Munich. It's bigger than just a world *war*.

JOE. In what way do you mean?

MAN. Well—things are never going to be the same as they were. That's all done with. The people who are fighting this one and paying for it and suffering its agonies are simply not going to let the old systems take up where they left off.

JOE. Are you talking about all people, or the people of England?

MAN. All people, I *hope*—the English certainly. We've discovered that the idea of every-man-for-himself, that the old class distinctions have outlived their usefulness—if they ever *were* useful. We've found out that when people allow incompetents and blunderers to manage their affairs, they run up a big bill in blood and grief and money.

JOE. But how are you going to do anything about it?

MAN. Well, by insisting on a new life—by demanding that the same tremendous sacrifice and energy, the same resources of men and material that are put into a successful war be put into a successful peace. [*Pause*] It staggers the mind to think of what could be done in the way of housing and health and education for the cost of what it takes to run a week of this war. The idea is first to win the war—and then to see that what *can* be done after this war, *will* be done. [*Pause*] That's what we're fighting for. Not the old stuff.

JOE [*After a pause*]. A silence falls between you; for a while you think over what he's said. Then fatigue sets in again, and you stop thinking and just sit.

The train hurries on. You must be approaching London, be-

cause the barrage balloons are getting thicker. Look like stubby
fish, all swimming the same way—into the wind. The train's
slowing down now, and you make ready to get off. As you
collect your forty-four pounds of luggage, your friend comes
over and takes you aside. . . .

MAN. One thing I wish you'd keep in mind when you're looking
about the country. Don't judge us by the occasional bounder you
may come across . . . there's that kind in every country. And
don't judge us by the lobbies of a few hotels in London. See
us as we are—see us in the towns and villages and on the streets
and in the factories and pubs and army camps and aerodromes
and schools. I think you'll like us. . . .

JOE. By this time the train has arrived, and passengers are crowding
out. . . .

MAN. It's been terribly good talking to you.

JOE. Thanks. It's been a pleasure for me.

MAN. I'm· Flying Officer Hill, Royal Air Force. . . .

JOE. You tell him who you are, and you shake hands. . . .

MAN. Good-bye. Good luck.

JOE. Good-bye. Good luck, sir. [*Pause*] And he's lost in the crowd.
You get out with your luggage and try to get a taxi. [*Up*] Taxi!
Hey, taxi!—Hey, you, how about it?

TAXI. Finished. Just enough petrol to get home.

JOE. What about you, there? [*Whistles*] Hey!

SECOND TAXI. Sorry. Through for the day.

JOE. If you think trying to get a taxi at the depot in *Washington*
is tough! [*Up*] Taxi! [*Down*] You wait an hour, and then
finally one comes along that has enough petrol to take you to
your hotel. You arrive. You get into your room. The curtains
are drawn over all windows. The bathroom window is painted
black. You're hungry. You feel you can eat *two* horses by now.
You order something to eat. . . .

WAITER. Did you ring, sir?

JOE. Yes. I'm starved. Can you bring me some milk?

WAITER. Oh, no, sir. Too late for that.

JOE. Soup?

WAITER. Sorry, sir. All gone by now.

JOE. What *can* you bring me?

WAITER. Some cold meat?

JOE. Okay. . . . The meal arrives, but when it's set on the table,
you can't eat it, because you're even more tired than you are
hungry.

It's getting on toward midnight now. You take a warm bath
and stagger into a robe. Then you switch off the lights and go
over to the window and pull back the curtains.

[*Music: London in the gloom of mid-war blackout*]

London is blacked out. The greatest city in the world lies in a
vast hush between battles. You see the rooftops faint in the light
of the waning moon. And you make out the Thames. You make
out the tall silhouette of Big Ben; you're surprised to find it
this close. [*Pause*] And as you stand at the open window, suddenly you hear airplanes overhead. They must be friendly planes,
or else you'd hear a siren—or wouldn't you? Is that distant
gunfire, or a train crossing a bridge somewhere? Is that a siren,
or a bus starting up in low gear?

The planes keep droning above you. They're heading east to
the attack. They'll be flying over swastikas twenty minutes from
now.

[*Big Ben begins to strike, off in Westminster. It is midnight*]
Ah! Big Ben! Fine, upstanding, outspoken Ben—telling the
world midnight has come again to this island in the third year
of its siege. You wonder how many midnights more will sound
before the siege is turned and *we* do the besieging? How many
midnights more before Big Ben is joined by all the bells in
England and in the whole wide world, proclaiming victory and
peace and the new world of Flying Officer Hill? [*He pauses and
reflects*]

Another plane flies up there somewhere in the black night of
England, bent on making that new world.

[*The twelfth bell, dissolving into:*]

[*Music: Conclusion*]

JAPANESE-AMERICANS

Harry Kleiner

IN THE EARLY years of the war, anti-Japanese feeling in parts of the United States became race hatred of the sort we were theoretically fighting against. This wave of racism threatened the lives and property of many loyal people. And, because it made good material for Japanese propaganda to the Chinese, the Burmese, etc., it was a danger to our position in Asia and throughout the world.

This program on Japanese-Americans can best be understood in perspective if we remember the factors it had to contend with. In the western United States, racism served the purposes of those anxious to eliminate the competition of Japanese-American truck gardeners. In the armed forces, race hatred probably helped, in a short-term sense, to promote a zeal for "killing Japs." These factors make it the more remarkable and creditable that the program was broadcast, that the initiative came from the War Department, and that the program was heard not only on the domestic air but also by our troops on all war fronts.

During 1942-43, the War Department's Armed Forces Radio Service built up a world-wide system of radio stations and sound systems for broadcasting to men overseas. At its peak this chain consisted of some two hundred stations and two hundred sound systems. Every week each of these outlets received, by air transport from the United States, a shipment of over one hundred recorded programs, totaling over fifty hours of broadcasting. Each station could supplement this material with local programs of its own, and with rebroadcasts of short-wave programs—particularly news and special events—beamed from the United States.

The vast AFRS network was at first used chiefly for entertainment and news. When it became increasingly desirable to include programs about the issues of the war, and programs of a general educational nature, the AFRS Education Unit was formed.

One of the first projects planned by this unit, in conjunction with the Army Education Branch, was a series dealing with the "contributions of various culture groups to the history and development of the United States and to the winning of the war." Largely to save army manpower and funds, the project was proposed to the NBC University of the Air, which offered to produce the series at its expense, with the editorial co-operation and supervision of the AFRS. The program pattern agreed on provided that each script should tell the family history behind an American in the armed forces. These case histories might be actual or composite stories. The series, broadcast during the summer of 1944, was given the title *They Call Me Joe. Japanese-Americans* was the eleventh and last in the series.

The programs were heard in the United States via NBC, overseas via the AFRS.

The series received a special citation from the National Conference of Christians and Jews. The programs were written by Frank Wells, Morton Wishengrad, Norman Rosten, Harry Kleiner, and others, and were directed by Frank Papp.

An important feature of the series was the strict avoidance of stereotype dialects; these, it was felt, would set groups apart, instead of emphasizing their community of interests. The character Matsumo had a very slight accent. The other Japanese and Japanese-Americans used no mispronounced l's, no breathy hisses, nor any of the other paraphernalia of a "Japanese" characterization.

Harry Kleiner came to the writing of this script with an interestingly intercultural background. Born in Russia, he traveled all over Europe as an infant, then moved to Havana long enough to learn the language, and came to the United States speaking only Spanish. Here his family was so much on the go that he attended fifteen different public schools. Nevertheless, he won a scholarship to Temple University and another to the Yale Drama School.

While still in college he wrote his own weekly experimental radio drama series for WFIL, Philadelphia. It was inspired by the *Columbia Workshop*. He continued the series from Yale, mailing his script to Philadelphia each week. "More than any other medium today," says Kleiner, "I feel that radio can restore to our literature the beauty of the spoken word, which it has lost since the Elizabethans."

During the war he has written scripts on war themes for a number of series. In a civilian capacity he wrote "industrial incentive" pictures for the Signal Corps Photographic Center. He is the writer of the screen play *Fallen Angel*.

JAPANESE-AMERICANS

[*Fade in sputter of star shells . . . distant artillery*]

SERGEANT [*Low . . . tense*]. Have you got it, everybody? By the time those star shells douse, their 88's will have our range. Pick out a shellhole up ahead—while you can still see. And if you don't make it in the dark before the Jerries send the next star shell up, you'll be a case for the medics. All right, wait till it gets dark . . . Are you ready? . . .

[*Music: Suspense chord . . . Hold under*]

PAUL. That shell crater . . . by what used to be a house . . . that's for me . . . that's for me. . . .

[*Pause*]

[*Whine of shells and explosions through*]

SERGEANT. There go the 88's! Up and over . . .

[*Barrage up. Man running, breathing hard, slide of body into rubble . . . thump. Barrage cuts abruptly same time*]

PAUL [*Frightened*]. Hey! Who's that? Who's that?

GEORGE [*Close, quiet*]. Might ask you the same?

PAUL [*Struggling*]. I'm asking! . . . Are you . . .

GEORGE. 133d Infantry, 34th Division. Take it easy.

PAUL. Whew . . . in the pitch black I was afraid you might be . . .

GEORGE. Keep your relief down, there's a Jerry patrol crawling this way.

PAUL. Right now?

GEORGE. Next star shell and they'll be on us. You're the answer to a prayer . . . Got enough grenades left?

PAUL. None.

GEORGE. Here's a couple. Reach out . . . Got 'em?

PAUL. Got 'em . . . What's that? There's something right ahead . . . I felt it! On the edge of the shell hole!

GEORGE. Sh!

PAUL. I tell you there's something near us—

GEORGE. Five of my buddies . . .

PAUL. Oh . . .

GEORGE. Dead. Those 88's on the ridge . . . Yesterday.

PAUL. You mean you been here with . . . them . . . since . . . ?

GEORGE. Orders were to hold. . . .

PAUL. They've been changed. You're to move ahead, now—

[*Star shells sputtering*]

GEORGE. There go the star shells! Keep down! And hold fire till that Jerry patrol's near enough to—

PAUL. Holy smoke! You're a Jap! A Jap in Italy!

[*Music sweeps in and hold under*]

GEORGE. I will never forget, father, the look on his face as he said: "Holy smoke! you're a Jap!" His face was tense, and he suddenly held his gun as if to jab the bayonet through me. There was hatred in his eyes. Later we went over the top together, and fought well side by side. Afterwards I learnt that this was his first night at Salerno . . . that's why he didn't know. But even now, long afterwards, I remember that look, and I am writing you about it, father, because it shows the problem we face . . . the problem of having America in our bones, but the look of Japan on our faces.

[*Music up and down*]

NISHIDA. Yes. my son at the front, we have a problem. I have never told you much about the story of our family, of how your great-grandfather and others came to America and became a part of it . . . I wanted you to look forward, not backward. But because the story may strengthen you in such moments as you wrote me of, I am writing you this now.

[*Music out*]

Over one hundred years ago, when Japan was a country sealed tight against the outside world, your great-grandfather Bunjii Morimitsu was blown out to sea in a small fishing boat. He was only a boy then. He was rescued by an American whaling ship, and spent ten years in Oregon, where he learned to chop trees [*Smile*], and also the American language. When he had mastered both, he longed to revisit the land of his birth, to see his family once more. Finally he found a ship that was willing to try to take him back [*Fade*] with six other shipwrecked Japanese sailors . . .

[*Sailing ship in wind*]

BUNJII. It's getting clearer now. Yes, that must be Yeddo Harbor. It must be!

CAPTAIN. Fine, Bunjii. That fishing boat starboard side. It's in shouting distance now. Tell 'em what we want. Ask 'em if they'll heave to and take you aboard—all seven of you. Tell 'em all we want them to do is take you ashore. If they'll do that, we won't sail another yard further.

BUNJII [*Shouts it in Japanese*].

VOICE [*Shouts something in Japanese from fishing boat*].

CAPTAIN [*Excitement*]. They're turning about! Are they coming? Are they, Bunjii?

BUNJII [*Disappointed*]. No . . . They're heading for shore, like all the rest of them. Fast as they can. They're frightened.

CAPTAIN. There they go, all right. Like we had the plague. What did they say?

BUNJII. They reminded us that those who leave Japan may never return.

CAPTAIN. Are you sure you want to go through with this, Bunjii?

BUNJII. I *must* see my parents again.

CAPTAIN. Suppose it means prison, or your head off.

BUNJII. Somehow, I must see them.

CAPTAIN. Tell you what I'll do. By now the shore authorities must know what our errand is . . . that we just want to deliver a human cargo, and leave. That our errand is one of mercy, and nothing else. We'll edge closer to the harbor entrance. If they'll let us take you in, we'll get by. If not—we'll know soon enough, I reckon. Port your helm, quartermaster!

VOICE. Aye, aye, sir.

CAPTAIN. Bunjii. On both sides of the harbor there—what do you make of them—heathen temples?

BUNJII. They might be forts.

CAPTAIN. That's what I thought. [*Calling*] Keep a sharp lookout there! Forts to port and starboard. [*On mike*] Bosun! Pipe all hands on deck! Unfurl the tops'l . . . Ready to tack at the first shot!

VOICE. Aye, aye, sir. [*Going off*] All hands on deck! Unfurl the tops'l!

[*Piping. Feet running, etc.*]

CAPTAIN. In two flaps of a sail we'll be on those forts—if that's what they are. Strange-lookin' things, all right.

VOICE [*Far off*]. All quiet at the forts.

CAPTAIN [*Exultant*]. I . . . I believe they're letting us in! . . . Bunjii, my lad, maybe we'll drop you right in the shogun's lap. Sliding right through their line of fire and nary a greeting—

[*Booming of guns, splash of shells in the water*]

VOICE [*Off*]. They're firing from the starboard fort.

CAPTAIN. Hard left, quartermaster.

VOICE. Aye, aye, sir.

[*Boom of cannon*]

CAPTAIN. Hope they don't open up on the portside and catch us in a crossfire.

[*Boom of cannon*]

VOICE. Fire from portside.

CAPTAIN. Straighten her up, quartermaster! Straighten her up.

VOICE. Aye, aye, sir.

CAPTAIN. Bunjii, my lad, that's as close as we'll ever come to those heathen shores. I guess we'll—hey! Where are you going? Come back! Come back!

BUNJII [*Way off*]. I must go! I must!

CAPTAIN. Hold him—hold him. Don't let him jump! Bunjii!

[*Splash*]

VOICE [*Off*]. Man overboard!

CAPTAIN. Bunjii! Bunjii!

VOICE [*In*]. What'll we do, captain?

CAPTAIN. Keep right on going. Get away from here as quick as we can.

VOICE. Look! He's swimming for shore!

CAPTAIN. And if he makes it—heaven help him then.

[*Music: Narrative theme under*]

NISHIDA. My son . . . your great-grandfather became a fugitive in his own land. Hiding by day, stumbling on by night . . . through bamboo saplings that cut the flesh . . . over the steaming marshes on the lava land . . . past hovels on the stony terraces . . . stealing through the lotus-filled estates of the war lords . . . your great-grandfather went, until he reached the lowly hut of his ancestors . . . home.

[*Music out*]

BUNJII. But . . . you *must* listen to me . . . you *must* . . . Don't you understand that—

FATHER. My eldest son will keep his tongue while his elders speak!

BUNJII. I will not be silent, father. I must speak.

UNCLE. Can such things come to pass in this household?

BUNJII. I mean no disrespect, old uncle. But don't you see . . . After ten years, I have at last returned to my home. And now, after all this, you tell me that—

FATHER. It must be, my son.

BUNJII. You too, father?

FATHER. I am an obedient subject.

BUNJII. But . . . I don't understand. *Why* must—

UNCLE. The all-wise shogun has decreed that whoever leaves Japan must never return.

BUNJII. But I was blown to sea, against my will. For five days I struggled against wind and waves, and then when I—

FATHER [*Interrupt*]. My son, the venerable uncle speaks for the Council of Relatives . . . Whatever the reason for leaving, you must be turned over to the mercy of the shogun.

BUNJII. What mercy is there in an ax?

FATHER [*Struggling*]. I have called the Council of Relatives into my house to decide what is to be done. They have determined you must be given up.

BUNJII. Have my honorable relatives asked *me* if I want to die?

VOICES. Ask him?
What is that he said?
Why should his relatives ask him?

FATHER [*Over voices*]. Have you forgotten the teachings of your youth, my son? It is the Council of Relatives which decides what to do with every life in a household.

UNCLE. And the shogun is the Supreme Will of all.

BUNJII. But it is *my* life. As long as I hurt no one, *I* should decide what to do with it.

[*Murmur of horror starts*]

This I have found in the land across the sea—

UNCLE [*Topping*]. Silence! Silence! [*Ad lib stops*] "Whosoever leaves the land, his Japanese spirit departeth also." So the thought controllers have said. It is your moral duty to die, my nephew. For whoever leaves the Land of the Gods cannot come back the same.

BUNJII [*Quiet*]. No . . . you are right . . . never the same! Because the shogun knows if we ever see how other men live—!

FATHER. Let my honorable relatives be poisoned no more by the words of my unworthy son! My eldest son . . . it is the will of the Council of your uncles . . . brothers-in-law . . . brother . . . and father . . . that you—

BUNJII [*Desperately*]. Father, no!

VOICES [*Together*]. Let us bring him to the Thought Police.

Let them come here!

To our household? He *must* go there, or shame us forever!

BUNJII [*Over them*]. Listen to me! *Try* to understand!

[*Voices out*]

It is more than for my life I beg you to understand me. If it were for some good reason, a man could die happily! But for this? . . . If you would only *think!* In the country across the sea a man can say to another—this is what *I* think. *I* think it is wrong, *I* think it is right. And their shogun does not kill him for it! Can you understand that?

FATHER. A strange country.

BUNJIA. A *free* country. In America I worked in their great forests. Trees wider than a hundred bamboo saplings fall to the axes of men of many different tongues, and of different colors. I chose that work myself. I was free to come to it and free to leave it. Their shogun does not rule them—they regard him more as their servant. For it is they who rule.

[*Subdued, shocked murmur begins*]

Father, I came here because I hoped to take you back to that land with me, to—

[*Murmur, up, with great horror*]

UNCLE [*Furious*]. Silence! How *dare* you!

FATHER [*Brokenly*]. My son, you have shamed me before my ancestors. Still, you are my eldest son, and it will be more honorable for you to commit suppuka—die at your own hands, than under the executioner's ax . . . Give him your sword, Chiura.

VOICE. Bunjii—here—

BUNJII. My brother . . .

VOICE [*Whispering*]. The sword is sharp. I have seen to it. It will not take long.

FATHER. Come, honorable relatives, we will wait in the next room. [*Coughing, shuffling, etc.*]

BUNJII [*Quietly, after they've gone*]. All you have been condemned, not I. To be a Japanese in Japan.

[*Music: bridge*]

[*Murmur*]

SETSUKO [*Weeping*]. Let me see my son . . . before . . . before . . .

FATHER. Stay. It will be over soon. Then, may his ancestors receive him with forgiveness.

SETSUKO. Ten years away from us . . . and now . . .

FATHER. Be still, woman! Be still. He came back lost.

UNCLE. We can go in. Come.

[*Pause, murmur out . . . off*]

Follow me. Your son's body!

VOICE. Father! He's not here!

[*Murmur of amazement . . . "He's gone," etc.*]

FATHER. Then he didn't . . . Before the oldest souls of my shamed ancestors, and before you, my relatives, I have no excuse for what my eldest son has failed to do! I am at your mercy.

UNCLE. I will speak for the Council of Relatives . . . Fill an urn with ashes, and bury it outside the shrine. And let us all join in a funeral chant for your son, who came back to his homeland —dead.

[*Music: Japanese theme up and segue to narrative and under*]

NISHIDA. Your great-grandfather was dead—to the land of his birth. But toward the new land that lay beyond many horizons, he ran, walked, stumbled, and finally set sail, in a stolen fishing boat. Across the East China Seas . . . blown off course to the lonely islands . . . past Aguna-Jima . . . Kuma-Shima . . . Koto-Sho . . . Polilo Island . . .

[*Music out*]

And then under a sun without wind . . . held in the [*Fade*] middle of nowhere fifty days. . . .

[*Ship's bell off*]

DOCTOR [*English*]. What do you make of it, captain?

CAPTAIN [*English*]. By the look of it through the glass, it was a bit of a boat all right . . . a spar and a sail's all that's left.

DOCTOR. And what of that rag on the spar?

CAPTAIN. Well, doc, it may be a man . . . We'll be on it in half an hour. [*Fading*] But if it's alive it'll sure be the eighth wonder.

[*Music: Bridge*]

NISHIDA. It was alive . . . and soon your great-grandfather was safe once more, his strength recovered. Then nine long years on many ships . . . Australia . . . Hawaii . . . and then . . .

[*Rhythmic chopping of trees . . . broad strokes*]

America once more . . . swinging great ax strokes in the Northwest forests . . . forests that were now spreading over the nation in railway ties, telegraph poles, wagons and homes that brought East to West. Your great-grandfather put his ax strokes in, for he was helping to build a nation, and building himself a home.

[*Sound out—music out*]

But something was missing.

MAN. I tank something be up, Bunjii. Sittin' there like a log, while inside a game be on.

BUNJII. Nothing wrong . . . Chris, what is one tree on a mountain? When it's windy, the tree bends alone. When it's cold . . . [*Fading*] . . . the tree must shiver alone. . . .

[*Music: Narrative theme in and under*]

NISHIDA. But while your great-grandfather worked, so did destiny . . .

[*Music up and out*]

[*Harbor noises*]

MASON. Well, commodore, there it is. Yeddo Harbor.

PERRY. What's the date back home, Mr. Mason?

MASON. July 7, 1853.

PERRY. Then unofficially, until history makes it otherwise, this is a day to remember . . .

[*Music in and under*]

Inform the emperor that what the United States wants is friendship, commerce, humane treatment of shipwrecked sailors . . .

[*Music up and down under*]

MAN. In return, Commodore Perry, the Son of Heaven desires to send a delegation to the United States, to see how you do— everything.

[*Music: Japanese theme with humorous American counterpoint, "Turkey in the Straw," etc.*]

JAP 1. Descendant of the gods, may my ancestors cast me out if it be false! There in America men lie down in what they call a tub, and water comes out like a spring after the rains. This they do every week—some even every day! And the women—they do not bathe in the water the men leave—as it is with us. But the women use fresh water. This I swear by my ancestors. . . .

[*Music: Bridge*]

JAP 2 [*Breathless*]. Divine One, it is the truth! A great marvel! They have an iron beast that puffs like a volcano and can go thirty miles in one hour!

[*Music: Bridge*]

JAP 3. Those are the guns I drew after I saw them, Wise One. And their ships are covered with metal and move with fire.

[*Music up discordantly: Segue to narrative theme*]

NISHIDA. And while Japan, under the Emperor Meiji, began to imitate the substance of America, a new day also came for your greatgrandfather. For now Japan permitted her people to leave. People —and women—

[*Music out*]

BUNJII. This picture.

MAN. Tama Kuraki is her name. You can be married by proxy in Japan, and the Emigration Company will bring the picture bride to the arms of her husband.

BUNJII. How long will it take?

MAN. One year.

BUNJII. How much will it cost?

MAN. Only a thousand dollars.

[*Music: Quick bridge*]

[*Steamboat whistle. Crowd at dock*]

BUNJII. You . . . you are Tama . . . my wife.

TAMA [*Low*]. I am Tama.

BUNJII. You and your picture are one . . . What are you doing down there on the pavement? . . . Get up, Tama!

TAMA. I will be an obedient wife.

BUNJII [*Embarrassed*]. Women here do not throw themselves at the feet of their husbands! . . . Come, we will go home.

[*Pause—Crowd up slightly*]

Tama! Tama, where are you? . . . Oh, there . . . Why don't you walk with me through this crowd?

TAMA. Walk beside—my husband?

BUNJII. Tama, look around you. In America women do not walk ten feet behind their husbands. Look. There goes a woman who walks ahead of her husband!

[*Music: Bridge*]

And then?

TAMA. My sister was sold by my father to pay his debts. I did not want him to sell me to a city house too. Then they said I could come over here and get married. . . .

BUNJII. Did my picture please you?

TAMA. Does it matter?

BUNJII. In Japan, I remember, there is a proverb: "There is nothing worse than to be born a woman." That is not true here, Tama. It does matter.

TAMA. Then, I did like your picture . . . And I will like it here! I will work as I did in my father's house, from sunrise to darkness, and I will eat little . . .

BUNJII. No, no, Tama! This is not your father's house—

TAMA. I have displeased you. I will always do as you tell me, give you no trouble.

BUNJII. I want you to give me trouble, if it pleases you.

[*Music: Narrative theme and under*]

NISHIDA. And Tama became an American woman, and gave him trouble. When the children came, she made him move out of the forest, go south toward the farmland, where other Japanese-Americans were settling. And after your great-grandparents had become part of this country, their son Manase and his wife helped make it flower . . .

[*Music out*]

[*Slight, hot wind in*]

MANASE [*Tired*]. Things will grow in the desert, in time. But the ground is thirsty, so thirsty.

MURA. The brook is only two hours away. I will help carry the water.

MANASE. No, my wife.

MURA. We will walk together, and we will carry more . . . Manase, look. The wind—it's blowing the sand. It's covering everything!

MANASE. Tomorrow, we will push the sand back again.

[*Music in and over: Segue to narrative under*]

NISHIDA. With their fingernails, with their bent backs, with their long hours of labor, your grandparents brought food up out of the American desert. . . .

[*Music out*]

OLD MAN [*Fading in*]. Imperial Valley . . . I remember it when it was nothing but waste! Getting so a desert rat don't have room to turn. All your boys workin' the ground, Manase?

MANASE. All but one, Nishida. His mother wants him to work in the city.

OLD MAN. Woman foolishness.

MANASE. Well, he's her son too. He'll work in a hotel, when he returns.

OLD MAN. Where from? Heh?

MANASE. To work in a Japanese hotel in Frisco, one must speak Japanese. And to learn that, where could you go? Japan!

[*Music in discordantly: Segue to narrative theme*]

NISHIDA. I do not regret those two years I spent at school back in Japan, my son. They taught me more than my father thought they would. Taught me to understand why our distant relatives behave as they do.

[*Music: Change to a Japanese military march*]

When a boy is seven years old, they give him a gun and a uniform and tell him—

JAP 1. Your imperial ancestors were Samurai! Great warriors who followed the code of Bushido! There is only one crime, failure! Only one aim—victory! Bushido means you may slice off the head of a captured enemy as a mark of chivalry! You too will follow the code of Bushido—with a sword and a gun.

NISHIDA. And from the beginning school children are taught—

BOY. "As infinite as the dome of heaven above us
Is the debt we owe our emperor.
The time has come to pay our debt."

JAP 2. The sun-goddess came out of a cave to create the Japanese people! You come from the gods and you will return to the gods. To die in battle for the divine emperor is the quickest way to heaven!

CHORUS. Banzai! . . . Banzai! . . . [*Fade*]

[*Music in and over: Segue to narrative and down under*]

NISHIDA. I did not think this insanity would reach across the ocean to us, so soon. I didn't know it until one day someone from the Japanese consulate came to see me . . .

[*Matsumo may use an accent. No one else in cast should*]

MATSUMO [*Fading in*]. Jinshu no jinshu yuen [*Pause*] Jinshu no jinshu yuen . . . Yes.

NISHIDA. I don't understand Japanese. . . .

MATSUMO [*Pleasantly*]. No? According to our files, you were a student in Japan twenty years ago. A good student. In your capacity as a hotelkeeper, you have occasion to use your native tongue.

NISHIDA. We are speaking my native tongue—now.

MATSUMO. Then perhaps a reminder! Jinshu no jinshu yuen . . . "The Divine Mission of Divine Japan—to conquer the world." Surely, you remember your Shinto faith?

NISHIDA. I remember—nothing.

MATSUMO. Then I will remind you. You have only one country, one faith—Japan!

NISHIDA. This is my country.

MATSUMO. Is it? In Nippon you heard: "Although my body is cast out to decay, yet my Japanese spirit will remain!" Your ancestors lying in Arizona and California have not lost their spirit—

NISHIDA. No. They found it there.

MATSUMO. You may still find yours . . .

NISHIDA. How?

MATSUMO. The San Francisco water front might be very interesting to us, someday . . . And your son, George Morimitsu . . . Of military age . . . passage will be arranged . . .

NISHIDA. I'm sure it will. By the American army.

MATSUMO [Gently]. Nishida Morimitsu, when the emperor-god arrives in America, there will be a day of judgment . . .

NISHIDA. You musubi—you riceball—

MATSUMO [Struggling]. What—what—

NISHIDA. Have a taste of what your emperor-god will get!

[Sock against jaw, body tumbling]

[Music in: Narrative theme holds under]

Well, my son, it is almost sundown and I must stop talking shop. As I look out on this war relocation camp, from where I am writing you, I see past the crisis that put those of Japanese ancestry here, because of a traitorous few. . . . I see a country which my father, and his father before him, found good. Now, does this country find us good? I hope so. . . . If you are not brutal, and do not glorify barbarism as the Japanese soldier does, it is because America made you otherwise. Good luck to you, son . . . . Your father.

[Music up and out]

ANNOUNCER. In Italy, the 100th Infantry Battalion of Japanese-American soldiers won a unit citation from Lieutenant General Mark Clark. The 442nd Regimental Combat Team of Japanese-Americans from the mainland and Hawaii has won high praise from the War Department. Its soldiers were the first to enter Pisa. An Irish-American officer in Italy said:

VOICE. There are crosses with Japanese names in the American cemeteries in the bitter Italian hills.

ANNOUNCER. At Saipan in the Pacific, five Americans with Japanese faces won Bronze Stars and a sixth was cited. Wherever they fight, they fight in the same cause as all Americans . . . the sons of men who came from many lands, to make a new land on American shores.

THE LONESOME
TRAIN

Millard Lampell

"FOLK CANTATA," "ballad opera," or what you will—radio is developing a dramatico-musical form and tradition of its own. It is one of its most interesting developments. *The Lonesome Train*, scored by Earl Robinson to Millard Lampell's words, is one of the fine accomplishments in this radio form.

Back in depression days Earl Robinson and John Latouche wrote, for the Federal Theatre stage production *Sing for Your Supper*, a composition called *Ballad of Uncle Sam*. Some time later Norman Corwin, directing the CBS series *Pursuit of Happiness*, came across it, worked out some cuts and revisions for radio, got Paul Robeson to star in it, and broadcast it. It was one of those moments in the arts when a new "trend" can clearly be put down as having been born. Many a later short radio opera, performed and unperformed, has drawn its inspiration from that broadcast.

Many factors may have contributed to it. Documentary drama had been in the air for some years, and *Ballad for Americans* was a musical wing of this development. Cabaret entertainment, in Europe more than in America, had taken on a political, documentary color; this too may have influenced the *Ballad*. Corwin himself, in the series *Words Without Music*, had experimented with radio dramatizations of poems, using some of the techniques which appeared, enormously heightened by the addition of music, in the *Pursuit of Happiness* production of *Ballad for Americans*, and in its radio descendants.

The *Ballad*, while it was music almost throughout, was at the same time poetry and at the same time drama. It was not primarily any one of these. Its narrator could sing or speak; so could its chorus. There was occasional spoken dialogue.

Maxwell Anderson and Kurt Weill, also for *Pursuit of Happiness*, used the same elements for a "ballad opera" called *Magna Charta*. Corwin again directed. Corwin, for one of his own CBS series, did a short radio-opera version of the Book of Esther, which continued the tradition. *Labor for Victory* has featured occasional short documentary operas.

In the *Lonesome Train*, Earl Robinson, by then a nationally recognized composer and the chief force behind the new form, again had a collaborator who was able to supply him with a script of literary merit in its own right. It is characteristic of Robinson that he is not easily satisfied with any other kind of script. The collaborators this time called their work a "folk cantata." It makes rich use of folk song, folk poetry, folk humor.

As with *Ballad for Americans*, *Magna Charta*, *Esther*, and other works in this form, a powerful factor in the impact of the piece was its topicality. World War II had its President-haters as did the Civil War, and whatever else *The Lonesome Train* may also have been, it was in the most important sense a political document, a cantata against Copperheads. When President Roosevelt died in the closing days of the European struggle, *The Lonesome Train* at once became the most-played radio program in America. Decca Records, Inc., had made phonograph recordings as well as radio transcriptions of *The Lonesome Train*. In the days following the President's death, particularly as the funeral train moved north, the transcriptions were broadcast by local stations across the length and breadth of the country. And in many communities, school assemblies and other groups listened solemnly to phonograph recordings of *The Lonesome Train*.

Millard Lampell was born in Paterson, New Jersey. He went to West Virginia University. There he got steeped in square dances and ballads, and bought a six-dollar guitar. Going to New York after graduation, he joined a group known as the Almanac Singers, which included Pete Seeger, banjo player and singer, and Woodie Guthrie, the talented Okie balladist and writer. They toured the country, singing at Grange meetings, union halls, Minnesota lumber camps, Montana copper miners' halls, and on ships on the West Coast. They played folk songs and picked up new ones. During this period Lampell began to feel that he wanted to devote himself in a literary way to the "poetry of working people on the job."

Lampell saw a radio studio for the first time in 1942, when Norman Corwin decided to use the Almanac Singers' square dance, *Round and Round Hitler's Grave*, on the *This Is War* series. Soon afterward Lampell went to work for Himan Brown, a very successful commercial producer who felt that soap-opera technique—corny organ, homey narrator—could be put to the service of the war effort by treating race discrimination, Lend-Lease, the black market, and similar themes. Lampell wrote for a while for *Green Valley, U.S.A.*, which tried the experiment with some success. This started him off in radio and he wrote for several other series. In 1944 Lampell, by then a member of the Army Air Corps, was assigned to New York to write for two of its official radio series, *First in the Air* and *Wings for Tomorrow*.

Lampell and Earl Robinson wrote *The Lonesome Train* in 1942. Warner Brothers bought it and then did nothing with it. The movie contract prevented radio performance until 1944, when Norman Corwin introduced it over the Columbia Broadcasting System. Raymond Massey was Lincoln. The singing narrator—the "Ballad Singer"—was Burl Ives. Earl Robinson was a speaking narrator. Lynn Murray conducted the orchestra and chorus.

THE LONESOME

TRAIN*

EARL [*Speaks throughout*]. The long war was over. And the tall man with the sad eyes and the stooping shoulders was tired. And so one night he did what everybody likes to do sometimes when they're tired. He went to a show. He went down to Ford's Theatre in Washington town and he sat in a box and it was the Number I box because he was a pretty big man.

Well, the play went on, and along about the middle of the evening something happened that wasn't on the program. I guess you all know what that was. The news spread pretty fast. . . .

BALLAD SANGER [*Sings throughout, unless indicated*].
They carried the news from Washington,
That Abraham Lincoln's time had come;
John Wilkes Booth shot Lincoln dead,
With a pistol bullet through the head!

The slaves were free, the war was won,
But the fight for freedom was just begun;
There were still slaves,
The hungry and poor,
Men who were not free to speak.

Freedom's a thing that has no ending,
It needs to be cared for, it needs defending;
A great long job for many hands,
Carrying freedom 'cross the land!

* THE LONESOME TRAIN by Millard Lampell. Copyright, 1944, by Decca Records, Inc., Assigned to Sun Music Co., Inc., Subsidiary of Decca Records, Inc.

EARL. A job for all the people,
      Carrying freedom across the land.
      A job for Lincoln's people!
      And you know who Lincoln's people were . . .
SINGER A. A Kansas farmer, a Brooklyn sailor,
      An Irish policeman, a Jewish tailor;
SINGER B. An old storekeeper shaking his head,
      Handing over a loaf of bread;
SINGER. C. A buffalo hunter telling a story,
      Out in the Oregon Territory.
BALLAD SINGER. They were his people, he was their man,
      You couldn't quite tell where the people left off,
      And where Abe Lincoln began.
WOMAN [*Alto*]. There was a silence in Washington town,
      When they carried Mr. Lincoln down.
CHORUS. A lonesome train on a lonesome track,
      Seven coaches painted black.
EARL. Mr. Lincoln's funeral train,
      Traveling the long road from Washington to Baltimore,
      Baltimore to Philadelphia, Philadelphia to New York.
SOLO VOICES. Albany, Syracuse, Cleveland, Chicago,
      To Springfield, Illinois.
CHORUS. A slow train, a quiet train,
      Carrying Lincoln home again.
BALLAD SINGER. It wasn't quite mist, it was almost rain,
      Falling down on that funeral train;
      There was a strange and a quiet crowd,
      Nobody wanting to talk out loud.
      Along the streets, across the square,
      Lincoln's people were waiting there.
EARL. A young soldier stood in the road and said:
SOLDIER [*Speaks*]. You'd think they'd have warned him; even a rattle-
      snake warns you.
EARL. And an old man answered:
OLD MAN [*Speaks*]. This one must have been a copperhead!

      [*Orchestra*]

CHORUS. A lonesome train on a lonesome track

Seven coaches painted black.
They carried Mr. Lincoln down,
The train started, the wheels went round,
You could hear the whistle for miles around,
  Crying, Free - dom!
      Free - dom!

BALLAD SINGER. They tell a story about that train,
  They say that Lincoln wasn't on that train;
  When that train started on its trip that day,
  Lincoln was in Alabama, miles away!
  [Speaks]
  Yes, sir, down in Alabama . . .
  [Sings]
  In an old wooden church,
  Didn't have no paint,
  Didn't have no floor,
  Didn't have no glass in the windows . . .
  [Speaks]
  Just a pulpit and some wooden benches.
NEGRO WOMAN [Moaning softly]. O Great God Almighty, Lord . . .
  [Amens and ad libs by congregation through following sequence]
BALLAD SINGER. Just a pulpit and some wooden benches,
  And Mr. Lincoln on the last bench away in the back,
  Listening to the sermon,
  Listening to the singing.
CHORUS [Softly]. Amen, brother, amen.
NEGRO PREACHER. You may bury me in the east,
  You may bury me in the west,
  But I'll hear the trumpet sound in the morning!
NEGRO WOMAN. In the morning, Lord, in the morning!
PREACHER. This evening, brothers and sisters,
  I come in the holiest manner,
  To tell how he died.
CHORUS. He died, yes, Lord, he's dead!
PREACHER. He was a-lyin' there,
  His blood on the ground,

Covering the ground;
And while he was lyin' there the sun rose,
And it recognized him;
Just as soon as the sun recognized him,
It clothed itself in sackcloth and ashes!
O, went down in mourning!

CHORUS. Lord, the sun went down! Yes, Lord, it went down!

PREACHER. He was a-lyin' there,
And the sky turned dark,
And seven angels leaped over the battlements of glory,
And come down to get him;
And just when they came near him, he rose,
Yes, Lord, he rose up and walked down among us,
Praise God,
He walked back down among his people!

WOMAN. Lord, he's living now!

PREACHER. We got a new land; my dear friends, we got a new land!
Ain't no riding boss with a whip, (no!)
Don't have no backbiters, (no!)
Liars can't go, cheaters can't go,
Ain't no separate kingdom,
No high sheriff to bring us back!

WOMAN'S VOICE. We got a new land!

PREACHER. You may bury me in the east,
You may bury me in the west,
But I'll hear the trumpet sound in the morning!

CHORUS. In the morning, Lord, in the morning!

BALLAD SINGER. Down in Alabama,
Nothing but a pulpit and some wooden benches,
And Mr. Lincoln sitting in the back, away in the back.

[Orchestra]

CHORUS. A lonesome train on a lonesome track,
Seven coaches painted black;
A slow train, a quiet train,
Carrying Lincoln home again.

SOLO VOICES. Washington, Baltimore, Harrisburg, Philadelphia . . .

CHORUS. Coming into New York town,
You could hear the whistle for miles around,
Crying, Free - dom!
Free - dom!

EARL. From Washington to New York people lined the tracks.

BALLAD SINGER. A strange crowd,
A quiet crowd;
Nobody wanting to talk out loud.

EARL. At lonely country crossroads there were farmers
And their wives and kids standing around for hours;
In Philadelphia, the line of mourners ran three miles;
And most of them were deep in mourning;
An old lady stood by the coffin and said:

OLD LADY [*Speaks*]. Mr. Lincoln, are you dead? Are you really dead?

EARL. And some wanted him dead for a long time.
A cotton speculator turned away from the coffin, saying:

SPECULATOR [*Speaks*]. All right, boys, the drinks are on me!

CHORUS. For there were those who cursed the Union,
Those who wanted the people apart;
While the sound of the freedom guns still echoed,
Copperheads struck at the people's heart!

BALLAD SINGER [*Speaks*].
I've heard it said that when that train pulled into New York town,
Mr. Lincoln wasn't around.
[*Sings*]
He was where there was work to be done,
Where there were people having fun;
When that funeral train pulled into New York . . .
Lincoln was down in a Kansas town,
Swinging his lady round and round!
[*Dance back around and ad libs through following*]

CALLER [*Fading in*]. Swing your maw, swing your paw,
Don't forget the gal from Arkansas!

CHORUS [*Men and ballad singer*].
When young Abe Lincoln came to dance,
Those Kansas boys didn't have a chance!

CALLER. Grab your gal and circle four,

Make sure she ain't your mother-in-law!
Now, promenade!
Feed your chickens, milk your cows,
Have just as much fun as the law allows!
CHORUS. They were dancing people, you could see,
They were folks who liked being free;
The men were tall and the girls were fair,
They had fought for the right to be dancing there!
CALLER. Pretty little gal, around she goes,
Swing your lady for a do-si-do!
First to the right, and then to the left,
And then to the gal that you love best!
Duck for the oyster, dig for the clam,
Pass right through to the promised land!
CHORUS. Those Kansas boys didn't have a chance,
When young Abe Lincoln came to dance!

[*Orchestra*]

A lonesome train on a lonesome track,
Seven coaches painted black,
The train started, the wheels went round,
On the way to Cleveland town,
Poughkeepsie, Albany, Utica, Syracuse, Cleveland . . .
You could hear the whistle for miles around,
Crying, Free - dom!
Free - dom!

EARL. In Cleveland the crowds were there;
Two hundred and fifty came from Meadville, Pa.;
Five hundred with two brass bands from Detroit,
A million people came from northern Ohio,
They came to mourn,
And some went home to celebrate.
BALLAD SINGER. Some in the north and some in the west,
And some by the President's side,
Cursed him every day that he lived,
And cheered on the day he died!
EARL. The Copperheads . . .

A New York politician who didn't like Lincoln . . .
An Ohio businessman who didn't like Negroes . . .
A Chicago newspaper editor who didn't like people . . .
GIRL ALTO [*Sings softly*].
    You couldn't quite tell where the people left off
    And where Abe Lincoln began.
EARL. Naturally the Copperheads went home to celebrate.
BALLAD SINGER. When that train rolled into Cleveland town,
    Mr. Lincoln wasn't around;
    Lincoln sat in a hospital ward, far from the funeral train,
    Lincoln sat in a hospital ward, talking to quiet a soldier's pain.
LINCOLN [*Speaks throughout*].
    Do you mind if I stand by the side of the bed?
SOLDIER. No, sir.
LINCOLN. Where were you wounded, son?
SOLDIER [Sings].
    At Bull Run, sir, and Chancellorsville,
    I was shot when we stormed the hill;
    And I've been worried since Chancellorsville,
    About killing, sir, it's wrong to kill.
LINCOLN. I admit, son, that's been bothering me;
    How to make the war and the Word agree.
CHORUS. Quiet and tall by the side of the bed . . .
LINCOLN. There is a reason.
CHORUS. There is a reason, Lincoln said.
LINCOLN. Until all men are equal, and all are free
    There will be no peace.
    While there are whips and chains,
    And men to use them,
    There will be no peace;
    After the battles,
    After the blood and wounded,
    When the chains are smashed,
    And the whips are broken,
    And the men who held the whips are dead!
    When men are brothers and men are free,
    The killing will end, the war will cease,
    When free men have a free men's peace!

BALLAD SINGER. I'll be going home, soon, the soldier said.
  Lincoln turned from the side of the bed.
LINCOLN. I'll see you there.
BALLAD SINGER. I'll see you there, Mr. Lincoln said.

[*Orchestra*]

CHORUS. A slow train, a funeral train,
  Carrying Lincoln home again.
CONDUCTOR. Last stop! Springfield, Illinois!
EARL. Lincoln's neighbors came,
  Farmers from over in the next county,
  Shopkeepers and shoemakers,
  Men who'd hired him for a lawyer,
  Men who'd split rails with him;
  They came from Matoon and Salem,
  Fellows who'd swapped stories with Abe Lincoln during those
      long Illinois winter nights;
  Lincoln's neighbors were there.
CHORUS. A slow rain, a warm rain,
  Falling down on the funeral train.
  (While the sound of the freedom guns still echoed,
  Copperheads struck at the peoples' heart!)
BALLAD SINGER. When that train pulled into Springfield, you know
      where Lincoln was?
  He was standing with his friends in the back of the crowd!
  Yes, sir!
CHORUS AND BALLAD SINGER. Standing tall, standing proud,
  Wearing a shawl instead of a shroud!
BALLAD SINGER. Abe Lincoln was with his friends, telling jokes!

[*Chorus hums behind*]

LINCOLN. I presume you all know who I am. I am humble Abraham
  Lincoln.
  My politics are short and sweet, like the old woman's dance.
MAN [*Speaks*]. Mr. Lincoln, isn't it right that some men should be
  masters and some should be slaves?
LINCOLN. Brother, if God intended some men to do all the work and
  no eating,

He would have made some men with all hands and no mouths.

CHORUS. Standing tall, standing proud.

WOMAN [*Speaks*]. Well, I say, America for Americans. What happens on the other side of the ocean shouldn't be any skin off our backs. Right, Mr. Lincoln?

LINCOLN. Well, I'll tell you, ma'am. It seems to me the strongest bond of human sympathy, outside your family of course, should be the one uniting all working people, of all *nations, tongues* and *kindreds.*

CHORUS. Wearing a shawl instead of a shroud.

WOMAN [*Speaks*]. Somehow, I wouldn't expect the President of the United States to be such a common man.

LINCOLN. I think God must have loved the common people—he made so many of them.

CHORUS. Wearing a shawl instead of a shroud.

CHILD [*Speaks*]. Mr. Lincoln, how does it feel to be President?

LINCOLN. Well, now; it feels sort of like the fellow they ran out of town on a rail. If it wasn't for the honor of it, I'd just as soon walk.

BALLAD SINGER. They were his people, he was their man,
You couldn't quite tell where the people left off,
And where Abe Lincoln began.

CHORUS. A lonesome train on a lonesome track,
Seven coaches painted black.

[*Orchestra*]

CHORUS. Abe Lincoln had an Illinois face,
And he came out of a pioneer race;
He knew how hard the fight would be,
But he liked the idea of being free.
His heart was tough as a railroad tie,
He was made of stuff that doesn't die;
He was made of hopes, he was made of fears,
He was made to last a million years!
Freedom's a thing that has no ending,
It needs to be cared for, it needs defending!
Free-dom!

THE "BOISE"

Ranald MacDougall

OLDER RADIO WRITERS—anyone over thirty-five—grew up in a newspaper-and-theater world, and learned radio as something new.

Ranald MacDougall, at the age of seven, in 1922 in the city of Schenectady, wound cotton-covered copper wire around an oatmeal box to make his first radio set. He wrote his first radio script, about pirates, at the age of twelve. He still has copies. His second script, written at fifteen, was at first rejected by NBC but was rewritten some years later and sold to the same network, retitled *The Ineffable Essence of Nothing*.

MacDougall moved to Brooklyn and kept turning up at NBC in the uniform of a Radio City Music Hall usher, and telling executives he was going to be one of the top writers in the business. NBC's George Nelson chuckled over this, and offered him a job in the mimeograph department. MacDougall took it, kept writing scripts, and worked his way onto the script staff, where he stayed several years.

Late in 1941 he got an idea for a series he called *Men at War*. Lewis H. Titterton, then head of the NBC Script Division, liked it but it was rejected on a higher level as too technical. Instead, MacDougall was put to work on an item called *Ted Steele's Studio Club*, which made him unhappy. He asked to have his $62.50 salary raised to $75.00; instead, his resignation was accepted—March, 1942.

Two weeks later he wrote a very successful script for the government series, *This Is War*, broadcast on all four major networks. CBS immediately offered him a contract. He then wrote two series for CBS: *The Twenty-Second Letter* and *The Man Behind the Gun*, the latter being the series he had tried to promote at NBC. It attracted enormous attention and in time acquired a sponsor: the Elgin National Watch Company. But after thirty-nine weeks MacDougall felt written out and went to "dabble in the Hollywood fleshpot—it makes nice dabbling."

For *The Man Behind the Gun* MacDougall wrote two scripts on the cruiser "Boise," his favorites in the series. The second of these is published here for the first time. Material for these scripts was obtained by interviews with three of the men who were aboard the cruiser during the action described. MacDougall and William N. Robson, producer-director of the series (notes on Robson will be found preceding his *Open Letter to the American People*, also in this volume) went aboard the "Boise" and saw what had happened. "For the first time in my life I realized the effect of an explosive on steel, and on men." The most fanatical kind of research and checking, often involving long trips up and down the Atlantic seaboard, preceded the writing of *The Man Behind the Gun* scripts. This paid off. The series was held in high regard by armed forces and civilians alike. In authenticity is was an object lesson to radio writers. Its minute attention to technical detail gave the series a special fascination.

Some of the seemingly irrelevant remarks in the script were, Mac-Dougall reports, actually made by the men of the "Boise" during the height of the engagement. The men interviewed remembered them, largely because of their odd irrelevancy. So they went in.

The Man Behind the Gun popularized in radio a novel device: narration in the second person. Third person narration was common in radio from the start. Oboler and Welles did most to establish "first person singular" narration. The "you" type of narration, unusual in most media, became a basic feature of *The Man Behind the Gun*—partly by accident. While writing the third program of the series, called *Tin Can*, Mac-Dougall was very tired. Wrestling with the technicalities of the script and with his own weariness, he made no headway until he unconsciously slipped into "you do this . . . you do that." The program then came with incredible ease, and the "you" narration was used thereafter. "I found afterwards that it had been used before, notably by Corwin, who has done just about everything before anybody else, but I don't think it had ever been used as the basis of a series."

MacDougall is grateful to Douglas Coulter, Davidson Taylor, and other executives at CBS, who not only gave him freedom to work in his own way but put publicity behind his efforts. As for his director and producer, William N. Robson, MacDougall writes: "He sweated out every script with me, and went to really impossible lengths to better my work. I wrote good scripts for him, but when he got through with them in the studio they were masterpieces. I cannot pay too much tribute to Bill. I have worked with many directors before, and have often got along with them better, but never until I worked with Robson did a director get more out of my scripts than I had put in. He's my boy."

MacDougall now writes for radio between pictures. This is how he feels about radio: "I served my apprenticeship when experimental radio was at its height—when Irving Reis, Milton Geiger, Oboler, and Corwin were developing radio drama as we know it now. There was plenty of sustaining time available in those days, and a writer could kick an idea to pieces on the airwaves without screams of agony from upstairs. Lewis Titterton at NBC and Max Wylie at CBS were both encouraging young writers to develop distinctive techniques in radio drama, and individual radio styles. This seemingly is no longer the case, largely, I suspect, because of the scarcity of free time." He feels that salaries also may have something to do with it.

THE "BOISE"

[Orchestra: Show opening]

NARRATOR. You're a chief bosun's mate aboard the "Boise"—a gun pointer—the guy that points and fires the fifteen big guns of the cruiser. Right now you're standing by for action—off Savo Island · —in the Solomons—it's nearly midnight on October 11, 1942. Your guns are manned, ready, loaded, and laid. You've sighted the enemy, and your eye is jammed into the telescopic gun sight, searching for a target. And now, very dimly, you see a light-gray spot on the lens . . . then another . . . and another—five of them. It's them! You can see them plainly.

BOSUN [Shouting]. Target sighted bearing one eight oh! There they are, Scotty . . . pick 'em up . . . pick 'em up—you farmer . . . right-right-right . . . steady, steady now . . . left-left-left . . . There—you're on! On target! Mark-mark-mark!

SCOTTY. Trainer on target!

BOSUN. Pointer on target! Control from Director One. One target.

CONTROL. Repeat, Director One. Are you on the target?

BOSUN. Director One, aye . . . I am on five targets.

CONTROL. Very well, pick out the biggest one and stand by to commence firing.

BOSUN. Aye, aye, pick up biggest target! Left a little . . . left-left-left . . . mark!

NARRATOR. Through your sights you center the cross wires on the largest enemy ship in the line, and then you pick up the two firing keys and curve your thumbs over them . . . This is it!

BOSUN. Director One . . . on target!

CONTROL. Open shutter—commence firing!

[Harsh sound of buzzer]

NARRATOR. You press the firing keys that set off the fifteen big guns, and as the searchlights on topside flash on for a moment you see the big enemy cruiser square in the cross hairs of your sight.

BOSUN. Commence! Commence! Commence!

[*Salvo*]

NARRATOR. Then your view is blurred by the shock of the explosion and the smoke of the guns—and now the Jap cruiser disappears behind mountainous spouts of water flung skyward by the bursts and you know that the first salvo has straddled its target.

[*Explosions on cue under above*]

CONTROL [*Battle talker*]. Check fire . . . Spot one.

BOSUN. Check-Check-Check. Spot one . . . Spot one . . .

CONTROL. Up one oh double oh . . . right oh two!

· BOSUN. Up one oh double oh, aye . . . right oh two . . . right-right-right!

CONTROL. Resume fire!

BOSUN. Resume fire!

[*From now on the war sounds are steady—there is the dull and regular poom-poom-poom of the five-inchers—and the heavier boom of the six-inchers*]

NARRATOR. Now the guns are firing as fast as they can be loaded and that's plenty fast . . . the shells are like tracer bullets from a machine gun, pouring into the enemy . . . and then, sudden, the Jap ship erupts into flame from stem to stern. . . .

BOSUN. That's right! Burn, you buzzards, burn!

FILTER [*Screaming*]. We got 'im! He's rolling over! Going down now! That's Number One for the "Boise!"

SPOTTER. Check fire!

BOSUN. Check-check-check!

[*The guns stop—not all at once*]

CONTROL. Director One . . . pick up next target!

BOSUN. Director One, aye . . . shifting target. Left a little, left a little . . . mark-mark-mark!

SCOTTY. Trainer on target!

BOSUN. Director One on target!

CONTROL. Commence firing! Salvo!

BOSUN. Salvo! Commence-commence-commence!

[*Harsh buzzer and then eruption of full salvo*]

SPOTTER. Check fire! Spot one!

BOSUN. Check-check-check. Spot one! Spot one! [*Excited*] Boy, this is fun, ain't it, Scotty? See the way that Jap split open?

SCOTTY. No stamina. No stamina.

CONTROL. Director One . . . pick up the next target.

BOSUN. Director One, aye . . . shifting target! Come on, Tojo—who's next? Find something, will you, Scotty? Don't leave us here with our guns hanging out.

SCOTTY. Cruiser on the left . . . left-left.

BOSUN. I got it. I'm on it. Pick it up! Mark-mark-mark!

SCOTTY. Trainer on target!

BOSUN. Director One on target!

LOUDSPEAKER. Open shutters! Commence firing!

[*Harsh buzzer as before*]

BOSUN [*Over*]. Commence-commence-commence!

[*The war sounds come back in as before*]

NARRATOR. Now the main battery of the "Boise" is pumping shells at a second Jap cruiser . . . in less than ten minutes three enemy ships have been destroyed . . . a cruiser and a destroyer by the main battery . . . and another destroyer by the secondary battery . . . this is the fourth Jap ship, and you pour everything you've got into her. You can see her plainly . . . silhouetted against the blazing ruin of the first cruiser you hit . . . and you can see the shells from your battery arching through the sky and hitting into her . . .

BOSUN. Ain't that pretty! Look at that, Scotty, ain't that pretty?

SCOTTY. Ask me later! Ask me later!

NARRATOR. You're throwing everything but the kitchen sink at the Jap . . . you can see the smearing glare of ricochets from his armor plating . . . but most of them go in, and then you see the dull white gleam of fires inside. . . .

BOSUN. Fry, you dogs, fry! Burn! Burn!

NARRATOR. You keep waiting for the Jap to explode, but he doesn't. He's taking everything you've got, and now you see huge balls of fire arching away from his forward deck . . . and suddenly you realize what it means.

BOSUN. Why, the dirty jerks! They're shooting back at us! They're shooting at us!

SCOTTY. Whadyah expect 'em to do? Blow you a kiss? Come on—keep your thumbs on that firing key!

BOSUN. If you don't like the way I handle this key you can shove it overboard.

CONTROL. Check fire!

BOSUN. Check-check-check!

[*The guns stop one by one*]

NARRATOR. The second cruiser is going down now . . . a flaming hulk. You take a quick look around and you see another Jap destroyer on her side and burning. The second battery has picked off another one while you were busy on the cruiser . . . five Jap ships sunk. Not bad.

BOSUN. Boy, we'll get a medal for this!

SCOTTY. Don't break your arm patting yourself.

[*The screech of a shell coming in and then an explosion*]

BOSUN. A hit! We've been hit! There's still some more Japs around. Where are they?

SCOTTY. They know where *we* are, bud.

CONTROL [*Snapping*]. Report the position of the hit!

FILTER. Five-inch gun out of commission. Captain's cabin demolished.

LOUDSPEAKER [*Frantic*]. Torpedo approaching the starboard bow! Another torpedo approaching the starboard bow!

BOSUN [*A low voice*]. Torpedoes. Here we go.

NARRATOR. The ship is quiet now . . . deathly quiet . . . it's turning . . . you can feel the slight list as it turns toward the torpedoes . . . . you cross your fingers . . .

BOSUN. Smile, Scotty, smile.

SCOTTY [*Weakly*]. Heh . . . heh . . . heh . . .

[*There is a pause*]

LOUDSPEAKER. First torpedo passing to port! [*A pause*] Second torpedo passing the starboard counter!

BOSUN [*Simultaneously*]. Missed us!

SCOTTY. Right between 'em! What a skipper!

NARRATOR. A miss is as good as a mile . . . and now the ship heels over again . . . going back into the battle line . . . over the electrician's circuit you can hear the smoke watcher describing the scene. . . .

FILTER. We're turning back now. There are two more Jap ships that we didn't spot the first time. I can see their guns firing now . . . evidently they're—

[*The screeching roar of incoming shells—then the roaring blasts of flame as they hit—muffled shouts and cries—continues*]

[*Music smashes in and wipes sound off—then down*]

NARRATOR [*Very quiet and objective*]. Now the "Boise" is taking it. As she turns to go back into the line of battle a Jap cruiser finds the range and begins pouring in six- and eight-inch shells. . . . Most of them miss, tossing tons of water over the forward deck and superstructure . . . but some of them are hitting and going in. The "Boise" is burning now. You sit there in the director with your eye jammed to the scope . . . centering the cross hairs. . . .

BOSUN. Come on—let's put the kill on those dogs! Left-left-left!

SCOTTY. Trainer on target!

BOSUN. Director One on target!

CONTROL. Resume fire!

BOSUN. Commence-commence-commence!

[*Harsh buzzer and then muffled reports of guns*]

NARRATOR. You're on target again, and firing . . . but not as fast . . . not as smoothly . . . and you're getting hit . . . you're taking it from stem to stern . . . you can feel the ship heel over and pick up speed . . . and you shout for the smoke watch. . . .

BOSUN. Hey, Money! Where are we hit? Can you see anything? Hey, Money! Where are we hit?

SCOTTY. Must have stopped one up there.

FILTER. We're bad hit—we're afire forward!

BOSUN. That you, Money? We thought you was dead.

FILTER. No, I ain't dead—the explosion knocked out my phone plug. I'm all right. It looks pretty bad.

[*A heavy shuddering explosion*]

TURRET 1 [*Battle talker*]. Number One turret to control . . . sir, I have a shell hit in the face plate of Number One gun turret. . . . I have a shell hit in the face plate . . . it's sticking through the armor . . . I think it's a dud, but it's still buzzing. I don't know—

[*He's cut off short by another racking explosion*]

[*Music takes it under*]

NARRATOR. The "Boise" is hit . . . and hit hard. Number One is filled with flame and smoke . . . the guns are silent. Up on the bridge the captain looks out over his ship and what he sees isn't pretty . . . fire. Fire in Number One turret. Fire forward . . . fire below . . . and the ship down by the head. . . .

OFFICER. We really caught it that time, sir.

CAPTAIN. Yeah. Get on the pipe. See if you can raise anybody in that gun turret.

OFFICER [*Slowly and distinctly*]. Turret One . . . control testing. Answer please. Turret One . . . answer please. Is anybody alive in there? Turret One . . . control testing. [*A pause*] Turret Three . . . can you raise Turret One?

TURRET 3 [*Battle talker*]. Turret One . . . Turret Three testing. Turret One . . . Turret Three testing. [*A long pause*] No control, I can't raise Turret One.

OFFICER [*Low voice*]. Very well. That's all then.

REPAIR [*Battle talker*]. Control. Repair Three. I have sent one of my men into Turret One . . . he's just coming out now. Stand by.

VOICE [*Off indistinct*]. No life in Turret One.

REPAIR. He reports . . . no life in Turret One.

OFFICER. Very well. [*Up*] No life in Turret One, sir.

CAPTAIN. Not anyone alive in there? No one?

OFFICER. No, sir. Tough.

CAPTAIN [*Shouting*]. Repair Three! Flood the turret! Put out those fires!

FILTER. Aye, aye, sir.

REPAIR 2. Bridge from Repair Two!

CAPTAIN. Bridge, aye!

REPAIR 2. One of my men has just come up from below forward . . . a shell or torpedo has hit in the forward magazine, sir!

CAPTAIN. In the magazine! There's enough stuff in there to blow us to bits. *Flood* the forward magazines!

REPAIR 2. Can't right away, sir. My hose connections are shot away. The electrician's mate is still working on them. The hit was below the water line about frame fifty. Maybe it'll flood itself from the sea.

CAPTAIN. Send one of your men down there to find out. Meanwhile . . . stick your fingers in your ears.

[*Music: Background.* . . . *Screaming subjective tension*]

NARRATOR. The ship is dead quiet now . . . everywhere men are frozen at their stations . . . looking forward with grim eyes and tight mouths . . . everybody is waiting to find out whether there's a fire in the forward magazine . . . the way you find out is simple. If the ship suddenly blows into little pieces . . . there was a fire in the magazine. And so everybody stands still and looks forward, waiting for the ship to erupt in flame and split open from end to end . . .

CAPTAIN. Wish I had a cup of jamoke.

OFFICER. Yes, sir. It would taste good, all right.

[*A pause*]

CAPTAIN. Without sugar. I wouldn't want any sugar.

OFFICER. No, sir.

[*Another pause*]

REPAIR 2. Repair Two. To control.

CAPTAIN [*Snapping*]. Control, aye!

, FILTER. The forward magazines have been flooded by the shell hit, sir. No fires.

CAPTAIN [*Emphatic*]. Very well. [*Shouting*] Repair parties from Repair Two and Three go below and make a full report on the bulkheads.

LOUDSPEAKER. Aye, aye.

CAPTAIN [*Down*]. Find out if there's any other damage, mister.

OFFICER. Aye, aye, sir. Control to all stations . . . any unreported damage?

REPAIR 1 [*Battle talker*]. Repair One, aye . . . a five-inch shell hit at frame seventy-eight . . .

OFFICER. Very well. [*Up*] Five-inch shell hit at frame seventy-eight.

CAPTAIN. Thank you. Now lemme think—shall we re-engage the enemy, or withdraw?

[*Music: Sneak in background*]

NARRATOR. The skipper stands there talking to himself . . . thinking out loud . . . and there's plenty to think about . . . one gun turret is blown out . . . the ship is down by the head, and the forward magazines are flooded . . . there are dead men aboard the "Boise" now—and fire. We can go back into the fight and go down still throwing steel . . . or we can leave the kill for the other ships in the task force, withdraw and save ourselves from sinking . . . with six Jap ships to our credit.

CAPTAIN. Six is enough for one day. We'll retire. Hard left rudder!

QUARTERMASTER. Hard left rudder it is, sir!

[*Music sweeps in and down*]

NARRATOR. So the battle is over for the "Boise." But there's no rest anywhere on board ship. For two hours every man jack is fighting fires and trying to win back control of the battered cruiser. And gradually it gets done. The fires are out, and the ship will float. But it's not pretty now. Not the trim, beautiful ship it was yesterday. Now the proud decks are heaved and twisted and scarred by shrapnel. The guns in the forward turret point this way and that . . . drunken fingers to the sky. And everywhere in the ship is smoke and dirt and grimy ashes . . . and the smell of oil and dead men mixed together . . . so that never again in all your life will you be able to smell fuel oil without remembering how it was on the "Boise" after the battle.

[*Music swells heavily and then down*]

[*Distant sound of gunfire*]

But finally the "Boise" is under control again, and you turn back toward the scene of battle. The two task forces have moved away, still fighting. And you pass by dark and nameless shapes floating in the water . . . and life rafts crowded with Japs who stare at you sullenly as you go by. And then over the loudspeaker the word is passed . . .

BATTLE TALKER. Target sighted bearing one eight oh.

CONTROL [*Filter*]. Can you make her out?

BATTLE TALKER. Looks like a large ship or group of ships.

CONTROL. Commence tracking! All hands to battle stations! Stand by for action starboard!

[*Bosun's pipe*]

LOUDSPEAKER. All hands! Man your battle stations . . . on the double!

NARRATOR. You take your station in the director turret again . . . and sit there staring into the dark through your telescope, waiting for the order to resume firing. That's all you think about now. Your mind seems dead and heavy. All you're waiting for is the order to resume firing. That's all you know or remember.

SCOTTY. I'm pooped.

BOSUN. *You're* pooped. Man, I'm half past six all the way down the line.

LOUDSPEAKER. Range ten . . . estimated range one five oh double oh.

BOSUN. I'd be just as happy if these ain't Japs we're closing with.

SCOTTY. A while ago there wasn't enough Japs to suit you.

BOSUN. Right now I could take a hundred years shore leave.

LOUDSPEAKER. Range ten . . . estimated range one three oh, double oh. Range is closing fast.

BOSUN. You ain't kidding, brother. *Too* fast.

SCOTTY. Well, we might as well get it over with.

BOSUN. Yeah. I can't hardly wait.

LOUDSPEAKER. Range ten . . . range is one one oh, double oh.

SCOTTY. We'll soon know whether they're Japs or not. Either way it's okay with me. Don't give up the ship, I always say.

BOSUN. [*Wearily*]. Look, John Paul . . . go bat your head, will yah?

LOUDSPEAKER. Range ten . . . range nine oh, double oh. Stand by to commence firing!

BOSUN [*Roaring*]. Stand by to commerce! Pick 'em up, Scotty! Pick 'em up. Left a little . . . left-left-left! Mark. On target!

SCOTTY. Trainer on target!

BOSUN. Director One on target!

[*A long pause*]

LOUDSPEAKER. Unidentified craft have been challenged. They are friendly.

BOSUN [*Long half groan . . . half sigh*]. Brother—I hear you talking.

LOUDSPEAKER. We are taking our station in column. At ease.

[*Music: Sweeps in triumphantly and then down*]

NARRATOR. At ease. But there's no at ease aboard a crippled ship. No at ease in waters where there are more Jap subs than fish. And when morning comes, the submarines come with it. Every forty-five minutes there's a torpedo alarm, and the destroyers alongside the wallowing "Boise" rush up and down dropping depth charges in a steady pattern. All day long. And you sit there at your battle station, ready for anything. You sit there where you've been sitting for nineteen hours straight . . . and no time and a half for overtime.

BOSUN. You tired, Scotty?

SCOTTY. Heck, no. I only look this way because I'm anemic.

BOSUN [Not laughing]. Very funny.

SCOTTY [After a pause]. I wish something would happen . . . Not serious or anything like that . . . but something to occupy my mind. I felt good when we was fighting . . . but now . . . I dunno, but I sure feel low down.

BOSUN. Yeah. You and me both. It's the reaction. Has something to do with the nervous system. I read about it in a book once. That's how I know.

SCOTTY. Yeah. Guess you're right. [A long pause] They taking the men out of the turret yet?

BOSUN. Yeah. All morning. [Pause] They found Johnson.

SCOTTY. What'll we do with the picture of his kid?

BOSUN. I dunno. They found him just the way he was standing when the blast went off. Just reaching back for the powder bag like he was still alive. All of them was like that in there. Even the electrician's mate . . . he was sitting down with his arms on his knees, looking ahead, just like he was when the blast went off. Ain't that funny?

SCOTTY. Maybe we oughta send the picture back to his wife. Whaddyuh think?

BOSUN. I don't know. Lissen, Scotty, why don't you get some shut-eye? Go ahead. Hit the sack.

SCOTTY. I'll toss you for it.

BOSUN. Naw, I ain't sleepy. You go ahead.

SCOTTY. Aw right. [Trying to laugh] Look—you make sure you wake me up if any Japs come along.

BOSUN. Yeah—sure. I'll do that.

[Music]

NARRATOR. That evening you get a sandwich and a cup of coffee. That night you get four hours' sleep. And the next day there's a notice on the bulletin board . . . and an announcement over the loudspeaker.

LOUDSPEAKER. Services for the dead will be held at twelve forty-five on
the fantail. All hands off watch fall in at quarters for the muster.

[*Music: Background: Marche funèbre à la Mer*]

[*Muffled conversations break out*]

NARRATOR. And so the men go aft . . . one by one they slip along the
battle-scarred decks. But Scotty stands there, trying to make up
his mind whether to go or not.

BOSUN. Come on, Scotty.

SCOTTY. I don't know whether I wanna go or not, chief.

BOSUN. Why not? They were all friends of ours.

SCOTTY. That's it. That's the point. The way I wanna remember them
is like they were. Not like the way they are now. I wanna remember Johnson with that big, dumb pan of his turning red on
account of nobody laughing at his stories about his kid. I wanna
remember Eddie with his ears flapping while he played the harmonica. 'Member those ears of his? He looked like a taxicab coming down the street with the doors open. [*He laughs and then
stops*] See? That's what I mean. I drank beer with those guys.
I wanna remember them like that, not sliding out from under a
flag into the ocean. I don't wanna go, chief.

BOSUN. Okay. Okay, Scotty. I know how you feel. I'll see you later
. . . afterwards.

[*Music: Sneak*]

NARRATOR. So you go aft alone . . . past the twisted, battle-scarred tur-
rets and the shell-pocked superstructure . . . aft to join the silent
crew of the "Boise," formed into a hollow U on the fantail. Astern,
as far as you can see, the white boiling wake of the ship is like
a broad highway. Then the captain comes and climbs up on a
capstan and reads to you . . . you can't hear everything he says,
but sentences come back to you as the wind shifts and changes . . .

CAPTAIN. I am the resurrection and the life . . .

NARRATOR. It's a beautiful day. Calm and peaceful. The air is sweet.

CAPTAIN. Since by man came death, by man came also the resurrection
of the dead . . .

NARRATOR. Not far away a sea gull rises and falls without moving its wings . . . the wake of the ship is white and straight as far as you can see.

CAPTAIN. Now this I say, brethren, that flesh and blood cannot inherit the kingdom of God . . . Behold, I show you a mystery; We shall not all sleep, but we shall all be changed . . .

NARRATOR. You have no feeling . . . no deep sadness in you. It might be you, lying there. It might still be you. And you know they felt like you do . . . if one comes along with your name on it, okay.

CAPTAIN. O death, where is thy sting? O grave, where is thy victory?

[*Sound of taps*]

NARRATOR. And then one by one the honored dead are draped in the flag for which they gave everything they had to give . . . and carried to the taffrail.

BOSUN. Adams, J. B., Seaman Second Class. [*Pause*]

[*Scrape of body slipping off board—after each name*]
Delong, L. H., Seaman First Class.
[*Pause*]
Van Hooser, R. G., Electricians Mate Third Class.
[*Pause*]
Polito, S. T., Seaman First Class.
[*Pause*]

NARRATOR. One by one they slip out from under the flag and into the sea . . . carried down to the depths by a six inch shell lashed between their feet . . . the honored dead of the United States ship . . . "Boise."

BOSUN. Kelley, G. H.
S1/c
White, J. W.
S1/c
Davis, G. M.
S1/c
Popovich
David,
S1/c

[*Music: Swells up and over and then down*]

NARRATOR. Do not weep for them . . . or feel sorry. One doesn't weep or feel sorry for men who have given their lives for their country. You try and make up for them.

GRANDPA AND THE
STATUE

Arthur Miller

Arthur Miller was born in Manhattan around the corner from P.S. 117, where he went to school. He now lives in Brooklyn, writes novels and plays, which are his chief interests, and many radio scripts. The editors of *Cavalcade of America* particularly value the quality of his writing.

When Miller writes a script, very real people generally emerge, who have an existence of their own far beyond the needs of the plot or subject he has been asked to handle.

As for *Grandpa and the Statue*, he tells it this way: "*Grandpa and the Statue* came out the way it did because I could not bear to do another Statue of Liberty show which would illustrate how friendly we are with France and how it will stand forever as a symbol of a symbol and so on. I believe the government and the Radio Writers' Guild ought to get together and decide on one Statue of Liberty script once and for all, and when the anniversary comes around just do it instead of making every writer knock his brains out trying to get a new idea about it. Everything that needs to be said about it was said by Emma Lazarus anyway.

"The story behind the script is the same as the story behind most *Cavalcade* scripts, and probably all other radio scripts. The man in the advertising office has a calendar with all the national holidays and celebrations and so on marked on it. I come in and we talk until I get depressed, and then go home and do the script and then try not to think of Washington's Birthday coming up. I will not deny though that I had a desire to make people realize that the Statue of Liberty was erected to signify America's former open-door policy. If people get the idea from the show that, Jew, Irish, Italian or what not, we were all welcome here once, that will be a great satisfaction to me."

Cavalcade of America, which has won innumerable awards through the years, is one of the few sponsored series that give an opportunity to Miller's type of talent, which doesn't readily let itself be poured into prescribed formulas.

Miller, after a childhood at the edge of Harlem, spent four years at the University of Michigan and wrote three stage plays, two of which won the Avery Hopwood Award, and another the Bureau of New Plays Prize. He worked on the movie *Story of GI Joe,* and published a book about that experience, called *Situation Normal.* His play, *The Man Who Had All the Luck,* was on Broadway in 1944. A new Miller novel is on the way.

GRANDPA AND THE
STATUE*

[*Music: Theme*]

ANNOUNCER. The scene is the fourth floor of a giant army hospital overlooking New York Harbor. A young man sitting in a wheel chair is looking out a window; just looking. After a while another young man in another wheel chair rolls over to him and they both look.

[*Music out*]

AUGUST. You want to play some checkers with me, Monaghan?

MONAGHAN. Not right now.

AUGUST. Okay. [*Slight pause*] You don't want to go feeling blue, Monaghan.

MONAGHAN. I'm not blue.

AUGUST. All you do most days is sit here looking out this window.

MONAGHAN. What do you want me to do, jump rope?

AUGUST. No, but what do you get out of it?

MONAGHAN. It's a beautiful view. Some companies make millions of dollars just printing that view on postcards.

AUGUST. Yeh, but nobody keeps looking at a postcard six, seven hours a day.

MONAGHAN. I come from around here, it reminds me of things. My young days.

AUGUST. That's right, you're Brooklyn, aren't you?

MONAGHAN. My house is only about a mile away.

AUGUST. That so. Tell me, are you looking at just the water all the time? I'm curious. I don't get a kick out of this view.

MONAGHAN. There's the Statue of Liberty out there. Don't you see it?

AUGUST. Oh, that's it. Yeh, that's nice to look at.

* GRANDPA AND THE STATUE by Arthur Miller. Copyright, 1945, by E. I. du Pont de Nemours & Co., Inc.

MONAGHAN. I like it. Reminds me of a lot of laughs.

AUGUST. Laughs? The Statue of Liberty?

MONAGHAN. Yeh, my grandfather. He got all twisted up with the Statue of Liberty.

AUGUST [*Laughs a little*]. That so? What happened?

MONAGHAN. Well. My grandfather was the stingiest man in Brooklyn. "Mercyless" Monaghan, they used to call him. He even used to save umbrella handles.

AUGUST. What for?

MONAGHAN. Just couldn't stand seeing anything go to waste. After a big windstorm there'd be a lot of broken umbrellas laying around in the streets.

AUGUST. Yeh?

MONAGHAN. He'd go around picking them up. In our house the closets were always full of umbrella handles. My grandma used to say that he would go across the Brooklyn Bridge on the trolley just because he could come back on the same nickel. See, if you stayed on the trolley they'd let you come back for the same nickel.

AUGUST. What'd he do, just go over and come back?

MONAGHAN. Yeh, it made him feel good. Savin' money. Two and a half cents.

AUGUST. So how'd he get twisted up with the Statue of Liberty?

MONAGHAN. Well, way back in 1887 around there they were living on Butler Street. Butler Street, Brooklyn, practically runs right down to the river. One day he's sitting on the front porch, reading a paper he borrowed from the neighbors, when along comes this man Jack Sheean who lived up the block.

[*Music: Sneak into above speech, then bridge, then out*]

SHEEAN [*Slight brogue*]. A good afternoon to you, Monaghan.

MONAGHAN. How're you, Sheean, how're ya?

SHEEAN. Fair, fair. And how's Mrs. Monaghan these days?

MONAGHAN. Warm. Same as everybody else in summer.

SHEEAN. I've come to talk to you about the fund, Monaghan.

MONAGHAN. What fund is that?

SHEEAN. The Statue of Liberty fund.

MONAGHAN. Oh, that.

SHEEAN. It's time we come to grips with the subject, Monaghan.

MONAGHAN. I'm not interested, Sheean.

SHEEAN. Now hold up on that a minute. Let me tell you the facts. This
here Frenchman has gone and built a fine statue of Liberty. It
costs the Lord knows how many millions to build. All they're
askin' us to do is contribute enough to put up a base for the
statue to stand on.

MONAGHAN. I'm not . . . !

SHEEAN. Before you answer me. People all over the whole United
States are puttin' in for it. Butler Street is doin' the same. We'd
like to hang up a flag on the corner saying—"Butler Street,
Brooklyn, is one hundred per cent behind the Statue of Liberty."
And Butler Street *is* a hundred per cent subscribed except for you.
Now will you give us a dime, Monaghan? One dime and we can
put up the flag. Now what do you say to that?

MONAGHAN. I'm not throwin' me good money away for somethin' I
don't even know exists.

SHEEAN. Now what do you mean by that?

MONAGHAN. Have you seen this statue?

SHEEAN. No, but it's in a warehouse. And as soon as we get the money
to build the pedestal they'll take it and put it up on that island
in the river, and all the boats comin' in from the old country
will see it there and it'll raise the hearts of the poor immigrants
to see such a fine sight on their first look at this country.

MONAGHAN. And how do I know it's in this here warehouse at all?

SHEEAN. You read your paper, don't you? It's been in all the papers
for the past year.

MONAGHAN. Ha, the papers! Last year I read in the paper that they
were about to pave Butler Street and take out all the holes. Turn
around and look at Butler Street, Mr. Sheean.

SHEEAN. All right. I'll do this: I'll take you to the warehouse and show
you the statue. Will you give me a dime then?

MONAGHAN. Well . . . I'm not sayin' I would, and I'm not sayin' I
wouldn't. But I'd be more *likely* if I saw the thing large as life,
I would.

SHEEAN [*Peeved*]. All right, then. Come along.

[*Music up and down and out*]

[*Footsteps, in a warehouse . . . echo . . . they come to halt*]
Now then. Do you see the Statue of Liberty or don't you see it?

MONAGHAN. I see it all right, but it's all broke!

SHEEAN. *Broke!* They brought it from France on a boat. They had to take it apart, didn't they?

MONAGHAN. You got a secondhand statute, that's what you got, and I'm not payin' for new when they've shipped us something that's all smashed to pieces.

SHEEAN. Now just a minute, just a minute. Visualize what I'm about to tell you, Monaghan, get the picture of it. When this statue is put together it's going to stand ten stories high. Could they get a thing ten stories high into a four-story building such as this is? Use your good sense, now, Monaghan.

MONAGHAN. What's that over there?

SHEEAN. Where?

MONAGHAN. That tablet there in her hand. What's it say? July Eye Vee (IV) MDCCLXXVI . . . what . . . what's all that?

SHEEAN. That means July 4, 1776. It's in Roman numbers. Very high class.

MONAGHAN. What's the good of it? If they're going to put a sign on her they ought to put it: Welcome All. That's it. Welcome All.

SHEEAN. They decided July 4, 1776, and July 4, 1776, it's going to be!

MONAGHAN. All right, then let them get their dime from somebody else!

SHEEAN. Monaghan!

MONAGHAN. No, sir! I'll tell you something. I didn't think there was a statue but there is. She's all broke, it's true, but she's here and maybe they can get her together. But even if they do, will you tell me what sort of a welcome to immigrants it'll be, to have a gigantic thing like that in the middle of the river and in her hand is July Eye Vee MCDVC . . . whatever it is?

SHEEAN. That's the date the country was made!

MONAGHAN. The divil with the date! A man comin' in from the sea wants a place to stay, not a date. When I come from the old country I git off at the dock and there's a feller says to me, "Would you care for a room for the night?" "I would that," I sez, and he sez, "All right then, follow me." He takes me to a rooming house. I no sooner sign me name on the register—which I was

able to do even at that time—when I look around and the feller
is gone clear away and took my valise in the bargain. A statue
anyway can't move off so fast, but if she's going to welcome let
her say welcome, not this MCDC. . . .

SHEEAN. All right, then, Monaghan. But all I can say is, you've laid
a disgrace on the name of Butler Street. I'll put the dime in
for ya.

MONAGHAN. Don't connect me with it! It's a swindle, is all it is. In
the first place, it's broke; in the second place, if they do put it
up it'll come down with the first high wind that strikes it.

SHEEAN. The engineers say it'll last forever!

MONAGHAN. And I say it'll topple into the river in a high wind! Look
at the inside of her. She's all hollow!

SHEEAN. I've heard everything now, Monaghan. Just about everything.
Good-bye.

MONAGHAN. What do you mean, good-bye? How am I to get back to
Butler Street from here?

SHEEAN. You've got legs to walk.

MONAGHAN. I'll remind you that I come on the trolley.

SHEEAN. And I'll remind you that I paid your fare and I'm not repeating the kindness.

MONAGHAN. Sheean? You've stranded me!

[Music up and down]

YOUNG MONAGHAN. That was grandpa. That's why I have to laugh
every time I look at the statue now.

AUGUST. Did he ever put the dime in?

YOUNG MONAGHAN. Well—in a way. What happened was this: His
daughters got married and finally my mom . . . put *me* out on
Butler Street. I got to be pretty attached to grandpa. He'd even
give me an umbrella handle and make a sword out of it for me.
Naturally, I wasn't very old before he began working on me
about the statue.

[High wind]

CHILD MONAGHAN [Softly, as though grandpa is in bed]. Grampa?

MONAGHAN [Awakened]. Heh? What are you doin' up?

CHILD MONAGHAN. Ssssh! Listen!

[Wind rising up and fading. Rising higher and fading]

MONAGHAN [*Gleefully*]. Aaaaaaaah! Yes, yes. This'll do it, boy. This'll do it! First thing in the morning we'll go down to the docks and I'll bet you me life that Mr. Sheean's statue is smashed down and layin' on the bottom of the bay. Go to sleep now, we'll have a look first thing.

[*Music up and down*]

[*Footsteps*]

CHILD MONAGHAN. If it fell down, all the people will get their dimes back, won't they, grampa? Slow down, I can't walk so fast.

MONAGHAN. Not only will they get their dimes back, but Mr. Sheean and the whole crew that engineered the collection are going to rot in jail. Now mark my words. Here, now, we'll take a short cut around this shed . . .

[*Footsteps continue a moment, then gradually . . . disappointedly they come to a halt*]

CHILD MONAGHAN. She's . . . she's still standing, grampa.

MONAGHAN. She is that. [*Uncomprehending*] I don't understand it. That was a terrible wind last night. Terrible.

CHILD MONAGHAN. Maybe she's weaker though. Heh?

MONAGHAN. Why . . . sure, that must be it. I'll wager she's hangin' by a thread. [*Realizing*] Of course! That's why they put her out there in the water so when she falls down she won't be flattening out a lot of poor innocent people. Hey—feel that?

CHILD MONAGHAN. The wind! It's starting to blow again!

MONAGHAN. Sure, and look at the sky blackening over!

[*Wind rising*]

Feel it comin' up! Take your last look at the statue, boy. If I don't mistake me eyes she's takin' a small list to Jersey already!

[*Music up and down*]

YOUNG MONAGHAN. It was getting embarrassing for me on the block. I kept promising the other kids that when the next wind came the statue would come down. We even had a game. Four or five kids would stand in a semicircle around one kid who was the statue. The statue kid had to stand on his heels and look right in our eyes. Then we'd all take a deep breath and blow in his face. He'd fall down like a stick of wood. They all believed me and grampa . . . until one day. We were standing around throwing rocks at an old milk can . . .

[*Banging of rocks against milk can*]

GEORGE [*Kid*]. What're you doin?

CHILD MONAGHAN. What do we look like we're doin'?

GEORGE. I'm going someplace tomorrow.

CHARLEY [*Kid*]. I know, church. Watch out, I'm throwin'.

[*Can being hit*]

GEORGE. I mean after church.

JACK. Where?

GEORGE. My old man's going to take me out on the Statue of Liberty boat.

[*Banging against can abruptly stops*]

CHILD MONAGHAN. You're not going out on the statue, though, are you?

GEORGE. Sure, that's where we're going.

CHILD MONAGHAN. But you're liable to get killed. Supposing there's a high wind tomorrow?

GEORGE. My old man says that statue couldn't fall down if all the wind in the world and John L. Sullivan hit it at the same time.

CHILD MONAGHAN. Is that so?

GEORGE. Yeh, that's so. My old man says that the only reason your grandfather's saying that it's going to fall down is that he's ashamed he didn't put a dime in for the pedestal.

CHILD MONAGHAN. Is that so?

GEORGE. Yeh, that's so.

CHILD MONAGHAN. Well, you tell your old man that if he gets killed tomorrow not to come around to my grandfather and say he didn't warn him!

JACK. Hey, George, would your father take me along?

GEORGE. I'll ask him, maybe he—

CHILD MONAGHAN. What, are you crazy, Jack?

MIKE. Ask him if he'd take me too, will ya, George?

CHILD MONAGHAN. Mike, what's the matter with you?

JOE. Me too, George, I'll ask my mother for money.

CHILD MONAGHAN. Joe! Didn't you hear what my grampa said?

JOE. Well . . . I don't really believe that any more.

CHILD MONAGHAN. You don't be . . .

MIKE. Me neither.

JACK. I don't really think your grampa knows what he's talkin' about.
CHILD MONAGHAN. He don't, heh? [*Ready to weep*] Okay . . . Okay.
[*Bursting out*] I just hope that wind blows tomorrow, boy! I just
hope that wind blows!

[*Music up and down*]

[*Creaking of a rocking chair*]
Grampa . . . ?
MONAGHAN. Huh?
CHILD MONAGHAN. Can you stop rocking for a minute?
[*Rocking stops*]
Can you put down your paper?
[*Rustle of paper*]
I—I read the weather report for tomorrow.
MONAGHAN. The weather report . . .
CHILD MONAGHAN. Yeh. It says fair and cool.
MONAGHAN. What of it?
CHILD MONAGHAN. I was wondering. Supposing you and me we went
on a boat tomorrow. You know, I see the water every day when
I go down to the docks to play, but I never sat on it. I mean
in a boat.
MONAGHAN. Oh. Well, we might take the ferry on the Jersey side. We
might do that.
CHILD MONAGHAN. Yeh, but there's nothing to see in Jersey.
MONAGHAN. You can't go to Europe tomorrow.
CHILD MONAGHAN. No, but couldn't we go toward the ocean? Just . . .
toward it?
MONAGHAN. Toward it. What—what is it on your mind, boy? What
is it now?
CHILD MONAGHAN. Well, I . . .
MONAGHAN. Oh, you want to take the Staten Island ferry. Sure, that's
in the direction of the sea.
CHILD MONAGHAN. No, grampa, not the Staten Island ferry.
MONOGHAN. You don't mean—[*Breaks off*] Boy!
CHILD MONAGHAN. All the kids are going tomorrow with Georgie's
old man.
MONAGHAN. You don't believe me any more.
CHILD MONAGHAN. I do, grampa, but . . .

MONAGHAN. You don't. If you did you'd stay clear of the Statue of Liberty for love of your life!

CHILD MONAGHAN. But, grampa, when is it going to fall down? All I do is wait and wait.

MONAGHAN [*With some uncertainty*]. You've got to have faith.

CHILD MONAGHAN. But every kid in my class went to see it and now the ones that didn't are going tomorrow. And they all keep talking about it and all I do . . . Well, I can't keep telling them it's a swindle. I—I wish we could see it, grampa. It don't cost so much to go.

MONAGHAN. As long as you put it that way I'll have to admit I'm a bit curious meself as to how it's managed to stand upright so long. Tell you what I'll do. Barrin' wind, we'll chance it to-morrow!

CHILD MONAGHAN. Oh, gramp!

MONAGHAN. But! If anyone should ask you where we went you'll say— Staten Island. Are y' on?

CHILD MONAGHAN. Okay, sure. Staten Island.

MONAGHAN [*Secretively*]. We'll take the early boat, then. Mum's the word, now. For if old man Sheean hears that I went out there I'll have no peace from the thief the rest of m' life.

[*Music up and down*]

[*Boat whistles*]

CHILD MONAGHAN. Gee, it's nice ridin' on a boat, ain't it, grampa?

MONAGHAN. Never said there was anything wrong with the boat. Boat's all right. You're sure now that Georgie's father is takin' the kids in the afternoon.

CHILD MONAGHAN. Yeh, that's when they're going. Gee, look at those two sea gulls. Wee!—look at them swoop! They caught a fish!

MONAGHAN. What I can't understand is what all these people see in that statue that they'll keep a boat like this full makin' the trip, year in year out. To hear the newspapers talk, if the statue was gone we'd be at war with the nation that stole her the followin' mornin' early. All it is is a big high pile of French copper.

CHILD MONAGHAN. The teacher says it shows us that we got liberty.

MONAGHAN. Bah! If you've got liberty you don't need a statue to tell you you got it; and if you haven't got liberty no statue's going to do you any good tellin' you you got it. It was a criminal waste of the people's money. [*Quietly*] And just to prove it to you I'll ask this feller sitting right over there what he sees in it. You'll see what a madness the whole thing was. Say, mister?

ALF. Hey?

MONAGHAN. I beg your pardon. I'm a little strange here, and curious. Could you tell me why you're going to the Statue of Liberty?

ALF. Me? Well, I tell ya. I always wanted to take an ocean voyage. This is a pretty big boat—bigger than the ferries—so on Sundays, sometimes, I take the trip. It's better than nothing.

MONAGHAN. Thank you. [*To the kid*] So much for the great meaning of that statue, me boy. We'll talk to this lady standing at the rail. I just want you to understand why I didn't give Sheean me dime. Madam, would you be good enough to . . . Oh pardon me. [*To kid*] Better pass her by, she don't look so good. We'll ask that girl there. Young lady, if you'll pardon the curiosity of an old man . . . could you tell me in a few good words what it is about that statue that brings you out here?

GIRL. What statue?

MONAGHAN. Why, the Statue of Liberty up 'head. We're coming up to it.

GIRL. Statue of Liberty! Is this the Statue of Liberty boat?

MONAGHAN. Well, what'd you think it was?

GIRL. Oh, my! I'm supposed to be on the Staten Island ferry! Where's the ticket man? [*Going away*] Ticket man! Where's the ticket man?

CHILD MONAGHAN. Gee whiz, nobody seems to want to see the statue.

MONAGHAN. Just to prove it, let's see this fellow sitting on this bench here. Young man, say . . .

YOUNG MAN. I can tell you in one word. For four days I haven't had a minute's peace. My kids are screaming, my wife is yelling, upstairs they play the piano all day long. The only place I can find that's quiet is a statue. That statue is my sweetheart. Every Sunday I beat it out to the island and sit next to her, and she don't talk.

CHILD MONAGHAN. I guess you were right, grampa. Nobody seems to think it means anything.

MONAGHAN. Not only doesn't mean anything, but if they'd used the

money to build an honest roomin' house on that island, the
immigrants would have a place to spend the night, their valises
wouldn't get robbed, and they—
MEGAPHONE VOICE. *Please keep your seats while the boat is docking.
Statue of Liberty—all out in five minutes!*
CHILD MONAGHAN. Look down there, gramp! There's a peanut stand!
Could I have some?
MONAGHAN. I feel the wind comin' up. I don't think we dare take
the time.

[*Music up and down*]

CHILD MONAGHAN. Sssssseuuuuuww! Look how far you can see! Look
at that ship way out in the ocean!
MONAGHAN. It is, it's quite a view. Don't let go of me hand now.
CHILD MONAGHAN. I betcha we could almost see California.
MONAGHAN. It's probably that grove of trees way out over there. They
do say it's beyond Jersey.
CHILD MONAGHAN. Feels funny. We're standing right inside her head.
Is that what you meant . . . July IV, MCD . . . ?
MONAGHAN. That's it. That tablet in her hand. Now shouldn't they
have put Welcome All on it instead of that foreign language?
Say! Do you feel her rockin'?
CHILD MONAGHAN. Yeah, she's moving a little bit. Listen, the wind!
[*Whistling of wind*]
MONAGHAN. We better get down, come on! This way!
CHILD MONAGHAN. No, the stairs are this way! Come on!
[*Running in echo. Then quick stop*]
MONAGHAN. No, I told you they're the other way! Come!
VETERAN [*Calm, quiet voice*]. Don't get excited, pop. She'll stand.
MONAGHAN. She's swayin' awful.
VETERAN. That's all right. I been up here thirty, forty times. She
gives with the wind, flexible. Enjoy the view, go on.
MONAGHAN. Did you say you've been up here forty times?
VETERAN. About that many.
MONAGHAN. What do you find here that's so interesting?
VETERAN. It calms my nerves.
MONAGHAN. Ah. It seems to me it would make you more nervous than
you were.

VETERAN. No, not me. It kinda means something to me.

MONAGHAN. Might I ask what?

VETERAN. Well . . . I was in the Philippine War . . . back in '98. Left my brother back there.

MONAGHAN. Oh, yes. Sorry I am to hear it. Young man, I suppose, eh?

VETERAN. Yeh. We were both young. This is his birthday today.

MONAGHAN. Oh, I understand.

VETERAN. Yeh, this statue is about the only stone he's got. In my mind I feel it is anyway. This statue kinda looks like what we believe. You know what I mean?

MONAGHAN. Looks like what we believe . . . I . . . I never thought of it that way. I . . . I see what you mean. It does look that way. [*Angrily*] See now, boy? If Sheean had put it that way I'd a give him me dime. [*Hurt*] Now, why do you suppose he didn't tell me that! Come down now. I'm sorry, sir, we've got to get out of here.

[*Music up and down*]

[*Footsteps under*]

Hurry now, I want to get out of here. I feel terrible. I do, boy. That Sheean, that fool. Why didn't he tell me that? You'd think . . .

CHILD MONAGHAN. What does this say?

[*Footsteps halt*]

MONAGHAN. Why, it's just a tablet, I suppose. I'll try it with me spectacles, just a minute. Why, it's a poem, I believe . . . "Give me your tired, your poor, your huddled masses yearning to breathe free, the wretched refuse of your teeming shore. Send these, the homeless, tempest-tost to me, I lift . . . my lamp beside . . . the golden door!" Oh, dear. [*Ready to weep*] It had Welcome All on it all the time. Why didn't Sheean tell me? I'd a given him a quarter! Boy . . . go over there and here's a nickel and buy yourself a bag of them peanuts.

CHILD MONAGHAN [*Astonished*]. Gramp!

MONAGHAN. Go on now, I want to study this a minute. And be sure the man gives you full count.

CHILD MONAGHAN. I'll be right back.

[*Footsteps running away*]

MONOGHAN. [*To himself*]. "Give me your tired, your poor, your huddled masses . . ."

[*Music swells from a sneak to full, then under to background*]

YOUNG MONAGHAN [*Soldier*]. I ran over and got my peanuts and stood there cracking them open, looking around. And I happened to glance over to grampa. He had his nose right up to that bronze tablet, reading it. And then he reached into his pocket and kinda spied around over his eyeglasses to see if anybody was looking, and then he took out a coin and stuck it in a crack of cement over the tablet.

[*Coin falling onto concrete*]

It fell out and before he could pick it up I got a look at it. It was a half a buck. He picked it up and pressed it into the crack so it stuck. And then he came over to me and we went home.

[*Music: Change to stronger, more forceful theme*]

That's why, when I look at her now through this window, I remember that time and that poem, and she really seems to say, Whoever you are, wherever you come from, Welcome All. Welcome Home.

[*Music: Flare up to finish*]

BOOKER T. WASHINGTON
IN ATLANTA

Langston Hughes

B *ooker T. Washington in Atlanta* was written at the invitation of Tuskegee Institute and the Columbia Broadcasting System, on the occasion of the issuing of a Booker T. Washington stamp by the Post Office Department. Hughes calls it "a special occasion script, as are most scripts dealing with Negro life—since we are not normally a part of radio drama, except as comedy relief."

In those few words Langston Hughes sums up American radio's tragic failure to give the Negro an even break. He goes on: "Radio furnishes some very good Negro entertainment, but comparatively little more, seldom touching on the drama or the problems of Negro life in America. . . . And it continues to keep alive the stereotype of the dialect-speaking, amiably moronic Negro servant as the chief representative of our racial group on the air."

The problem is, of course, complicated by several facts. Some of the programs that help keep alive the stereotype, such as the Jack Benny program with "Rochester," are popular with Negroes, because only through such programs do they find themselves regularly represented in big-time radio. And many brilliant Negro artists can find no outlets for their talents except through likewise helping to perpetuate the vicious circle.

In this generally discouraging picture there are occasional bright spots. There are a few important local series, like New York City's *New World A-Comin'*—see *The Negro Domestic* by Roi Ottley, in this volume. And networks from time to time feature important special programs. William N. Robson's *Open Letter on Race Hatred,* also included in this collection, is a hard-hitting example. But the potential effect of such programs is lessened by the fact that networks generally "warn" 'member stations about them in advance, so that those which wish—southern stations, in particular—can arrange to drop off the network and play phonograph records instead.

Booker T. Washington in Atlanta is more typical of special programs on the Negro, in that it deals with an outstanding individual. This approach to racial subjects is the one preferred by networks because it lends itself to "stressing the positive angle." This kind of script can emphasize Negro accomplishments instead of our society's failure toward him. It can give the Negro encouragement without raising anyone's temperature. There is probably a great deal of value in this strategy, especially when the writing is in the hands of someone like Langston Hughes, who can create believable people with a real humanity about them. However, this limited strategy cannot do all that needs to be done, cannot tell the whole story.

The question has often been raised: Why doesn't a network start a daytime serial about a Negro family, treating its members seriously as human beings, as people are treated on a program like *One Man's Family?* Merely to ask such a question is to point out the gap between what radio has accomplished and what it might and should do.

Langston Hughes has often been suggested as an ideal writer for such a venture. He has several times been invited to discuss the idea with network executives, but they "can't seem to carry it through."

Langston Hughes has published several volumes of verse, *The Weary Blues, The Dream Keeper,* and *Shakespeare in Harlem;* a novel, *Not Without Laughter;* a book of short stories, *The Ways of White Folks;* an autobiography, *The Big Sea.* He writes a weekly column, *Here to Yonder,* for the Chicago *Defender.* His verse play, *Don't You Want to Be Free,* ran for 135 performances in Harlem, and he has written songs and other material for several musical shows. He has written radio scripts from time to time, but does not feel that radio offers much opportunity for a writer on Negro life.

Hughes first attracted wide attention as a writer when Vachel Lindsay, at a performance at Washington's Wardman Park Hotel in 1925, read three unpublished poems by a young Negro poet. The poet, Langston Hughes, was a bus boy at the hotel.

BOOKER T. WASHINGTON

IN ATLANTA*

[*Clop-clop of hoofs . . . Sound of carriage*]

WIFE. Booker!

BOOKER. Yes?

WIFE. Why do you look so woebegone?

BOOKER. Margaret, to tell the truth, I feel like a man on the way to the gallows.

CHILD. Papa, they won't hang you for making another speech, will they?

BOOKER. Not hardly, Portia! But the wrong word said—and my usefulness in the South would be finished.

WIFE. You're always nervous before a speech, Booker, as often as you've made them. But tomorrow in Atlanta, I'm sure you'll give the best talk you've ever made. There's nothing to worry about.

BOY. Geeminy! It'll be wonderful to see Atlanta, won't it, mom?

GIRL. And the Cotton Exposition!

BOY. Papa, will there be a merry-go-round for colored children?

BOOKER. I reckon so, son. One of the biggest buildings on the grounds is the colored people's building.

GIRL. Will there be a Ferris wheel?

BOY. And firecrackers?

WIFE. Booker T. Junior, don't bother your father with firecrackers! He's tired—working all night on his speech. And besides, if he opens his mouth, clay dust'll get in his throat and he'll be hoarse.

BOOKER. Margaret, dust can't hurt a country boy like me. When I was Junior's age I was working in a coal mine twelve hours a day—and I've still got my voice.

WIFE. Well, save it for speaking and I'll take care of these children.

* BOOKER T. WASHINGTON IN ATLANTA by Langston Hughes. Copyright, by Langston Hughes.

Lucius, slow Jennie down a bit. There's plenty of time to make the train.

LUCIUS. Yes, ma'am, Mis' Washington.

BOY. Here comes Farmer Krenshaw in his old mule wagon, papa.

GIRL. He's one of the nicest white men around.

BOOKER. Lucius, you might stop a moment.

[*Horse slowing down*]

FARMER. Howdy, folks.

BOOKER. Howdy-do, Mr. Krenshaw. Nice sun for cotton, isn't it?

FARMER. Plenty! I hear you gonna make a speech tomorrow, Washington, the .opening of the Exposition?

BOOKER. It looks like I am, sir.

FARMER. Well, you pretty good. You've spoke in front of northern white folks, and southern colored folks, and us farmers around here too. But in Atlanta tomorrow you gonna have city folks *and* country folks, Yankees *and* Southerners—and colored folks added to that. Now, how you gonna please all them different kind o' folks, Washington? I figger you got yourself in a kinder tight place.

BOOKER [*Laughing*]. I'm afraid I have! But when I come back, I'll tell you what I said.

FARMER. Well, good luck to you, Washington.

BOOKER. Thank you, Mr. Krenshaw.

[*Horse speeds up, blending into*]

[*Music: Hoofbeat transition*]

[*Train pulling in*]

[*Ad libs of "good-bye," "good luck," etc.*]

STATION PORTER. Get you-all's bags and bundles together! Here she comes. You children get back from the track. . . . Auburn, Opelika, West Point, La Grange, Hogansville, Trimble, Atlanta! . . . Stand back 'cause she's a-blowin'!

[*Train comes to a stop*]

'Board! All 'board!

STUDENT. We with you, Dr. Washington.

SECOND STUDENT. God bless you, Mr. Washington.

THIRD STUDENT. Good luck to you-all. Happy journey!

[*Bell of departing train*]

ALL. Good-bye! Good-bye! Good-bye!
[*Train starting into*]

[*Music: Special pullman car . . . Music cross-fading to*]

[*Wheel sounds*]

BOOKER. The way my students believe in me, Margaret, I can't let then down at Atlanta.

WIFE. You won't, Booker. They believe in you because you have never let them down. And they know you started out like they did, poor and ignorant, no book learning, nobody to help you—but you kept on.

BOOKER. Out of slavery, and the coal mine.

WIFE. And tomorrow you'll sit on the platform with the Governor of Georgia!

BOOKER. It's been a long haul, Margaret, from a slave plantation in Virginia where I didn't know my father's name—a one-room cabin and a bundle of rags on the floor.

GIRL. Papa, you promised to tell us about it again sometime.

BOY. And about the cat hole.

GIRL. But you're always too busy.

BOY. Why don't you tell us now?

GIRL. Tell us, please, papa.

WIFE. Children—

BOY. Tell us about the cat hole.

BOOKER. Well, Junior, you see my mother's cabin on the plantation didn't have any windows in it—but there were plenty of holes where the rain leaked through. And there was a rickety door, and a cat hole cut in the wall for the cat to pass in and out during the night.

BOY. Why, couldn't the cat go out the door?

BOOKER. Could've. There were plenty of cracks in it. But *everybody* had a cat hole—so we had one, too.

BOY. And did your mother feed the cat?

BOOKER. She hardly had time to feed *us*. She was a slave. Why, I can remember . . .

[*Train sounds fade out*]

MOTHER [*Fading on*]. Get up, you-all chillun—if you wants to eat this corn pone. It mighty nigh daybreak. I got to go to my work.

CHILD [*Drowsily*]. Yes'm, we's comin'.

BOY. I's sleepy, ma.

MOTHER. Sleepy, nothin'! You got no time to be sleepy. [*Gently*] Here, eat this, son.

BOY. Yes'm.

MOTHER. And get on down yonder to de fields—'cause I don't want my chillun to get no floggin' this mornin'.

[*Fade in train*]

GIRL. I don't like to hear about floggings, papa.

BOY. Tell us about freedom.

GIRL. And the war.

BOOKER. I didn't see the war. But I heard the white folks talking about the war, as I fanned the flies away from them at dinnertime. And I knew it meant freedom—if the Yankees won. In the slave cabins at night . . .

[*Fade train out*]

SLAVE. Mars Lincoln, dey say he gonna sot us free!

SECOND SLAVE. Mars Lincoln, he gonna sign a paper that say . . .

THIRD SLAVE. No mo' work in de fields.

SLAVE. No mo' chillun sold away.

SECOND SLAVE. No mo' floggin's.

THIRD SLAVE. First thing I gwine do is learn to read.

SLAVE. First thing I gwine do is *rest*.

SECOND SLAVE. Yes, indeedy! Uh-hum-mmmmm!

THIRD SLAVE. Won't it be fun to be free!

[*Train in*]

BOOKER. Yet none of us wanted harm to come to our master's family.

BOY. But when freedom came, you went away?

BOOKER. Yes, my mother took us children to West Virginia and I went to work in the salt furnaces. I was a big boy, yet I couldn't read or write. But the number on my salt barrel was . . .

[*Train out*]

FOREMAN. Eighteen. Take that barrel and fill it, boy.

BOOKER. Eigh-teen? Is that what them two numbers mean, boss?

FOREMAN. A one and a eight, that's eighteen.

BOOKER. A one and a eight . . . one and eight . . . eigh-teen.

[*Train in*]

So I learned to make those numbers and to read them. And I

wanted to learn more. I talked so much about learning till my mother finally got me a battered blue-backed speller somewhere, and all alone I studied the alphabet.

GIRL. Why didn't you get somebody to help you?

BOOKER. There wasn't a colored person in town who knew how to read. They had all been slaves.

GIRL. Oh!

BOY. And there was no school?

BOOKER. No, son, there was no school. And when a school was finally established, it was a *pay* school and I couldn't go because I had to work. But at night I studied my blue-backed speller by the firelight.

BOY. Like Lincoln did.

BOOKER. And finally I got my chance to go to school—by rising at daybreak and working until classtime, then going back to work after school. There were many big boys in the first grade then, so being large didn't embarrass me. But what did embarrass me was that first day when the teacher was making out the roll, because I noticed all the other children had at least two names, or even three—but I had just been called Booker all my life. I didn't know what I would say when he got to me. And he was coming down the line.

   [*Train out*]

TEACHER. Your name, son?

BOY. Aloysius Wilkrus Jones, suh.

TEACHER. And yours?

GIRL. Mary Mackabee Johnson.

TEACHER. Yours?

SECOND BOY. Franklin Wadson Hall.

TEACHER. Yours, please.

THIRD BOY. I'm Robert E. Lee Grant.

   [*Train in*]

BOOKER. And all the time he kept getting closer to me, and I didn't know what I was going to say. I was mighty puzzled. I felt like I wanted to cry. But suddenly a bright idea came to me and when he said:

   [*Train out*]

TEACHER. And your name is . . . ?

BOOKER. Booker T. Washington.
[*Train in*]
It popped out just like that—as if I'd known it all my life. And ever since, that's been my name.

GIRL. Then you christened yourself, didn't you, papa?

BOOKER. I christened myself!
[*Laughter*]

BOY. But you didn't stay long in school, did you, papa?

BOOKER. No. I had to go to work again, this time in the coal mines, a mile down in the dark.

GIRL. Weren't you afraid?

BOOKER. Yes. There were often explosions, and falling slate, and gas. But one day down there I happened to hear two miners talking about a great school for colored people somewhere in Virginia, so I crept as close as I could to hear what they were saying.
[*Train out*]

MINER. They calls it Hampton. And if a boy ain't got no money, he can just work for his education.

SECOND MINER. How about his board and keep?

MINER. They say he can work for that too.

SECOND MINER. Dog scat my eyes! Where's it at?

MINER. Somewhere 'way 'cross Virginny. I'm . . .
[*Train in*]

BOOKER. I didn't know how far Hampton was, nor how to get to it, but I made up my mind then and there to go.

BOY. And when you got there, they weren't sure they wanted to let you in, were they, papa?

BOOKER. No, son, because I got there in rags, with no money, and I'd slept the night before under a sidewalk in Richmond. The school was crowded. There were so many students some of us slept in tents. And sometimes at night the tents blew away in the dead of winter—but we wanted an education—and we got it!

GIRL. It's nicer at Tuskegee.

BOOKER. But it wasn't always. We began in a stable and a hen house. We made our own bricks. I pawned my watch for materials, and begged for money. Then a white man gave us *ten thousand dollars*.

WIFE. Our first big sum.

BOOKER. And once an old colored woman over seventy brought a gift. She hobbled in in rags—but clean—leaning on a cane. She held out her gift.

[*Train out*]

OLD WOMAN. Mr. Washington, I's spent de best days o' my life in slavery. And God knows I's ignorant and po'. But I knows what you's tryin' to do. You tryin' to make better men and women for de cullud race. I ain't got no money, but I wants you to take dese here six eggs what I been savin' up, and I wants you to put these six eggs into de edication of dese boys and girls.

[*Train in*]

BOOKER. And so we struggled! But I'm glad we had to struggle. We built Tuskegee from the ground up. Now, when a new student is tempted to mar some building by carving his initials on it with a jackknife, I've often heard an old student say, "Don't do that. That's *our* building. I helped to put it up." In the beginning folks said we would fail. But I have no patience with the man who talks of failure, children. I believe only in the man who talks success.

WIFE. And that's what you should say in your speech tomorrow, Booker.

BOOKER. My speech is ready, Margaret. It's not what I'm going to say that worries me, but how they'll take it. Will the Southerners be displeased? Will the Negroes be worried? Will the northern whites think I've compromised? For they'll all be there—former slaves and former slaveowners, graduates from Tuskegee, and teachers from Hampton. And thousands of Georgians . . .

WIFE. And when Governor Bullock introduces you in Exposition Hall . . .

[*Fade out train scene*]

GOVERNOR. Ladies and gentlemen, we have with us here today a representative of Negro civilization in the South, Professor Booker T. Washington of Tuskegee.

[*A flurry of applause . . . A few cheers . . . Then dead silence*]

BOOKER. Mr. President, Gentlemen of the Board of Directors, Citizens: One-third of the population of the South is of the Negro race. No enterprise seeking the material, civil, or moral welfare of this section can disregard this element of our population and reach the highest success. Once a ship lost at sea for many days suddenly sighted a friendly vessel. From the mast of the unfortunate vessel was seen a signal, "Water, water; we die of thirst!" The answer from the friendly vessel came back, "Cast your bucket where you are." A second time the signal, "Water, water; send us water!" ran up the distressed vessel, and was answered, "Cast down your bucket where you are." And a third and fourth signal for water was answered, "Cast down your bucket where you are." The captain of the distressed vessel, at last heeding the injunction, cast down his bucket, and it came up full of fresh, sparkling water from the mouth of the Amazon River. To those of my race who underestimate the importance of cultivating friendly relations with the southern white man, who is their next-door neighbor, I would say, "Cast down your bucket where you are." Cast it down in making friends in every manly way of the people of all races by whom we are surrounded. Cast it down in agriculture, mechanics, in commerce, in domestic service, and in the professions. No race can prosper till it learns there is as much dignity in tilling a field as in writing a poem.

To those of the white race, I would repeat what I say to my own race, "Cast down your bucket where you are." Cast it down among the eight millions of Negroes whose habits you know, whose fidelity you have tested. Cast down your bucket among these people who have tilled your fields, cleared your forests, and brought forth treasures from the bowels of the earth. Cast down your bucket among my people, help and encourage them to the education of head, hand, and heart. Then you will find that they will buy your surplus land, make blossom the waste places in your fields, and run your factories. But there is no defense or security for any of us except in the highest intelligence and development of all.

Gentlemen of the Exposition, I pledge that in your effort to work out the intricate problem which God has laid at the doors of the South, you shall have at all times the help of my race. Only let this be constantly in mind . . .

[*Music in*]

that far beyond material benefits will be that higher good which, let us pray God, will result in a blotting out of sectional differences and racial animosities and suspicions, in a determination to administer absolute justice, and in a willing obedience among all classes to the mandates of law.

[*Music: Up to finish*]

NORTH ATLANTIC
TESTAMENT

Father Timothy J. Mulvey

D RAMA was born of religion. In radio we find it once more called into the service of religion.

At first religious radio programs were almost exclusively sermons, perhaps introduced and followed by religious music. But in recent years several denominations have also begun to use drama for religious messages.

North Atlantic Testament was written for the *Catholic Hour*. This series, presented by the National Council of Catholic Men, in co-operation with NBC, generally presents talks, but now also occasionally features dramatic programs.

Father Timothy J. Mulvey was born in New York City. He attended Canisius High School and Canisius College in Buffalo—both schools under the supervision of the Jesuits. Immediately after being ordained by Archbishop Francis J. Spellman as a priest in the Congregation of the Oblates of Mary Immaculate, he took up the study of speech and radio, first in Brookline, Massachusetts, then at the Catholic University Workshop, Washington, D. C. He received an M.A. degree, after writing a thesis on the development of radio dramatic techniques in the United States.

He has a particularly fine feeling for the use of music and sound for emotional effect in radio drama. He has written a number of plays for the *Catholic Hour*. *North Atlantic Testament* was repeated on *Words at War*.

The *Catholic Hour's* experiments with drama have apparently been very successful. Audience reaction has been overwhelmingly favorable. Father Mulvey's scripts won a special citation from the Institute for Education by Radio, as the most effective religious programs of 1944.

Speaking of the religious dramatic program, Father Mulvey says: "Like the radio sermon, it can be only an accessory. But a good radio play, employing the best professional standards, can be at once entertaining, instructive, and inspiring. In this, I feel that the radio play still remains to do religion a great good."

NORTH ATLANTIC
TESTAMENT

[*Music: Feathering of violins . . . Hold behind*]

ANNOUNCER. To the chaplains of the Armed Forces of the United States . . . to the young priests who traded the quiet flame of a sanctuary lamp for the ravaging flames of war . . . to the priests who walked from a peaceful world of chapel chimes and the Sanctus bell . . . to a world that rocked with the thunder of artillery . . .

[*Music: Punctuate . . . Cut*]

To Father Aloysius Schmitt of the navy, who went down with the battleship "Oklahoma" at Pearl Harbor . . .

[*Music: Punctuate . . . Cut*]

To Father Clement Falter of the army, who fell beneath enemy shells on the shores of North Africa . . .

[*Music: Punctuate . . . Cut*]

To Father Thomas Brady of the army, who crawled with the wounds of death into a foxhole at twilight . . .

[*Music: Punctuate . . . Cut*]

To Fathers James Liston and Valmore Savignac, who died under the lashing fury of the North Atlantic.

[*Music: Punctuate . . . Cut*]

To Father Neil Doyle of the army . . .

[*Music: Punctuate . . . Cut*]

To Father Michael Duggan . . .

[*Music: Punctuate . . . Cut*]

Lawrence Gough . . .

[*Music: Punctuate . . . Cut*]

Eugene Polheumus . . .

[*Music: Punctuate . . . Cut*]

James Flynn . . .

[*Music: Punctuate . . . Cut*]

To these chaplains . . . and to many others who have made the great sacrifice in this World War . . .

[*Music: Sneak in softly behind*]

We offer, this day, the humble tribute of our love and prayers . . .

[*Music: Sweep up . . . Then fast segue to "Requiem" on organ . . . Hold behind*]

May their souls . . . and the souls of all the faithful departed through the mercy of God . . . rest in peace. Amen.

[*Music: Organ up fast . . . Hold . . . Then drop behind music to mood . . . Hold under*]

Nor have we forgotten *him* . . . Father John P. Washington of the United States Army. We shall never forget him . . . for it was Father Washington . . . who, in the early, black hours of a February morning . . . gave to the world his . . .

[*Music: Punctuate . . . Hold up . . . Behind*]

NORTH ATLANTIC TESTAMENT!

[*Music: Up to peak . . . Hold . . . Then down softly behind*]

NARRATOR. This is a story about a boy you might have known . . .

[*Music: Out*]

It began very quietly one day . . . not so long ago . . . when John walked into a kitchen . . .

[*Fade in with washing of dishes . . . Hold behind*]

MRS. W. [*Humming distractedly*].

JOHN. [*Quietly*]. Mother.

MRS. W. Yes, John.

[*Cut dishes*]

JOHN. [*Not at ease*]. Would you . . . would you mind putting those dishes aside for a minute, I'd like to talk to you about . . . something.

MRS. W. Why . . .

JOHN. Wait a minute. I'll close the door.

[*Close door*]

MRS. W. Well . . . what's the trouble, John?

JOHN. Sit down, mother. [*Pause*] There's a . . . sort of problem that's been . . . on my mind.

MRS. W. Problem?

JOHN. Yes. [*Pause*] It's a . . . well, I don't know how to begin exactly . . .

MRS. W. [*Laughing softly*]. Why . . . what's the *matter* with you, John? You look as if . . .

JOHN. It's . . . it's simply this. [*Breath*] I've been a long time in school . . . You've spent a lot of money . . . educating me . . . you and pop—I know the sacrifices you've both had to make . . . And I know the sacrifices you *still* have to make . . . for the rest of the kids.

MRS. W. [*Laughing it off easily*]. Sacrifices! Why . . . six children, John, are nothing at all . . . Now, you take . . . for instance . . . that poor Mrs. —

JOHN. I understand, mother . . . but . . . what I *want* to say is . . . that . . . being the oldest . . . I have the responsibility . . . now . . . of . . . getting out into the world, and helping to pay back some of —

MRS. W. [*Cajoling*] Now, wait a minute, John.

JOHN. [*Easily*]. Oh, I know what you're going to say, mom. But the fact is I *do* owe you and the rest of the family a debt . . . [*Then seriously*] a debt which I may never be able to pay.

MRS. W. [*Smiling on the words*]. John . . . will you please tell me just *what* is on your mind?

JOHN. [*Pause . . . then hesitant*]. Mother . . . would it make much difference . . . if . . . [*Pause*] . . . I mean . . .

MRS. W. You mean . . . you want to become a priest . . . John?

JOHN. [*Pause*]. Yes.

MRS. W. Sure and didn't I know it all the while?

JOHN. [*Rapidly*]. It would mean more years of work and worry for you, and pop . . . That's what I wanted to talk to you about. It would mean that you—

MRS. W. Wait a minute, son. [*Pause*] You're talking about work and worry. Sure . . . and what greater blessing could I work and worry for . . . than the privilege of being the mother of a priest?

[*Music: Sneak in softly behind*]

I used to dream about seeing a son of mine . . . a priest. I dreamed . . . Oh, I guess I dreamed it a thousand times . . . or more . . . even when you were *that* small . . . John . . . even before you were born.

[*Music gathering exultantly behind*]

And I was thinking . . . that it would be a great day, John . . . sitting there with your father in the front pew . . . with the candles lit . . . and the incense floating like a white cloud over your head . . . with the altar boys in their red cassocks, and the grand organ filling the church . . . I was thinking . . . *that* would be the great day when I could look up and say . . . [*Trembling on the words*] . . . there he is! . . . there he is! . . . my *own* . . . Father John.

[*Music: Topping grandly . . . Then down behind*]

NARRATOR. Such was the dreaming of her who once was a young girl . . . playing on the green hills of Kilglass . . . County Roscommon . . . And such was the answer to her dreaming . . . a young priest-son . . . who once played on the streets of Newark, New Jersey!

[*Music: Almost to peak . . . Hold behind . . . Bring in heavy church bells . . . Hold up with music . . . Then bring down behind*]

[*Talking above music and bells*]. And so . . . on June the fifteenth, nineteen hundred and thirty-five . . . before the members of his family . . . and at the hands of the Most Reverend Thomas Joseph Walsh . . . Archbishop of Newark . . . John Washington was ordained a priest!

[*Music: Up to peak for five seconds . . . Then slightly down behind . . . Bells to peak for five seconds . . . Then slightly down behind*]

The bells rang joyously that day at St. Rose's . . .
[*Hold one bell way off mike . . . Ringing distantly . . . Behind*]
And for five years . . . at St. Stephen's in Arlington . . . a bell rang peacefully . . . [*Pause*] But time can bring strange accents to a peaceful world!
[*Music out*]
[*Cross-fade bell with distant thunder . . . Hold thunder off behind. Point up*]
[*Point up*] Pearl Harbor!
[*Bring thunder in with crash . . . Also sneak in, with thunder, faint battle call of bugle*]
Pearl Harbor turned bells to bugles!
[*Crash in with thunder again . . . Bring bugle closer . . . Behind*]
Pearl Harbor was a scream of pain in the afternoon!

[*Music: Immediate trembling of minor chord . . . Hold behind . . . Thunder rumbling off . . . Fade bugle out behind*]

Pearl Harbor was a face . . . twisted in surprised agony! . . . and the face was the face of your brother!
[*Music out*]
[*Sound out*]
Pearl Harbor was war!
[*Topping with one last distant rumble of thunder . . . Then cross-fade thunder with heavy marching of feet . . . Build gradually behind*]

[*Music: Sneak in martial stuff to tempo of feet . . . Build behind*]

VOICE 1 [*Above sound and music*]. Just wanted to say "so long" to you, Father Washington. I'm heading for boot camp at Sampson.
JOHN. Good-bye, Jimmy. Take good care of yourself.
[*Marching feet coming closer . . . Hold up behind*]

[*Music: Increase with marching feet . . . Hold up behind*]

VOICE 2 [*Above sound and music . . . on cue*]. Yeah . . . I'm goin'
to join the Marines, father. Quantico!

JOHN. Good going, Tommy.

VOICE 2. So I guess I'll say good-bye. [*Going off mike*] Don't forget
to write.

JOHN [*Calling after him*]. I won't, Tommy . . . God bless you.
[*Feet coming on mike stronger . . . Hold up behind*]

[*Music: Increase with marching feet . . . Hold up behind*]

VOICE 3 [*Above music and sound . . . on cue*]. Thought I'd drop over
to St. Stephen's before I left . . .

JOHN. So it's the army, eh, Jack?

VOICE 3. You bet. Dere's nuttin' like de army, fadder. Dem Marines
. . . huh . . . dey tink dey can run de whole show . . . Baloney!
[*Marching feet close to peak . . . Hold up behind*]

[*Music: Close to peak . . . Hold behind*]

VOICE 1 [*Way off mikke . . . Shouting*], So long, father!

VOICE 2 [*Way off mike . . . Shouting*]. We'll be seeing you!

VOACE 3 [*Way off mike . . . Shouting*]. Good-bye! . . . [*Almost swal-
lowed in sound and music*] Good-bye!

JOHN [*Calling after them above sound and music*]. Good-bye, fellows!
Good— [*Pause . . . then excitedly*] Wait a minute ! . . . WAIT
A MINUTE, FELLOWS!
[*Hold marching feet at complete peak for three seconds . . .
Then fade out behind music*]

[*Music: Catch marching feet at their peak . . . Then super-
impose heavy staccato beat chords to tempo . . . And "march"
gradually out to "dead" air*]

VOICE. So . . . you want to become an army chaplain, Father Washington!

JOHN. Yes, I do. I've been working with boys for over five years.
I *know* boys . . . know the scrapes they can get into . . . at times.
And I know how much they need priests.

VOICE [*Jokingly*]. And so you're going to desert your poor, old archbishop, are you? [*Laughing deeply*] Father Washington . . . I want you to understand that you have my wholehearted approval. I'm proud of you. And I know that wherever you go . . . you'll be a credit to your country and your God!

[*Music: Fast curtain . . . and out*]

NARRATOR. And so . . . Father Washington, curate at St. Stephen's, Arlington, New Jersey . . . became First Lieutenant Washington . . . chaplain in the United States Army. First it was the Chaplain School [*Fading*] at Fort Benjamin Harrison, Indiana.

VOICE [*Fading in on slight echo*] . . . something that every chaplain must bear in mind. For the primary aim of all military life is to prepare men . . . mentally . . . morally . . . physically . . . so that in time of combat they can bring their flag to victory against every foe. [*Fading*] Therefore . . . the duty of the chaplain lies with the men of his command. You will have to minister to the sick . . . to the wounded . . . to the dying . . . to prisoners . . .

NARRATOR. And from the Chaplain School . . . Chaplain Washington went next to the 76th Division Artillery . . . Fort Meade, Maryland. Then came orders!

VOICE. Chaplain Washington . . . you are assigned to overseas duty with a special group. You will proceed immediately to the Port of Embarkation.

[*Music: Topping . . . Hold . . . Cut on cue*]

[*Sneak telephone bell into tail end of music . . . Ring it again in the clear . . . Then lift receiver*]

MRS. W. Hello.

JOHN [*Over phone*]. Hello, mother.

MRS. W. [*Excited*]. John . . . is it . . . is it . . . *you?*

JOHN [*Laughing*]. Don't get excited, mother.

MRS. W. Where *are* you?

JOHN. Take a guess.

MRS. W. What's that?

JOHN. I said . . . take . . . a . . . guess.

MRS. W. Oh . . . um . . . [*Eagerly*] Are you coming home?

JOHN. No . . . I don't think I'll be home . . . for a while . . . yet.

MRS. W. [*Deflated*] Oh . . . I see . . . well . . . I guess . . .

JOHN. Mother.

MRS. W. Yes.

JOHN. Now listen real well . . . Can you hear me?

MRS. W. Yes, dear.

JOHN. Mother . . . this . . . this may be the last time you'll hear from me for . . . well . . . a little while.

MRS. W. [*Apprehensively*]. John . . . you're not going . . .

JOHN. I can't say anything, mother. You understand?

MRS. W. [*After slight pause*]. Yes . . . I understand, son.

JOHN. I just thought I'd call you . . . to let you know I'll be . . . thinking about you. [*Pause*] Can you hear me?

MRS. W. Yes, John.

JOHN. Mother . . . [*Slight pause*] . . . I never told you this before . . . in words.

   [*Music: Very distant . . . Hold behind*]
   There are so many things I've never said to you . . . face to face . . . But *now* I'm going to say it . . . [*Pause*] . . . I want you to know that you're the dearest thing God ever gave me on this earth . . . I want you to be happy . . . Do you hear?

MRS. W. [*Close to tears*]. Yes . . . John.

JOHN. Give my love to the kids . . . and . . . and . . . do you know what?

MRS. W. What?

JOHN [*Trying to joke*]. Why . . . before you know it . . . I'll be back again . . . and we'll . . . we'll have our ice-cream sodas . . . together again . . . Okay? [*Pause*] Okay, mom?

VOICE [*Typical girl operator voice*]. Your three minutes are up, sir!

JOHN. The three minutes are up, mom.

MRS. W. [*Slight pause . . . then breaking down easily on the words*] Yes . . . the three minutes are up . . . son.

   [*Music: Sweep in . . . Large and sad . . . Then segue slowly to broad ocean background . . . Hold up well behind*]

NARRATOR. Convoy moving in the night. Convoy carrying men and material for the United Nations. Convoy moving up into the cold . . . black stretches of the North Atlantic . . . moving up into the great sea lanes where icebergs that thunder loose out of the Greenland fiords . . . come drifting south . . . like wallowing . . . white mountains. Convoy stepping cautiously in the night over waters that are treacherous with enemy submarines.

[*Music out*]

Below the deck of a troop transport . . . four chaplains are sitting in Officers' Quarters. Then suddenly . . . there's a knock on the door.

[*Door creaking open*]

JIM [*Typical New Yorkese . . . off mike*]. Is dis de chaplains' quarters?

JOHN. Step right in, Jimmy.

JIM [*Fading in fast*]. Mmmm . . . nice and warm down here.

JOHN. Gentlemen . . . I want you to meet Jimmy . . . our new orderly . . . Jimmy . . . this is Chaplain Poling.

JIM. Pleased to meet ya.

POLING. How do you do, Jimmy.

JOHN. And this is Chaplain Goode . . . and over here . . . Chaplain Fox.

FOX. How are you?

JIM. Pleased to meet yez.

GOODE. Glad to know you, Jimmy.

JIM. Bein' as that I got de altar all fixed up . . . what I wanta know now is . . . who follows who in de choich soivices?

JOHN. I'm saying Mass at seven o'clock, Jimmy.

JIM. I know dat, fadder . . . but what I wanta know is . . . does de Jewish soivice *follow* you . . . or does the Protes'ant?

JOHN [*Slightly puzzled about it*]. Well . . . perhaps Chaplain Poling might explain.

POLING. If you don't mind, Jimmy, you can arrange the altar for Protestant service after Father Washington says Mass. I believe that was the arrangement. Is that agreeable to you, rabbi?

GOODE. Perfectly all right with me. I'm holding services at six . . . if it doesn't make any difference to Chaplain Fox.

FOX. Not at all.

JIM. I gotcha. In udder woids . . . foist it's de Jewish soivice . . . with *no* cross, and de altar toined around . . . Right?

GOODE. Right.

JIM. Den . . . it's de Cat'lic soivice . . . *with* de cross . . . and de altar toined around de udder way . . . Right?

JOHN. Right.

JIM. Next . . . it's de Protes'ant soivice . . . with . . . with . . . de altar toined around again . . . Right? And den . . . den— [*Flustered*] Whew! Ya know, chaplains . . . [*Gay*] . . . dis would be a heck of a lot easier . . . if yez all could only get *togedder* sometime!!

CAST [*Laughter*]

> [*Music: Wash out laughter to mood . . . Then quick segue to heavy sea background . . . Hold well up behind*]

NARRATOR. The convoy was still moving north in the night. Out on the screening lines . . . the escort destroyers were getting nervous. Right now . . . they knew they were riding deep into Germany's North Atlantic submarine zone.

> [*Music: Punctuate and cut for two strokes of cabin bell*]

SKIPPER [*Sea-doggish*]. It's black as pitch out there tonight, Jackson.

JACKSON. Yes, sir.

> [*Bring in wind fitfully . . . Hold behind . . . Bring in rhythmic wash of seas . . . Off mike . . . Hold behind*]

SKIPPER [*Immediately*]. Any reports yet?

JACKSON. No, sir . . . except we're running into high seas, sir.

SKIPPER. What did you expect? Zephyrs in the North Atlantic? Let's see the chart.

> [*Rustling of paper*]

JACKSON. Here it is, sir.

SKIPPER [*As if studying chart*]. Mmmmm. 5 to 7 . . . Beaufort Scale.

JACKSON. 5 to 7? . . . Let me see . . . That would be . . . roughly . . .

SKIPPER. Roughly, a 32-knot gale, Jackson.

JACKSON. Yes, sir.

SKIPPER. And we'll be running against it all the way in.

JACKSON. No doubt, sir.

SKIPPER [*Thinking*]. Mmmm . . . Jackson . . . what would you do . . . if a submarine suddenly pulled up along your port side?

JACKSON. Why . . . I'd . . . I'd *run* for it, sir.

SKIPPER. You'd run for it, eh? With a 32-knot gale hitting you in the teeth . . . you'd run for it, eh?

JACKSON. Yes, sir.

SKIPPER. And *where* would you run to, Jackson?

JACKSON. With a submarine patrolling us in a 32-knot gale, sir . . . I'd run for kingdom come!

[*Music: Topping . . . Then resume broad ocean background . . . Behind . . . up on wind and waves . . . Then hold behind*]

NARRATOR. And these were the sounds that night. The large sounds of wind and wave . . . And the small . . . friendly sounds of lifeboats swinging on the davits . . .

[*Wind and waves brought appreciably under . . . Behind*]
The sudden . . . bright sound of laughter from the galley . . . and the muffled . . . gray sound of boots . . . keeping vigil on the bridge . . . the jesting of boys at games . . . and the whispering of a boy at confession . . .

[*Fade music and sound to "dead" air*]
And there was silence . . . too. Silence for thinking. A priest had plenty of time to think . . . lying there on his bunk . . . aboard a troop transport.

[*Music: Very distant . . . Whimsical reverie . . . Hold softly behind*]

JOHN [*Softly on mike*]. Seems as though . . . a lot of people are depending on you . . . John. They're out there in the staterooms . . . talking. And you're in here . . . thinking. And you're thinking . . . how small you are . . . after all. It's only when you close your eyes . . . like this . . . in the dark . . . which makes it . . . double dark . . . it's only when you close your eyes like this . . . and run your finger tips over this small chaplain's cross on your lapel . . . it's only then that you begin to know why people . . . kids . . . look at you . . . and bank on you . . . It's the cross. [*Pause*] Strange . . . when you close your eyes like this . . . and run your fingers over a cross . . . strange how it seems to grow and grow . . . under your finger tips . . . in the dark . . . Just concentrating on this cross . . . with your eyes closed like this . . . seems to make it grow bigger and bigger . . . It's getting bigger than this room . . . It's getting bigger. [*Sighing*]

[*Music: Subtle shift to "Juravit"—Cardinal O'Connel—Hold softly behind*]

Seems only yesterday . . . that you were standing there . . . And because you were standing *there* . . . then . . . that's why you're lying *here* . . . *now* . . . on a bunk. You were standing there in a half circle . . . with the fellows . . . You were clothed in white linen and cincture . . . that morning . . . with a chasuble over your arm . . . and a candle in your hand . . . You were waiting nervously . . . joyously . . .for the ordination . . . for the pressure of the archbishop's hands. . . . And standing there . . . you tried to realize what it all meant . . . You remembered the professor telling you . . .

PROFESSOR [*On slight echo*] . . . and so you are going to be ordained? [*Pause*] Ordained for what? To wear a Roman collar? . . . No. To wear a cassock . . . gold vestments? . . . No. To walk out of a seminary with a trunkful of notes on Moral and Dogmatic Theology? . . . No. You will have to look past the walls of a church to find the answer . . . past the walls of cities. You will have to look down a long avenue of twenty centuries to find the answer. And the answer? You'll find it on the lips of . . . [*Whispering*] . . . the Galilean! "This is my Body" . . . He said . . . *His* Words . . . and . . . *your* words . . . [*Point up*] The answer is . . . you are ordained to be . . . [*Whispering*] another Christ!

[*Music: Punctuate easily . . . Then down behind*]

JOHN. That was it . . . another Christ! Another Christ . . . with a small cross on your shoulder . . . that grows . . . somehow . . . in a dark room . . . grows to be bigger than . . .

[*Music up slightly, then down behind*]

[*Whispering*]. Lord . . . Jesus . . . You who walked rough waters . . . watch over us.

[*Music: Echo prayer . . . Then hold softly behind*]

NARRATOR. These were his priest-thoughts.

[*Music: Lift slightly . . . Then cut*]

And he had *other* thoughts, too . . . warm . . . lively . . . memories . . .

[*Two bars of "Honeysuckle Rose" whistled distractedly . . . Off mike*]

. . . just the smallest bit of "Honeysuckle Rose" from one soldier whistling in a crowd . . . and . . .

[*Lively chorus of honeysuckle rose in piano . . . Hold behind*]

. . . he was back again in the little house on South Twelfth Street playing the piano. He liked a piano. Liked Fats Waller . . . In fact, he had Fats Waller's album at home right now . . . Left it in the dining room before he went away. . . . Of course . . . you *did* have to admit . . . Fats wasn't exactly a nightingale when it came to singing . . . *but he knew how to use his fingers.*

[*Fade out "Honeysuckle Rose" behind*]

And Frankie Carle . . . Now, you take Frankie Carle's "Sunrise Serenade" . . .

[*Sneak in "Sunrise Serenade" on piano . . . Hold behind*]

Never quite could get that run the way Frankie played it.

[*Up on "Sunrise Serenade" . . . Behind*]

The tune was there in your head, all right . . . but . . . somehow . . .

[*Music: Catch "Sunrise Serenade" with gradual upsweep . . . Swallow it . . . Then lean ponderously on former ocean background . . . Down . . . Behind*]

Memories . . . lying in your bunk aboard a troop transport. That's right . . . "*transport.*" . . . Almost forgot for a moment where you were . . .

[*In with wailing sea winds . . . Hold behind*]

But that night . . . you couldn't forget where you were . . .

[*Sneak out music behind sound*]

[*Hold up winds . . . Mix with rhythmic washing of heavy seas . . . Then down behind*]

SKIPPER [*Impatient*]. All right, Jackson . . . what's the bearing?

JACKSON. We're out of formation, sir.

SKIPPER. Sure we're out of formation. [*Barking*] What do they think we can do? . . . Walk a straight line with high seas running like this? [*Slight pause*] Where *are* we?

JACKSON. Here's the chart, sir.

SKIPPER [*As if studying the chart*]. Mmmmmm . . . that leaves us mighty close to Greenland.

JACKSON. Too close for comfort, sir.

SKIPPER. What are we making *now?*

JACKSON. Roughly . . . three knots, sir.

SKIPPER [*Exasperated*]. Three knots! Running out of formation at three knots! You know what *that* means, Jackson?

JACKSON. I presume it means, sir . . .

SKIPPER. It means . . . [*Point up*] . . . we're going to be easy pickin's for any submarine that decides to operate off the mainland tonight.

[*Music: Topping . . . Then slowly down behind*]

[*Wind and waves . . . Up and down behind*]

NARRATOR. They waited that night. . . . They stared into the dark . . . They listened for sounds . . .

[*Music: Shivering off with premonition . . . Hold behind*]

And then . . . *suddenly—*
[*Cut music and sound*]
. . . *this* . . . *this* sound . . .

VOICE [*Bang in over phone—excitedly*]. Calling all hands . . . calling all hands . . . "Escanaba" to all ships in convoy . . . We got a contact . . . It's good . . . It's good . . . Acknowledge.

ANOTHER VOICE. Calling "Escanaba" . . . "Escanaba" . . . We got you . . . 5-9-9 . . . Come back . . .

VOICE [*Over phone*]. "Escanaba" to all ships . . . Enemy submarines contacted . . . Enemy submarines bearing down on convoy . . . direction 0-3-5 . . . bearing 0-3-5. . . . Wind velocity seven . . . Increase speed to maximum . . . Over.

[*Music: Topping whirlwind fashion . . . Quick fade-out behind*]

[*Frantic ringing of electric alarm bell* . . . *Bang in behind music* . . . *Hold in the clear for three seconds* . . . *Then fast fade-out behind*]

[*Over loudspeaker*]. All hands alert . . . Submarine contacted . . . Gun crews . . . gun crews in position . . . All hands prepare for emergency . . .

[*Up fast with excited mob* . . . *Running feet* . . . *Mix up with high winds and washing of sea*]

NARRATOR [*In fast with sound—rapid recitation*]. The men came piling out of the cabins . . . wardrooms . . . They lined the rails, asked questions . . . looked out into the night . . . and waited . . . waited with the awful tension of men who dread the blow that strikes from the dark. . . .

TOMMY [*From out of the crowd—off mike*]. Father! . . . Father Washington!

JOHN [*Calling to him*]. Come over here, Tommy . . . Hang on this rail . . .

TOMMY [*Coming on mike*]. I've been looking all over for you.

JOHN. What is it, Tommy?

TOMMY [*Scared*]. Do you . . . do you think . . . there's really . . . *submarines* out there?

JOHN. Could be, Tommy.

VOICE 1 [*Shouting off mike*]. Ready ammunition on deck, sir!

VOICE 2 [*Shouting off mike*]. Gun crews . . . stand by!

JOHN. They're certainly preparing for *something,* anyway.

TOMMY [*Frightened*]. Yeah.

JOHN [*Startled*]. Tommy . . . where's your life jacket?

TOMMY. My life jacket? I guess . . . I must've left it somewhere. [*Suddenly terrified*] Father . . . I . . . I gotta see you about something.

JOHN. What's the matter?

TOMMY. I got to go to confession . . . [*Getting frantic*] I got to go to confession . . . Somethin' tells me . . .

JOHN. Easy, Tommy.

TOMMY. If anything happens . . .

JOHN [*Quieting him*]. All right, son . . . Go ahead.

TOMMY [*Panting on mike*]. Bless me . . . father . . . [*fading*] . . . for I have sinned . . .

[*Swallow with wind and waves . . . Hold . . . Then down behind*]

[*Fading in*] . . . to confess my sins . . . to do penance . . . and to amend my life. . . . Amen.

JOHN. There you are . . . Everything better now?

TOMMY [*Relieved*]. Everything's better, father . . . everything.

JOHN [*Stern*]. All right. . . . Now get your life jacket—and *fast*.

[*Music: In with depth and suspense. . . . Hold behind*]

NARRATOR. These were the sounds that night. Wind and wave . . . Murmuring of anxious men . . . Whispering of penitent men . . . Breathing of a priest in absolution. These were the sounds that night as men played a dreadful game of hide-and-seek on the high seas. [*With premonition*] But the sound they were still waiting for . . . the sound they dreaded to hear . . .

[*Music: A lightning pyramid . . . And cut*]

VOICE [*Shouting with terror off mike*]. Look out! There it is! Torpedo!!!!

[*Music: Eddying up to the explosion . . . Then lightning cut for explosion . . . One piercing discord . . . Hold up behind*]

NARRATOR [*Talking over ·discord*]. Just as quickly as that . . . the torpedo struck!

[*In fast with mob background . . . Hooting of ship's whistle . . . Running feet . . . Drop on cue behind narrator*]

CAST [*In fast with sound . . . Montage of following voices . . . All voices shouting off mike*].

(1) Hey, Freddie . . . *Freddie*, where are you?

(2) This way fellows . . .

(3) Where are you, Jackie? Hey, Newton . . . where are you?

(4) Sure it's a torpedo . . . Come on . . .

(5) By the stairway . . . you left it over there . . . Go back . . . go back and get it.

(6) Sure it's a torpedo. Didn't you hear it? Come on . . . We got to make those life boats . . .

NARRATOR. The transport shuddered for an instant . . . The deck was alive with running, shouting men. They didn't know it then . . .

but their ship was gaping with a wound from which she would never heal.

VOICE [*On loud speaker*]. Abandon ship . . . Abandon ship!

NARRATOR [*In fast behind voice*]. They *had* to abandon ship . . . They leaped into lifeboats . . . jumped over the side . . . and some . . . *some* stood terrified at the rail. [*Point up*] *Then it happened!*

[*Up strong with wind and waves . . . Then down behind*]

JOHN [*Calling off mike*]. Is that you . . . Chaplain Fox?

FOX. Yes, father.

JOHN [*Fading in panting*]. I guess . . . there's nothing more we can do now . . . ship's settling fast.

FOX. Where are the other two chaplains?

JOHN. Wait . . . I think . . . Here they come now. [*Calling*] You all right, Chaplain Poling?

POLING [*Fading in panting*]. All right . . . all right. It's . . . just . . . that we had trouble . . . getting that last batch over the side.

JOHN. How are you, rabbi?

GOODE. [*Big breath, weary*]. So far . . . so good.

JOHN. Wait a minute . . . over there . . . look! . . . Those kids along the rail!

FOX. They're going mad.

POLING. No life jackets . . . *they haven't any life jackets!*

JOHN [*Pause*]. Well . . . [*Breath on the decision*] Gentlemen . . . there's . . . there's only one thing left for us to do.

POLING [*Pause*]. Yes . . . you're right . . . only one thing left to do.

FOX. Come on!

GOODE. So, let's do it!

[*Up high with wind and waves . . . Slightly down behind*]

BOY [*Sobbing hysterically off mike*].

JOHN [*Quivering under the strain*]. All right, son . . . Stand up. [*Straining as if lifting the boy*] That's it . . . against the rail.

BOY [*Hysterically*]. I can't die . . . I can't die . . . father . . . I can't . . .

JOHN [*Almost fiercely*]. Stop that! [*Panting*] Hold up your arms. . . . Here . . . you'd better take this life jacket.

BOY [*Dazed*]. Life . . . jacket . . . [*Panting heavily*] But what . . . what are *you* going to do?

JOHN. Tie it on . . . that's it . . . tie it on tight. [*Pause*] Now you're all set.

BOY [*Whimpering*]. Thanks . . . thanks . . .

JOHN. Now . . . jump.

BOY [*Frightened again*]. Jump?

JOHN [*Almost shouting*]. Jump quick . . . if you want to get clear of this boat . . . she's . . . she's . . . going down fast.

BOY [*Whimpering*]. But I'll be alone.

JOHN. Get up there on the rail . . . [*As if hoisting him*] That's it.

BOY [*Slightly off mike*]. But I'll be alone, father.

JOHN. You won't be alone . . . Go ahead . . . jump . . . that's it . . . JUMP! [*Audible breath on mike . . . pause . . . then very quietly*] You won't be alone, now . . . kid . . . whoever you are. [*Half choked*] Nobody . . . nobody can *ever* be alone!

> [*Top with three seconds of wailing wind . . . Then fade out behind*]

> [*Music: Sneak in on top of wind . . . Playing with wind motif . . . Then resolve to mood behind*]

NARRATOR. In the early hours of a February morning . . . nineteen hundred and forty-three . . . four chaplains removed their life jackets . . . and placed them about the shivering bodies of four boys . . . and then . . . as the last lifeboats moved away in the night . . . a rabbi . . . two ministers . . . and a priest stood together on a listing deck. . . .

> [*Music: Fade out behind*]
> [*Catch music with wind, and boiling seas . . . Hold up . . . Then slightly down behind*]

JOHN [*Tense*]. I guess . . . we're all here . . . gentlemen.

GOODE. All present . . . and accounted for . . . Washington . . . Wait!

FOX [*Quietly*]. Just the lights, rabbi . . . The lights are gone out.

JOHN. I guess . . . we don't need that kind of light . . . now . . . chaplain.

POLING [*Tired*]. No . . . I guess we don't.

> [*Swirl in waters . . . hold behind*]

GOODE [*Trying hard to control his voice*]. Water's . . . water's coming over the deck . . . now.

FOX. She's starting to go . . . Washington.

JOHN [*Pause for the final admission*]. Yes . . . she's starting to
go . . . Well . . . gentlemen . . .
[*Music very far back . . . Tenderly . . . Behind*]
It was nice knowing you. And now . . . I suppose it's about
time . . . we got down on our knees . . . It's . . .
[*Water swirling into mike*]
. . . it's . . . just about . . . time . . .

[*Music: Hold the ship poised with a trembling chord . . .
Behind*]

NARRATOR. The ship poised for an instant . . .

[*Music: Swallow the ship with a whirlpool . . . All the way
down to "dead" air*]

The ship sank . . . [*Pause*] The ship sank . . .

[*Music: Sneak in softly behind*]

. . . but in that moment . . . [*Triumphant*] In that moment
. . . a miracle of self-sacrificing love converted her slippery deck
. . . once and forever . . . into a great altar . . . from which
four men offered their gallant souls to God!

[*Music: Pyramid to majestic resolution . . . Then cut*]

ANNOUNCER [*Quietly*]. On an occasion like this . . . no more fitting
tribute could be paid to man, for work well done . . . than the
tribute of his own Chief of Service. We take you, therefore, to
Washington, D. C., and to Chaplain W. R. Arnold . . . brigadier
general . . . chief of chaplains . . . of the United States Army.
Chaplain Arnold.

ARNOLD. Ladies and gentlemen! The loss of any chaplain is not only
an official loss . . . not only a statistical loss. It is above all . . .
a personal loss. Tonight . . . a Gold Star is hanging in a window
in New Jersey. And there are other Gold Stars hanging in
windows tonight. To these parents . . . relatives . . . friends . . .
I can only offer my heartfelt sympathy. Yet . . . I would have
them remember this. The memory of Chaplains John P. Washington, George L. Fox, Alexander D. Goode, and Clark V.
Poling shall be revered by a grateful nation . . . and cherished

wherever self-sacrifice commands the respect of men. As Catholics
. . . we pray this night . . . that a Merciful God shall give them
their just reward. To all our chaplains actively engaged in the
terrific struggle of war . . . to our wounded and sick chaplains
. . . and to those who are now prisoners . . . we offer the humble
tribute of our admiration . . . and thanks. Finally . . . to Father
John Washington, my brother priest . . . we pledge . . . not only
our prayers . . . but a dedication of our personal life . . . to those
Christlike principles of which his life and death were a reality.

[*Music softly behind*]

His North Atlantic Testament . . . was the testament of love . . .
and . . . "*Greater love than this hath no man . . . that a man
lay down his life for his friends.*"

[*Music: Up to resolution*]

TYPHUS

Bernard Victor Dryer

BERNARD VICTOR DRYER's script on Typhus was written for *The Human Adventure,* a series broadcast by MBS and created by the University of Chicago, which also has to its credit the *University of Chicago Round Table.*

In 1945 *The Human Adventure* won a Peabody Award as the outstanding educational series in American radio. Under its versatile producer Sherman H. Dryer—not related to Bernard Dryer—the series has been consistently informative and showmanly, treating a vast range of subjects that has included *The Einstein Theory, American Humor, The Story of Human Birth, The Causes of Nazism, The Origin of the Earth.* The series has made brilliant use of the dramatic possibilities of music.

The Human Adventure had a successful run on CBS in 1939-40, then reappeared on Mutual in 1943. At that time WGN Chicago paid the bulk of production costs, while the University contributed funds for scripts and cast. Later the Revere Copper and Brass Company became the series' sponsor. Each script is reviewed by members of the University faculty, and often goes through painstaking revision, either by the original writer or by the *Human Adventure's* staff writer Wentzle Ruml, or by others.

When the series won the 1945 Peabody Award, radio's closest equivalent to a Pulitzer Prize, trade journals edited in New York were puzzled, since they were not even aware the series was on the air.

Here is why: During the war the sale of radio time to sponsors underwent such an abnormal boom that public service features on all networks were pushed into obscure periods and sometimes off the air. The cause of the boom was chiefly that the government permitted advertising expenses to be deducted, for tax purposes, as essential expenditures. Companies paying high excess profit taxes often preferred to pour into advertising money which they would have had to pay in taxes anyway. Thus the government tax policy really subsidized advertising during wartime. The shortage of paper channeled most of this revenue into radio.

Here is the story of how the boom affected *The Human Adventure* on just one station—WOR, New York. This case history is told merely as one example of what happened to quite a few sustaining programs on quite a few stations during radio's war boom.

The series was produced at WGN, Chicago, and in the usual way sent to all Mutual stations via the network lines. Each station could broadcast the program if it wished to. When the series was launched, in a weekday evening period, a large network, including WOR, New York, carried it. This station then sold the time locally to a sponsor. For a time it recorded

The Human Adventure "off the line" each week and broadcast the recording at a later time: Sunday, 4:30 P.M. Then this time was sold and the
program moved to Sunday, 4:00 P.M. Presently this time was sold and the
program moved to Sunday, 9:00 A.M. Listeners who had managed to
follow the program thus far then found it dropped altogether—although
the series was still being sent out from Chicago each week. After the
series won the Peabody Award, the New York station reinstated the series—
on Saturdays, 2:00 P.M.

It is ironic that the "outstanding educational series" was later rescued
from obscurity by the very war boom which had been hounding it. Revere
Copper and Brass Company decided to sponsor the series in an evening
period, over a coast-to-coast Mutual network.

Bernard Victor Dryer is the sort of writer radio increasingly needs;
one who is not only a skilful craftsman but also has knowledge of a
special subject. Dryer started out to be a doctor, but after several years
of pre-medical training at Wesleyan University he won a prize in a national
playwriting contest conducted by six motion picture companies, and decided to turn to writing. While studying at Yale's 47 Workshop he got
his first radio experience at WICC Bridgeport. He was then engaged for
The Human Adventure; his schooling in bio-chemistry made him particularly valuable writing on scientific subjects. He then went to Washington to write for the NBC-Library of Congress series, *Hidden History.*

After Pearl Harbor he took on the job of assistant editorial chief for
the U. S. Public Health Service, writing both radio and motion pictures.
After working as liaison man to an OWI crew making a film on malaria
in the South, Surgeon-General Ross McIntire requested that he be loaned
to the Navy. Those were the days of Guadalcanal and South Pacific
malaria, and Dryer wrote *Clinical Malaria,* the Navy's first motion picture
for professional medical audiences. Going into uniform, he was assigned to
the Bureau of Medicine and Surgery's motion picture branch, eventually
becoming Officer-in-Charge of its editorial section. Several times during
the war he was despatched by plane to distant spots on the globe where
some special medical problem existed; as writer-director of a camera crew
he went to Africa to make a film of a bubonic plague epidemic. He was
with the First and Third Armies through their campaign in Central
Germany, preparing for some films on plastic surgery.

The conquest of typhus in Naples had been the subject of a Navy
film whose production Bernard Dryer directed. Because *The Human Adventure* was being broadcast to Army and Navy personnel throughout the
world by the Armed Forces Radio Service, the Navy gave him permission
to write a script on the same subject for *The Human Adventure.*

TYPHUS*

[*Music under*]

NARRATOR. Naples is brother to the centuries—and Naples is the city of typhus. Naples was old when Julius Caesar was a child and when General Mark Clark's Fifth Army liberated Naples in 1943, the ancient cobblestones of the streets echoed with a ghostly marching—the tramping of long-forgotten medieval armies. . . . And because Naples is the city of typhus, some of these armies had won the battle and lost the war. In 1528, four hundred years before Mark Clark, a different general faced a different battle of Naples—a struggle which was to decide the fate of Europe.

[*Music swells*]

LAUTREC [*As narrator*]. I am the general who won a battle, yet lost a war. I am Vicomte Odet de Foix Lautrec, maréchal of the armies of his Majesty, Francis the First of France. In the year of our gracious Lord 1528, my valiant men had cut Naples off from the rest of Italy. Like a heart without arteries, the city lay dying. My allies and I—Pope Clement VII and Count Sforza, of the Republic of Venice—we prepared for the final coup de grâce.

[*Music: Chord and out*]

SFORZA. And victory is certain, your Holiness. The Spanish troops in Naples live on bread and water.

CLEMENT. But, Count Sforza, if Lautrec here takes Naples, will we not be simply taking the city out of Spanish domination and putting it under French domination?

LAUTREC. Do you not prefer the French velvet glove to the Spanish iron hand, your Holiness?

CLEMENT. We prefer peace and independence, M'sieu le Maréchal.

---

* TYPHUS by Bernard Victor Dryer. Copyright, 1945, by the University of Chicago.

LAUTREC. But the issue involves the future of all Europe, your Holiness.

SFORZA. Naples is the pivot!

LAUTREC [*For all it's worth*]. No bell sounds within the city. No church is open, your Holiness, and no mass is read. The corpses in the street are gnawed by dogs. The city lies at our feet like a broken woman. Within a few days my troops will be provisioned and ready. Within a month Naples will be ours.

[*Music: Bridge*]

[*Horses stomp and neigh*]

LAUTREC [*Low as on-the-spot narrator*]. My army was ready. I walked through the camp on a final inspection.

VOICE [*Off . . . salutes*]. Mon maréchal . . .

LAUTREC. It was as any other time . . .

VOICE [*Tired*]. Mon maréchal . . .

LAUTREC. The men a little tired, perhaps . . .

VOICE [*More tired*]. Mon maréchal . . .

LAUTREC. It had been a hard campaign . . . [*Stronger*] Yet victory was certain.

VOICE [*Sick*]. Mon . . . maréchal . . .

LAUTREC. But why should they be tired? Why should they be sick? Then—suddenly—I saw some fresh graves being dug—being dug for a group funeral.

PRIEST [*Fades on*]. Te igitur clementissime Pater . . . miseratur vestri omnipotens Deus . . . Pater noster in coelis es . . . sanctificetur nomen tuum . . . [*Continues background*]

LAUTREC [*Low*]. Sergeant . . .

SERGEANT. Mon maréchal.

LAUTREC. There has been no fighting. How did these men die?

SERGEANT. I-I-I-I do not know, mon maréchal.

LAUTREC. I'll have your tongue cut out.

SERGEANT. But, mon maréchal, I—

LAUTREC [*Up*]. Priest!

PRIEST [*Cuts short . . . fading on*]. Please, mon maréchal, a prayer for—

LAUTREC. I do not like this sudden, quiet dying within my camp. Of what did these men die? [*Pause for no answer*] Sergeant! Lift this coffin lid!

SERGEANT. But, mon—

LAUTREC. Lift it!

[*Creaks open*]

PRIEST [*Close on . . . very low*]. Oui, mon maréchal. It is the fever.

LAUTREC [*Quiet with fear*]. Spots on the chest. The others?

PRIEST. The same. Bloodshot eyes. Spots on the chest. We must bury them quickly.

LAUTREC [*Tough*]. There will be no burial!

MEN [*Protest*].

LAUTREC. Fill in the graves, you dogs! Those bodies will be burned!

[*Music: Up and down*]

[*Strumming of lute. Lute stops*]

WOMAN [*Tired*]. Do you wish that I play the lute more, sire? My head—

LAUTREC [*Taut*]. Play till I bid you stop!

WOMAN [*Murmurs*]. Oui, sire.

[*Lute in background*]

LAUTREC. Page! Page! Where is the physician?

PAGE. He is here now, sire. . . . Please come in, doctor.

DOCTOR [*Fades on breathless*]. I came as quickly as I—

LAUTREC. I've a mind to bleed you myself, you leechmonger. Give me news.

DOCTOR. The fever spreads, mon maréchal. Every tent has its sick or dying. Even the camp followers are deserting their men.

LAUTREC. That means the fever is bad—getting worse . . . [*Up*] It must be stopped!

DOCTOR [*Wagging his finger*]. The planets are in evil conjunction, mon maréchal. Saturn upon Mars, and there is blood upon the moon.

LAUTREC. Well? Will you cure the disease or move the planets?

DOCTOR. Please, mon maréchal. This is a serious—

LAUTREC [*Snaps*]. I know it's serious, you fool!

WOMAN [*Gasps*]. Sire!

[*Music out cold. Crash of falling lute*]

LAUTREC. What's that?

DOCTOR. The lute player—she has collapsed.

[*Few footsteps*]

LAUTREC. Is she—dead?

DOCTOR. No, mon maréchal . . . But within a few days . . .

LAUTREC. The—fever?

DOCTOR. Yes, mon maréchal. Within your own tent.

[*Music: "Dead March" . . . Slow ominous tympani . . . And under*]

LAUTREC. Typhus walked the dirty streets of my camp, and to every second man typhus said: You. From twenty-eight thousand my army died away to fifteen, then ten, then five. With all Europe trembling in my grasp, I had no army. I, personally, had neither strength nor life, for typhus had entered my house and said: You.

[*Music: To tag*]

ANNOUNCER. And now your host on the Human Adventure, Mr. Walter Yust.

YUST. The French marshal Lautrec was nowhere near being the first, or the last, man to whom the dread typhus said the single word "You," and Naples is neither the first nor the last city where typhus has struck. But the events which took place in Marshal Lautrec's army in Naples in 1528 are typical of the attack of epidemic typhus. For centuries, wherever armies fought, typhus marched behind the troops like an invisible executioner. Today, four hundred odd years after Lautrec, the Mutual Broadcasting System and the University of Chicago bring you the story of typhus research and the answer of modern science to the dread threat of this disease. For typhus is both an ancient and a modern international killer, and the modern answer to the riddle of typhus illustrates an important and beneficial trend in medical research—a trend written as today's chapter in those fascinating notebooks of science which recount the Human Adventure.

[*Music up and down*]

NARRATOR. As the long years passed, typhus prowled back and forth across Europe, a winter wolf, a dark traveler driven by a bitter wind. . . . Centuries passed, and no man knew the cause of typhus . . . no one knew how typhus spread from a man to his wife to his children. . . . Typhus became an international murderer, a mystery. . . .

[*Music: Swell and segue*]

MYRA [*As narrator*]. My husband was one of the first men to begin solving the mystery. Dr. Howard Ricketts. He was a research bacteriologist at the University of Chicago in the early 1900's, the golden age of bacteriology. . . .

[*Music out*]

[*Door slams off*]

RICK [*Fading on*]. Myra . . . Myra . . .

MYRA. In here, dear.

RICK [*On*]. Hello, dear, hello . . .

MYRA. Sit down, Howard. Catch your breath.

RICK [*Gasps air*]. Myra, how would you like a vacation?

MYRA [*Disbelief*]. What in the world!

RICK. I'm serious, Myra. Mexico City. [*Fades to background*] It'll be a wonderful trip, dear. A remarkable chance to work on some ideas I've had in the back of my mind for a long time. . . .

MYRA [*On . . . low*]. If we had only known then what was going to happen in Mexico City . . . If we had only known . . .

RICK [*Up*]. Here's the story, dear.

MYRA. Don't say it like that, Howard.

RICK. What do you mean?

MYRA. You sound like the beginning of a lecture when you talk like that.

RICK [*Laughs*]. All right, I won't tell. I'll keep it a secret.

[*Music: Sneak*]

MYRA [*As narrator*]. The secret was typhus. In Montana, Howard had just proved that Rocky Mountain spotted fever was carried by the bite of an insect, the tick. Typhus presented what Howard called a "similar clinical picture" and he wondered whether there might not be more in common between the two diseases, something more than just symptoms. So he closed his laboratory at the

university and went to a hospital where he could find typhus—in
Mexico City.

[*Music: Bridge*]

MEXICAN [*Fades on*]. Buenos días, señor. Buenos días.

RICK. Good morning, sir.

MEXICAN. It is said in the city that the American doctor pays money
for strange things.

RICK. Well, that depends. What do you have to sell?

MEXICAN. My beard, señor. This fine, long bush of a beard.

RICK. Yes, that is a nice beard. A fine specimen.

MEXICAN. It is said—perhaps just idle talk, señor—one does not know—
but it is *said* that you comb beards and pay to do it.

RICK [*Laughs*]. Well, it's true. We're looking for lice.

MEXICAN [*Faking offense*]. Lice? In *my* beard?

RICK [*Straight*]. Yes. Lice. In your beard.

MEXICAN. Oh, fine, fine! And how much do you pay for combing the
head also?

MYRA [*As narrator*]. A research scientist has to be everything—
diplomat, salesman, and mostly a hard worker. And Howard
was all of them. He did so much painstaking microscope work
that his faithful eyes, as he put it, began to complain. . . .

[*Clock off mike strikes two as door opens on mike*]

MYRA. It's getting awfully late, dear.

RICK [*Preoccupied*]. Finish up in a minute.

MYRA. Twenty hours a day, Howard. It's too much.

[*Sound like a small meat grinder . . . Continue under*]

RICK. See this little insect, Myra?

MYRA. Howard, it's late and you're tired and another louse doesn't—

RICK. This is a special louse, dear. It took a bite from a man dying of
typhus. So I slice the bug into thin little strips on the microtome . . .

MYRA. Here, let me crank it for you.

RICK. Now, just hold out one of the slides . . .

[*Microtome out . . . Clink of glass*]

MYRA. Here.

RICK. Now. A slice of the specimen. Turn on the microscope lamp,
please, dear. Now a drop of stain, and . . .

MYRA. Howard, I'm dying to look at him. Just *one* look.

RICK. All right, you can look. A section of a louse magnified several thousand times.

MYRA. But what are all those little black dots clumped together?

RICK. I think they're the microbes of typhus, Myra.

MYRA. No!

RICK. Yes . . . I think so. I think I can prove that the common body louse carries typhus by carrying that particular microbe.

MYRA. Well, if we can prove that, Howard . . .

RICK. Mm?

MYRA. You're sort of wonderful.

RICK. Just *sort of* wonderful? But—I'm awfully tired, dear. Awfully tired.

[*Music: Sneak*]

MYRA [*As narrator*]. That was long ago—April, 1910. Howard had made his discovery but two weeks later he came down with typhus. He fought against the disease just as he fought for knowledge, but a week later we closed his eyes . . .

[*Music up and down*]

NARRATOR. Ricketts went, then von Prowazek; Schussler came down with typhus, Luthje, Jochmann, Conneff, and Cornet. Casualties in the line of duty in the unending battle with the unknown. Yet some, if not all, of these lives could have been saved. For long before their time there was a hint—a small clue, which no one suspected would help lift the black shroud of mystery from the dread of the disease typhus.

[*Music: Bridge*]

ZIEDLER. While I was alive, I was a German, and my name was Othman Ziedler. I am telling this story because it was I who first synthesised the chemical called dichloro-diphenyl-trichloro-ethane. I was a student of Strasbourg in 1874, doing research for a higher degree—useless research, in the best German tradition . . .

[*Music: German beer hall tune in background . . . a kind of Germanic "Pony Boy"*]

KLAUS. Hey, Ziedler! Ziedler! Come over! Sit down and have a stein!

ZIEDLER [*Fades on*]. Oh, thank you, Klaus. Good evening, Heinrich . . . Robert . . . Otto . . .

HEINRICH. Come, Ziedler, sit down. We must have all a drink together.

ZIEDLER. Ah, perhaps. Perhaps. Perhaps just one.

ROBERT. Only one, Ziedler? But you—the beer-hall scholar of Strasbourg!

ZIEDLER. I know. But tonight—tonight I must work.

OTTO. Work, Ziedler?

ZIEDLER. Indeed. In fact, my dear Otto, I must say that I came here only to tell you all one thing—that I have finally succeeded in synthesising a chemical.

ALL [*Ad lib congratulations*]

KLAUS. That is excellent, Ziedler. This means you will get your degree.

HEINRICH. So it will, Klaus. But tell me, Ziedler, what is the chemical?

ZIEDLER. From its chemical formula, its name is dichloro-diphenyl-trichloroethane.

ROBERT. Agh! That's a tough name for even a chemist fellow, eh, boys?

OTTO. Well, then Ziedler, you have done it. Tonight—too bad you can have only one—your beer will be bought by us.

[*Music: Beer hall up and down to fade out behind*]

ZIEDLER [*As narrator*]. Yes, indeed, I had done it. And as soon as I had written up the complicated report of my technical experiments which led to their useless result, I presented them to my dean, and my dean said simply:

DEAN. Very well, Ziedler. You have synthesised your chemical, you have presented your thesis, you will receive your degree.

ZIEDLER. To the dean, dichloro-diphenyl-trichloroethane meant one more thesis, one more useless chemical and one more degree, all to be classified, passed upon, and filed, in the proper German order. To me, dichloro-diphenyl-trichloroethane meant only one thing—a degree. . . . In proper German order, my thesis was filed, and to the best of my knowledge, remained buried in dust for some sixty-five years . . . along with the name of its discoverer, one Othman Ziedler, a doctor of science from Strasbourg. . . .

I do not know, personally, how the formula was ever found in all the dust of those files. But the next report I heard on my chemical came from Switzerland, and it came in a manner which astounded me.

[*Fade in small airplane under Ziedler above . . . Gun motors as it passes mike and fade to background as it flies off*]

MULLER. Well Pierre, what do you think of the chemical now?

PIERRE. Ah, it certainly makes a fine white spray as the airplane drops it—almost like snow, we hope, for the potato crop.

PIERRE. You mean this is not just decoration for the fields?

MULLER. [*Laughs*]. No, Pierre, artistic as that would be, I'm afraid it isn't so. . . . This is a test to learn whether the powder will kill insects.

ZIEDLER [*As narrator*]. Yes, my white powder killed insects, the industrial chemist learned. And he found for it too, a trade name . . . he shortened dichloro-diphenyl-trichloroethane to Gesarol . . . And when next I heard of it, it was in 1942, and the newly mobilized American army had a problem being studied by an impressive number of organizations—the Gorgas Memorial Laboratory in Panama, the Rockefeller Foundation, the Food and Drug Administration, the Department of Agriculture, and the National Research Council . . . [*Fades*] All of them studying this single powder.

COLONEL. What we need most—what you chemists can give us—is a new insecticide . . . something that can be made synthetically—something neither man nor weather can keep us from getting—and we want it fast.

CHEMIST. Tough assignment, colonel, it will take time.

COLONEL. Put your whole staff on it then.

SECOND CHEMIST. But, colonel, even with all the chemists in the country—[*Fade*]

ZIEDLER [*As narrator*]. They were American scientists—but the job was done by a German chemical, developed by a company in Switzerland. My little chemical, the useless chemical I first synthesised for the benefit of one thesis, one degree, one diploma, was accepted, I am proud to say, by the Army and Navy of the United States.

COLONEL. All right, gentlemen. The army has tested your insecticide.

The Medical Corps says it's okay. If you can start production—
CHEMIST. It can be started immediately, sir.

COLONEL. Excellent. Now, for the writing of the requisition—what's its name?

CHEMIST. Dichloro-diphenyl-trichloroethane.

COLONEL. We couldn't get that on a whole pad of requisition blanks.

CHEMIST. Well, we do abbreviate it around the lab. Dichloro—that's D . . . diphenyl—another D . . . trichloroethane—a T . . . Dichloro-diphenyl-trichloroethane—DDT.

[*Music: Triple punctuation and under*]

ZIEDLER [*As narrator*]. And thus, as DDT, my little discovery has become famous. It is no longer a dusty thesis in the libraries at Strasbourg, no longer a snowlike cloud drifting from one of your modern airplanes in Switzerland. My name, Othman Ziedler, is one you will probably never hear again—for I am what you Americans would call a scientific also-ran. But I have achieved sufficient immortality. I can remember always and forever—those three letters DDT.

[*Music up and out*]

NARRATOR. This was DDT. It killed the body lice of typhus in the laboratory, to be sure. It killed many insects, not only in the laboratory but also in the field—under conditions where insects were naturally found. But typhus? Would it kill the lice of typhus under natural conditions? No man knew. No man was sure. Then, last year, the ancient, dark, international murderer was back, wandering along the ancient, smashed cobblestone streets of Naples. Typhus—epidemic typhus, the quick and silent killer—had returned.

[*Music up and down*]

GUY. I'm a tech sergeant in the Medical Corps. Even if I told you my name you wouldn't know me from a hole in the ground. Here we're tryin' to make Naples a big port to unload supplies . . .

[*Music: out into*]
[*Trucks grinding by in low gear*]

[*No pause*]. Trucks day and night . . . But that wasn't all—
the Germans seen us comin'—left blockbusters and the time
bombs all over the place. No electricity, no gas, no food, no heat,
no soap. But one thing we did have—lice. More lice than people,
and twice as happy, too . . . Okay, that's the beginning of the
story, and, as I get it, this is the way the *medical* war began.
There was five spearheads, and the first . . .

    [*Trucks out on door shut . . . Follow man walking and stop*]

MAJOR. Is everybody here?

CAST [*A chorus of "yes"*].

MAJOR. Fine. We're organized to be a sort of flying squadron on this
  typhus-control job. The Nazis are shoving refugees through our
  lines at night. We're to make sure these people aren't carrying
  typhus. We'll have to come through the suburbs of Naples and
  find *all* suspected cases of typhus . . . Any questions? Okay. Let's
  roll.

GUY. That flying squad was our first spearhead against typhus. The
  second was vaccination. Maybe you call it inoculation—same difference. We went after the key people that kept Naples going—
  doctors, nurses, police, firemen . . .

VOICE [*Off . . . Italian*]. Vine cua! Uno navoete.

CAPTAIN. Lots of customers today, sergeant. Better boil another batch
  of needles.

GUY. Yes, sir.

    [*Clink of metal tray . . . Water pouring*]

SOLDIER [*A little off*]. Okay, Mac.

ITALIAN [*A little off . . . in Italian*]. Voia me?

SOLDIER. Yeah, you, Mac. Let's go. This won't hardly hurt a-tall.

ITALIAN [*On . . . in English*]. Thank . . . you.

SOLDIER. Next. Let's go now.

ITALIAN 2. Thank . . . you.

GUY. Lot different from the day we vaccinated all them GIs, eh,
  Shorty?

ITALIAN 3. Thank you.

SOLDIER. Yeah. At least these guys say, Thank you. [*Fading*] All
  right. Let's keep the line moving. One man at a time.

GUY [*Topping*]. The next job—spearhead number three—was tough.

We had to locate people sick with typhus and separate them from healthy people—same as in scarlet fever or measles.

[*Knock on door*]

DOCTOR. This is the right address, isn't it, Pete?

PETE. Number fourteen's right, sir.

[*Knock again . . . Harder . . . Door creaks open a little*]

WOMAN [*Afraid . . . in Italian*]. Che vo tete?

DOCTOR. Tell her we've come to help her.

PETE [*In Italian*]. Vanime a darte ainta. Dottore Mericano.

[*Door creaks open*]

WOMAN. Trovate lo malato?

PETE. Sì . . . This is it, major. Over there in the corner.

LUIGI [*Off*]. Oeee—oeee!

WOMAN [*Italian*]. Queste sono dottore Mericani.

DOCTOR [*Terrific American accent*]. Sono un Americano dottore, vostro amico. Sarete al sicuro.

LUIGI. Tantie grazie.

DOCTOR. Let's see your chest—il petto. Pete, tell her he has typhus and has to go to the contagious hospital for isolation.

PETE [*In Italian*]. Mi dispiacio! Tene "typhus." Deve ir a lo spedale.

WOMAN [*In Italian*]. No, no! Sta neglio qua! No!

DOCTOR [*Tops and cuts*]. Tell her it's for her own protection . . . Tell her maybe we can save him.

PETE [*In Italian . . . fades*]. Questa e lunica manera di solvarlo a aintarti.

GUY [*Topping*]. It was a tough job, not just the treatment but taking 'em away from their families too. Everything that guy owned had to be sterilized with steam, and there were hundreds like him. . . . Attack number four, going on at the same time, was aimed at the low-down little louse. When somebody got sick, we dusted everybody that knew him with DDT powder. . . . And attack number five was the same, but bigger. Contact or not, we dusted everybody with DDT. Yeah, everybody—about a million people.

[*Streetcar in under above . . . Up . . . Stop . . . Bell clangs . . . Crowd noises*]

Well, cap'n, shall we tackle this bunch on the streetcar?

CAPTAIN. Don't see why not. Get the men and powder ready.

[*Bell clangs*]

[*In Italian . . . shouts while fading*]. Questa palvera e bona per tutti—si chiana DDT . . . [*Repeat*]

GUY [*As narrator*]. The captain laid the law down to the crowd, and we lined up and started using our guns. Powder guns—same kind you use against flies.

SOLDIER [*Off*]. Okay, sarge, ready down here.

GUY. Okay. How about you, Jim?

JIM [*A little off*]. All set.

GUY. Lift your right arm, please. Okay, Allen. Powder down his sleeve.

[*Shoosh of powder gun*]

CAPTAIN [*Fades on*]. All organized here, sergeant?

GUY. Yes, sir . . . Open your shirt now . . .

[*Whoosh*]

Top of your pants . . .

SOLDIER [*Fades on*]. Captain . . . captain, how we gonna dust all these women on the streetcar?

CAPTAIN. Well—uh—I'll take over here. [*Fades*] You organize the group inside the streetcar.

GUY [*As narrator*]. We started our counterattack against typhus in January, '44, when they were getting sick almost a hundred a day in Naples. In a month, typhus was hitting only half a dozen people a day. By this time—a year ago—we'd stopped a big typhus epidemic in midwinter—the first time in history. . . .

[*Music: Down*]

We're not perfect, but the story as I get it is this. Only two American servicemen have been hit by typhus. One got it because he didn't follow his antityphus orders. The case of the other one was so mild that we had to go through a long string of tests to be sure he really had it. I think that's pretty good—almost perfect. I think you can call that—victory over typhus.

[*Music: Finale*]

ANNOUNCER. And now your host on the Human Adventure, the editor of the Encyclopaedia Britannica, Mr. Walter Yust.

YUST. To the scientist, DDT means more than victory over typhus. DDT has been found to be excellent against most of the insects usually encountered by men, domestic animals, and domestic plants. But its theoretical importance is even greater. For, since the time when Louis Pasteur proved that bacteria can cause disease, science has sought to conquer disease by conquering bacteria. This, often if not always, required the disease to be present. The emphasis was upon cure. Here, with DDT, we have a better process—for the intention in the process is to *keep bacteria from the body* by killing the carriers of bacteria. Here, the emphasis is upon prevention. I know that the method has been tried before —as with malaria—but never with such success. This method means the saving of millions of dollars and millions of lives— dollars and lives which, if they are used wisely, will be used in that drama of knowledge which is the Human Adventure.

[*Music: To tag*]

PACIFIC TASK
FORCE

T Sgt. Lawrence Lader

Among the most interesting wartime developments in radio have been the Armed Forces Radio stations and sound systems operated overseas by the army and navy, broadcasting to our troops. These were set up wherever American servicemen were stationed: not only in battle zones, but also at many lonely outposts, air bases, weather stations. Servicemen with radio backgrounds in Dubuque or Tuscaloosa found themselves sent to operate radio stations in Tehran or Myitkyina. Half a dozen men, headed by one officer, could run a station.

Program material at each station consisted of: (1) domestic network programs, "decommercialized" in the case of sponsored programs, recorded at Armed Forces Radio Service headquarters in Los Angeles and either flown or short-waved to overseas outlets; (2) original AFRS programs, for troops only, produced in the United States and distributed in the same ways; (3) original productions of the local stations.

Because each war theater had its own problems, the local programs often had an important local job to do. The following script is an example of such a program, broadcast over the Mosquito Network. This was a group of four AFRS stations in the South Pacific: on Guadalcanal, at Noumea in New Caledonia, at Espiritu Santo in the New Hebrides, and at Auckland, New Zealand.

The writer, T/Sgt. Lawrence Lader, worked for the Blue Network before induction, but probably his most valuable radio experience was on the Harvard campus, where he was program director for the Crimson Network, one of the "wired-wireless" stations that, before the war, sprung up on more than a score of college campuses. Many servicemen with this kind of experience found it particularly valuable at the overseas stations, where the same resourcefulness and versatility were needed.

"When the station staff arrived at Guadalcanal," Sgt. Lader writes, "the crates with all their equipment were carried in by 'seeps' and dumped on the beach. Engineers, announcers, and program men stood around without the slightest idea of where or when the station was to be built. The officer in charge set off with his men on a reconnaissance of the island, leaving one shaking corporal with a .45 automatic to guard the crates. The danger was not from Japs but from the Americans themselves, who in those freebooting days of Guadalcanal considered any unguarded property on the beach open to all comers."

A convoy making a new landing often brought a new station with it, complete with a couple of weeks of programing. The station was sometimes set up and put into operation within a few days after the landing of the first wave.

In some South Pacific islands, where malaria was a constant danger, one of the station's jobs was to hammer endlessly at the men to take daily doses of atabrine and use insect repellents. The campaign was carried on in every possible vein. "Are you repellent?" an announcer would say in the accents of home. "Use Toujours Gai—it keeps the mosquitoes away." This campaign was so successful that the mosquito, painted on microphones and other equipment, became the symbol of the Guadalcanal station and eventually of the group of stations which took the name "Mosquito Network."

No other means of communication meant as much to the men overseas. Broadcasters who have seen scores of servicemen crowded around one radio set at a distant beachhead will never forget the sight.

Theater commands, realizing the hold of these stations, used them effectively for keeping in touch with their men. Sgt. Lader was assigned to the Information and Education Section at South Pacific Base Command headquarters. One of his jobs was to write and produce a weekly *Report to the Troops*, which was heard on all stations of the Mosquito Network. The following script is from this series. The purpose was simply to make every man feel his combat or service job as part of large and important events. The series was launched in the summer of 1944.

As in many radio series designed to convey information, the program uses drama followed by a short talk. Drama is the curtain raiser, the attention getter, the background sketcher. The speaker then speaks with the voice of authority.

While the style of the sketch resembles that of *The Man Behind the Gun*, the construction is far simpler. The script was written for a small cast. There were only two turntables for playing music and sound effect recordings—a limitation that had to be born in mind in writing the script.

Radio will do well to keep an eye and a door open for the writers who, at a couple of hundred stations throughout the world, have set up typewriter in huts, tents, and ruins and banged out programs for their fellow troops.

PACIFIC TASK

FORCE

ANNOUNCER 2. Pacific Task Force!

ANNOUNCER 1. The dramatized story of the raid on Manila which was flashed to the world just twenty-four hours ago, and an analysis of task force strategy in the Pacific by an officer of General Gilbreath's staff . . .

ANNOUNCER 2. Brought to you by the Information and Education Section of the South Pacific Base Command on your . . .

ANNOUNCER 1. Report to the Troops!

[*Music: Beethoven's Fifth . . . Two bars and out*]

Two months ago at his conference in Hawaii with Admiral Nimitz and General MacArthur, the President of the United States leaned forward towards a circle of newspaper reporters and said quietly:

VOICE 1 [*With determined simplicity*]. We are going back to the Philippines!

ANNOUNCER 1. That was two months ago. This week, we were on our way! General MacArthur's troops invaded Morotai, only three hundred miles from the Philippines. Vice-Admiral Wilkinson's amphibious forces landed in the Palau group, six hundred miles from the Philippines. But even closer than that, sometimes just a few miles offshore, the carriers and battlewagons of Admiral Halsey's Third Fleet, and of the Pacific Fleet, were prowling the Philippine coast. Hundreds of ships moving forward, sniffing for the enemy. Hundreds of ships stretched out across the ocean farther than the eye could see. In the center were the carriers. In front of them, in back of them, on their flanks, divisions of destroyers and cruisers. Leading the way, light scouting forces . . .

[*Fade in slowly drone of airplane motors*]

And hundreds of miles ahead, radiating out from the task force in carefully planned, geometric lanes—the search planes.

[*Bring plane motors up strong for a second . . . Then fade and hold in background*]

VOICE 2. X 51 to Hot Mamma. How'm I coming in?

VOICE 3 [*Filter*]. Hot Mamma to X 51. Like the Brooklyn express, honey. What's new out your way?

VOICE 2. No visitors all morning. Wake the cook up, will you? I'm heading home.

ANNOUNCER 1. That's the way it goes, hour after hour. Back and forth in their radiating lanes, the search planes fly, scanning the waters for hundreds of miles, reporting back to the flagship. And in the flag plot—the small room behind the bridge—each report is taken down carefully, digested, put together into the total plan of coming battle. All over the ship, there is movement and expectancy, like feet hurrying down the street before the storm. The crews in their bright linen helmets and gloves stand talking in nervous circles. On the flight deck, row on row of dive bombers, torpedo bombers, and fighters are crowded together. Mechanics tinker with last-minute repairs. Crew chiefs hover over the engines like expectant fathers, talking just to fill the empty time . . .

VOICE 4. You fixed the number two supercharger, Mickey?

VOICE 5. Don't worry, chief. Like a dream, I fixed it.

VOICE 4. Sure now?

VOICE 5. How do yuh like that? Am I sure I had beans for breakfast?

ANNOUNCER 1. In the ready room, the pilots are sitting and waiting in little knots, talking quietly. Then the operations officer comes into the room and stands in front of the big map.

[*Tap with pointer on board*]

VOICE 6. Your attention please, gentlemen. [*Pause*] I don't like speeches any more than you do but I want to say this. The mission you're carrying out today—and I say this with knowledge of all the missions you've flown before—may turn out to be the most important of them all. [*Then very businesslike*] Okay. Now here it is. You take off at 0600.

[*Fade behind but hold in background*]

Torpedo 6 will follow a straight course, right through . . . and . . .

ANNOUNCER I. He goes on talking, giving the altitude, weather conditions, where the enemy might try to intercept, and where the flak will be heaviest. On and on, fact after fact, in the same unchanging voice. Then suddenly he stops—and looks around. And you stuff your notebook in your pocket and wait for the next words because you know the next words are going to be the words that count.

[*Bring background mumble to a halt . . . Pause, then*]

VOICE 6. Your objective, gentlemen, is the northern Philippines. Your objective is—Manila!

[*Music: Quick stab up to climax*]

ANNOUNCER I. It takes a moment for the words to sink in, but suddenly it hits you, and you know that every man is thinking the same thing. This is the beginning of the road back. You're going back to Manila for the first time since March, 1942. Back to Manila and Clark Field and Cavite. [*Slight pause*] And then everyone is running for his plane. All along the great flight deck, motors are turning over, turning over and blending into one convulsive roar.

[*Roar of motors starting up strong under previous speech, holding in background*]

At the other end of the deck, the launching officer is standing with an orange and blue flag in each outstretched hand. Then his arms come down, sweeping through the air in giant arcs, waving the planes off the deck, one after another, almost faster than the eye can follow. It's your turn now, and you throttle your motor hard, and give it the gun.

[*Motors up to roar and off into the air*]

For a second, just for a second, you see the deck whirling past you, and then you ease the stick forward. Tail up. Stick back. You feel the air catch and lift you in an elevator of sky. And then you're clear and the Pacific is racing below you. You start to climb. Down below, the fleet is spread out to the horizon. You knew what to expect, but seeing it is different. Seeing it is like something Hollywood had been dreaming up for twenty years. Carrier after carrier. One, two, three, four, five, six, seven . . . You can't count them all. And then the big cruisers on the flanks, and the destroyers, zigzagging through the waters, darting back and forth like anxious parents. [*Pause*] Then you leave the fleet behind, and you're alone. Nothing but the long, gray sheet of water running into the sky. The motors drone on and on. It seems like hours, but you know it isn't. You know it isn't because suddenly you see a cluster of islands off your starboard wing. You look on your map. Right on the nose. In a couple of minutes, you'll be over the coast of Luzon. You'll be hitting the town of Aparri. [*Slight pause*] The name catches in your mind. Aparri. Aparri. You try to forget it but the name keeps coming back like the refrain of an old song. Aparri, Aparri . . .

[*Fading and holding in background*]
Appari. Aparri . . .

VOICE 7 [*Filter*]. Kelley to bombardier. We're over Aparri. Take a look down below.

ANNOUNCER 1. Aparri, Aparri. First the name gets you. And now it's voices.

VOICE 7 [*Filter*]. Kelley to bombardier. We're over Aparri. Take a look down below.

ANNOUNCER 1. Now you know you heard it. Kelley to bombardier. Kelley . . . Kelley . . . There's nobody named Kelley in your squadron. Maybe some guy from another squadron is off his course. You crane your neck around but you don't see anything. You're all alone, but somebody's talking on your frequency. You're all alone but words keep pounding in your ears.

VOICE 7 [*Filter*]. Kelley to bombardier. . . . Hey, Levin. Do you see that big fat son of a gun down there?

ANNOUNCER 1 [*Mechanically*]. Kelley to Levin. Do you see that— [*The take*] Kelley to Levin! Then it hits you like a sliver of ice up your spine. It comes back to you in a rush. Everything comes back to you—Aparri. December 10, 1941. Four days after Pearl Harbor. The big fortress taking off from Clark Field. Colin Kelley at the controls. Donald Robbins, copilot. Meyer Levin, bombardier. North over Luzon. At Aparri they saw it. The perfect target. Sitting down there in the water like a fat duck.

voice 7 [*Filter*]. Kelley to bombardier. Shall we go down and get it?
[*Keep repeating low in background, "Shall we go down and get it?"*]

ANNOUNCER 1. Instinctively, you look down. You know you're crazy . . . but you look down. There can't be anything there but the water. There can't be anything but the coast and the white houses of Aparri. But then you see it. You blink your eyes and look again, but you still see it. Sitting in the water, big and gray. A Jap transport just waiting for you. A Jap transport just itching for a stick of bombs in its midriff . . .

voice 7 [*Comes up strong from background*]. Kelley to bombardier. Shall we go down and get it?

ANNOUNCER 1. Shall we go down and get it? You want to shout. You want to stand up in the cockpit and shout . . .

voice 8. You're damn right, we'll go down. It's our turn now. We told you we'd be back, and now we're back for good. Are you ready? [*To climax*] We're coming down!
[*Roar of plane into long dive, segue*]

[*Music: Strong Air Corps theme up to climax*]

ANNOUNCER 2. To bring you now an analysis of task force strategy in the Pacific, Report to the Troops calls in its military expert, Lieutenant Colonel F. P. Todd of Major General Gilbreath's staff.

COLONEL TODD. One of the most significant statements to come out of the recent Quebec Conference is that there will be no single commander in the Pacific, as there was for the invasion of Europe. Instead there will be three commands, as there are at present: a naval commander in the Pacific Ocean areas; another in Southeast Asia; and an army commander in the Southwest Pacific. All this centers attention on the way the fleets and the amphibious forces under Admiral Chester W. Nimitz and General Douglas MacArthur will act in concert to achieve a common goal.

Available to Admiral Nimitz is the largest aggregation of naval strength the world has ever seen. As commander in chief of the Pacific Fleet he has under him four fleets, each led by a separate fleet commander. . . .

The fleets vary in size, depending on the job before them. Each is composed of task forces designed to meet particular conditions.

For an invasion, they are usually divided into an invasion task force and a carrier task force. As an example of the latter, we have Vice-Admiral Marc Mitscher's fast carrier task force which blasted the Japanese at Hollandia, Truk, and the Marianas. Then, it was part of Spruance's Fifth Fleet and included a good part of the twenty-two first-class carriers commissioned since Pearl Harbor. Described as "the largest and most destructive force in naval history," it has its own battleships, cruisers, destroyers, and auxiliary vessels. It is "able to carry its own fuel, food, replacement aircraft and pilots wherever it goes . . ." as the Japanese Admiral Shimada discovered at Saipan. It can launch more than one thousand planes and fire more than three hundred and fifty large naval guns.

The Third and Fifth Fleets constitute two complete teams. Each has its amphibious force commander. Under Admiral Halsey is the Third Amphibious Force, consisting of transports, cargo vessels, and naval support, and the Third Amphibious Corps, composed of the troops who are to make the landing. Admiral Spruance's fleet has the Fifth Amphibious Force and the Fifth Amphibious Corps. Both teams are completely equipped and trained to raid enemy bases, attack Japanese fleet units and convoys, and land on hostile shores. While the carriers search the seas far to the front and strike the enemy at his strong points, the amphibious forces in the rear, protected and assisted by units of the fleet, make the landings. With two such potent striking forces already in operation, Admiral Nimitz has said that he will hit the Japanese with heavy and continuous blows. While the Fifth Fleet executes one operation, Halsey and his staff will plan another, which they will execute as soon as Spruance completes his task. They will thus give the Japanese no rest.

The landings on Saipan, Guam, and Palau illustrated this technique. . . .

In the invasion of Palau, Admiral Mitscher's fast carrier task force, now a part of Halsey's Third Fleet, ranged far ahead of the invasion group. In four days of raids, he destroyed 173 Japanese ships and 500 planes. The amphibious forces then moved in to make the landing, protected by naval units estimated to consist of 23 battleships and 19 cruisers with 8-inch guns, and 40 more with 6-inch guns. This powerful force hit Yap, Ulithi, Mindanao in the Southern Philippines, and yesterday ventured as far as Manila Bay.

While these operations go on, Admiral Spruance and his staff plan and prepare others to follow. The tempo of the war in the Pacific increases; the pattern for invasion is established.

[*Music: Bridge*]

ANNOUNCER 1. Just one month ago, Vice-Admiral Aubrey Fitch said that Task Force 58 "was just a sweet summer breeze compared to the arrangement of ships, planes, and other weapons . . . which are ready to lash out now." Last week, Palau felt the power of one of those task forces. And today, as the news keeps coming in of the raid against Manila, a raid which sent 11 Japanese warships and probably 26 more to the bottom, and destroyed 205 planes, the greatest concentration of naval power ever gathered in the Pacific seems to be thrown against the Philippines. And today also the time is coming closer when General MacArthur's promise will be fulfilled. The promise that he made to return to the Philippines, the promise he made to his soldiers on Bataan . . .

VOICE 9. I shall keep the soldier's faith. I came through and I shall return.

[*Music: Beethoven's Fifth . . . Two bars and out*]

AGAINST THE STORM

Sandra Michael

ONE OF RADIO's most celebrated conflicts is that over the daytime serial, often under attack from women's clubs, educators, psychologists, and others. Denunciations of the daytime serial sometimes make exception of individual serials; among the exceptions most often singled out for praise have been *Vic and Sade, The Goldbergs,* and *Against the Storm.*

In 1942 Sandra Michael's *Against the Storm* won a Peabody Award as radio's most distinguished dramatic program. The fact that a *serial* won the award—which in other years has gone to Norman Corwin, *Cavalcade of America,* etc.—caused a great deal of comment, and helped focus attention on the literary possibilities of the serial form.

Sandra Michael was born in Denmark, went to school in Montana and in Chicago, and attended the University of Illinois and the University of Chicago. Her father was an architect, and her ancestors were clergymen, teachers, and farmers.

She wanted to be a newspaper reporter, but went straight from school into radio when one of her brothers got her a job at a station in Milwaukee. Soon radio seemed to her the most immediate and powerful means of communicating ideas, giving the writer a new dimension denied the novelist, without the physical limitations of stage or screen. She began to think about a *radio novel.* "I wanted to write a story set in a contemporary world, related to the forces that were at work in the social, economic, and political phases of our lives."

This was heresy in the field of the daytime serial, which exists in a land where troubles stem from bad people and are solved by courage. Another essential of her plan was that her characters, as in a good novel, should develop and change. This too was heresy. Most daytime serials are constructed around standardized formulas, which require their characters to remain always the same, so that they can keep on going through the same plot routines, and dispensing the same sort of standardized satisfactions they have led their listeners to expect.

Sandra Michael's ideas found little response until John Gibbs, her manager—and husband, met William Ramsey of Procter and Gamble, who persuaded his company to sponsor Sandra Michael's work—and thereby to make one of the few important decisions that have brought life and meaning to the daytime serial.

The first episode of *Against the Storm* was written the day war was declared by France and Great Britain—September 3, 1939. The war inevitably became a principal character in the story. Gerda Michael, the

ithor's sister, had that summer gone with their mother to Denmark, and
i the fall brought back firsthand material on the European scene that
icame part of *Against the Storm*. In 1942, Gerda became coauthor of the
iries. Their brother Peter was writing a regional serial, *Lone Journey*,
it in the Montana country where they had lived during their first days
i America. Another brother, Asger, photographed the real-life settings
ir published stories about the latter series, so that the whole family was
orking together, sharing experiences and interests.

Against the Storm ranged over two continents, involved many char-
cters, and occasionally went back in time to sketch in the background
f a character or situation. The simple episode published here does not
epend on knowledge of previous plot.

Against the Storm excited many people and won a large audience,
ut it has not revolutionized the daytime serial, which goes on as it was.
Vhen any new serial is launched, which is not often, it generally imitates
ie formula of one of the two or three serials getting at the moment the
ighest ratings in the telephone surveys. This is defended by some as in
ie public interest, since it "gives the American public what it wants." But
ie public appetite grows by what it feeds on. Thus, it is pandered to
ither than satisfied.

Sandra Michael feels this way about serials: "As books and drama
ave for centuries been activating forces in world history, so radio drama
as a part to play in the future—if given the chance."

Against the Storm was directed by Axel Gruenberg—"brilliantly,"
andra Michael feels. "Ax always knew what I had been trying to say,
/hat effect I had hoped for." The following episode, the 814th of *Against
ie Storm*, was broadcast on November 26, 1942.

AGAINST THE STORM

ANNOUNCER. Professor Jason McKinley Allen slept a little beyond his usual hour for rising. Then he heard a well-remembered and a well-beloved voice; it came from a distance of forty-five years or more. . . .

PORKY. Ja-son! Oh, Jason! Jason McKinley Allen, aren't you *up* yet? Ja-son!

PROFESSOR [*Aloud, but half in sleep*]. Yes, Porky! Of course I'm up, I—[*Awake now*] My word . . .

    [*Knock on door*]

SIRI [*Distance*]. Professor Jason McKinley Allen! Aren't you up yet?

PROFESSOR. What? Is that you, Siri? Come in! [*As if turning to look at his wife in bed*] Margaret, Siri seems to be up, what time—[*Stops. . . . Sees she isn't in her bed*] Well, for goodness—

    [*Door opens during above*]

SIRI [*Distance*]. Good morning, father! Who are you talking to?

PROFESSOR [*Half bewildered, half annoyed*]. Well, your mother, of course—except that she doesn't seem to be here. When did she get up? And what's all this?

SIRI [*Fading in*]. Quarter of a cup of coffee to wake you up. We thought you'd sleep all day if we didn't wake you.

PROFESSOR. Well, what time *is* it? Why didn't your mother call me when *she* got up? You *know* I don't like to oversleep . . .

SIRI. You didn't. It isn't late at all. For some reason or other the rest of us just happened to wake earlier.

PROFESSOR. And you've all had breakfast?

SIRI. No, no. Take your coffee, professor, and don't look so cross. Mother and Penny are getting breakfast, and Kathy's setting the table.

PROFESSOR. Well, that's better. Thank you, Siri . . . this coffee smells very good. Hate to drink it, if it's my quota for the day.

SIRI. It's just a quarter of a cup. Father, do you know what I thought

348

you said when I knocked on the door and asked if you weren't up?

PROFESSOR. No. What *did* I say?

SIRI. It *sounded* as if you said, "Yes, Porky! Of course I'm up."

PROFESSOR [*Smiles*]. I believe I did say that.

SIRI. You were dreaming . . .

PROFESSOR. I was dreaming. I thought I was at home on the farm. It was Thanksgiving morning. Porky Mason was on the scene before I was out of bed . . . he always was, on a holiday. He'd stand out in the yard and yell up at my window . . .

PORKY [*Under next speech by professor*]. Ja-son! Oh, Jason! Jason McKinley Allen, aren't you *up* yet?

PROFESSOR. I'd fly out of bed, and dash over to the window, in my bare feet, on the bare floor, and it seems to me in those days we had colder weather for Thanksgiving. Colder and maybe snow. Sometimes there'd be snow on the window sill. I can remember the touch of it on my hands as I leaned out to talk to Porky.

PORKY [*Distance*]. Say, Jason, aren't you ever going to get up? [*He's looking up from yard below*] I already tested the ice on the river and—Oh! There you are!

JASON. Hello, Porky. You certainly got over here early.

PORKY. Pa went to town in the sled to meet my aunt and uncle and I rode along as far as here. He's going to stop on the way back and see if you can come home with us.

JASON. It's Thanksgiving, Porky. I have to stay home.

PORKY. You can go home for *dinner*. . . . It's my uncle that knows all the parlor tricks, Jason . . .

JASON. It *is?* I'd like to see *him!*

PORKY. He's got an invention for a balloon, too. He'll show us how to make one to jump off the barn with.

JASON [*Fading*]. *Maybe* I could go home with you till dinnertime, Porky. I'll ask ma and see . . .

PROFESSOR [*Fading in*]. I'd close the window then, gather up my clothes, and rush out to the ice-cold hall, down the ice-cold stairs, and into the kitchen.

SIRI [*Laughing*]. Oh, father, I hope the *kitchen* wasn't ice-cold!

PROFESSOR. It wasn't. In fact it was the warmest and coziest place on earth. We were allowed to wash ourselves in the kitchen on really cold winter mornings . . . when the water was frozen in the pitchers upstairs . . . and then I'd stand in a corner on the far side of the stove, in my long woolen underwear, and pull into my clothes. It was quite a trick to fold the legs of my long under-drawers into my wool stockings . . . if I was careful, and took my time about it, I could get a pretty smooth effect, but if I was in a hurry . . . with Porky champing at the bit . . . the result was casual, to say the least. My stockings would be full of bumps and bulges, which made no difference to me, except after a time when the underwear would work itself up out of my shoe tops, and that was a nuisance. [*Laughs, or smiles and draws a deep breath*] Oh, my word . . . strange stuff the mind remembers and holds on to . . .

SIRI. Was that a better world, father?

PROFESSOR [*Absently*]. Mm? . . . [*Double take*] Better world? When I was a boy?

SIRI. Yes. When you and Porky Mason used to go skating and hunt-ing together on your father's farms . . . and nobody had heard of automobiles or airplanes . . . or dive bombers . . .

PROFESSOR. It's easy to think it was a better world. Our country wasn't at war. The Civil War graves in the cemetery were thirty years old, and war seemed like something that belonged to our history book, and to the old soldiers who sat around Courthouse Square in town . . . [*Briskly, decisively*] But of course it wasn't a better world, Siri; as a stage of development in the history of mankind, it wasn't nearly as good a world as this is today.

SIRI. But, *father!* With all the horror and death and destruction . . .

PROFESSOR. I know, I know, but that was all there *potentially,* years ago. Only the surface was calm . . . and it wasn't as calm for everyone, by any means, as it happened to be for my family up on the farm. All the germs of war were being nurtured in those days, Siri, only most of us didn't know it. Sometime look up the economic facts about those fine old days, and you'll see what I mean. Child labor, no limit on working hours, no compulsion about education, no planning to protect the farmer against the whims of weather or any of the other circum-stances beyond his control. No program to conserve natural resources. Very few laws to protect man against himself. The most provincial attitude toward everything and everyone in the world outside our own borders. For a few of us, a lovely, simple period of life; for a great many more people, a struggling, empty, hopeless time. Yes. Maybe what I *should* have said is that we're *nearer* a better world now. The disease began long ago. Right now I think it's probably at its very height. This is the crisis. This is the hour before dawn, when life and death match their strength . . . And life is going to win, Siri. In the new day, when the fever is gone, all the old evils should have been burned away, dishonored, destroyed forever. I think they will be. I refuse to believe anything else.

SIRI [*Not an exclamation . . . a quiet comment*]. Bravo, father. Those are good hopeful words to hear.

PROFESSOR. Ah, I'm just an old professor in flannel pajamas . . . talking my head off before breakfast. It doesn't much matter what *I* say. But there are great voices speaking for the future, Siri. Roosevelt, Wallace . . . listen to *them* . . . They speak for the new day, and the better world . . . And now run downstairs, child, and tell your mother I'll be down for breakfast in ten minutes.

SIRI [*Distance*]. All right, father!

PROFESSOR. And thank you for the coffee.

SIRI [*Distance*]. You're welcome!

[*Door closes, not loudly, at a distance*]

[*Music*]

ANNOUNCER. The professor leaned back against the pillows and closed his eyes for a moment . . .

GORKY [*Voice off, or over music*]. Jason! Jason McKinley Allen! It's a wonderful day and it's *Thanksgiving*, Jason! Aren't you awake yet?

PROFESSOR. Yes, old friend . . . I think we are awake. And it *is* a wonderful day . . .

THE NEGRO DOMESTIC

Roi Ottley

*T*he *Negro Domestic,* by Roi Ottley, is from the local New York series, *New World A-Coming*—an outstanding example of local public service programing.

When WMCA, New York, under the management of Nathan Straus, decided to put aside a weekly half-hour period each Sunday afternoon for a series on Negro life, it purchased the broadcast rights and title of Roi Ottley's famous book, *New World A-Coming.* The series was not to be a radio adaptation of the book; rather, it would carry out in radio the book's general theme and purpose.

The series has been presented under auspices of the City-Wide Citizens' Committee on Harlem, by special endowment of WMCA. The series was launched in March, 1944.

Seldom has a community rallied to the support of a radio series as did the Negro community of New York to *New World A-Coming.* And non-Negroes have been equally anxious to take part in and help the project.

Duke Ellington composed a special theme. Among performers who have appeared on this local series have been Marian Anderson, Muriel Smith, Canada Lee, Miriam Hopkins, Hazel Scott, Josh White, Hilda Simms, and innumerable others. Scripts have been written by Roi Ottley, Owen Dodson, Michael Sklar, Mitchell Grayson, Saul Carson, Sol Panitz and others.

Mitchell Grayson has produced and directed the series from its start, giving it the kind of detailed and skillful attention it has deserved. The music has been by James Lozito.

The series has won a number of honors, including citations from the National Conference of Christians and Jews and from the Writers' War Board. In 1945 the station, because of this series, won the annual award of the Schomburg Collection of Negro Literature of the New York Public Library. Dr. Lawrence D. Reddick, curator, in making the award, said: "Generally speaking, radio does not have a good record in the field of race relations. . . . This radio station assumes its responsibility for improving race relations in our society by utilizing its facilities for exposing social evil and interpreting what is socially good."

Roi Ottley was born in New York in 1906. Like several other writers in this volume, he went to the University of Michigan. After three years there he studied law for two years. Then, after periods as redcap, bellhop, and soda jerker, he became a newspaperman and for seven years was

:porter, editor, and columnist for the *Amsterdam Star News*. He then id public relations work for the Congress of Industrial Organizations. .fter the publication of his widely praised book, *New World A-Coming,* e became a war correspondent overseas.

He writes occasional scripts for the *New World A-Coming* series.

THE NEGRO DOMESTIC

NARRATOR. If there is one thing that irritates Negroes today—it is the "mammy" legend often romanticized in song and story. Yes, of course, the mammy did exist—once. For at least two centuries she was an institution of the Old South. Even today—here and there—one can be found. But today the Old South as we knew it is disappearing and mammy is rapidly passing away with her. Today—mammy has become largely a fiction—a museum piece of slavery days. Yes—it's true that mammy—the epitome of the patient, contented slave—doesn't live here any more! Yet, you will still hear some people saying . . .

WOMAN. Why, Old Sarah? She is really one of us. She thinks more of us—almost—than we do of ourselves.

MAN. Why, suh! We cherish Martha. She's a black diamond. Been in our family for years. And can she cook! Someday they'll need a wafflemaker in heaven, and we'll lose her.

WOMAN. The dear old horse. There isn't a thing she wouldn't do for me. And the best of it is that, no matter what or how much she does, she never seems to get the "misery" in her back.

NARRATOR. While such people exalt mammy verbally, they often don't seem to understand that she has developed strong feelings—about her role as a servant—about her own identity—and particularly about her own race. It is this development that has lately caused conflicts between a Negro servant and her white employer. Take, for instance, the experiences of a Negro domestic in the home of Mr. and Mrs. Frederick Millburn. Her name is Martha Howard.

[Music up then under]

MARTHA *[Pleasantly]*. I'm Martha Howard. I worked for the Millburns for ten years. Ever since Junior was born. The Millburns were like most folks—nice people. And Junior—I watched him

grow up just like my own boy who is now in the army.
[*Chuckles*] I liked little Junior [*Modestly*] and I think he liked
me. He was a *good* boy, bright, quick, smart as most children are,
well behaved, a little gentleman. I came to work for the Millburns in the depression, when it was awfully hard to get a job.
[*Quickly adds*] Of course, it isn't like that now . . . with war
work and such . . . nowadays. In all fairness, if you asked the
Millburns, I think they would say that I did my work well—and
when I say *work,* that's exactly what I mean. I was called on to
do all sorts of things—like, for instance, whenever Junior got sick
I would be the one to look after him. The last time he was sick
was just a few weeks ago . . .

[*Door opening and closing*]

JUNIOR. Good morning, Martha.

MARTHA [*Cheerfully*]. Good morning', Junior. How you feelin'?

JUNIOR [*Brightly*]. Oh, I feel fine.

MARTHA. Well, let me put these shades up an' see. . . .

[*Shades lifted*]

MARTHA. Yesssss . . . You do look better! I guess you'll be ready to
get up tomorrow.

JUNIOR. Tomorrow, not today?

MARTHA. Another day in bed and your cold will completely go away.

JUNIOR. Okay, if you say so. Is mother up yet?

MARTHA. Yes, she jes' had her breakfast. She'll be in in a minute.
[*New tone*] Here now, let me fix that pillow back o' your head.

[*Door opens*]

MOTHER. Good morning, son.

JUNIOR. Good morning, mother. Mother, Martha says I'll be all right
by tomorrow.

MARTHA. Yes, ma'am. He's gettin' along fine.

MOTHER. I think by tomorrow you'll be well enough to go back to
school. [*To Martha*] Martha, I don't know *what* we'd do without you. Did you get enough sleep last night?

MARTHA. Yes, ma'am. I only got up twice during the night to get
him some water.

MOTHER. Well, if you're not too tired, you'd better go out and do the
shopping now. I'll stay here with Junior.

MARTHA. Yes, ma'am.

MOTHER. Oh, Martha, we have special friends coming to dinner to-morrow night . . . and I'd like everything to be just right! The Richards are coming for dinner and bridge.

MARTHA. Yes, ma'am. I'll do my best. I remember that Mr. Richards likes apple pie.

MOTHER. Yes, he does!

JUNIOR [Cuts in]. Martha, before you go, will you bring me my break-fast, please?

MOTHER. I'll get you your breakfast, darling. Martha has other things to do. And, Martha, don't forget to give the house an extra special cleaning today. Dust the bookshelves, wash the woodwork, and vacuum-clean all the rugs. [Start fading] And make sure to polish the silver.

[Music up and out]

MARTHA. Now that day was pretty much like any other. Days get so that one day just runs into another when you're washin', cookin', shoppin', and doin' round the house. [Pause] The next day didn't seem any different—except for one thing. That morning I got a letter from my boy Charlie, in the army. It was a letter telling me that he'd got a furlough an' he was 'specially comin' in that night to see me. I got all choked up—as 'most any mother would—when I thought about it. I must have read it about a dozen times. That same day I was in the kitchen workin' an' thinkin', when Junior came in. At first, I didn't hear him . . .

JUNIOR [Off mike]. Martha!

[Rattling pans, pots, dishes]

[Approaching] Martha! [Pause] Martha, what are you thinkin' about?

MARTHA. Pardon me, Junior, but I was just lost in thought . . .

JUNIOR. About what, Martha?

MARTHA. Oh, I got a letter this morning from my boy Charlie . . .

JUNIOR [Excitedly]. Charlie? In the army?

MARTHA. Yes. He's comin' here tonight. He's got a furlough.

JUNIOR [All agog]. Where's he been fighting?

MARTHA. Well, now, he hasn't been fighting yet. He's just finishing his basic training—but I guess he'll be goin' overseas 'most any day now.

JUNIOR. Where's he goin', Martha?

MARTHA. Well, chile, I'm sure he don't know that himself.

JUNIOR. *Gosh,* I wish *I* could be a soldier!

MARTHA. Good land, this war'll be over long before that. I hope. [*Reflectively*] Hmmmm . . . That's one reason why Charlie's in a uniform. So's you won't have to go when you grow up.

JUNIOR. I wish I could see him . . . is he an officer?

MARTHA. No, Junior. He's only a private. Same as every other GI Joe.

JUNIOR. Will I be awake when he comes here tonight?

MARTHA. I don't know. Depends on what time his train comes in.

JUNIOR. I'd *like* to see him . . . even if he gets here when I'm sleeping . . .

MARTHA. We'll have to ask your mother about that. You've got to get up in time for school in the morning.

JUNIOR. I'll ask mother right away. I want to see Charlie.

MARTHA [*Smiling*]. Seems like only yesterday he was no bigger than you—runnin' around in short pants—I can hardly believe he's old enough to be in the army.

JUNIOR. I'm going to join the Air Force when I grow up. I'm going to get in an airplane and ah-ah-ah-ah-ah all the Nazis and Japs in the sky. I'll dive right into 'em . . . and ZOOOOOMMMMMM up . . . and then circle round . . . I'll get every one of 'em!

MARTHA. Yes . . . I believe you would . . . and get a chestful of medals, too. . . . But your poor mother . . . she's spared the things I go through each time I think of something happening to Charlie. [*Shooing him away*] Now you go out an' let me finish my work. I gotta get this dinner ready on time for your mother's friends. [*Fade*]

[*Music up and out*]

[*Chuckles*] He sure was a bright little fellow—an' always knew what was goin' on. An' what he didn't know, he tried to find out. [*Pause*] Well, that night, Mr. and Mrs. Richards from up the street came to dinner. Everything had gone smoothly . . . and when they got to the dessert . . . the apple pie . . . Mr. Richards was feelin' fine.

[*Music up and out*]

[*Dinner table . . . knives and forks . . . plates, etc.*]

RICHARDS. By Golly, Mrs. Millburn, that was certainly a fine piece of pie.

MOTHER. Did you really like it, Mr. Richards?

RICHARDS. Like it? That's the best pie I've had in years! That cook of yours is sure wonderful.

MOTHER. I guess we're pretty lucky that we still have Martha.

MRS. RICHARDS. We've got a girl like her, too.

MOTHER. Really, Mrs. Richards?

MRS. RICHARDS. Why, you've never in your life tasted fried chicken like she makes it. We wouldn't part with her for the world.

MOTHER. I don't blame you. The way things are, it's terribly hard to find good servants these days.

FATHER. Yeah, the war industries gobble them all up. You never know when they'll skip off . . .

MOTHER [*Interrupts*]. Why, Frederick, we don't have to worry about that! Martha's happy here with us. And Junior loves her. [*Joking*] Almost as much as he does me.

FATHER. Well, if he does, it's because he sees more of her than he does you, darling.

MOTHER. Now, Frederick . . .

FATHER [*Smiling*]. Well, I think you spoil Martha . . .
  [*Doorbell rings off mike*]

FATHER. Now who in the world could that be? Are you expecting anyone else this evening?

MOTHER [*Startled*]. Oh, my goodness! Yes! I forgot all about it.

FATHER. Who?

MOTHER. Martha's son Charlie—the one who's in the army . . . got a furlough . . . and wrote her that he was coming here tonight to see her.

JUNIOR [*Rushing in, excitedly*]. Mother, mother, guess who's here? Guess who's here, mother?

MOTHER. Why, Junior, what are you so excited about?

JUNIOR. Charlie is here, mother! In uniform an' everything!

MOTHER. Hush, darling, lower your voice. There's no need to shout.

JUNIOR [*Complying*] Yes, mother. [*Hushed excitement*] And you know what, dad?

FATHER. What, Junior?

JUNIOR. He's got wings on his sleeve . . . he's in the Air Corps!

FATHER. Well, that's fine!

MRS. RICHARDS [Chuckling]. Why, Junior, do you think you'll be able to sleep tonight with all this excitement?

MR. RICHARDS. I guess he wouldn't mind being in the Air Corps himself. Would you, Junior?

JUNIOR. Who, me? Yes, sir! I'm going to be a pilot . . . when I'm old enough.

MOTHER. Frederick, I think it would be a nice thing if we invited Martha and her son into the living room while we're having our coffee. I think that would be a nice thing to do, don't you?

FATHER [Hesitating]. Er . . . well . . . darling . . .

JUNIOR. I'll ask them to come in, mother. [Fading] I'll bring them in.

FATHER [Raising voice]. Er, Junior?

JUNIOR [Off mike]. Yes, dad?

FATHER. Er . . . never mind . . . go ahead.

JUNIOR. Okay, dad!

FATHER. Well . . . I guess that sort of breaks up our bridge game for this evening.

MOTHER. Oh, Frederick . . . I don't think so.

FATHER. I'm sorry, Mr. Richards.

MR. RICHARDS. Oh, that's all right. Forget it.

MRS. RICHARDS. [With effort]. Of course. Besides, I didn't see how you could get out of it with Junior so persistent . . . [Laughs uneasily]

MOTHER. Well, shall we go into the living room?

[Ad lib agreement]

[Music up . . . Short bridge and out]

Charles, would you like another cup of coffee?

CHARLIE. No, thank you, Mrs. Millburn.

FATHER. So, you're in the Air Corps, eh, Charles?

CHARLIE. Yes, sir. And I've just been accepted for further training at the flying school.

JUNIOR. Boy, that's swell! Isn't it, dad?

FATHER [Interrupts]. You mean, ground crew . . . don't you?

CHARLIE. Why, no. As a pilot, sir.

FATHER. Aren't the qualifications pretty stiff?

CHARLIE. Yes, sir. But I just made it. I was lucky that I had completed two years of college before I went into the service. That helped plenty. I'll tell you.

FATHER. Well, er, that's fine . . .

JUNIOR. Mother, one of the boys in our school . . . one of the older boys . . .

MOTHER. Junior, your father's talking. It isn't polite to interrupt.

JUNIOR. I'm sorry. [*Adding quickly*] But, mother, the Air Corps wants lots of boys.

FATHER [*Patronizingly*]. Well, I guess you're learning a whole lot in the army. Negroes are getting opportunities for the first time, I hear.

CHARLIE. Yes, sir.

FATHER. You seem to be doing well, and I hope you'll make the most of your opportunities. I suppose your people have their own training grounds and divisions. . . .

CHARLIE. Well, sir, that's one thing about the army none of us likes. Especially when they say this is a war for democracy! That kind of treatment . . . Negro this and white that . . . doesn't seem fair to us. But I guess that will be all reckoned with in the future.

MOTHER. How do you mean that, Charles?

CHARLIE. Well, Mrs. Millburn, when you're in the army . . . and you fight for something . . . you fight for something that's right. That's the reason why I think we're fighting this war . . . for things that are right. Everybody in a uniform takes a chance on giving up his life. Negro soldiers are not different. We believe we're fighting for something that's right. And we don't think we ought to be separated on any 'count.

MOTHER. I see what you mean, Charles.

CHARLIE. And I think there's some headway being made, too.

MOTHER. Yes, Charles, go on.

CHARLIE. Well, in a few months, if I make the grade, I'll be in a flier's uniform. That's a little headway, I think. There were no Negro fliers in the last war.

JUNIOR. Gosh, Charles, I wish I were flying with you!

MRS. RICHARDS. Now, Junior, you know you can't do that.

JUNIOR. Why, Mrs. Richards?

MRS. RICHARDS. Well, it's just not done, that's all.

MOTHER. I think, Junior, Mrs. Richards means that you're not old enough to be in a uniform. Only boys who are in the army can fly in army planes.

JUNIOR. Well, gosh, I hope when I'm old enough to get in the army they'll let me fly with Charlie.

MOTHER. Well, perhaps someday. [*Changing subject*] Martha, you've been quiet all evening . . . you've hardly said a word.

MARTHA [*Quietly*]. I'm just so glad to see Charlie—I guess there's just nothing to say.

FATHER. Junior, I think you ought to get to bed now, don't you? It's long past your bedtime.

JUNIOR. Must I go so early, dad?

FATHER. Yes, I think so.

MARTHA. Come on, boy, I'll take you upstairs.

JUNIOR. Ohhhhhh, Martha . . . Okaaaaaaay.

MARTHA. And, Charlie, you can wait for me in my room. I'll be down in a little while.

CHARLIE. Yes, mom. Mr. Millburn . . . Mrs. Millburn . . . Mr. and Mrs. Richards . . . Thank you for everything and goodnight.

ALL [*Ad lib*]. Goodnight, Charlie . . . You must come and see us again before you go . . . Thank you . . .

[*Music: Bridge up and out*]

MARTHA. I took young Junior upstairs and put him to bed . . . opened the windows . . . pulled the shades down . . . said good night to him . . . closed the door softly behind me . . . and started down the stairs toward my room. On the way down I heard Mrs. Richards talking loudly. What she said gave me a start.

MRS. RICHARDS [*Fading in, acidly*]. Well, my dear, your son certainly seemed interested in your cook's son.

MOTHER. Oh, that's quite natural. All young boys idolize soldiers in uniform.

MRS. RICHARDS. Yes . . . but he doesn't seem to realize that your cook's son is a Negro!

MOTHER. Mrs. Richards, I don't think there's anything to fear in that. Martha is a Negro, but she is also an American woman . . . and the mother of a very intelligent boy who would be a credit to any parent.

MRS. RICHARDS. Well, I wouldn't encourage that kind of relationship in my home.

MR. RICHARDS. Oh, come now, what difference does it make? Let's play some bridge. . . . What do you say, Mr. Millburn?

FATHER. Yes, Mr. Richards. Let's . . . er . . . play some bridge . . . [*Fading*] I'll get the cards and the score pad . . .

[*Music: Strings . . . Ominous punctuation . . . Then under*]

MARTHA. I was hurt by Mrs. Richards' remarks . . . I guess it was more than that! I was stunned! . . . In the ten years that I had been working in the Millburns' home . . . this was the first time that I had ever heard any talk about color. I walked into my room and found my boy waiting for me . . . my own boy . . . in uniform. He noticed at once that something was wrong . . . but I got around that all right . . . I didn't let on what I had heard. That night, Charlie slept at my brother's home, and we arranged to see each other sometime during the next day. I guess I would have forgotten the whole thing except that next mornin', when I went upstairs, I happened to pass Junior's room and heard Mr. Millburn talkin' to Junior. Again, I didn't mean to listen . . . but he was harpin' on that color question again. . . .

FATHER. Naturally, we are very fond of Charlie, but he is—not like us, you know.

JUNIOR. I know, dad. Perhaps not. Maybe we're all a little different. But they say everybody should get a chance in a democracy. We talked about it in school . . .

FATHER. Well, that's not exactly what I mean. Why—it's just this. Your skin is white, whereas Charlie's is dark.

JUNIOR. Does that make any difference?

FATHER. DOES IT?????????

JUNIOR. Well . . . does it?

FATHER. Well, Junior, it means that Charlie is a very good, nice person, but not white . . . and therefore not in the same class.

JUNIOR. You mean because his skin is a different color?

FATHER. Yes, Junior.

JUNIOR. Dad, are you sure?

FATHER. Sure, I'm sure. Color makes a lot of difference.

JUNIOR. Gee, it just doesn't make sense.

FATHER. Let me put it this way, son. How would you like it, if I took Martha to the movies tonight?

JUNIOR. What's playing?

FATHER [*Raising voice*]. Now. what difference does that—Say, if I took a Negro to the movies, we would be ostracized by polite society! Nobody would play with you any more.

JUNIOR. Do you really think so, dad?

FATHER. Yes! People would say I had a son who was being brought up wrong.

JUNIOR. Is there a law which says people with dark skins are not equal people to people with white skins?

FATHER. Well, it's practically a law.

JUNIOR [*Triumphantly*]. Yes, but it isn't really a law, is it?

FATHER. Junior, I'm not going to argue with you. I want you to understand what I've said to you. Do you understand?

JUNIOR. No, dad.

[*Music up . . . then under*]

MARTHA. When they came out of the room—I lowered my head so our eyes wouldn't meet and walked past them. Junior said . . .

JUNIOR [*Gloomily*]. Hello, Martha.

MARTHA. I don't know whether I answered him or not. I was all choked up, incensed. I knew there was only one thing to do. I tried to calm myself, keep my head about me, but it was no use, my head was spinning like a top. This whole thing happened so sudden . . . I couldn't believe it! When I got to my room, I packed up my things and then walked into Mrs. Millburn's room. She was talkin' on the phone . . .

MOTHER. Why, of course, Jean. We'd love to have you and Bill come over for dinner . . . Think nothing of it . . . Just a minute, dear, someone came into the room . . . What is it, Martha?

MARTHA. I'll wait, Mrs. Millburn, till you're finished.

MOTHER. Why, Martha, you look so, so—what's happened?

MARTHA. I'm leavin'!

MOTHER [*Amazed*]. Leaving?

MARTHA. I can't work in this house a minute longer.

MOTHER. What! My goodness! This is terrible! What's come over you, Martha?

MARTHA. Nothin' 'cept I'm leavin', Mrs. Millburn.

MOTHER. Wait just a minute . . . [*On phone off mike*] Jean . . . Darling . . . I'll call you back in a few minutes . . . No, no, it's all right . . . Yes, in a very few minutes . . .

[*Phone hook on receiver*]

Now, Martha, what's all this about?

MARTHA. It's somethin' I can't repeat. I don't want to talk about it. I came to get my money for a week's work. I can't work here no more.

MOTHER. Martha, you just can't leave this way. After ten years! What's happened? Whatever it is, I'll straighten it out.

MARTHA. I'm 'fraid you can't straighten this out, Mrs. Millburn.

MOTHER. I have no idea what you're talking about!

MARTHA. Ask Mr. Millburn . . . he can tell you. Or talk to your son . . . Junior will tell you.

MOTHER. Wait a second.

[*Door opens*]

Frederick! Frederick!

FATHER [*Off mike*]. Yes, Millicent.

MOTHER. Frederick! Come up here, please.

FATHER [*Coming on*]. Coming! [*Then on mike*] What's up, Millicent?

MOTHER. Frederick, what did you say to Martha?

FATHER. Martha, why . . .

MOTHER. Martha says she's leaving.

FATHER. Leaving? Why?

MARTHA [*Choked up*]. I have worked for you for ten years—to the day. I never got too much pay. I came here in the depression 'cause I couldn't do no better. I stayed on and did my work—and you all seemed to like me.

MOTHER. Why . . . we do, Martha, we do! We're very fond of you.

MARTHA. Workin' here, I couldn't look after my own son right. I gave you most of my time . . . day and night . . . whenever you asked me to do extra things like that dinner last night . . . and even when you didn't ask me. I wasn't in love with the work . . . but I tried to do a good day's work an' not complain.

MOTHER. Yes, we're perfectly satisfied with you, Martha.

MARTHA [*Continuing as though uninterrupted*]. I always liked your boy. He's a good boy. I treated him like I did my own.

MOTHER. And he loves you, too, Martha.

MARTHA. But after what I just heard Mr. Millburn tell your boy . . . I don't belong here!

FATHER [*Amazed*]. You heard what I told Junior?

MARTHA. Only by accident. I was comin' up the stairs, the door was open . . . anyway, I'm glad to know how you feel.

MOTHER. What . . . now, what did you tell Junior, Frederick?

MARTHA. You had nothin' against me, Mr. Millburn, but the things you told your son only helps to turn his mind against me an' my race . . . people who's done nothin' wrong to you.

FATHER. I only tried to show him . . . to try and explain to him . . . Well, you know, Martha . . .

MARTHA. Yes, I know, Mr. Millburn. An' I'm sorry for you because you're teachin' your own flesh and blood to have prejudice.

MOTHER. Martha, I wish you'd reconsider what you're doing. I'm sure Mr. Millburn meant no harm. Why . . . where will you go if you leave here?

MARTHA. Oh, I don't need to worry 'bout that. There's plenty of places for me to go.

MOTHER. I wish you wouldn't do anything hasty. [*New tone*] Why don't you take the rest of the day off, Martha, think it over before you make any decisions?

MARTHA. I wouldn't have any respect for myself if I didn't do jes' what I'm doin' now!

MOTHER. Then you've definitely made up your mind about leaving.

MARTHA. Yes.

MOTHER. Well, while you say good-bye to Junior, I'll make out your check.

MARTHA. No, Mrs. Millburn, I'd rather not see him now.

MOTHER. Why, he'll feel bad when he hears that you've gone without saying good-bye.

MARTHA. Some other time, maybe . . . but I don't want to interfere with what his father said!

FATHER. I'm terribly sorry, Martha. [*Fade*]

[*Music: Slow, deep, sad theme which segues . . . not too quickly . . . into light, airy, brighter theme under*]

MARTHA. I never really explained to Charlie why I left the Millburns. I figured he was in the army . . . and soon enough he'd be over, there fighting for the things we believed in . . . I didn't want him to get bitter because he had enough to worry about right now. I think he must have known, though, that something was wrong. You can't fool bright young people. And even if I must say it myself, Charlie is a bright boy. I told him that I wanted a job in a war plant, that I wanted to be part of this war too. And as a matter of fact, about a week later I got a job in a parachute factory . . . sewing parachutes. Then one afternoon . . . it was Sunday after church . . . I came home to my newly rented house and . . . well . . . [*Smile*] who do you think was sitting on my doorstep?

JUNIOR. Hello, Martha . . .

MARTHA. Why, Junior, bless your heart. Did you come 'way up here to see me?

JUNIOR [*Smile*]. Yes, Martha, I did.

MARTHA. Does your mother know you're here?

JUNIOR. Yes, she does an' father does too!

MARTHA. Your father?

JUNIOR. Yes. Dad took back what he said.

MARTHA. And your mother—what did she say?

JUNIOR. Mother felt very bad. I think they both did. Gee, mother hasn't been able to get anyone in the house to stay with us.

MARTHA. Maybe 'cause it's such hard work being a servant. Awfully hard sometimes. Now, since I got my job in the parachute factory, I got more time for myself. And I make more money, too. Isn't that good?

JUNIOR. It sure is. I'm glad for you. Martha . . . You look so nice in that blue dress.

MARTHA. You like it, Junior?

JUNIOR. I sure do.

MARTHA. Well, come on inside and let me show you my *own* house . . .

JUNIOR. May I?

MARTHA. Sure. . . . In my house friends are always welcome.

   [*Music: Theme*]

JAPAN'S ADVANCE BASE: THE BONIN ISLANDS

Arnold Marquis

*J*apan's *Advance Base: the Bonin Islands* is from the *Pacific Story* series, written and directed by Arnold Marquis. Marquis has never been to Asia or to any of the islands of the Pacific he has written about on this series, but his programs are so authoritative and packed with fact that he is constantly consulted about the Pacific area. When Truk was still considered an impregnable fortress about which nothing was known, *Pacific Story* did a half-hour program about it. When three days later our forces bombed the fortress for the first time, the New York *Daily News* put in a long-distance call to Marquis in Los Angeles, to get inside information on Truk. Mothers with sons fighting in the Pacific have written him constantly to ask questions about the islands where their boys are stationed. He answers all the letters. Schools use *Pacific Story* scripts as text material. The University of California Press sells individual scripts in mimeographed form.

Tireless research is behind *Pacific Story*. Unlike many "educational" series on the air, the series does not sacrifice facts for drama. When approaching a new subject, Marquis and his research assistant, Mary Behner, dig into every possible source and discuss the subject with consultants.

Like several other of the more successful writers of educational scripts, Marquis himself had an odd education. He was born of immigrant parents in the factory town of Racine, Wisconsin, one of ten children. He was expelled from high school in his sophomore year, and at fifteen joined the navy. After World War I, a veteran of seventeen, he balked at the idea of sitting next to high school sophomore "kids." The University of Wisconsin wouldn't take him because he hadn't finished school.

But Stevens Point College would. After two very happy and fruitful college years there he left and went into newspaperwork, for papers in Kenosha, Chicago and Milwaukee. Then he wrote some books, many articles, and plays. He wasn't doing so well in the depression, when he had a talk with the program director at NBC in San Francisco. Marquis told him frankly he'd never been inside a radio studio and had never seen a script. The program director suggested he try writing one. He wrote it that night, and next day NBC bought it and hired him.

Moving to Los Angeles, Marquis later wrote and produced the science series *Unlimited Horizons*. When war came, and science became increasingly hush-hush, *Pacific Story* took the place of *Unlimited Horizons* on NBC's program schedule.

Pacific Story has been conducted on a genuinely adult level, with an enormous respect for facts. Marquis turns his back on the mistaken notion, held by many in radio, that listeners don't really want information, and that it has to be spoon-fed to them with generous swallows of boy-girl plot. Marquis occasionally uses fictional narrators but never to dilute content. *Pacific Story* aims always to be as informative as possible. And it is objective. In programs on Japan, it has not suppressed facts that might do her credit or that might be uncomfortable to us. His aim is to put facts in correct perspective, to clarify complex problems.

A *Pacific Story* program is really a dramatized article. The series has won an enthusiastic following, although it has always been scheduled at almost the worst time available: 11:30 P.M. to midnight in most large cities.

Japan's Advance Base: the Bonin Islands was first broadcast on July 2, 1944.

JAPAN'S ADVANCE BASE:

THE BONIN ISLANDS

[*Harbor sounds: Buoys . . . Foghorns, etc. . . . . Ad libs in background*]

MASTER. Well, Mr. Hunikara, we're getting under way in a few minutes now. I'll say good-bye to you.

HUNIKARA. Yes. Good-bye, captain.

MASTER. Thanks for all your hospitality. Man needs that after the long passage here.

HUNIKARA. You are welcome.

MASTER. I always like to call at Port Lloyd here, and I hate to leave. Well, see you when we call here again next year.

HUNIKARA. I am afraid you will not, captain.

MASTER [*Puzzled . . . amused*]. You figuring on something happening to you in the next year. Mr. Hunikara?

HUNIKARA. You are not coming back here.

MASTER. Hmmmm? [*Chuckles*] Nothing's going to happen to *me*.

HUNIKARA. Because of the gravity of the world situation, henceforth no foreign ships will be permitted to put in here.

MASTER. You mean just here at Port Lloyd?

HUNIKARA. No. Anywhere in the Bonin Islands.

MASTER. Look, Mr. Hunikara, you're taking that situation in Europe too seriously. There isn't going to be any war over there. Lot of noise, but—

HUNIKARA. Perhaps.

MASTER. I've been calling here at the Bonin Islands nearly every year for, well, twenty-five years and—

HUNIKARA. This is 1939, and the world situation has changed.

MASTER. Well, yes, if you—

HUNIKARA. Henceforth no foreign ships will be permitted to put in here.

MASTER. Well . . . See you again sometime, Mr. Hunikara. [*Fades*]
Thank you for everything . . . and good-bye.

HUNIKARA. Good-bye, captain. [*Coldly*]

[*Whistle of ship . . . Ad libs as ship gets under way*]

MASTER. I am the last white man to leave the Bonin Islands. As we got under way and stood out to sea, I had a strange feeling. I stood on the bridge and looked back at Port Lloyd and wondered if I would ever see the Bonins again. As master of the "Lottie D" I had called at the Bonins for years. And years before that I had sailed the waters around the Bonins, and I knew them by heart. As the islands receded, all that I had learned about the Bonins in my years of trading fell together in a clear picture. The islands were Japanese now, and were being closed to the world. We were being excluded, and yet once the United States occupied them, the British occupied them, and [*Fades*] neither country realized how important they would one day become.

[*Oscillator . . . Builds full . . . Drops to background*]

NEWSVOICE. The Bonin Islands, which were bombed again today, are the last group of islands between the Marianas, where the Americans have landed on Saipan, and Japan itself. The Bonins are some eight hundred miles north of the Marianas, and only two hours' flying time from Japan.

[*Oscillator . . . Swells and fades out*]

MASTER. The Bonins are mighty important today. And some Americans and some Britishers had the notion the islands were important a hundred years ago and more.

MAZARRO. I am Matteo Mazarro. I am an Italian, but I came to the Bonin Islands in a British ship.

MASTER. When Mazarro got there in 1830, some problems had to be settled with an American named Nathaniel Savory.

SAVORY. On what basis, Mazarro, do you claim these islands in the name of Britain?

MAZARRO. Captain Beechey landed here three years ago in his Majesty's ship "Blossom" and took possession of them in the name of George IV.

SAVORY. Three years ago?

MAZARRO. Yes, in 1827.

SAVORY. An American whaler, the "Transit," with Captain Coffin as master, landed here four years before that, in 1823.

MAZARRO. But the American ship captain did not claim the islands, and the British captain did.

SAVORY. The Americans were here before the British.

MAZARRO. I have orders from the British consul in Honolulu that I am to take over the islands, and that I am to be the governor.

SAVORY. Mr. Mazarro, you and I cannot decide which country is to hold these islands. That is for Britain and the United States to decide. If we are to live here, all of us, we must have some kind of law and order. And *that* is what we should be putting our minds to. [*Fades out*]

MASTER. Well, Mazarro, the Italian, became the governor in the name of Britain, but Savory, the American, really was the boss. They tell about some of his first orders.

SAVORY. There is no sense to the way the goats on these islands are being slaughtered. This must stop.

MASTER. He issued an order about women.

SAVORY. There are few women on these islands. Hereafter it is against the law to steal a woman.

MASTER. He looked to the days ahead.

SAVORY. If we are going to grow and thrive here on these islands, we must have contact with the outside world. We must not depend on the visits of ships. We must have ships of our own.

MASTER. They worked out a pretty satisfactory sort of government, far's I've been able to find out. After they'd been there eighteen years, Mazarro died, and Savory became governor. An American citizen, governor of a group of islands claimed by Britain! I shouldn't say claimed by Britain because, at this stage at least, the British in London had no such idea.

LONDONER. What do we want with those islands in the Pacific? No one will quarrel with those British subjects who roam over the world and go to unheard-of places, but as for Britain supplying them protection and the like, that, of course, is out of the question.

MASTER. When Savory became governor, he appealed to Washington to take over the islands officially.

AMERICAN. No, no, no, no. It's foolishness. If the Americans in the Bonin Islands wish to live under the American flag, they should

come back to this country. The policy of the United States has
been, historically, never to accept any lands which would require
the navy to defend them. The United States is not interested in
the Bonin Islands.

[*Orchestra: Dynamic attack . . . Courageous . . . Hold in
background*]

MASTER. Well, the British flag went on flying over the Bonins, and
Savory, the American, went on being governor. It was along
about 1853 that another American came to the islands, Commodore Perry. He came to establish coaling stations at various
points across the Pacific. With a whole squadron of American
warships he came to open a sea route to China.

[*Orchestra: Sweeps up briefly, dynamically . . . Fades out*]

The commodore ran the American flag up over the Bonins, and
made a deal with Nathaniel Savory.

PERRY [*Pompous . . . bluff*]. You see, Mr. Savory, by this document
we are paying you fifty dollars and other benefits for this part of
Port Lloyd right here.

SAVORY [*Old man now*]. How much of the port will you require
for this coaling station, Commodore Perry?

PERRY. It's this section right here on this chart . . .

[*Rattle of chart*]

SAVORY. Ummm hmmmm.

PERRY. It's set forth here. You see it reads that our part of Port Lloyd
will include both sides of the creek which empties into the said
harbor called Ten Fathom Hole.

SAVORY. Yes.

PERRY. And I propose to set up an American code of government here
and have you elected by the people as chief magistrate.

SAVORY. But that's the same as the United States taking over the
islands, and we've been flying the British flag ever since we
came here.

PERRY. You're an American, aren't you?

SAVORY. Yes. I was born in the United States.

PERRY. As of now, Mr. Savory, you will be the agent of the United
States Naval Squadron and as such you will be attached to the

Navy of the United States and have all its privileges. [*Fades*] The government of the United States will . . .

MASTER. The people of the Bonins did elect Savory as chief magistrate, and although Savory was the British governor, he also became the agent of the United States Naval Squadron. When the British government in London learned about this, they suddenly took an interest in the Bonins.

LONDONER. By what right does Commodore Perry make a deal of this kind with our governor on the Bonin Islands. The islands were claimed by Captain Beechey in his Majesty's ship "Blossom" in 1827.

MASTER. When the word got around to Commodore Perry, he had an answer.

PERRY. In 1823, three years before the visit of Captain Beechey in his Majesty's ship "Blossom," the Bonin Islands were visited by the American whaling vessel "Transit" under command of Captain Coffin. In addition to this, the Japanese landed on these islands 230 years before that, in 1593, and the Spanish explorer, Villalobos, landed there fifty years *before the Japanese,* in 1543.

MASTER. The question went to the American government. Perry saw the value of the Bonins to the United States.

PERRY. Each passing day strengthens my opinion that the large and increasing commerce of the United States with the Far East makes it not only desirable, but indispensable that ports of refuge should be established in this part of the world. Unless we establish such ports, other powers, less scrupulous, may slip in and seize upon the advantage which should rightly belong to us.

MASTER. They listened to Perry's arguments in Washington, but that was about all. They disposed of the question once and for all.

AMERICAN. The policy of the United States is *still* not to accept any territory that would require the navy to defend it. The United States is not interested in the Bonin Islands.

MASTER. The dispute brought the Bonins to the attention of the Japanese once more. You see, by this time Commodore Perry had opened up Japan and, for the first time in more than two and a half centuries, the Japanese were looking out beyond their own islands.

JAP 1. The Bonin Islands rightfully belong to Japan.

MASTER [*Aside*]. They saw the value of the Bonins.

JAP 1. The Bonin Islands were discovered by Ogasawara in 1593.

MASTER [*Aside*]. They conveniently overlooked that the Spaniards had discovered the Bonins fifty years before *that*.

JAP 1. The United States and Britain are now quibbling over the Bonins. But the United States is fighting for its life in civil war, and the British actually have little interest in the islands.

MASTER. The Japanese saw their opportunity.

JAP 1. *This* is the time for us to move in.

MASTER. They made careful plans. They knew that Nathaniel Savory and a colony of Americans and Britishers were occupying the islands. As daylight was breaking one fine morning one of the settlers at Port Lloyd came hurriedly to Nathaniel Savory.

SETTLER 1. [*Coming in*]. Mr. Savory . . . Mr. Savory . . . down on the beach . . .

SAVORY [*Old*]. Hmmmm? What about the beach?

SETTLER 1. [*Excited*]. Down on the beach . . . there is a whole party of . . . of . . .

SAVORY. Calm yourself. What is it?

SETTLER 1. A whole party of strangers. They're on the beach.

SAVORY. Who are they? What do they want?

SETTLER 1. I cannot understand what they say, Mr. Savory. There are men and women and children, and they are strange and—

SAVORY [*Fades*]. Well, let us go down to the beach and have a look at them.

MASTER. Down at the beach they saw a ship heading out to sea. And on the beach was a party of about twenty-five Japanese families. They had all their belongings with them. They'd come to stay.

[*Beach . . . Surf . . . Ad libs of Japs*]

JAP 2. Oh, there are people here on these islands?

SAVORY. We've been here for more than thirty years.

JAP 2. Oh, we did not know these islands had people on them.

SAVORY. You people came here with the idea of living here?

JAP 2. The captain of the ship put us off here.

SAVORY. Must have put you and your people ashore here before daylight.

JAP 2. Yes. We thought there was no one here.

SAVORY. That ship captain didn't waste any time. Just put your party ashore and pulled out right away.

JAP 2. Yes. [*Grins*] You can show us where we can live here?

SAVORY. I don't know what we're going to do with you. [*Fades*] We'll have to look around and see if we can . . .

MASTER. Well, Savory had the twenty-five Japanese families on his hands. He had no vessel to send them away. He had to make some kind of arrangement for them. So he gave them quite a plot of land . . . told them to work it . . . raise their own food. They went to work on it and developed it. Probably Savory watched the Japanese and knew what they were up to, and maybe he didn't. But one day the head of the Japanese group came to Savory . . .

JAP 2. We are very happy to have you here in these islands, Mr. Savory.

SAVORY. What do you mean . . . have *us* here?

JAP 2. [*Grinning*]. There has been a small mistake. These islands really belong to the imperial government of Japan.

SAVORY. Japan? We've been here for over thirty years, and Americans and British landed here before that.

JAP 2. Slight misunderstanding. Ogasawara landed here more than two hundred years ago, in 1593. These islands should not be called Bonin Islands. From now on they will be called Ogasawara Islands. But we are very happy to have you here. Under the imperial Japanese government, you are now the commissioner of the Ogasawara Islands.

MASTER. The Japanese had worked out their plans well. They knew that the government of the United States was in no position to throw them out—the Civil War was on. And as for Britain . . .

LONDONER. Our subjects never had any business there in the first place.

MASTER. So the Japanese took over. And from that time they worked to make the Bonins as Japanese as Japan itself.

[*Orchestra: Dire threat and peril . . . Hold in background*]

I heard a great deal about Nathaniel Savory in my many visits to the Bonins. He lived quite a life . . . sort of a colonizing adventurer . . . opportunist. But neither he nor Commodore Perry could get the United States government to see the value of the

Bonins. He died in the Bonins when he was about eighty. As the years went by, more and more Japanese came in, and the white settlers really became the outsiders. You could see that it was going to be only a matter of time until no more white people would be admitted in the Bonin Islands.

[*Orchestra: Swells briefly . . . Menace . . . Down and out*]

JAP 3. Hereafter, no people but Japanese will be permitted to settle in Ogasawara. Only people from Japan itself will have entry.

MASTER. Most of the white settlers saw what was coming . . .

SETTLER 1. No, there's nothing here for us any more.

SETTLER 2. These Japanese aren't going to interfere with you.

SETTLER 1. All the schools are Japanese. They teach Japanese to everyone, whites and Japanese alike.

SETTLER 2. When you're in Rome you have to do as the Romans do.

SETTLER 1. I don't want my children to grow up Japanese. I'm leaving with my family.

SETTLER 2. Wherever you go, you'll have to start all over.

SETTLER 1. Are you going to stay?

SETTLER 2. Yes.

SETTLER 1. In another generation there won't be one white person in the Bonins who will be able to speak anything but Japanese; everything about them will be Japanese . . . even the way they think. No . . . [*Fades*] I'm taking my family out.

MASTER. I took out a good many of the whites who left the Bonins. On the long voyage, they told me what was happening there. They told me about the people. Some of them even remember Nathaniel Savory himself. And most of them felt as Savory had felt about the coming importance of the islands. They not only felt that they had lost the home they had worked for so long, but that their country had made a mistake.

SETTLER 3 [*Coming in*]. They are really remarkable islands, captain.

MASTER. I've thought that a good many times.

SETTLER 3. Take Peel Island . . . the main island. Why, the beaches are beautiful. And the climate is wonderful . . . 75 degrees all year around.

MASTER. Yes, and Port Lloyd on Peel Island could be made into a naval base.

SETTLER 3. Ah, it sickens me, captain. It's not only Peel Island. There are 26 other islands, and probably 60 or 70 islets.

MASTER. Even if there were just Peel Island, it would be a valuable base for us to have.

SETTLER 3. I've walked over nearly every foot of Peel Island . . . and over many of the other islands too. There are palms and wild pineapples, and the valleys are filled with wild beans and taro . . . and there are sugar-cane plantations. Almost everything will grow in those valleys . . . maize, vegetables, tobacco. And up on the hills there are all kinds of valuable timber: cedar . . . rosewood . . . ironwood . . . sandalwood . . . oak. When I was young I used to go fishing in the bays for green turtles. We caught many of them, and sometimes we caught a shark. The waters are filled with fish. [*Fades*] And when those Japanese came in . . .

MASTER. Nearly all of the settlers that I took out of the Bonins felt the same way about it. One of them was a geologist.

SETTLER 4 [*Coming in*]. You see, captain, the islands are high and bold and rocky, and that's one of the valuable things about them.

MASTER. Yes; Port Lloyd, on Peel Island, is a sort of shelter cove. All those hills around it.

SETTLER 4. The harbor of Port Lloyd is actually the crater of a volcano. All the Bonins are of volcanic formation. You've probably noticed that sometimes the sea comes surging up on the beaches, and sometimes it is so low that boats are left high and dry.

MASTER. I've noticed that, yes.

SETTLER 4. That's because of the submarine earthquakes . . . upheavals and disturbances on the floor of the ocean.

MASTER. I recall that one of the islands I saw one year was missing when I came back the next year.

SETTLER 4. That has happened a number of times. The smaller islands have changed in the passing centuries, but the Japanese have shown that they know the value of the bigger islands.

MASTER. Yes. I remember when they gave all of them Japanese names.

SETTLER 4. They named them after members of the family . . . father, mother, older sister, younger brother, and so on.

MASTER. Members of the family, eh?

SETTLER 4. Yes, they renamed Peel Island Chichi Jima, which means Father Island, and they named another Haha Jima, which means

Mother Island, and [*Fades*] still another Ototo Jima, which means . . .

MASTER. The Japanese completely Japanized the islands. They put in their own system of weights and measures, their own customs, and their own currency. The rest of the world call the islands by their English names—Bailey Island, Beechey Island, Peel Island, and so on—but this is about all that is not Japanese in the Bonin Islands.

[*Orchestra: Japanese motif . . . Conquest . . . Hold in background*]

In those last years when I called in the "Lottie D" at Port Lloyd, I got to know Mr. Hunikara quite well. He was a typical Japanese official . . . pleasant, a little conscious of the responsibility of his office . . . and always a little standoffish. It did not occur to me until the day he told me that the islands would thereafter be closed to all foreign ships, that in the several previous visits he had cleverly avoided showing me around the island, as he had always done before.

[*Music out*]

HUNIKARA. I am sorry, captain, that the pressure of official business keeps me at my desk.

MASTER. Sure, sure, I understand, Mr. Hunikara. I'll just take a look around myself. [*Chuckles*] Stretch my legs.

HUNIKARA. Some of the streets and roads are torn up. If you will be good enough to wait until tomorrow, perhaps [*Fades*] I shall have the pleasure of showing you around.

MASTER. But when the next day came, there were other excuses why he could not spare the time with me. And so it went until sailing time came. I never got out of Port Lloyd. When the war broke out in the Pacific, the attention of important men turned to the Bonins.

OBSERVER. Did you notice any changes in the islands in the course of those last few calls, captain?

MASTER. I remember that the tops of the hills looked changed. Many of them had been graded off. There were installations on them.

OBSERVER. Did you see any gun mounts?

MASTER. I did not actually see the guns but, now that I look back, I am sure that those were heavy gun emplacements on the tops of the hills commanding the approaches.

OBSERVER. What about airfields?

MASTER. There were always planes over the islands, but I never got inside to see if there were airfields.

OBSERVER. They must have made an early start in fortifying the Bonins.

MASTER. I remember seeing quite a number of soldiers in Port Lloyd.

OBSERVER. That confirms what we've thought for a long time: Japan pledged at the Washington conference in 1922 *not* to fortify the Bonins, but she fortified them anyway. Japan knows that the Bonins command her southern approaches.

MASTER. As a matter of fact, Port Lloyd is the only harbor of any importance between Guam and Japan.

OBSERVER. You've sailed in and out of that harbor many times. Would you say, captain, that it has possibilities as a naval base?

MASTER. It is an excellent harbor. They were working on it when I made that last call there in 1939.

OBSERVER. They've probably worked on it a great deal more in the years since then.

MASTER. Yes, probably.

OBSERVER. How many Japanese would you say were there in 1939?

MASTER. I remember asking Mr. Hunikara that. I noticed that there seemed to be more Japanese around than I'd ever seen there before. He said there were about five thousand Japanese in the Bonin group.

OBSERVER. Five thousand. Hmmmm. And there's no telling how many troops were there. It's my guess that we're going to have to keep our eyes [*Fades*] on the Bonins ...

MASTER. For the next few months I was so busy that I didn't have a chance to think of the Bonins. The Japanese took the Philippines, and Singapore, and the Dutch Indies ... and the Bonins were thousands of miles behind their lines. And during those months in the "Lottie D" we carried war supplies to the Southwest Pacific ... we kept on carrying them until this happened.

[*Ship at sea ... Siren warning of submarine attack*]

LOOKOUT [*Off ... calling*]. Submarine. Submarine ... two points off the starboard beam. Submarine.

[*Bell for general quarters*]

MATE. Battle stations. Man your guns.

[*Ad libs of men jumping to guns*]

MASTER [*Order on bridge*]. Hard right rudder. Hard right rudder.

LOOKOUT. Torpedo—on the starboard beam! Torpedo!

[*Spinning of steering wheel*]

MATE. Torpedo, sir! Coming straight for us.

MASTER. Full speed ahead, Mr. Martin. Hard right rudder.

MATE. Yes, sir.

LOOKOUT. Torpedo . . . on the starboard beam.

[*Explosion of torpedo . . . Wild ad libs of crew*]

MASTER. Mr. Martin . . . go and see how badly we're hit.

MATE. Yes, sir.

LOOKOUT. Torpedo. Torpedo. Another torpedo.

[*Ad libs*]

[*Explosion of torpedo*]

[*Orchestra: Sweeps out . . . Wipes out sound . . . Dramatic . . . hold in background*]

MATE. Ladies and gentlemen, I was the mate on the "Lottie D." I was on my way aft when the second torpedo struck. It exploded under the bridge, and almost immediately the fo'c'sle and most of the topside forward were in flames. She started to settle by the bow. The captain gave the order to abandon ship, but he refused to leave the vessel until every man . . . all who were living . . . were in the boats. The "Lottie D" sank in a few minutes. It wasn't until we got the captain into our boat that we saw how badly burned he was. [*Pause*] We talked about everything during those days we were drifting. About our home towns . . . people we knew . . . going to Sunday school . . . experiences we'd had . . . women . . . places we'd been. Everything. The captain told about the many ports he'd called on. On the fifth day he started telling about Port Lloyd and the Bonin Islands. No one else in our boat had ever been there. He talked about the Bonins—all the things I've told you—for nine days. How they looked, the harbors and the hills, about the people, about Savory and Mazarro and all the rest, and how the Japs came there and took over. We figured that he never got over being told by Hunikara that he could never come back there. On the fourteenth day, he started to get worse. He drifted into a sort of coma. We did everything for him we could. On the seventeenth day, he died. We slid him over the side. If he could have lived four days more, until we were picked up, he'd probably be here now. [*Pause*] He made the Bonin Islands mean something to me . . . something special. I've watched the war move back toward the Bonins.

[*Music out*]

[*Oscillator . . . Up and fade to background*]

VOICE 1 [*Filter*]. American forces have stormed ashore at Kwajalein!

VOICE 2 [*Filter*]. Landings are being made on Eniwetok!

VOICE 3 [*Filter*]. Ponape and Truk are being blasted by waves of American bombers.

MATE. I watched them push westward, through the Marshalls and over the Carolinas, back toward the Bonins and Japan. I traced their progress on the map.

[*Oscillator: Up and fade to background*]

VOICE 1 [*Filter*]. A powerful American task force has raided Marcus Island.

VOICE 2 [*Filter*]. Americans have landed in force on Saipan in the Marianas, just fourteen hundred miles from Japan.

VOICE 3 [*Filter*]. Strong American formations of bombers have struck at the Bonin Islands—the advance base of the Japanese—just two hours' flying time from the coast of Japan.

[*Sound out*]

MATE. As the captain said, maybe one of these days we'll find out that that fellow Savory and Commodore Perry were right about the Bonin Islands.

[*Orchestra: Dramatic play-off*]

THE HOUSE I
LIVE IN

Arch Oboler

ARCH OBOLER is one of the most widely known radio writers. Several collections of his scripts have appeared in book form, the most recent being *An Oboler Omnibus.*

Oboler was born in Chicago in 1909 and attended the University of Chicago. His radio career got off to a symbolic start when he wrote a sketch entitled *Futuristics,* broadcast by NBC for the opening of Radio City in New York. Oboler then wrote a number of short, startling sketches for *Vallee Varieties.* On the basis of their success he tried to persuade NBC in Chicago to let him start a "maturely experimental" series on the lines of CBS's *Columbia Workshop.* Instead, NBC put him to work on *Lights Out,* a late-night horror series. Oboler managed to devote a percentage of these plays to themes of current significance. This suggests the pattern of much of Oboler's career. While capitalizing on his skill in melodrama, he has fought for the privilege of expressing himself, through plays, on world problems.

After short trips to Hollywood and Europe, Oboler was invited by NBC to launch a series devoted entirely to his own work, and produced by him. This series, *Arch Oboler's Plays,* was the first radio-drama series to be named after its writer. It ran fifty-two weeks. Although the acting budget provided for no higher salaries than the union minimum of twenty-one dollars per performance, a number of high-priced stars volunteered to appear in the plays. Oboler's scripts are always highly actable, and give the player something to bite his teeth into. Oboler is also an extremely precise and effective director. Under his direction every performer knows exactly what is expected of him; the orchestra leader knows at just what syllable the music must start or stop.

During the 1940-41 season Oboler's plays were sponsored briefly by Procter & Gamble under the title *Everyman's Theatre.* In this period, when war was coming closer to America, radio became increasingly nervous about unneutral drama, fearing the charge of warmongering. It took a cross-country flight by Oboler and Raymond Massey, the star, to persuade NBC officials to permit the broadcasting of the second script Oboler wrote for *Everyman's Theatre—This Precious Freedom.* Later the Institute for Education by Radio, at its annual meeting in Columbus, Ohio, named this the outstanding commercial broadcast of the year.

Paradoxically, America's involvement in the war freed radio drama from its most repressed and frustrated period. Soon after Pearl Harbor, NBC invited Oboler to produce a series that would stimulate the American war effort. In the resulting series, *Plays for Americans,* Oboler was at his most effective. Through illustrative stories, never through direct rhetorical appeal, he prodded the consciences and energies of Americans, group by group. Many of the plays written for this series, as for the later *To the President* and *Free World Theatre,* were of very temporary meaning. They were aimed at the needs of the moment. They persuaded the air-raid warden to stay on the job. They stimulated blood donations. They told the soldier he would not return to exactly the same world he left behind. They fought premature optimism.

In 1945 *Arch Oboler's Plays* returned to the air over MBS. *The House I Live In,* broadcast on this series, was another editorial for the day.

THE HOUSE I

LIVE IN*

[*Music: Quiet, brooding, cellos predominating, then down and continuing behind*]

ROGERS. I want to tell you about the house I live in. I want to tell you how the house that had been mine lost its walls and all the rooms were filled with rubble and a dust arose, and when I looked again, the house was gone.

[*Music: Rises swiftly, then down behind*]

VOICE. Was it a bomb that fell?

ROGERS. Bomb? [*Amused*] Bomber over Elm Street, U.S.A.? No . . .

WOMAN'S VOICE. But you say your house disappeared? How did it disappear?

[*Music out*]

ROGERS. I am going to tell you . . .

[*Music: Of morning begins, continuing behind*]

The morning began as so many others had begun since . . . Tom and Elsa had gone. . . . Again I hadn't slept—I opened the front door, and stood on the front porch and watched the daylight slowly wake up the street. It had rained during the night—I had listened to every drop—and now the light lit up the wet leaves as the trees shook themselves in the morning wind. . . . Another day . . . and I was waiting . . . for eight o'clock . . .

[*Whistle of postman, back*]

POSTMAN [*Back*]. Sorry, Mr. Rogers—nothing today.

ROGERS. Are you sure? Perhaps the letter—

POSTMAN. Sorry, Mr. Rogers. Nothing today. . . . Maybe it'll come tomorrow. . . .

---

* THE HOUSE I LIVE IN by Arch Oboler. Copyright, by Arch Oboler.

ROGERS [*Flatly*]. I already knew about tomorrow. . . .

POSTMAN [*Back*]. Sorry, Mr. Rogers. Nothing today. . . . You know, it takes a long time for a letter to get to Elm Street from Japan.

[*Music: Hits, then down and continuing behind*]

ROGERS. I went back into the house. Chairs, table, sofa—the piano Elsa had played.

[*Piano begins to play softly, then fades slowly out as the orchestra comes in behind*]

I went upstairs . . .

[*Sound of opening door*]

Tom's room just as it had been—his bed, his typewriter on the desk, his track shoes hanging from the side of the chair he had made in manual training. . . . Just the way it had been that last night.

[*Music: Goes into Elsa's theme behind*]

[*Sound of opening door*]

Elsa's room—the "silly room" I'd called it with its frippery—billowing curtains—cretonne flounces on the dressing table at which she'd sat so many times covering with glamour a face that was so very young . . .

[*Music: Hits chord, holding behind*]

Everything as it had been— [*His voice tightens, quickens*] —but now a place I couldn't stay in!

[*Music: Rises, in transition, then down broodingly behind*]

Out into the street—to walk as I had done so many times before until the circle of my aimless steps brought me back to this *empty* house I lived in. . . . I'd made the walk so many times . . . fifty steps and . . .

[*Dog barking back*]

that silly little Pekinese of Mrs. Engelhart's would see me pass and yap at me. . . . Another dozen steps and the broken piece of sidewalk in front of the Andrews place. . . . Then the iron picket fence Tom used to run along when he was small, banging a stick along the iron picket . . .

[*Sound of picket fence being banged*]
as he ran, so half the neighborhood knew his nibs was free of
school for another day. . . . I passed the big oak tree where
Elsa'd stand with her girl friends when she was very young . . .
　　[*Sound of girls giggling*]
and giggle when the latest football hero passed. . . .
　　[*Children laughing far, far back*]
Laughter—children's laughter. *They'd* laughed too—they'd been
full of laughter, my children. . . .

　　[*Music: Hits chord holding behind*]

My steps went past the children's laughter—the endless circle
of my aimless steps.

　　[*Music: Rises, then down and continuing behind*]

BOY. Hullo, Mr. Rogers.
ROGERS. The Johnsons' boy suddenly was there, walking alongside
　　of me.
BOY. Kin I walk with you, Mr. Rogers?
ROGERS. All right . . .
BOY. I heard a funny joke today. A man was riding along and he
　　got losted—you know, he didn't know where he was, and he
　　went up to a farmer and he said to the farmer, where's the
　　road to town, and the farmer said I don't know and the fellow
　　said well where's the road to the other town and the farmer
　　says I don't know and the fellow says well where's the road to
　　some other town and the farmer says I don't know and the
　　fellow says you don't know much do you and the farmer said
　　nope but I ain't lost. Funny joke, huh, Mr. Rogers?
ROGERS. Yes, very funny.
　　[*Music out*]
　　[*Sound of wind*]
BOY. I gotta new harmonica.
ROGERS. Have you?
BOY. Do you play the harmonica?
ROGERS. No. . . .
BOY. I can.

[*Boy begins to play "The House I Live In" softly, then breaks off the tune with*]

My ma said, "Please get out of the house if you're gonna play that—I gotta headache." [*He plays a loud run on the harmonica*] Why do heads ache, Mr. Rogers?

ROGERS. Loud noises—unnecessary conversations—worries.

BOY. You got worries, Mr. Rogers?

ROGERS [*Evading the question*]. What's that song you were playing? I mean, a moment ago.

BOY. I dunno. . . . You got worries, Mr. Rogers?

ROGERS [*Softly*]. Play your harmonica, son.

BOY. Okay.

[*He begins to play "The House I Live In" softly, simply—the tune fades back*]

[*Music: Orchestra begins a paraphrase of the song behind*]

ROGERS. He kept playing as he walked alongside of me. And suddenly I realized that his eyes were on me as if he wanted to say something to me, yet was afraid to speak. . . . And then he did speak . . .

[*Music: Orchestra out*]

[*Harmonica in full, then stops with*]

BOY [*A little breathlessly*]. You—you take such big steps, Mr. Rogers!

ROGERS. Sorry. . . . That better?

BOY. Yes . . .

[*Begins to play softly on harmonica*]

ROGERS. Are you going anywhere in particular, son?

BOY. No, sir.

ROGERS. No school today?

BOY. It's Saturday!

ROGERS. Oh . . . I forgot . . .

BOY [*In wonder*]. You didn't know it was Saturday?

ROGERS. Sometimes one day . . . gets to be like another . . .

BOY [*Suddenly bursts out*]. Mr. Rogers, listen! You must wait! Jimmy Doolittle'll go over with a thousand thousand Flying Forts and he'll get Tom out, you just wait and see! . . . Jimmy Doolittle'll get him away from those Japs! Honest he will!

[*Music: Hits, then down and continuing behind*]

ROGERS. And then he was gone . . . I kept on walking . . .

[*Tempo of the music quickens*]

Then, this thought: The boy, this neighbor boy—his meeting and walking with me had not been accidental. He had *wanted* to walk with me and say what he had said! [*Sardonically*] A thousand thousand Flying Fortresses! Headed up by Superman, I supposed, with Tarzan of the Apes leading a charge of elephants toward my son's prison camp! Prison camp! I didn't even know if he was *in* a prison camp! Those devils—what had they done to my son?

[*Music: Rises, then down and continuing behind*]

WOMAN. Good morning, Mr. Rogers. How are you this morning? I'm your neighbor, Mrs. Gibson.

[*Music: Rises slightly, then down and continuing behind*]

ROGERS. A woman—yes—a neighbor—I had seen her once or twice as I'd walked by—and now she was there walking with me, a grocery bag on her arm, and talking to me . . .

[*Music up and out*]

WOMAN. It must have rained quite hard last night.

ROGERS. Yes, it did.

WOMAN. All the rain this spring has certainly done wonders for our lawns—I've noticed yours—it's very lovely.

ROGERS. Yes . . .

WOMAN. Of course the whole problem is to get someone to do the mowing! I saw you talking to little David Miller—I guess the smaller boys of this neighborhood will come into their own, this year, what with the twelve- and fourteen-year-olds all going off to help on the farms during their vacations.

ROGERS [*Quietly*]. If the grass grows tall, there'll be no harm.

WOMAN [*Looks at him*]. No, of course, no . . . Did you hear about the Griffith boy?

ROGERS. No . . .

WOMAN. He was out flying a kite and it fell across those high-tension wires over on Oak Street and he and some of the other boys got a ladder and put it across the telegraph post and were half-

way up when Mr. Griffith came along. The Griffith boy had a
metal fishing rod that he was going to use to lift the kite off the
wires. Can you imagine that? He'd have been electrocuted if
Mr. Griffith hadn't just happened to leave work early that day!
If you ever expect them to grow up, you certainly have to watch
your children every minute . . . [*She stops as she realizes what
she had started to say*] I mean— [*Nervously*] Mr. Rogers, I
wonder if I could ask you something.

ROGERS. Yes?

WOMAN. Well—I—I know your daughter Elsa has been overseas for a
long time, but my daughter Peggy is joining up, and—and you
can understand how excited I've been, and I was wondering if
you could tell me anything that— [*She suddenly stops*]

ROGERS. You were saying . . .

WOMAN [*Quietly, tightly*]. I was just finding an excuse to talk to
you. Peggy's joined up and gone and I've watched you walk by
my house every day, and—and—today I started off to market, just
at this time, just so that I could have an excuse to tell you that—
that Mr. Gibson and I would like very much to have you come
to dinner some night this week. No, don't say yes or no now.
Think about it, and whenever you'd like to come over, just let
us know. [*Fade*] Good-bye!

[*Music: Hits, then down and continuing behind*]

ROGERS. She turned and went. [*With tempo*] I'd walked along this
street morning after morning—hundreds of mornings from the
day after the news came that Tom wouldn't be back, and Elsa
left the house to join up! Morning after morning, and always it
had been *alone!* And now this—a boy, a woman—childish prattle
—feminine dinner-making—What *was* this today?

[*Music: Rises, then down softly in counterpoint*]

[*Colored woman begins to hum the song, "The House I Live
In" in the distance. She has a deep vibrant voice*]
Suddenly I heard *that* tune again—the one the boy had been
playing! One of the houses along the street—a colored woman
singing as she swept the front porch.

[*Orchestra out*]

COLORED WOMAN [*In full, singing*].
    "The house I live in,
    A plot of earth, a street,
    The grocer and the butcher
    And the people that I meet;
    The children in the playground,
    The faces that I see;
    All races, all religions,
    That's America to me.

    The house that I live in,
    My neighbors, white and black,
    The people who just came here,
    Or from generations back,
    The town hall and the soap box,
    The torch of liberty,
    The Home for all God's children,
    That's America to me." *

    [*Music: Hits, then down and continuing behind*]

ROGERS [*Repeats slowly*]. "The house I live in" . . . [*Sharply*] The
    house I lived in was an *empty* house!

    [*Music: Rises, swirls, then through it we hear*]

ANN [*Filter*]. That's a wonderful song, isn't it, Mr. Rogers?

    [*Music: Hits, then down and continues agitato behind*]

ROGERS. I turned! Who? And then I saw it was Ann—my Tom's Ann!
    [*Music out*]
ANN [*Fade in*]. I said that's a wonderful song.
ROGERS. Hello, Ann!
ANN. Hello. You going anywhere in particular?
ROGERS. I was just walking . . .
ANN. [*Looks at him*]. Mind if I walk with you?
ROGERS. No, of course not. I'm glad to see you! . . .

[*Colored woman begins singing again, far back—Her song slowly fades out as the two walk away from her*]
How have you been?

ANN. Fine, Mr. Rogers. Fine.

ROGERS. I haven't seen you for quite some time.

ANN. Almost a year.

ROGERS [*In surprise*]. Has it been that long?

ANN [*Tightly*]. Yes . . . it has . . .

ROGERS. I had no idea.

[*Far in the distance we can hear the end of the song*]

ANN. Mother and I have wanted very much to see you.

ROGERS. I'm sorry—I've been very busy.

ANN. I know—your war work. . . . And yet surely you could have found some time to come visit us.

ROGERS. I'm sorry . . .

ANN. It's going well . . .

ROGERS. What's going well?

ANN. The war . . .

ROGERS [*Flatly*]. Is it . . .

ANN. Did you know it rained last night?

ROGERS. Yes, I know . . .

ANN. I opened my window and lay on the bed and watched it . . . It was a strange sort of rain. So soft and fine—it wasn't as if it was rain at all, and when it began to get light every drop seemed to be dancing as it fell . . .

ROGERS. You didn't sleep . . .

ANN. I—I was thinking. . . . Oh, Mr. Rogers, we've missed you very much! Why didn't you come to see us?

ROGERS. I'm sorry, dear. I don't go out these days at all. I go down to the plant—I do everything I can—when I come home, I like to shut the door and be quite alone. I'm sure you understand. . . .

ANN [*Softly*]. And yet each morning you come out of the house and walk the street.

ROGERS. How do you know that?

ANN. I've watched you—we *all* have. . . . [*She whispers*] You're very lonely, Mr. Rogers.

ROGERS [*Looks at her*]. Yes . . . I am . . .

ANN. I was, too . . .

ROGERS [*In wonder*]. Was? [*Eagerly*] You've heard from Tom?

ANN [*Quickly*]. No, no, I didn't—

ROGERS. The—the War Department? Why should they write *you?* Why not *me?* Why didn't they—

ANN [*Breaking through*]. Mr. Rogers! Please! . . . There's been noth-ing—no letter—

ROGERS. Then *what?—Tell* me!

ANN. I—I don't know how!

ROGERS. I see! All right, that's natural—why not?—he's been away so long—why shouldn't you find someone else?

ANN. Oh, no! No! That's not it! Of course not! Why won't you understand?

ROGERS. Understand what? You say you're not lonely any more and I'm supposed to understand! Understand what—that you're young —that you can forget! But can *I* forget my son? Can *I* forget what he said, how he looked, how he . . . [*He chokes up*] What have I got left but a lonely house? . . .

ANN. I stopped being lonely the day someone—one of the neighbor-hood women—stopped me on the street, and asked me where she and some of the others could send packages to Tom.

ROGERS [*In wonder*]. Our Tom?

ANN. Yes . . . ours.

ROGERS [*Quietly*]. I—I *don't* understand . . . Why should they—what was Tom to *them?*

ANN [*Speaking almost to herself*]. Tom mattered to a lot of people— on this street—yes, and I suddenly began to realize that he mattered on many other streets where they didn't know his name or who he was.

ROGERS [*Softly*]. Why, Ann? *Why?*

ANN. Because Tom wasn't just ours any more. What had happened to him mattered to everybody back home who has a sweetheart in this war—or a husband— [*She looks up at him*] —or a son . . .

[*Music: Hits in a great rending climax of the shattering of metal walls. When it dies out we hear the singing of strings which continues behind*]

ROGERS. All in a moment the house that I lived in lost its walls, and all the rooms were filled with rubble, and a dust arose and when I looked again, my empty house was gone!

[*Music: The full orchestra hits, then slowly, very slowly, the strings begin to build behind*]

And suddenly a new house arose, and it was filled with people—all the people to whom Tom mattered even though they had never seen him, or didn't even know his name. All the people whose hearts were filled with the work, and the troubles, and the hopes of this war that my son and my daughter—yes, and I—were fighting!

[*Music: Is singing now behind*]

So this is the house I live in: a house of *people!* And there can be no walls! For sorrow knows no walls—and determination knows no walls—and there are no walls for *faith.*

[*Music: Rises to glowing curtain*]

Lightning Source UK Ltd.
Milton Keynes UK
05 March 2011

168714UK00001B/34/P